THE POLITICS OF
APOLLONIUS RHODIUS'
ARGONAUTICA

Apollonius Rhodius' epic poem, the *Argonautica*, is one of the most important and influential literary productions of the Hellenistic period. This book shows how the retelling of a heroic adventure set in the generation before the Trojan War engages the political, religious, and ethical dynamics of its day by alluding to the real-world context of the early Ptolemaic dynasty as well as to poetic and other models. Through a hegemonic typology that ranges from the just and theocratic to the duplicitous and lawless, Apollonius characterizes the political heirs of Alexander the Great as pious, civilized rulers. This interpretation goes beyond previous studies by examining the political resonance of religious activity in the poem, and by relating these formulations (especially where they concern Apollonius' departures from his literary predecessors) to the ideological construction of Hellenic identity in third-century Egypt.

ANATOLE MORI is Associate Professor of Classics at the University of Missouri-Columbia.

Bronze cult statuette of Alexander Aigiochos ("Aegis-Bearing") with *chlamys*-shaped aegis. Roman copy from Alexandria (London, British Museum). Original dated to late fourth century BC. Photo courtesy of the British Museum, © The Trustees of the British Museum

THE POLITICS OF APOLLONIUS RHODIUS' *ARGONAUTICA*

ANATOLE MORI

CAMBRIDGE UNIVERSITY PRESS
Cambridge, New York, Melbourne, Madrid, Cape Town, Singapore, São Paulo, Delhi

Cambridge University Press
The Edinburgh Building, Cambridge CB2 8RU, UK

Published in the United States of America by Cambridge University Press, New York

www.cambridge.org
Information on this title: www.cambridge.org/9780521882255

© Anatole Mori 2008

This publication is in copyright. Subject to statutory exception
and to the provisions of relevant collective licensing agreements,
no reproduction of any part may take place without
the written permission of Cambridge University Press.

First published 2008

Printed in the United Kingdom at the University Press, Cambridge

A catalogue record for this publication is available from the British Library

Library of Congress Cataloging in Publication data
Mori, Anatole, 1960–
The politics of Apollonius Rhodius' Argonautica / Anatole Mori.
p. cm.
Includes bibliographical references and index.
ISBN 978-0-521-88225-5 (hardback)
1. Apollonius, Rhodius. Argonautica.   2. Argonauts (Greek mythology)–Poetry.
3. Epic poetry, Greek–History and criticism.   I. Title.

PA3872.Z4M74   2008
883'.01–dc22   2008019590

ISBN 978-0-521-88225-5 hardback

Cambridge University Press has no responsibility for the persistence or
accuracy of URLs for external or third-party internet websites referred to
in this publication, and does not guarantee that any content on such
websites is, or will remain, accurate or appropriate.

Contents

List of tables	*page*	vi
Acknowledgments		vii
List of abbreviations		viii
1 Introduction		1
2 The politics of Alexandrian poetry		19
3 Strife and restraint among the Argonauts		52
4 Sexual politics in Lemnos, Colchis, and Drepane		91
5 Piety, mediation, and the favor of the gods		140
6 The bones of Apsyrtus		187
7 *Quid denique restat*: Apollonius and Virgil		224
Bibliography		236
Index		256

Tables

4.1	The early Ptolemies.	page 97
5.1	Sacrifices in the *Argonautica*.	157
5.2	Implied sacrifices in the *Argonautica*.	160

Acknowledgments

It is difficult for me to imagine how I could have completed this project without the help of Richard Hunter, who saw it in its initial stages as a University of Chicago dissertation and whose wise counsel in recent years has been of greater value to me than I can say. I have benefited from perceptive criticism offered by Alex Sens (who has read through more than one incarnation of the manuscript), James Clauss, Graham Shipley, and Susan Stephens, all of whom have saved me from an embarrassment of errors. Earlier versions of several sections from Chapter 3 first appeared in the *American Journal of Philology* 126.2 © 2005 by The Johns Hopkins University Press and are here reprinted with their kind permission. I am grateful to the Loeb Classical Library Foundation for their generous support in 2004–2005, and to the Department of Classical Studies at the University of Missouri-Columbia for arranging a leave from teaching in the winter of 2004.

For their encouragement and learned advice, I am greatly indebted to my colleagues John Miles Foley, Richard Foley, Raymond Marks, Charles Saylor, Dennis Trout, and Barbara Wallach. For their thoughtful responses to several chapters I thank David Schenker, James McGlew, and especially Daniel Hooley, whose judicious suggestions substantially improved the whole manuscript. I owe a debt of thanks to Ian Worthington for important corrections to an early draft and for his guidance in general, to Stefani Engelstein for comparing notes as our respective labors evolved, and to Nicole Monnier for helping me keep things in perspective. Most of all, I want to thank my colleague (and husband), Michael Barnes, with whom I share a dangerous passion for the poetry of Apollonius, and it is to him that I dedicate this book.

Abbreviations

Spelling and abbreviation generally adhere to the onomastic conventions of the *Oxford Classical Dictionary*. Modern periodicals and multivolume reference works are abbreviated as in *L'Année Philologique*. Apollonius is cited from Vian 2002; Virgil from Mynors 1969. All translations are my own except where indicated otherwise.

AB	C. Austin and G. Bastianini (eds.) *Posidippi Pellaei quae supersunt omnia*. Milan, 2002.
ABV	J. D. Beazley. *Attic Black-Figure Vase-Painters*. Oxford, 1956.
CAH	F. W. Walbank, A. E. Astin, and M. W. Frederiksen (eds.) *The Cambridge Ancient History*. Vol. 7.1: The Hellenistic World. 2nd edn. Cambridge, 1984.
CG	*Catalogue générale des antiquités égyptiennes du Musée du Caire* (with monument number).
Etym. M.	T. Gaisford (ed.) *Etymologicon magnum*. Amsterdam, 1962.
FGrH	F. Jacoby (ed.) *Die Fragmente der griechischen Historiker*. Berlin and Leiden, 1923–40; 1940–59; 1994–.
GP	A. S. F. Gow and D. L. Page (eds.) *The Greek Anthology: Hellenistic Epigrams*. 2 vols. Cambridge, 1965.
IG II	*Inscriptiones Graecae* II/III, Part 1: Inscriptiones Atticae Euclidis anno posteriores, fasc. i: decreta annorum 403/2–230/29. 2nd edn. Ed. J. Kirchner. Berlin, 1913.
IG VII	*Inscriptiones Graecae* VII: Inscriptiones Megaridis et Boeotiae. Ed. W. Dittenberger. Berlin, 1982.
IG XI	*Inscriptiones Graecae* XI, fasc. iv: Inscriptiones Deli. Ed. P. Roussel. Berlin, 1914.
IG XII	*Inscriptiones Graecae* XII: Inscriptiones maris Aegeai praeter Delum, fasc. iii, supplement. Ed. F. H. de Gaetringen. Berlin, 1904; fasc. vii. Ed. F. H. de Gaetringen. Berlin, 1908.

List of abbreviations

LIMC	H. C. Ackermann and J.-R. Gisler (eds.) *Lexicon iconographicum mythologiae classicae*. Zurich, 1981–.
LSJ	H. G. Liddell and R. Scott (eds.) *A Greek–English Lexison*. Oxford, 1968.
OGIS	W. Dittenberger (ed.) *Orientis Graeci inscriptiones selectae*. 2 vols. Leipzig, 1903–5.
P. Cair. Zen.	C. C. Edgar (ed.) *Zenon Papyri: Catalogue général des antiquités égyptiennes du Musée du Caire*. 5 vols. Cairo, 1925–40.
P. Eleph.	O. Rubensohn (ed.) *Aegyptische Urkunden aus den Königlichen Museen zu Berlin: Griechische Urkunden*, Sonderheft: Elephantine-Papyri. Berlin, 1907.
P. Giss.	O. Eger, E. Kornemann, and P. M. Meyer (eds.) *Griechische Papyri im Museum des oberhessischen Geschichtsvereins zu Giessen*. Leipzig and Berlin, 1910–12.
P. Lille	*Papyrus grecs*. Institute papyrologique de l'Université de Lille, 1907–12.
P. Mil. Vogl.	*Papiri dell'Università degli Studi di Milano*. Milan, 1937–.
P. Oxy.	*The Oxyrhynchus Papyri*. London, 1898–.
Pfeiffer i	R. Pfeiffer (ed.) *Callimachus: Fragmenta*. Vol. 1. Oxford, 1949.
Pfeiffer ii	R. Pfeiffer (ed.) *Callimachus: Hymni et Epigrammata*. Vol. 2. Oxford, 1953.
SEG	*Supplementum epigraphicum Graecum*. Amsterdam, 1923–.
SH	H. Lloyd-Jones and P. Parsons (eds.) *Supplementum Hellenisticum*. Berlin, 1983.
Suda	A. Adler (ed.) *Suidae Lexicon*. 5 vols. Stuttgart, 1967–71.
Syll.	W. Dittenberger (ed.) *Sylloge inscriptionum Graecarum*. 3rd edn. 4 vols. Leipzig, 1915–24. (Reprint 1960.)

CHAPTER 1

Introduction

Anyone accustomed to Homeric tales of heroic honor and undying glory is liable to be perplexed by Apollonius' *Argonautica*. Nearly every line of the poem recalls an event or an expression from the *Iliad* or the *Odyssey*, yet from a dramatic perspective there is little to compare with Achilles' wrath, Hector's death, or Odysseus' revenge against the Suitors. If the *Iliad* is a poem of force, the *Argonautica* is a poem of political alternatives. It is a crisis for the Achaeans when Achilles refuses to fight after ten years of battle, while the Argonauts' conflict with the Colchian army is patched up in only a few days. Their losses during the entire voyage are hardly Iliadic (four die unexpectedly, one is lost, two are left behind), and although their return, like the *nostos* of Odysseus, is delayed, it is a matter of weeks rather than years.[1]

One of the delays occurs when the Argo is washed up by a shallow flood tide and stranded in the shoals of the Syrtes Gulf along the coast of Libya.[2] The Argonauts lose hope and go their separate ways expecting a slow anonymous death in the desert sun. The guardian nymphs of Libya, called the Herossae, take pity on them and tell Jason that they must repay a debt to their mother if they wish to return home (4.1305–36).[3] Jason reports this to the rest, and they are all then startled to see a massive horse, dripping with briny sea water, rising out of the sand and galloping off. The

---

[1] The length of Argo's round trip voyage from Thessaly to Colchis has been estimated at about six months, from mid-June to early December; Green 1997 *ad* 1.559–68; 2.1097–99; and 4.1775–81. See also Severin 1985, whose one-way voyage in a replica of the Argo from the Bay of Volos to the mouth of the Rhioni River in Georgia took eighty days (May 3–July 21).

[2] The Egyptian shores from Paraetonium in Libya to Alexandria, lying several hundred miles to the east, were notoriously dangerous: see Diod. 1.30.1–5; Plin. *HN* 5.26; Procop. *Aed.* 6.3. Cf. Agatharchides on the grounding of elephant cargo ships along the African coast in the Arabian gulf, and the terrible suffering of the crews (Diod. 3.40). For discussion of this episode see Andrews 1989.

[3] Nelis 2001b, 123, n. 238 notes and provides references for the parallel between this scene and the shipwrecked Odysseus, who is aided by the sea nymph Leucothoe as well as by Nausicaa and her maidens.

1

Argonauts are pleased by Peleus' interpretation of these portents: they are to bear the Argo (their symbolic mother) on their shoulders as they follow the horse's tracks toward an inland sea (4.1370–79).

The episode is at once familiar and strange. In some ways the apparition of the Herossae is reminiscent of a Homeric dream vision, as when the ghost of Patroclus comes to the sleeping Achilles with a request for swift burial (*Il.* 23.65–92).[4] But the Libyan scene is set at noon, not night; the hero is awake, not asleep; and the Herossae are strangers to him.[5] The narrator also compares Jason to a lion whose roar terrifies cattle and herdsmen (*Argon.* 4.1337–44), a simile that recalls Homeric descriptions of warriors in battle. When Menelaus catches sight of Paris, for example, he is said to feel like a starving, hunted lion that stops to devour a carcass though dogs are in pursuit (*Il.* 3.23–26). The Argonautic narrator again undermines the audience's expectations, however, by observing that Jason's voice, unlike the lion's roar, does not really threaten those nearby (*Argon.* 4.1337–44).[6]

In addition, many details of the episode are absent from one of Apollonius' literary models, Pindar's *Fourth Pythian Ode*. The first section of the celebratory ode rehearses Medea's prophecy about the foundation of Cyrene, a theme well suited to the chariot victory of King Arcesilaus. Of the portage of the Argo (4.25–27), Medea says only that

> δώδεκα δὲ πρότερον
> ἀμέρας ἐξ Ὠκεανοῦ φέρομεν νώτων ὕπερ γαίας ἐρήμων
> ἐννάλιον δόρυ, μήδεσιν ἀνσπάσσαντες ἀμοῖς.
>
> twelve days earlier
> On my counsel we drew our ship from Ocean and bore it
> Over desolate ridges of earth.[7]

To this brief passage Apollonius adds descriptions of the Argonauts' anguish, the two apparitions, and Peleus' interpretation. He also expands Jason's role, presumably in keeping with another source, the historian Herodotus, who relates how Triton offered to guide Jason through the shallows in exchange for a tripod, though Herodotus does not say whether the Argonauts actually

---

[4] Cf. also the evil dream that misleads Agamemnon in the likeness of Nestor (*Il.* 2.16–36). Virgil has Aeneas dream of the dead Hector (*Aen.* 2.268–97) and the dead Anchises (*Aen.* 5.721–45).
[5] Vian 2002, 3:191, n. 1314; Green 1997, 342, n. 1312ff.
[6] See Vian 2002 *ad loc.* on the similarity to *Od.* 6.130–34; cf. the fiercely roaring lion at *Il.* 5.299–302 (= Aeneas). On the subversion of the traditional epic simile, see Hunter 1993, 133; Goldhill 1991, 307–8.
[7] Bowra 1947.

Introduction 3

carried the Argo (4.179).[8] In contrast to Pindar, then, both Herodotus and Apollonius focus on Jason and say next to nothing about Medea.[9]

Especially curious in terms of verisimilitude is the idea that Peleus' plan to carry the Argo would "please everyone" (4.1380).[10] While his interpretation fits the portents, it is hard to see why the starving[11] Argonauts would enthusiastically agree to haul the Argo for days in the scorching heat toward an unknown destination. The narrator, who typically comments on unusual practices (e.g., the Colchian treatment of the dead, 3.200–9) and decisions that may have unpleasant consequences (the Boreads' reproof of Telamon, 1.1298–309), acknowledges the extraordinary nature of the deed by insisting on its historical veracity. Shifting from third-person narrative to second-person invocation, the poet praises the Argonauts' strength and endurance (4.1381–92) and claims that he has heard this story "infallibly" (πανατρεκὲς, 1382) from the Muses, noting that, as the descendants of the gods, the Argonauts were born for such exploits (4.1389). The audience is thus given a more or less logical justification for the success of the venture,[12] but no psychological explanation is given for the Argonauts' abrupt emotional reversal.

One might try to intuit some kind of internal motivation. Perhaps the Argonauts, who are aware that Zeus was angry with Jason and Medea, are encouraged by these signs of divine immanence, or perhaps they are simply relieved to be doing something, however laborious, instead of waiting for death to take them. Such readings are plausible in the absence of evidence to the contrary, but inasmuch as the psychology of Apollonius' characters is no more transparent here than it is elsewhere in the poem (with the obvious exception of Medea in Books 3 and 4), they are not only speculative but also, and more importantly, they fail to account for the narrative choices that Apollonius is making here. Why does Apollonius place greater weight upon this scene than Pindar? Medea's aid is as crucial in the *Argonautica* as it is in *Pythian* 4, so why does Apollonius follow Herodotus here by placing Jason in the central role? What is it, exactly, about the plan to carry the Argo that makes it seem appropriate to the Argonauts? What would the

---

[8] See Murray 1972, 203 with nn. 5–7, on Herodotean echoes in Callimachus and Apollonius.
[9] The narrator of the *Argonautica* does comment that the serving women around Medea were wailing like birds (4.1296–304).
[10] Green 1997, 344, nn. 1370–79, 1381–87 comments that the seemingly more rational alternative of floating the Argo back to the coast is not entertained because quicksands were common in the area, but observes that the heroic portage must be relegated to the realm of fantasy.
[11] *Argon.* 4.1295 ἄκμηνοι καὶ ἄπαστοι, cf. Achilles' grief at the death of Patroclus, *Il.* 19.346 ἄκμηνος καὶ ἄπαστος.
[12] Fränkel 1968 *ad* 4.1382; Livrea 1973 *ad* 4.1381.

image of the Argonauts carrying the boat have suggested to an Alexandrian audience of the third century BC?

The present volume sets out to answer these and other questions by taking into consideration the historical context of the *Argonautica* and the formation of Ptolemaic political ideology. I explore how Apollonius' epic retelling of a heroic adventure set in the generation before the Trojan War engages the external world: the religious, socio-political, and ethical dynamics of Apollonius' day. The political tenor of Apollonius' other poems, all now lost, about the founding of cities like Alexandria, Naucratis, Caunus, Cnidus, and Rhodes, suggests that the *Argonautica* is informed by a similar consciousness of the political value of epic poetry,[13] and that its consistent elaboration of the religious activity of leaders is rooted in the cultic ethos of contemporary politics. The aim of my argument is twofold: first, to explore the political resonance of religious activity in the epic, and second, to relate these poetic formulations of such activity (especially where they concern Apollonius' departures from his literary predecessors) to the ideological construction of Ptolemaic kingship and Hellenic identity in Egypt. By "religious activity" I mean formal communication with the gods, such as prayer and sacrifice, as well as practices that are less immediately connected with worship, such as the institution of new cults or shrines. Where previous historical studies have largely concentrated on Apollonius' life, career, literary chronology, and professional rivalries,[14] I am principally interested in the effect of the Alexandrian political context on the imagery, characterizations, and motifs of the *Argonautica*.

As will become clear in subsequent chapters, Apollonius' heroes are composite figures, poetic renderings of Alexander the Great, the Ptolemies, and other historical figures, not to mention archaic epic heroes and characters from other genres.[15] At times the components of their characterization can be contradictory and difficult to reconcile, particularly when it comes to the use of force: the Argonauts prefer diplomacy to aggression and yet are shown to be as dangerous in combat as their Homeric counterparts; Jason reveres the gods and yet commits a murder that violates the laws of Zeus. With these contradictions in mind I address not only the ramifications of

---

[13] For this argument and additional references, see Hunter 1989, 10. Unfortunately, Apollonius' foundation (*ktisis*) poems do not survive, for the most part. Hunter (1989, 5) observes that while the subject matter of several (Caunus, Cnidus, and Rhodes) might lead one to imagine that they were composed during Apollonius' putative time in Rhodes, Ptolemaic interest in those areas was too pronounced to make the composition of these poems in Alexandria unlikely.

[14] E.g., Fraser 1972; Pfeiffer 1968, 140–49.

[15] In this respect, as in others, Virgil's rendering of Aeneas is comparable to Apollonius' construction of Jason. Boyle 1993b, 83, observes of Aeneas: "There is much in him, for example, of Mark Antony, Julius Caesar, Marius, Scipio Africanus, Camillus, Romulus and other Roman heroes." On the relation between the *Aeneid* and the *Argonautica*, see Chapter 7.

religious activity for authority figures in the *Argonautica* but also a number of related questions concerning Jason's status as a hero and as the leader of the Argonauts. My interpretative strategy has been to concentrate on the aspects of the epic that are least "Homeric" and have aroused much critical attention, for the most part unfavorable. Jason's reticence, Medea's dominance and recklessness, and their collusion in the deceptive murder of Apsyrtus have all been damned as departures from the heroic epic tradition. These incongruities look different, however, when they are set against alternative historical, literary, and mythological paradigms: what were taken as structural inconsistencies, ruptures, and flaws begin to cohere and fall into place.

Since this book is intended for those who are reading the *Argonautica* for the first time as well as for specialists in Hellenistic poetry, the remainder of this introduction considers the poem's historical and literary background. Here and elsewhere I treat historical and literary material separately, and although this structure may give the impression that discussion has been split into constituent analyses, my hope is that the reader will regard this comparative approach as a developmental and progressive strategy rather than as an exercise in the incommensurable. The conceptual boundaries between poetic and historical discussions can (and should) be acknowledged in a diagnostic framework, but it is important to recognize the artificiality of these same distinctions as a concession to scholarly discourse.

I begin by considering what Hellenistic poetry is, or at least what it has traditionally been thought to be. The term "Hellenistic" ("Hellenistisch") was first adopted by the nineteenth-century German historian J. G. Droysen, to distinguish what he saw as a dynamic new Hellenism in the historical period bounded by the death of Alexander the Great in 323 and Octavian's defeat of Antony and Cleopatra in 30. By "Alexandrian poetry" I mean poetry that was produced in and around Egyptian Alexandria early in the Hellenistic period, roughly from the end of the fourth century to the middle of the third century. Apart from these loose temporal and geographical parameters, it is not so easy to define what is uniquely "Alexandrian" or "Hellenistic" about such works because so much material from the fifth, fourth, and third centuries has been lost. Not much is known of fifth-century epic, elegy, and non-dramatic poetry, likewise obscure is nearly everything from the fourth century (apart from the New Comedy of the Attic playwright Menander) as well as the bulk of the poetry produced in the first twenty years of the third century.[16] With so many missing links, it is impossible to speak with precision about the evolution of the literary

---

[16] Hutchinson 1988, 10–11.

tradition down to Apollonius' time, and informed hypotheses have necessarily taken the place of evidence.

In what might be seen as a compensatory move, scholars have turned to the historical background of Alexandrian poetry in order to sketch the outlines of its new thought-world. Here again contemporary material is in comparatively short supply,[17] and the decline of Athenian power after the fifth century has often been used to set the discursive stage. Readings of Hellenistic poetry have been informed by a sense of belatedness and decline that is exemplified by this passage from Rudolf Pfeiffer's famous address to the 1954 Jubilee Meeting of the Classical Association: "The [Alexandrian] poets were in a unique historical position. They could no longer speak as free citizens to a political and spiritual community as audience; their only chance was to write books for smaller circles of well-educated connoisseurs."[18] According to this view Apollonius and the other scholar-poets associated with the Library of Alexandria had essentially abandoned the public sphere and devoted themselves to learned poetry because their "political and spiritual community" had been compromised: they were living under autocratic rule far from Athens – which at this time was Athens more or less in name only, her citizens having yielded their long-cherished autonomy to Macedon and the rich and powerful Hellenistic kingdoms.[19]

In retrospect, this assessment seems too restrictive: democratic citizenship was not a prerequisite for poetic expression in ancient Greece, and in any case it is possible for politically sensitive poetry to emerge outside (or at least in the margins of) liberal forms of government. Then, too, it is possible to characterize the *Argonautica* as a political epic because it is thematically concerned with the effects of royal power, although something more seems to be in play here. The Ptolemaic monarchy may not be "political" in the narrow sense of a legislative body (whether oligarchic or democratic) whose members discuss and vote on binding resolutions,[20] but even if one holds to a rigid definition of what constitutes genuinely political institutions

---

[17] For the first seventy years of the third century, a period of Macedonian ascendancy that apparently held little interest for later (i.e., Roman) writers, no contemporary history survives. On the historiography and non-literary texts of the period, see Shipley 2000, 1–32; on ancient (and modern) historical sources for Alexander, see Worthington 2004, 234–42.
[18] Pfeiffer 1955.
[19] Although the Athenians were weakened militarily, they maintained the democracy at a local level: Lape 2004 shows how civic institutions like the theater continued to be politically engaged and helped to reformulate a new model of citizenship based on kinship and the retrenchment of citizenship requirements in the absence of an active military.
[20] Finley 1983, 50–51.

(i.e., representative rather than monarchical), the poetry produced in Alexandria at this time was inherently political because of its prominence in the politicized culture of the royal court and its contribution toward the expression of Ptolemaic ideology.

Nevertheless, the idea of a literary schism that divided the world of authentic public performance in politically engaged fifth-century Athens from the isolated and derivative culture of the written word and private study in Alexandria has continued to inform attitudes toward Hellenistic poetry.[21] Sir Kenneth Dover traced this idea back to the ancient perception, arising early in the fourth century, that the great age of Greek poetry ended with the deaths of the Athenian dramatists Euripides and Sophocles in 407/6, to be replaced by a diminished, essentially custodial age dedicated to the preservation and nostalgic cultivation of the canon. On his view the major post-classical Greek poets – meaning Callimachus, Theocritus, and Apollonius Rhodius – were steeped in the archaic and classical tradition and therefore managed to produce works of technical brilliance, although they unfortunately failed to "bring their intelligence to bear upon profound issues which excite the intellect and emotions simultaneously."[22] Clever, yes, but shallow and derivative: this view of the Alexandrians still holds sway in some circles, though it has long been called into question.[23] Peter Parsons, citing Dover ("If one wants an epoch, it should come with Euripides"), allows for the utility of treating the Hellenistic period as a discrete unit, but despairs of structuring it in terms of "dividing lines, new beginnings, universal characteristics, and unique preoccupations," for, as he rightly concludes, "it is normally not a question of absolute novelties, but of novel emphases."[24] However one chooses to characterize Hellenistic poetry, the "novel emphases" that define the *Argonautica* are consistent with those of other poems that were circulating in Alexandria and elsewhere in the Mediterranean early in the Hellenistic period (see Chapter 2).

---

[21] See Bing 1988; Easterling and Knox 1985, 543: "To sum up, poetry had experienced a radical shift of direction by the Hellenistic period"; against this view see Cameron 1995. On the difficulty of definition see also Heinrich's discussion of papers by Gelzer and Parsons in Bulloch *et al.*, 1993, esp. 171–87.
[22] Dover 1971, lxix, lxxi.
[23] See, e.g., Pfeiffer 1968, who assigns a Renaissance-like creativity to the third-century poets, after the deadly fourth-century doldrums; Bulloch 1984, who discusses differing critical views of Callimachus' piety, arguing for the genuine solemnity of his hymns; and Lloyd-Jones 1990, who explicitly counters Dover's interpretation (cited above), arguing that a fifth-century audience would not have been taken aback by the passages he cites as overly learned or disrespectful of the gods.
[24] Parsons 1993, 155.

An examination of the contemporary context hardly qualifies as a new approach to interpreting ancient Greek poetry,[25] but what scholars of Hellenistic poetry have sought to do in recent years is to focus less on what has been lost, in terms of the manuscript tradition or political institutions, and more on what is known of Alexandria as the center of a group of scholar-poets who explored and experimented with poetic tradition in celebrating, among other subjects, their newly established royal patrons. This cross-disciplinary approach has proved to be most insightful, to judge by recent studies that are grounded in both the political as well as the literary context of Hellenistic poetry.[26] The work of Richard Hunter in particular has advanced our knowledge and deepened our appreciation of these works. Most significant, for my purposes, is his exploration of the ways in which the *Argonautica* not only encodes the activity of world travelers like the ancient Egyptian ruler Sesostris, the Athenian Xenophon, and Alexander, but also integrates into an epic format a wide range of topics that were relevant to the Ptolemaic political agenda, such as, for example, the geography of Libya, the Aegean, and the Black Sea, or the religious cults of Homonoia ("Concord"), the mysterious Samothracian gods, the Dioscuri (Castor and Pollux), and the goddess Tyche ("Fortune").[27] What Hunter has shown is that the *Argonautica* is far more politically engaged than was previously supposed, and the same can be said of works by other Alexandrian poets. "Callimachus' writing takes shape as part and parcel of the Ptolemaic reorganization of society and state," writes Daniel Selden, "a hymn by Callimachus turns out to be as much a concrete embodiment of Ptolemaic ideology as the law courts, onomastic codes, the Pithom Stele, or Museion."[28] While the aesthetic sensibility of these works may not immediately strike the reader as explicitly political, they are nonetheless politically encoded, as Peter Bing demonstrates in a recent discussion of the Ptolemaic orientation of Posidippus' λιθικά epigrams ("On Gemstones").[29] In short, the artistry and personal ambition of the Alexandrians dovetailed with the

---

[25] Hutchinson 1988, 9–10 cautions: "I should by inclination be pleased to illuminate the poems through their historical setting. But the character of the evidence, and of the literature and of other aspects of the time, seems to discourage attempts to approach the literature by constructing the period."
[26] A representative, if not exhaustive, list includes Foster 2006; Gutzwiller 2005; Mori 2005; Stephens 2005; Depew 2004; Stephens 2003; Mori 2001; Stephens 2001; Reed 2000; Pietsch 1999; Selden 1998; Burton 1995; Rostropowicz 1995; Bulloch *et al.*, 1993; Koenen 1993; Zanker 1987; Rostropowicz 1983; Merkelbach 1981; Griffiths 1979.
[27] See Fantuzzi and Hunter 2004, 128–32; Hunter 1995 *passim*; 1993, 152–69, 1991, esp. 82–90.
[28] Selden 1998, 406.
[29] Bing 2005, 130: "The stones exemplify in their geographical distribution and social construction both the territorial and cultural/artistic aims of the Ptolemies and their poet, Posidippus."

desire of the first Ptolemies to be celebrated as the heirs to Alexander's empire, both in Egypt and beyond.

Of those scholars who are currently working on the political resonance of Alexandrian poetry, Susan Stephens has gone the farthest in demonstrating how the poets refashioned Greek ideas about kingship in the light of ancient Egyptian mythology, images, and symbols.[30] In her discussion of the *Argonautica* in *Seeing Double: Intercultural Poetics in Ptolemaic Alexandria*, Stephens explores how Apollonius sets up "competing centers of authority in his text by deploying Egyptian mythology in the epic as a conscious articulation of a new idea of kingship."[31] I am very much indebted to Stephens' work and regularly guided by her observations, though in the end I take a slightly different view of the *Argonautica* because I do not agree that "[a]ny message of Greek cultural supremacy or of the transforming quality of Greek values is rendered moot."[32] On my view the poem frames the connection between the practical forms of (Greco-Macedonian) political authority and the celebration of (mainly Greek) cult practice for a Greek-speaking audience, one that would have been gratified by tales of a divine mandate for Hellenic rule over Egypt. The visual spectacle of ruler cult, from its monuments, processions, and public celebrations to its physical insinuation within Egyptian temples, was a foil for the redefinition of political identity, helping to legitimate (and at the same time to screen) the reality of the military and economic foundations of the Ptolemaic dynasty. That the Ptolemies would have exploited native institutions to strengthen the monarchy by positioning it as favorable to Egyptians, had little bearing on the actual self-image of the colonizing Macedonians and Greeks. From my perspective, then, it follows that any identification between Greek and Egyptian culture in the *Argonautica* necessarily privileged the politically dominant group.

As part of the community of scholar-poets working under Ptolemaic patronage Apollonius was well positioned to appreciate their political interests. According to the sources that have come down to us with the surviving manuscripts of the poem,[33] it was probably during the reign of Ptolemy II Philadelphus (308–246; ruled 282–246) that Apollonius served as royal tutor, an honorific office held in association with the post of Chief Librarian, to Philadelphus' heir, the young Euergetes.[34] In recent years the composition of the poem has also been dated to Philadelphus' rule, between

---

[30] See Stephens 2005; 2003; 2000.   [31] Stephens 2003, 235.   [32] Stephens 2003, 235.
[33] On the ancient sources for Apollonius' life, see the section on Poetry under the Ptolemies in Chapter 2.
[34] Hunter 1989, 4.

270 and 260,[35] somewhat earlier than was previously thought (between 250 and 240).[36] Whichever decade one prefers, Apollonius composed the *Argonautica* in the formative years of the dynasty: roughly two generations after Alexander took control of Egypt (332),[37] a land in which the religious image of the king was arguably more important, ideologically speaking, than it was elsewhere in the ancient Mediterranean world. The Ptolemies took the place not only of Alexander, who had forced the Persians out of Egypt, but also of the Egyptian pharaohs, who were traditionally seen as divine intermediaries between gods and mortals. Native opposition to the Macedonian occupation would increase over time,[38] as nationalistic literature like the *Demotic Chronicle* suggests,[39] but civil unrest was less problematic at the beginning of Ptolemaic governance than the external threat posed by the armies of the other Macedonian Diadochs ("Successors"), who had served as Alexander's generals. Those who survived the tumultuous years after Alexander's death in 323 would eventually assume royal titles as they fought to secure territory in Europe, North Africa, and Asia. Like other rulers of the Hellenistic period, the Ptolemies maintained a complex network of systems of power,[40] some intentional, others not, and it is fair to say that the security of Ptolemaic Egypt was founded on a powerful military, combined with the ideological promotion of the dynasty as both pious and divine in its own right.[41]

One of my main concerns, then, is to show how the *Argonautica*'s preoccupation with the religious agency of authority figures communicates the ideological interdependence of Ptolemaic politics and cult. The Ptolemies configured their rule in accordance with the expectations of their Egyptian

---

[35] Hunter 1989, 1–9.
[36] Vian 2002, 1:xiii views Callimachus' *Hymn to Apollo*, written after 246, as contemporary with a revised version of the *Argonautica*, but Hunter (see previous note) suggests that similarities between these poems may be the result of earlier versions of the hymn, which probably circulated for some years among those who worked in the Library of Alexandria.
[37] See Chapter 2, n. 68 on the date of the poem.
[38] The first native revolt occurred in 245, at the beginning of the reign of Ptolemy III. The famed Rosetta stone (*OGIS* 1:90) reflects the concern of Ptolemy V (210–180) for the internal security of Egypt. For a translation, see Burstein 1985, no. 103, pp. 131–34. See also McGing 1997, 274–75.
[39] The *Demotic Chronicle* of the mid-third century romanticizes the age of the pharaohs before Macedonian rule. The "Oracle of the Potter," a religious text dated to 130–115 BC, prophesies the eventual collapse of latter-day Alexandria (see Burstein's translation in Koenen 1968). Parts of the third-century AD "Alexander-Romance" (Pseudo-Callisthenes), may date as far back as the third century BC; the depiction of pharaoh Nectanebo as the father of Alexander suggests Egyptian bias; see Stoneman 1994, and the introduction to his 1991 translation.
[40] On horizontal and vertical networks of suzerainty in the Hellenistic period, see Davies 2002.
[41] Koenen 1993, 80.

as well as their Greek-speaking subjects,[42] and religious cults were instrumental in this process. The royal image was a hybrid, fashioned by the kings and their advisors out of the political customs, cultural expectations, and religious practices of the ancient Egyptians, Greeks, and Macedonians. Ptolemaic displays of piety took numerous forms, from the recovery of cult artifacts to the foundation and support of native Egyptian shrines and temples. The initial formulations of Ptolemy I Soter and later developments under his son and successor, Ptolemy II Philadelphus, show that the formation of the royal image was a dynamic process, subject to periodic revisions as the rulers first emphasized their ties to Alexander and later introduced and expanded cults dedicated both to the dynasty and to individual members of the royal house. Cults associated with particular family members were established with a view to the prestige of the dynasty among both indigenous and immigrant populations, not only in Egypt, but also in Greece, the Aegean islands, and Asia.[43] The authority of the Ptolemies was thus entwined with their religious activity, making participation in the cults of the royal family tantamount to an affirmation of political support.[44]

In coming to terms with a work that arose out of a complex assortment of political influences and literary traditions, I am guided, methodologically speaking, by the assumption that the *Argonautica* supplies the audience with sufficient information to understand its characters' behavior – despite the fact that we are only infrequently given access to the thinking of heroes like Jason or Heracles. The thoughts, doubts, and desires of Homeric heroes are quite openly on display, as Eric Auerbach argued in the classic study *Mimesis*,[45] but Apollonius is much more restricted in this regard – frustratingly so, to many. If Apollonius was attempting a Homeric epic, the consensus is that he failed – and yet the portrait of Medea, whose anxieties are so masterfully explored in the second half of the poem, suggests

---

[42] Macedonians spoke their own language, though Alexander and other members of the Macedonian elite were able to speak Greek. Despite the Macedonian military presence in Alexandria and in the Fayuum – a swampy bottomland (Lake Moeris) drained by the first two Ptolemies for settlement by Macedonian soldiers – the Greek language was more widely used. On the decline of the ethnic Macedonian population in Egypt, see Fraser 1972, 1:53–54, 80–81, 129, and 223, *passim*. On Greek attitudes toward Macedonia, see Vasunia 2001, 252–53.

[43] For Ptolemaic cult practice, see Hölbl 2001, 77–112; Shipley 2000, 156–76; Koenen 1993; Fraser 1972, 1:189–301; Cerfaux and Tondriau 1957, 189–227.

[44] There is an element of mild coercion connected, for example, with the local celebration of Arsinoë during the Arsinoeia, as well as the politically inflected establishment of cult centers elsewhere, as in Rhodes, to thank Ptolemy I Soter for his aid against Demetrius Poliorcetes (Diod. 20.100.3–4). See further Hölbl 2001, 92–93, 104.

[45] Auerbach 1953, 9.

that Apollonius' limitations in this area are neither accidental nor without purpose.[46] I suggest that the tone and resonance of those episodes that are less explicit from a psychological perspective are nevertheless reliably cued by other modes of expression, such as background settings, external behaviors, visual images, symbols, and allusions both to texts and to historical and political contexts. This range of expressive modes generates a higher intertextual register than has been previously considered, allowing the reader a greater range of comparanda not only among Apollonius' poetic predecessors and contemporaries, but also among Hellenic (and to a limited extent, Egyptian) customs, the political and cultic protocols observed by Alexander, and the projects of the Ptolemies themselves. In a very real sense this book applies to Apollonius M. A. Harder's close study of literary allusion in the *Aetia*, particularly her recognition that allusivity was for Callimachus "an important means for extending his dense and compact text on behalf of the reader," who is able "to situate the text he is reading in its literary and socio-cultural context."[47] The same claim can be made of Apollonius, with the central goal of exploring how the political focus of the *Argonautica* reinterprets concrete historical events and inflects them with more abstract ideological constructions and considerations.

In the following chapters I demonstrate that the multiple roles and responsibilities of kings and heroes in this epic draw on the real world context of Alexander and the early Ptolemies as well as material from Homeric epic, the epic cycle, and other poetic works. Chapter 2 examines more closely a number of relevant topics, from Alexander's arrival in Egypt to the organization of the Ptolemaic dynasty, and from the character of Alexandrian poetry in general to the literary controversies specifically associated with the *Argonautica*. Chapter 3 addresses the representation of conflict and resolution in Book 1 – the election, the conflict with Idas, and the quarrel with Telamon – from the perspective of Macedonian political protocols as well as philosophical ideals of self-restraint, while Chapter 4 weighs the prominence of female characters like Medea and the Lemnian ruler Hypsipyle against the political activity of the queens Arsinoë II, wife of Ptolemy II Philadelphus, and Berenice II, wife of Ptolemy III Euergetes. Chapter 5 surveys the religious responsibilities of Alexander and the early Ptolemies in order to evaluate the representation of kings like Alcinous and the Colchian Aeëtes. To show that Apsyrtus' death represents another realistic (albeit problematic) aspect of Hellenistic political power, Chapter 6

---

[46] Book 3 focuses on Medea's emotional turmoil after falling in love with Jason (esp. 3.616–912, 948–1162), while Book 4 details her fear at the possibility of betrayal and capture (e.g., 4.11–108, 338–444).
[47] Harder 2002a, 223.

contrasts the ambush of Apsyrtus with the murders by stealth that were committed by the agents of Alexander and the Ptolemies. Finally, in Chapter 7, I explore some of the ways that this new reading of the *Argonautica* inflects our understanding of Virgil's *Aeneid*.

While I am particularly concerned with the historical models provided by the activity of late fourth- and early third-century rulers and military leaders, analysis of poetic influences on the *Argonautica* remains pivotal inasmuch as the poem responds to literary models in contrasting the behavior of good (i.e., peaceful, pious, diplomatic) leaders with that of bad (violent, unstable) ones. This is not to say that such contrasts are absent from Homeric epic. Agamemnon in *Iliad* 1 is the antithesis of Nestor in *Odyssey* 3, for example, but the difference is that the *Argonautica* is a single epic that displays the relative strengths and shortcomings of the rulers encountered by the Argonauts. The poem is unified in its formulation of a hegemonic typology, ranging from the just and theocratic to the duplicitous and lawless, for an audience who viewed themselves as civilized conquerors: just towards allies and subjects, scrupulous with respect to ritual observance and the will of the gods, and called by destiny to rule in foreign lands.[48] Apollonius places greater emphasis than Homer on the religious activity not only of kings but also of the heroes themselves: the Argonauts' frequent sacrifices, their concern to establish shrines, their influence on local customs. Homeric heroes like Achilles and Odysseus enjoy a familial closeness with certain gods, but these characters are predominantly defined by their social isolation and intense desire for punitive vengeance, whereas it is religious activity of one kind or another that distinguishes Jason and other leaders in this poem. Thus, while many Argonautic scenes depicting religious activity may call up Homeric and other poetic precedents, they have also been reformulated in ways that suggest they owe much to the politics of cult practice in Ptolemaic Egypt.

A particularly telling example of this kind of reformulation appears in the portage of the Argo, described at the beginning of this chapter. Certain aspects of this episode recall an Egyptian ritual that is significant, at least from a Greco-Macedonian point of view, because of its association with Alexander. This particular cultural referent goes a long way toward explaining Medea's reduced role in this episode as well as the Argonauts' lack of concern about the dangers of the proposed adventure. Peleus' odd plan

---

[48] For a study of the stereotype of the Hellenistic good king as a model for Virgil's Aeneas, see Cairns 1988, 1–28, esp. 17–21 for a list of specific characteristics: e.g., preeminence in, among other things, virtue, military strength, self-control, mercy, strict observance of the law, desire for *homonoia/concordia*, good appearance, and so on.

does not seem odd to them because it mimes the ritual transport of an image of the god Amon-Re in a portable solar boat during festival processions that took place all over Egypt. One of the most important of these processions occurred in the second month of the Nile flood season as part of the annual Opet festival at Karnak.[49] During the festival priests carried an image of the god over land from the temple of Amon in Karnak to Luxor temple. The solar boat would respond to questions from the public during this procession: a forward inclination would indicate yes, while a retreat would indicate no. On rare occasions an individual might be admitted to a private audience with the god inside the temple, although the meeting was mediated by priests. The purpose of the Opet festival was the divine rejuvenation of the pharaoh, who accompanied the procession and at its conclusion would emerge from Luxor temple to be reunited with his people, renewed and symbolically reborn with Amon-Re.[50]

Alexander witnessed a ritual of this type during his visit to the oracle of Zeus Amon at Siwah, where the aniconic image of the god was carried in a golden boat by eighty priests after private consultation with the king.[51] In contrast to Luxor temple, where commoners might be admitted to an audience with the god, Siwah was a royal oracle, to be questioned only by the pharaoh. Alexander was unique in personally consulting this oracle, for no Egyptian pharaoh had ever made the arduous journey into the desert.[52] Zeus had long been identified by the Greeks with the Egyptian god Amon; the Hellenic renown of Siwah had increased after the foundation of nearby Cyrene (c. 500) and likely prompted Alexander's visit. As Phiroze Vasunia puts it: "The weight of mainland Greek lore about the foreign god Ammon, combined with whatever Alexander learned in and around Egypt and whatever personal desires he nurtured inside himself, helped propel the new ruler to Siwah."[53]

The procession of the Argonauts to Lake Triton thus enacts an "appropriate" cultic response to a numinous apparition in Libya, with certain features of such Egyptian boat processions reimagined here and elsewhere in the poem.[54] Greek precedents can, of course, be found: the traditional processions that enacted the advent of Dionysus (a most fitting parallel, especially for Alexander) using ship-like chariots that were sometimes wheeled,

---

[49] See Kemp 1991, 206. [50] Kemp 1991, 208.
[51] On the golden boat: Diod. 17.50.6; Just. 4.7.24; on the entire journey to Siwah: Arr. 3.3–4; Plut. *Alex.* 26–27; Diod. 17.49.2–51.4; Curt. 4.7.5; Just. 4.7.5–32. See further Hölbl 2001, 11. Cf. Reed 2000, 326 on the Osiris festival, which included sacred boat processions. Stephens 2003, 231 compares this episode with the Egyptian myth of the underworld progress of the solar boat.
[52] Vasunia 2001, 274. [53] Vasunia 2001, 274–75.
[54] See Stephens 2003, 218–37 for discussion of possible connections between the Argo's return and the progress of the solar boat.

but sometimes carried by men.⁵⁵ So, too, for example, the association of Zeus with Amon suggests an additional connection between the "talking" solar boat and Argo's revelatory speech through the beam of Dodona that occurs earlier in Book 4 (4.580–83).⁵⁶ The oak of Dodona is imagined as a metonym for Zeus, for while it is Hera who ensures that the oak communicates with the Argonauts, what it communicates is the true judgment of Zeus regarding the Argonauts' fate.⁵⁷

What is more, the portage of the Argo revisits and completes an event at the beginning of the *Argonautica* itself: Jason's cardinal act of piety in bearing the goddess Hera, a maternal protector, upon his shoulders through the spring flood waters of the River Anaurus (1.8–11; 3.64–73). Just as Hera favors Jason above all others for honoring her in this way (3.74), so the Argonauts' portage of the Argo marks them as favored sons of the gods (4.1389–90):

> ἔμπεδον ἀθανάτων ἔσαν αἵματος, οἷον ὑπέσταν
> ἔργον ἀναγκαίῃ βεβιημένοι.
>
> Necessity compelled them to so great a deed
> That surely theirs was the blood of immortals.

Certain Argonauts are introduced early in the poem as the sons of Olympian gods,⁵⁸ but Apollonius is more evasive about the Argonauts' ties to the gods elsewhere, and only in this passage does he come close to an explicit statement about the divine heritage of the Argonauts as a group.⁵⁹ It is telling that the Argonauts' blood kinship with the gods is brought into relief in Libya, a setting where divine ancestry carried considerable political weight. Alexander's capacity to endure the extremes of the Libyan Desert as he made the trip to Siwah was similarly understood, at least by him, as a mark of divine heroism.⁶⁰

Like his Greek-speaking audience, Apollonius would have been interested in the Egyptian culture that surrounded him, but such interest would

---

⁵⁵ See Burkert 1985, 100–1, 166.
⁵⁶ Like the barque of Amon, the oracle of Zeus at Dodona gave simple yes or no responses to questions. In Greece such exchanges were not gestural but rather inscribed on lead tablets: Burkert 1985, 114.
⁵⁷ Hera's role as transmitter of Zeus's judgment in this scene is comparable to Arete's role in transmitting the judgment of Alcinous in Book 4 to the Argonauts (see Chapter 4).
⁵⁸ E.g., Heracles and the Dioscuri (or at least Polydeuces) are sons of Zeus (1.146–50; 1188); Erytus and Echion are sons of Hermes (1.51–52).
⁵⁹ The narrator observes that the better part of the Argonauts claim blood kinship with daughters of Minyas, a son of Poseidon (1.231–32), and Peleus observes that the Argonauts are very nearly (σχεδόν) of the blood of the immortals (2.1223).
⁶⁰ According to Callisthenes, Alexander's court historian, the king was inspired to go to the oracle by the examples of Perseus and Heracles (Strabo, 17.1.43). Strabo rejects the rumor that Alexander was saved by providential rains and the guidance of two crows. See also Arr. 3.3.1.

also have presumed an Egypt that naturally accepted and even eagerly recognized Macedonian sovereignty. Accordingly, the manifestation of the Herossae is as "nationalistic," in its way, as Aeneas' vision of the Penates at *Aeneid* 3.147–71.[61] Hunter, who has noted this parallel, suggests that while the "nationalist religious resonance" of the Penates helps to unify the *Aeneid*, the Herossae are more evocative of the fractured structure of the *Argonautica*.[62] I would add that the parallel is still closer since the welcome extended to the Greeks by the native gods makes explicit the ideological framework, unifying it in a way that Virgil evidently appreciated. Peleus' interpretation of the Argo as the "mother" mentioned by the Herossae recasts the Argonauts' near death during a flood tide in Libya as a preparation for a symbolic rebirth, and a possible allusion to the pharaoh's rebirth at the climax of the Opet festival. But where the *Argonautica* experiments with traditional epic by quite literally exalting maternal figures, the *Aeneid* restores patriarchal order as Aeneas bears his father Anchises on his shoulders, not across the River Anaurus, not out of the burning Libyan sands, but out of the burning city of Troy.

In effect, the portage of the Argo is a colonizing aition, an explanatory account that recasts a traditional Egyptian ritual as the analogue of a labor that was originally performed by Greek heroes.[63] Broadly speaking, the episode is framed as aetiological: what happened long ago in the Syrtes Gulf looks ahead to the same things "that happen even today"[64] – although the stranding of Argo has no causal bearing on later misfortunes. Granted, this episode is not included in discussions of Apollonian aitia, and it must fall into the category of implicit aetiologies since it is not marked by the linguistic formulae (e.g., εἰσέτι νῦν "still today"; ἔτι νῦν περ "still to this very day") that often (though not always) introduce the aition proper. Nor, for that matter, does it confirm, as aitia often do, the historicity of an event – indeed the opposite is true since the narrator must appeal to the authority of the Muses in order to vindicate it: Μουσάων ὅδε μῦθος (4.1381). Nevertheless, in characterizing the portage as aetiological my purpose is not to identify yet another species of what is known to be a versatile, even protean figure,[65] but rather to acknowledge its participation in a programmatic articulation of the link between the remote past and the Ptolemaic

---

[61] The Penates are the household deities whose effigies are brought safely by Aeneas out of Troy; they appear during the night and advise Aeneas to leave Crete and settle instead in their homeland Hesperia (Italy).
[62] Hunter 1993, 174.
[63] On "linguistic colonialism," see Barnes 2003, 22; Stephens 2000, 208; Dougherty 1994.
[64] On the various types of aitia in the *Argonautica* see Barnes 2003; Valverde Sanchez 1989.
[65] Barnes 2003, 175–76.

present, fixing an epic precedent for an incongruous ritual that would have embodied, to Greek eyes, the otherness of Egypt.

Two modes of thought are at work here. First, the image of dozens of men carrying a ship inland would have looked "Egyptian" to Apollonius' Greek audience, not only because there were such rituals, but also because it is a paradoxical inversion of "normal" (i.e., Greek) behavior. Such inversions constituted the essence of Egyptian custom according to Herodotus, who, it should be noted, continued to be widely read in the Hellenistic period.[66] Peleus' suggestion would have made sense, metapoetically speaking, to both the Argonauts and their audience, because strange things were to be expected in places like the Libyan Desert. At the same time, however, Herodotus, like many Greeks and, for that matter, many Egyptians (Diod. 1.23–25), viewed Egyptian religion as anterior and therefore to some degree formative of Hellenic beliefs and practices. Ancient Greek philosophers and logographers consistently posited some kind of generative relation between these two cultures, with this connection becoming more pronounced in Alexandrian poetry.[67] The closer the cultural parallels, so the ethnographic logic goes, the closer the bonds between the ethnic groups in question. So, for example, the inhabitants of Colchis were thought to be descended from Egyptian colonists left behind by Sesostris because both groups practiced circumcision in the manner of Egyptian Jews (Diod. 1.55.4–5; cf. 1.29.5–6).[68] In this case, a Greek response to crisis (the men must carry the ship because it is stuck) acts as a rational model for a peculiar Egyptian ritual. The portage of the Argo represents a cultural link between Greece and Egypt, but more importantly it is a link that privileges the anteriority of the Greek side of the equation.

One of the implications of this episode is that Ptolemaic rule and religious protocols, from the institution of dynastic and private cults down to the celebration of royal figures on a spectacular scale, are not merely borrowed from Egyptian archetypes: on the contrary, Egyptian culture is anachronistically coded in the *Argonautica* as originally Greek. Alexander's participation in the Siwah ritual served to naturalize aspects of the cult of Amon, bringing it within the compass of a Hellenized Egyptian experience. Then, too, the ethnocentric mirroring of Egyptian cult activity in

---

[66] Herodotus 2.35. On Herodotus' influence on Hellenistic ethnography, see Vasunia 2001; Murray 1972, 256–57. On Hecataeus as a corrector of Herodotus' popular history, see Burstein 1992.
[67] Stephens 2003, 24–25.
[68] On the traditional connection between Colchis and Libya/Egypt, see Stephens 2003, 175, n. 8; Clare 2002, 33–38 with notes; Braund 1994, 9, 17–19, 25. Stephens argues that the association of Egypt with Colchis points toward the establishment of competing ethnic registers in the poem (2003, 235).

the Libyan episode reinforces Jason's standing in turn as an "Alexander figure."[69] His unusual interview with the Herossae not only sets him apart from Medea and the other Argonauts but also underscores his privileged standing as a chosen intermediary between them and the Egyptian gods.

But even as the episode assimilates an Egyptian ritual to Greek heroic epic it also constructs a new version of Greek heroism that is at odds with traditional epic formulations. In privileging *homonoia* over conflict and representing it, together with piety, as the prerogative of a particular ethnic group, the *Argonautica* also prefigures the *Aeneid*.[70] Of interest in this regard is the mutual influence of poetic and political ideals on mythic characterization and personal image-making.[71] Alexander had emulated the behavior of Homeric warriors and imagined himself a new Achilles;[72] conversely, the tale of the Argonauts was shaped, to a certain extent, by newer, more "politically correct" versions of Alexander's exploits. Achilles may have inspired Alexander to expand the boundaries of the Hellenic world, but the consolidation of power in this new world called for a revised heroic paradigm, one that tempered the stylized violence and tragic alienation of traditional epic with a modern alloy of mutual cooperation, peaceful reconciliation, and divine stewardship.

---

[69] On the resonance of the Alexander legend in the *Argonautica*, see Solomon 1998. Jason's vision of the Herossae also recalls Ptolemy Soter's vision of the statue of Pluto at Sinope, which demanded to be brought to Alexandria (Plut. *De Is. et Os.* 29). Ptolemy, like Jason, requires aid in interpreting the dream, and the statue is eventually identified with Sarapis.

[70] See Cairns 1988, 125: "Nationalism in the *Aeneid* and its geographical signals are therefore aspects of the theme of *concordia* after a civil war, which is one of the major preoccupations of the *Aeneid*."

[71] Rostropowicz 1983, 61 sees Philadelphus as a model for Jason's diplomatic character, citing in particular his charitable aid to characters in need, such as Phineus and Phrixus. She observes that the idealized portrait of the Hellenistic king as a defender of the weak can also be seen in Alcinous, the Phaeacian king.

[72] On Alexander's self-identification with Achilles, see Vasunia 2001, 254; Stewart 1993, 78–86.

CHAPTER 2

The politics of Alexandrian poetry

ALEXANDER AND THE PTOLEMIES IN EGYPT

In comparing Jason with Alexander the Great, among others, it is not my intention to argue for anything resembling consistent parallelism. That there is a loosely selective parallelism between these two figures has already been discussed by scholars like Hunter and Rostropowicz, and it has no doubt also been recognized privately by countless others. Jason's voyage with the Argonauts from Thessaly to the Black Sea shares the broadest of outlines with Alexander's expedition from Macedonia to the far reaches of India. Both are young leaders, confronting political opponents before and during foreign campaigns; both marry eastern princesses and survive the rigors of prolonged travel. Yet there are also countless differences between them, foremost among them being, for example, Alexander's Achillean battle lust and Jason's unheroic domestic overthrow by Medea. The argument of this book is not that Apollonius seeks to reconcile these extremes but that the *Argonautica* splits aspects of Alexander's character into separate wavelengths, like bands of light in a prism, some of which are reflected at times in Jason, while others may appear in Heracles, and so on. Jason in his turn is a composite figure, now a warlike Alexander or Ares (3.1282–83), now radiant like Apollo (1.307–11; 3.1283) as a kind of Ptolemaic precursor.[1] His complex character is thus metaphorically evoked by the seven varied scenes on his cloak (1.721–67), whose unity is essentially predicated on the fact that they are grouped together: their coherence is local rather than thematic, spatial rather than logically sequential.

The *Argonautica*, moreover, does not articulate the historical details of Alexander's conquest but is instead concerned with the political implications of that conquest and its ideological afterlife in Ptolemaic Egypt. Of special importance in this regard were the religious activities that helped

---

[1] On the politically significant association of Jason with light and the sun, see Stephens 2003, 214–15.

to define the divine status of Alexander and his royal successors. Images associated with Egyptian religion were, as I noted in the Introduction, influential in the organization of Ptolemaic rule, although differences with Hellenic traditions and practices were obvious. Alexander and his father had largely promoted their piety or kinship ties with the gods for political ends, but Egyptian kingship was another matter because it explicitly conferred divinity upon the pharaoh during his lifetime. Yet because the concept of a godly mortal, while unusual, was not entirely alien to the Greek world, the dynastic cults associated with the Ptolemies developed out of a combination of Egyptian and Greek influences. By way of framing the multiple perspectives that are implicit in the portrayal of the Argonauts, then, this chapter explores how divine kingship, as well as religious activity in general, were promoted by Alexander, the early Ptolemies, and the scholar-poets of the Alexandrian Library, with an emphasis on the aesthetic ties between the works of other contemporary poets and the *Argonautica* as an epic exploration of the archaic origins of cults, customs, and the Greek presence in North Africa.

Alexander visited Egypt only once, but during those six months he established the foundations of what would later become the Ptolemaic monarchy, and ultimately played a pivotal role in justifying its reign both to the native Egyptian population and throughout the Mediterranean.[2] Egypt had been occupied by Persia with few interruptions since Cambyses' conquest in 525, but when Alexander, fresh from a string of victories in Asia, sailed to Memphis in 332,[3] the satrap Mazaces fled, surrendering Persian control of the country.[4] Alexander celebrated his victory with public games and sacrifices, having secured Egypt without shedding a drop of Macedonian, Greek, Persian, or Egyptian blood.[5] A recently discovered epigram by Posidippus celebrates the fierce glance of an Alexander statue crafted by Lysippus, the king's official court sculptor, and comments that the Persians could hardly be blamed for scattering like cows before a lion.[6] Macedonian authority in Egypt was thus founded on the threat rather than the exercise of force, and this fortunate turn of events helped to shore up a beneficent

---

[2] On the ideological importance of Alexander's kingship for the early Ptolemies, see Stephens 2003, 75.
[3] Memphis had become the capital of Egypt and the residence of the pharaohs in 663 after the Assyrian sack of the ancient capital, Thebes.
[4] Persian troops garrisoned in Egypt had been sent to the battle of Issus with the previous satrap, who was killed there (Arr. 3.1.1–3, 2.11.8).
[5] Bosworth 1993, 70.
[6] 65 AB. The Persian defeat by Alexander is likewise celebrated in epigrams 31 and 35, while 70 seems to have compared Lysippus' skill with that of Polyclitus; cf. 62 AB.

royal ideology – for Alexander as well as the Ptolemies – that was based on "divine descent, warrior prowess, reverence toward the gods, and generosity toward men."[7]

Divine descent was a matter of particular significance. When Alexander visited the oracle of Amon in the Siwah oasis, he made much of a slip by a priest who approached him (so goes the claim), not with the greeting "My son" (*O paidion*) but rather "Son of Zeus" (*O pai Dios*).[8] Such tokens (rumors?) of divinity counted for much in Macedonia and in a land accustomed to the rule of pharaohs,[9] and Alexander evidently recognized piety as an associative idiom that could quickly secure Greco-Macedonian hegemony.[10] He embraced Egyptian custom, sacrificing to Apis in the temple of Ptah in Memphis (Arr. 3.1.2–4) and restoring the temple of Ba'al, which had previously been destroyed by the Persians (Arr. 3.16.4; 7.17.1–3).[11] Alexander's position was founded on military strength, but his consultation with the oracle of Amon and his respect for Egyptian religion in general undoubtedly helped to win the approval of the native population, not least because of the contrast with the earlier intolerance of the Persians, who had either ignored or dishonored the local gods.[12]

The priestly bureaucracy did not go so far as to regard Alexander as the equivalent of a native-born pharaoh, however. While Alexander's political authority was acknowledged, he was not crowned in a traditional Egyptian ceremony,[13] and in fact it is unclear whether any of the early Ptolemies were, at least not until the beginning of the second century.[14] What is more, the Egyptian construct of a divine kingship supported by a priestly

---

[7] Samuel 1993, 181

[8] Plut. *Alex.* 27.5; cf. Arr. 3.3–4; Diod. 17.49–51. See also Worthington 2004, 86–89; Bosworth 1993, 72–74 for detailed descriptions of the visit to the oasis. It is probably not a coincidence that the Oracle of Apollo at Didyma and the Sibyl at Erythrae both came to Memphis shortly after Alexander's return with confirmation of his divine paternity (Callisthenes *FGrH* 124 F 14a).

[9] See Hölbl 2001, 10, 78, and 98–99 on the significance of the visit and the link between the cult of Zeus Amon in Siwah and the worship of Libyan Amon in Greece and Macedonia.

[10] Merkelbach 1981, 28–29.   [11] See further Vasunia 2001, 266–67.

[12] Alexander was not always supportive. The destruction of the citadel of Persepolis, sacred capital of Ahuramazda, avenged the Persian destruction of Greek temples in 480/79, and undermined a nearly monotheistic cult that was incompatible with Greco-Macedonian polytheism (Fredricksmeyer 2003, 259–60).

[13] Worthington 2004, 85; Bosworth 1993, 71; Burstein 1991. According to the "Alexander Romance," Alexander was formally crowned, but this account is not reliable.

[14] See Mooren 1982, 208–9, n. 10 on the first real evidence for an Egyptian coronation in Memphis, that of Ptolemy V Epiphanes in 196, which is recorded on the Rosetta stone. Cf. Koenen 1977, 58–63, who argues that Ptolemy II Philadelphus (and possibly Ptolemy I Soter as well) became not only *basileus* ("king") upon the death of his predecessor, but was crowned pharaoh in a formal Egyptian ceremony. Neither of Alexander's immediate heirs, his half-brother Philip III and son Alexander IV, went to Egypt at any time (Hölbl 2001, 13).

bureaucracy could not have been easily accepted by the Macedonians and Greeks themselves: after Alexander's arrival in India the Macedonian army is said to have mocked his claim to be a god, the son of Amon (Diod. 17.108.3; Arr. 7.8.3).

Certain Greeks are thought to have granted divine honors to living men in the past, but such treatment tended to be the exception, and cults in honor of fallen city founders or heroes remained the rule. In 422, for example, the people of Amphipolis replaced the memorials of the Athenian Hagnon, who had founded the city in 437/6 and was still alive, with memorials for the Spartan general Brasidas, who was mortally wounded defending the city against Athens and was to be honored thereafter as a hero with annual sacrifices (Thuc. 5.11.1). Then, too, Alexander's father, Philip II, was celebrated in ways that might imply divinity: his image was housed as a *synnaos* in the temple of Artemis on Ephesus, and the inhabitants of Eresos on Lesbos dedicated altars to Zeus Philippios.[15] While everyone would agree that these are signs of extraordinary gratitude and esteem, many scholars are reluctant to conclude that these cults were actually honoring Philip himself as a god.[16] Interestingly, the king chose to include his own image in a procession of statues of the Twelve Gods during the wedding celebration of his daughter at Aegae (Diod. 16.92.5), and while this might be thought to indicate immodest aspirations, it was likely meant only as a public acknowledgment of royal piety.[17] Since the Twelve Gods were portrayed on the Parthenon frieze and were primarily associated with Athens,[18] and since there is no evidence for this particular cult in Macedonia prior to the procession, it was probably intended to illustrate the support of the Greek gods for the planned invasion of Asia.[19]

Setting these controversial examples aside, we can be certain of only one cult being dedicated to a living man, and it continues to be an anomaly. The Spartan general Lysander was granted divine honors, complete with sacrifices, contests, and paeans, on Samos for the remainder of his life,

---

[15] Statue in Ephesus: Arr. 1.17.11; altars in Eresus: Tod 1948, no. 191.6.
[16] Worthington 2004, 200 observes that Zeus was marked as Philip's protector rather than identified with him on Lesbos; Bosworth 1993, 281 comments that the erection of a statue on Ephesus did not in itself constitute an act of deification. On Philip's political influence in this region see Habicht 1970, 15–16.
[17] Worthington 2004, 201.
[18] The Twelve Gods were Aphrodite, Apollo, Ares, Artemis, Athena, Demeter, Dionysus, Hephaestus, Hera, Hermes, Poseidon, and Zeus, though local versions varied, and Greek textual evidence focuses primarily on the number rather than the individual names of the gods. See Long 1987, 141.
[19] Long 1987, 210. After surveying the evidence Long concludes on p. 230 that Hellenistic rulers apparently avoided association with the Twelve for almost a century, possibly because of the tragic ends of those who promoted it (Philip, Alexander, Antigonus the One-Eyed, and Demetrius).

Alexander and the Ptolemies in Egypt

and was presumably the first Greek to be celebrated in this fashion.[20] But in any event the range of meaning for the Greek term *theos* ("god") was quite expansive, and as the social historian Diana Delia observes: "It might denote an Olympian god, a demigod, a hero, or a Hellenistic sovereign."[21] As she explains, to the ancient Greeks divinity "was not construed as an absolute, but instead was an unstructured abstract signifying varying levels and nuances of power."[22] Because the celebration of deceased founders, heroes, and kings was traditionally expressed through cult worship, the concept of a divine ruler was less of an absolute contradiction than an adaptation of already existing religious categories to the accomplishments of an exceptional figure.[23]

So, while the dynastic cult of the Ptolemies undoubtedly owed something to the divine status of the Egyptian pharaoh, it also looked back to the hero cult of Alexander the Founder, established by Alexander's successor in Egypt, Ptolemy I Soter, son of Lagus.[24] At Alexander's death, practical governance of Egypt passed to Ptolemy (Diod. 18.3.1; Arr. *Succ.* 1.6). Alexander had earlier selected the site for Alexandria en route to the oracle of Zeus Amon noted above. Conveniently situated on an isthmus between Lake Mareotis and the sea (Arr. 3.1),[25] the new city had access to two harbors as well as the Nile (via canal), and it soon became the administrative center of the country and an important commercial port – there being so few navigable harbors in the area.[26] Ptolemy followed Alexander's example in treating the Egyptians well (Diod. 18.14.1),[27] and in maintaining good relations with the temples, as the Satrap Stele, issued in 311, indicates.[28]

---

[20] Plut. *Lys.* 18; Paus. 6.3.14–15; Duris *ap.* Athen. 15.696e. Habicht 1970, 2–6 argues that the story has been wrongly called into question: Lysander was awarded these honors on Samos by the previously exiled oligarchs who had been restored to power by him; for further discussion of this and several other examples see Hölbl 2001, 92–98; Bosworth 1993, 280; Certaux and Londrlau 1957, 109.

[21] Delia 1993, 197.   [22] Delia 1993, 197.

[23] See Shipley 2000, 158–63 on the relation between the Greek practice of extending divine honors and Hellenistic ruler cult.

[24] Préaux 1978–92, 1:225–57. For additional reading on this subject, see Delia's response to Samuel (Delia 1993, 196 with n. 24).

[25] On the location see Shipley 2000, 214–16; Bosworth 1993, 246–47.

[26] When Alexander left Egypt in 331, he assigned financial control of the region to Cleomenes of Naucratis (Arr. 3.5.1–5), whose corrupt abuse of his office did not impede his rapid promotion to satrap. To secure his position, Ptolemy later used the 8,000 talents from Cleomenes' treasury to hire Greco-Macedonian troops and mercenaries, who were encouraged to take up residence in Egypt through land grants (*kleroi*) (Diod. 18.14.1–2). He also arranged for the murder of Cleomenes, an unpopular figure whom he rightly suspected of disloyalty (Paus. 1.6.3). On the Ptolemaic army and navy, see Lewis 1986, 20–27; Bevan 1968, 165–177. On *kleroi*, see also Manning 2003, *passim*; Shipley 2000, 217–19; Van 'T Dack 1988, 1–46, esp. 7–9; Lewis 1986, 24–25.

[27] On the Hellenistic kings' reliance on the support of their cities, see Davies 2002, 6–7.

[28] On the Satrap Stele (Cairo Museum CG 22182; for hieroglyphs see Sethe 1904–16, 1:11–22; for English translation see Rittner 2003, 392–97), dated to 311, Soter recounts his recovery of artifacts from the

He helped to finance the elaborate burial of the Apis bull (Diod. 1.84.8), returned lands that had been taken away from the Egyptian temples by the Persian satraps, and allowed the priests to retain control of their lands and cult practices.[29]

In religious matters, Soter was advised by Timotheus, an Athenian high priest of ceremonies at Eleusis, and Manetho, an Egyptian high priest at Heliopolis. On their recommendation Soter promoted a cult dedicated to Sarapis, a deity blending elements of the Egyptian Osiris with the Greek Dionysus.[30] Along with the worship of "the Egyptian gods" (Sarapis, Isis, and her son Harpocrates), Soter introduced the cult of Alexander the Founder and an eponymous priesthood dedicated to Alexander.[31] By acquiring Alexander's body from the funeral cortege en route to Siwah for burial (Diod. 28.3.5) and by capitalizing on – or at least not contradicting – the rumor that he was Alexander's half-brother,[32] Ptolemy presented himself as the rightful successor to the Egyptian throne, both in the eyes of Egyptians and the other Diadochs – the officers who had divided Alexander's empire among themselves after the king's death.[33] Ptolemy waited until at least 306

Persians and his return of the land of Pe and Dep to the Egyptians. Ptolemy II Philadelphus makes similar claims on the Pithom Stele of 264 (CG 22183; see Sethe 1904–16, 2:81–104), as does Ptolemy III Euergetes in the Canopus decree of 238 (*OGIS* 1:56; for hieroglyphs from the stele found at Tanis [= CG 22187] see Sethe 1904–16, 2:124–54; for English translation see Simpson 1996, 224–41. See Manning 2003, 68; Stephens 2003, 13–14. As Egyptians believed hieroglyphs to be the representation of divine speech (Ray 1994, 52), the shift to demotic and administrative Greek under the Ptolemies had considerable religious implications. On the rise of a bilingual bureaucratic class in Egypt, see Thompson 1994, 72–79. On these and other priestly decrees, see Stanwick 2002, 6–14.

[29] Thompson 1988, 109.

[30] Plut. *De Is. et Os.* 28. See also Stephens 2003, 15–16. Shipley 2000, 165–66 notes that the god Sarapis can be dated back to the life of Alexander. The cult would extend beyond Egypt, though it would never be as popular as the worship of Isis. The most famous temples were at Alexandria and Memphis; the Athenians also honored Ptolemy by erecting a temple to Sarapis (Paus. 1.18.4).

[31] The state cult of Alexander the Founder was unrelated to the eponymous priesthood of the royal cult (Habicht 1970, 36).

[32] Among the Macedonians the story circulated that Soter's mother was pregnant by Philip II before her marriage to Lagus, which if true, would have made Soter an illegitimate brother of Alexander (Paus. 1.6.2; Curt. 9.8.2).

[33] Coinage was also very important for publicizing Ptolemy's association with Alexander. Ptolemy promoted his military service by minting coins such as the cast of a gold stater which shows Ptolemy I on one side and on the other, Alexander in an elephant quadriga, an allusion to the Indian campaign (London, British Museum; see Stewart 1993, black and white figure no. 76c). Unlike the other Successors, who continued to mint Alexander's coinage even after they assumed royal standing (Mørkholm 1991, 59), Ptolemy was quick to innovate. By 321 or 320 he had minted silver tetradrachms that paired a standard reverse of a seated Zeus and inscription marking the coin as Alexander's, with a new obverse: the head of a deified Alexander wearing an elephant scalp headdress, the ram's horn of Zeus Amon, and the royal diadem (Mørkholm 1991, 63). After Ptolemy assumed the royal title, he exchanged the image of Alexander on the obverse for his own image (Mørkholm 1991, 27), and by 298 or 297, his reign was sufficiently established to forgo the numismatic nod to Alexander entirely. Gold and silver coins thereafter featured Ptolemy on the obverse with the Ptolemaic eagle standing on a thunderbolt on the reverse (Mørkholm 1980, 157). On the eagle as a Ptolemaic symbol, see Stephens 2003, 158–59.

to adopt the royal title,[34] and he made sure that his connection to Alexander was well established and highly visible. As Andrew Stewart comments, "By the time Ptolemy [I Soter] retired in 285 and died in 283, Alexander must have been a familiar sight."[35] The body of the king was on display in the magnificent tomb known as the Sema, and numerous cult statues and commemorative paintings were scattered throughout the city.[36]

Alexander's divine legacy would therefore prove to be as useful to the Ptolemies as his original appetite for conquest had been. Beginning with Ptolemy II Philadelphus, the Ptolemies would receive cult offerings.[37] Philadelphus continued Soter's practice of supporting Egyptian cults, especially that of Isis, for which he built a temple on the island of Philae.[38] But he also inaugurated cults to honor his parents as the *Theoi Soteres* ("Savior Gods"), and himself and his sister Arsinoë II, whom he took as his second wife, as the *Theoi Adelphoi* ("Sibling Gods").[39] Like Alexander, Philadelphus shored up his divine status by tracing his lineage to Zeus, if somewhat less directly through Heracles and Dionysus.[40] *Idyll* 17, an encomium composed by the Syracusan poet Theocritus in honor of Philadelphus, celebrates Heracles as the ancestor of both Alexander and Soter (17.26–27).[41] The divine ancestry of the Ptolemies was similarly promoted in official documents like the Adulis inscription, which commemorated Euergetes'

---

[34] The death of Alexander's young son Alexander IV cleared the way for Antigonus the One-Eyed, Cassander (the son of Antipater), Ptolemy, and Lysimachus to claim royal status in their respective territories. Evidently the first to assume the royal title was Antigonus the One-Eyed, soon after the defeat of Ptolemy's fleet off the coast of Cyprus in 306; he immediately named his son Demetrius as co-regent. For discussion see Billows 1990, 135–60.

[35] Stewart 1993, 252.

[36] Stewart 1993, 163, 243–52 identifies four types of freestanding representations of Alexander in Alexandria. We possess late antique descriptions of two: an equestrian statue of Alexander the Founder (*ktistes*), and a statue of Alexander being crowned by Ge, who is herself crowned by Fortune, from the temple of Fortune that adjoined the Museum. Six replicas have survived of the so-called "Fouquet Alexander," a standing heroic nude with spear in the left hand, as have seventeen replicas of the Alexander Aigiochos, a statue of Alexander wearing a goatskin aegis: see Frontispiece.

[37] On the duality of Ptolemaic kingship, see Koenen 1993; on the divinity of the Egyptian pharaoh, Pernigotti 1997, 132–33; on the rise of Greek dynastic cult, see Thompson 1988, 125–38.

[38] Hölbl 2001, 86.

[39] The dynastic cult grew out of the original royal cult dedicated to Alexander with an eponymous priesthood (Hölbl 2001, 94–95). On the cult dedicated to Ptolemy II (with temple and priesthood) by the people of Byzantium, see Habicht 1970, 116–21.

[40] Kinship with both Heracles and Dionysus is evoked by a cult statuette of Ptolemy Philadelphus holding a club, the standard weapon, along with the bow, of Heracles, and wearing an elephant headdress, an updated version of Heracles' lion headdress (bronze statuettes of Ptolemy II and Arsinoë II: London, British Museum no. 38442). The elephant headdress symbolized Alexander's Indian exploits, which were in turn associated with the travels of Dionysus. The cult image thus alludes to the king's divine ancestry, and is paired with a statuette of Arsinoë II, identified here by the double cornucopia.

[41] Maehler 1988 suggests that artistic and poetic depictions of Heracles were popular not because of the hero's ties to the Ptolemaic dynasty but as compensation for the loss of real political power under their rule.

expedition into Asia and his recovery of objects taken by the Persians: "The great king Ptolemy (III), son of King Ptolemy and of Queen Arsinoë, the *Theoi Adelphoi*, the children of King Ptolemy and of Queen Berenice, the *Theoi Soteres*, descended through his father from Heracles, the son of Zeus, and through his mother from Dionysus, the son of Zeus."[42]

Dionysus was even more vigorously worshipped than Heracles, and was especially conspicuous in the famous Grand Procession (*pompe*), Philadelphus' sumptuous tribute to the late king.[43] The *pompe* staged a number of scenes from Dionysus' life, and included several oversized statues of Dionysus, such as a fifteen-foot statue of the god clad in a purple tunic, saffron coat, and purple mantle, surrounded by gold vessels and Bacchic trappings. In addition, the god's political role was signaled by statues of Alexander and Soter and by images of the Greek islands and cities. Alexander's connection with Dionysus was illustrated by a twelve-foot-tall automated image of Nysa (the nymph associated with the god's place of birth) that could stand, drink a libation, and reseat itself. The *pompe* demonstrated both the strength of the Ptolemies' army and the enormity of their wealth, reckoned at 740,000 talents by Appian (*Praef.* 10), but it also associated them, before an audience that included visiting dignitaries and other guests of political importance, with the Indian campaigns of Dionysus and of the new Dionysus, Alexander.

What all this means is that it was as important for the Ptolemies to demonstrate a divine heritage that satisfied the Hellenic community as it was to establish themselves in Egyptian terms as the heirs to the Egyptian throne. Intimations of Ptolemaic divinity are evident in some of the *Idylls* of Theocritus, whose seventeenth *Idyll* (noted above) hymns the apotheosis of Soter (13–18) as well as the pious and godlike behavior of Philadelphus (121–34). In the *Hymn to Delos* Callimachus also alludes to Philadelphus' divinity when the as-yet-unborn Apollo forbids his mother, the goddess Leto, from giving birth to him on the island of Cos because, as he prophetically declares, it will be the birthplace of another god (*theos allos*), namely Philadelphus: "But on it by the Fates some other god is destined to be

---

[42] *OGIS* 1:54: translation by Burstein 1985, no. 99, p. 125, with slight modifications. Burstein notes that Ptolemy III was the biological son of Ptolemy II and Arsinoë I, his first wife, and was later adopted by Arsinoë II, and that both Ptolemy II and Arsinoë II claimed descent from Heracles and Dionysus.

[43] The year of the Ptolemaieia, the festival during which this procession took place, is not certain. Soter died in 283/2, and a generous estimate for the Ptolemaieia is at some point between 280 and 270. Hölbl 2001, 94 dates it to 279/8; Rice 1983, 5, 165 suggests that 280–275 is likely; additional bibliography is cited in Hunter 2003, 2, n. 6. Callixenus composed the surviving account of the procession (*pompe*) by consulting state records more than one hundred years after the event. His description is preserved in the *Deipnosophistae* of Athenaeus (Athen. 197d–e), dating from the second to third century AD.

born, a most high-born descendant of the Savior Gods."[44] Likewise, in the *Hymn to Zeus* Callimachus praises the Ptolemies for their generosity, power, and close association with the Olympian gods,[45] linking the pharaoh with the Egyptian deity Horus-the-Child, a cult association that was actively promoted by the Ptolemies.[46]

To a Hellenic audience, then, Ptolemy presented himself as the divine son of Zeus by descent through Heracles and Dionysus, while to an Egyptian audience he was seen as the embodiment of Horus and the son of Amon-Re. Such ethnic distinctions were preserved, at least in the early years of the dynasty, because a straightforward assertion of divinity expressed in foreign (i.e., Egyptian) terms might have been taken less seriously or even rejected, as was the case in India when the Macedonians mocked Alexander's claim of descent from Amon-Re. The Greek and Egyptian cultural idioms accordingly remained separate even when they were recognized as closely related.[47] It is important to keep these ideas of cultural difference and transferability in mind with respect to the *Argonautica* not only because it translates Egyptian concepts into Greek ones, as is the case with the portage of the Argo, but also because it translates contemporary military and political images (whether Hellenic or Egyptian) into forms that are more appropriate to epic poetry.

POETRY UNDER THE PTOLEMIES: EPIC AND ENCOMIUM

In amassing an unprecedented collection of papyri in the Library of Alexandria, the Ptolemaic dynasty became the center of attention for a new circle of literary scholars and poets. The bulk of this laudatory industry was devoted not so much to the Ptolemaic kings as to their queens. Arsinoë II, Philadelphus' second wife, was especially admired, presumably because of her extensive involvement in cultural events. A glimpse of her patronage can be found in Theocritus' *Idyll* 15, which follows two women attending the festival celebration of Adonis that has been sponsored by the queen in the royal palace. As Andrew Foster shows in a recent article, Theocritus praises Arsinoë by comparing her with Homeric characters like Arete, Circe, and Helen:

---

[44] 4.165–66 Pfeiffer ii. On the date of the poem and occasion of *Hymn* 4, see Mineur 1984, 15–18; Fraser 1972, 1:657–58. Cf. Virgil's elliptical references to Augustus as *deus* (*Ecl.* 1.6–7).
[45] *Hymn* 1.85–90 Pfeiffer ii. For discussion of the controversial identification of Ptolemy with Zeus in Callimachus' *Hymn* 1, see Stephens 2003, 77–79.
[46] Stephens 2003, 104.   [47] Koenen 1993, 29.

A low mimetic genre amalgamated with a lyric hymn recast into hexameters becomes the framework by which Theocritus not only presents a slice from the upper crust of Greek domestic life, but also adorns his representation of Arsinoe's Adonia with an encomiastic façade created from allusions to high epic hospitality scenes.[48]

Theocritus selects details from the tapestries of Homeric epic and reweaves them into allusive contexts that honor their royal patrons and also flatter their wit and cultivation. To the educated audience of the Ptolemaic court, the poem indicates that Arsinoë's wealth is not merely comparable to the fortune of Helen in the *Odyssey*, it surpasses it.[49]

The Alexandrians prized ingenuity and variety, and subtle differences are apparent in their encomiastic styles. Arsinoë was publicly associated with Olympian goddesses, perhaps during her lifetime. For example, two papyri, one dated to the middle of the third century and the other to the beginning of the second,[50] list numerous streets, perhaps with local shrines, that assimilated her name with the cult titles of other deities.[51] But the Alexandrian poets are inconsistent in this regard: Arsinoë's divinity is sometimes emphasized and sometimes avoided, apparently deliberately. The new Milan papyrus roll (*P. Mil. Vogl.* VIII 309) has yielded over a hundred new epigrams by the Macedonian poet Posidippus. Several of these (36–39 AB) are dedicated to Arsinoë, with one in particular (39 AB) referring to the temple of Arsinoë-Aphrodite on the headland of Zephyrion.[52] Stephens shows that both Posidippus and this temple, which displayed a single cult statue rather than two, identify Arsinoë entirely with Aphrodite.[53] Callimachus, on the other hand, seems to hesitate when it comes to associating Arsinoë with Olympian goddesses.[54] In contrast to Posidippus, who openly celebrates Arsinoë's identification with Aphrodite, Callimachus downplays her divinity, placing greater emphasis on everyday matters.[55] Even after the queen's death removed her from the mortal

---

[48] Foster 2006, 147.   [49] Foster 2006, 142–43.   [50] Fraser 1972, 1:237–38.
[51] E.g., the Street of Arsinoë Chalkioikos ("Of the Bronze House" = Athena), the Street of Arsinoë Karpophoros ("Bearer of Fruit" = Demeter), the Street of Arsinoë Teleia ("Fulfiller" = Hera). See Fraser 1972, 1:35–36, who notes that no streets were named for any other members of the royal house.
[52] Fantuzzi and Hunter 2004, 377–403, esp. 379, 384–85. On Posidippus and Arsinoë, see Stephens 2005, 243–48; Thompson 2005, 270–74.
[53] Stephens 2005, 247, noting that Posidippus refers to the queen as Cypris-Arsinoë (116 and 119 AB) and gives her Aphrodite's cult title "Euploia" in 39 AB.
[54] As we saw in Chapter 1, Apollonius is similarly reluctant to assign divinity to the Argonauts.
[55] Stephens 2005, 245: "Callimachus' approach is to highlight the insignificant or mundane while consigning manifestation of the royal house to the background," referring to the queen's depiction in "The Nautilus" (*Epigr.* 5 Pfeiffer ii). We possess a fragment from an epithalamium dedicated to her as well (fr. 392 Pfeiffer i).

sphere, Callimachus' "Apotheosis of Arsinoë" (fr. 228 Pfeiffer i) avoids explicit identification with an Olympian goddess, although the poem does indicate her divine status by describing the Arsinoeion, a shrine dedicated to her by Philadelphus. Stephens concludes that Callimachus' stylistic differences from Posidippus in this regard do not imply that the two were fierce competitors caught up in a theological dispute so much as friendly rivals, competing for innovative ways of celebrating their royal patrons.

Callimachus also praises Berenice II, the wife of Philadelphus' successor Euergetes, in two poems that frame the second half of the *Aetia*.[56] The *Aetia* is a lengthy elegiac poem that traces the *aitia* ("origins") of various cults and practices and comprises a loosely connected series of ancient and often fantastic tales, typically focusing on neglected or seemingly insignificant details.[57] The third book of the *Aetia* begins with an epinician elegy, called the *Victoria Berenices* ("Victory Song of Berenice"), which honors the success of the queen's entry in a chariot race at the Nemean games.[58] Much of this ode has not been preserved, but the surviving fragments indicate that Callimachus acknowledges Berenice's blood relation to the *Theoi Adelphoi* even though he continues to avoid identifying the living queen with Olympian goddesses, focusing instead on the struggles of a poor farmer named Molorchus. The fourth book of the *Aetia*, on the other hand, ends with an epithalamium, or marriage ode, called the *Coma Berenices* ("Lock of Berenice"),[59] which takes as its starting point the newly married queen's dedication of a lock of hair in exchange for Euergetes' safe return from the Third Syrian War (247–246). The story of the lock's unexpected displacement to the heavens is laced with allusions to Euergetes' invasion of Syrian territory and to Xerxes' naval expedition against the Greeks.[60] Once again the poet avoids describing the living queen as a divinity, though he now refers to the long deceased and deified Arsinoë – the heavenly agent behind

---

[56] This "royal frame" parallels the first half of the poem, which begins with a Prologue reference to Arsinoë as the tenth Muse in Book 1 (reconstructed from the word δεκάς, "tenth" [fr. 1.41 Pfeiffer i] and the Scholiast's comment [*Schol. Lond.* fr. 1.16–45 *ad* v. 41 Pfeiffer i and ends with a reference to her as a Muse in the Epilogue of Book 2 (Pfeiffer locates this at the end of Book 4: fr. 112 Pfeiffer i; cf. Cameron 1995, 141–62).

[57] Selden 1998, 324: "In a particularly fragmentary way, it brings together disjoint pieces of tradition, procured from different times, places, peoples, and milieus, cataloguing the contemporary world as one vast collection of memorials, each with its own peculiar character and disposition."

[58] *P. Lille* 82 (= *SH* 254). The date of the *Aetia* is uncertain, but the first half seems to belong to the 270s, whereas the second probably dates to the mid-240s. Fantuzzi and Hunter 2004, 42. Parsons 1977, 49–50 located the *Victoria Berenices* at the beginning of *Aetia* 3.

[59] Fr. 110 Pfeiffer i. Cf. Posidippus' epithalamium of Arsinoë and Ptolemy (*114 AB).

[60] Xerxes: fr. 110.45–46 Pfeiffer i. Euergetes: lines supplied by Catullus' translation (66.11–12): *qua rex tempestate novo auctus hymenaeo / vastatum finis iuerat Assyrios*. For interpretation of the elements of Egyptian ideology present in the poem, see Selden 1998, 329–54.

the catasterism of the lock – by Aphrodite's titles: Cypris and Zephyritis (fr. 110.56–57 Pfeiffer i). Like Theocritus and Posidippus, Callimachus commemorates these queens with works that are loosely framed by references, both overt and implied, to the royal cult, blending mundane realism with literal flights of fancy, the historical with the fabulous.[61]

The Alexandrian poets, so called because of their association with the Library (whether or not they actually worked there in an official capacity), delighted in these kinds of stylistic variations, in the "deliberate and novel conflation of elements from separate genres, so as to use say a dialect abnormal for the meter, or a meter abnormal for the type of poem."[62] In addition to this contrapuntal approach to poetic form and substance, these poets explored the exotic and obscure details of local myths, cults, and legends, juxtaposing the ancient with the contemporary, the epic with the pedestrian, and the wondrous with the quotidian. They traced the well known and familiar back to its unexpected origins as they sought out the causes and explanations for a multitude of cults and cultural events. Such apparently recondite interests have given the impression that these works would have held little appeal for a wide audience, but this position underestimates the popularity and political value of regional mythmaking. As Alan Cameron explains:

Every new city the length and breadth of the Hellenistic world devised links of one sort or another with the mythical past, declaring some itinerant god or hero (Dionysus, Heracles, Perseus or Orestes) its founder and proclaiming his name on the coinage, in the hope that some day a poet or historian would work out a connected narrative.[63]

In his 1995 book, *Callimachus and his Critics*, Cameron attacks the "ivory-tower" image of the Alexandrian poets, and tries to redefine critical assumptions about their aesthetic disagreements. The debate about Callimachus' professional rivalries has consequently intensified in recent years, with the prologue to the *Aetia*, known as the *Reply to the Telchines*,[64] at the center of the controversy. In the *Reply* Callimachus rails against certain literary enemies (called Telchines after a group of mythical shape-shifting artisans from Crete) who fault him for failing to write "a continuous poem

---

[61] On Callimachus' "genre-crossing" experiments with epinician and lyric, see Fuhrer 1993.
[62] Hutchinson 1988, 15, though he cautions that such mixing of genres was by no means unique to this period, and that on the whole the Hellenistic poets were primarily concerned with tonal or stylistic variation rather than generic variation (8–25).
[63] Cameron 1995, 26.
[64] The exact date and original placement of this fifty-line passage within the poem are uncertain. Fantuzzi and Hunter 2004, 66–76.

(ἓν ἄεισμα διηνεκὲς) in many thousands of lines on kings or heroes."[65] This passage is usually cited as evidence of his dislike for lengthy heroic epics like the *Argonautica*.[66] Callimachus and Apollonius are indeed said to have launched literary squibs against each other,[67] and the theory of a rift between the two, possibly caused by Apollonius' promotion to Chief Librarian, has lent credence to late biographical accounts of Apollonius' withdrawal to Rhodes after an unsuccessful public reading of an early version of the epic.[68] Such a narrative would conveniently account for Apollonius' incongruous geographical epithet "Rhodius" (he is typically assumed to have been a native of Alexandria), but the scholarly consensus is that all the evidence for the quarrel, the two substantially different editions, and the retreat to Rhodes, is unreliable.[69]

Even so, the possibility of Apollonius' unsuccessful recitation of the *Argonautica* does bring up questions about the popularity and performance contexts of epic during the Hellenistic period. As part of their cultural program the Ptolemies sought to preserve the Homeric epics, and papyrus finds

[65] Callimachus also refers to professional jealousy and literary quarrels in *Iambi* 1, 4, and 13 (= frr. 191, 194, 203 Pfeiffer i), at the end of the *Hymn to Apollo*, and in *Epigram* 21 Pfeiffer ii (= *Anth. Pal.* 7.525).

[66] Cf. Hunter 1993, 190–95, who suggests that although the phrase ἓν ἄεισμα διηνεκὲς can be taken to mean "a unified and consistent [i.e., non-episodic] poem" (193), which the *Aetia* is not, it could instead reflect Aristotelian principles and refer to a poem that is at once single (edited) and yet paradoxically continuous or unbroken (unedited). The Telchines would thus have foolishly admonished Callimachus for failing to do the impossible: write a single action (like the *Iliad*, which Aristotle praises) that is at the same time continuous and unbroken (like a history or the cyclic epics, which Aristotle condemns).

[67] An epigram, variously ascribed as the work of Apollonius the Grammarian, Apollonius of Rhodes, or an anonymous author, attacks the *Aetia* in two mock encyclopedia entries; Callimachus is thought to have written a poem titled "The Ibis," which presumably likened the *Argonautica* to a carrion bird. For further details, see Pfeiffer 1968, 141–43, who dismisses this evidence as poor. Cf. Green 1990, 201–2, in favor of the historicity of these sources (see also p. 783, n. 1).

[68] The ancient sources preserved with the manuscripts include a brief second- or third-century AD papyrus from the garbage dumps at Oxyrhynchus in Middle Egypt. The papyrus names Apollonius as a teacher of Ptolemy I (generally thought to be confused here with Ptolemy III) and the second chief librarian (after Zenodotus and before Eratosthenes); an entry in the Byzantine encyclopedia called the *Suda* dates him to the life of Euergetes and lists him as the third chief librarian (after Eratosthenes), and there are also two biographical notes (possibly late first century BC). *Vita* A states that Apollonius, a native of Alexandria, was Callimachus' pupil; after a reading of the *Argonautica* met with disapproval he went to Rhodes where the revised version was completed and celebrated. *Vita* B is similar but notes that his mother's name was Rhode and that he returned to Alexandria after the exile and was buried next to Callimachus. See Lefkowitz 2001 for a thorough evaluation of this evidence.

[69] That there were *somewhat* different versions is suggested by the scholiasts' references to six variants in an early text (*proekdosis*). See further Lefkowitz 2001; Cameron 1995; Rengakos 1992; Hunter 1989, 1–6; Lefkowitz 1980 rejects the story of the quarrel (214–19), but accepts the retreat to Rhodes (26). Stephens 2005 advances the argument that the quarrel (if it existed) was likely a playful debate about whether to praise the throne in Egyptian terms, as Callimachus does, or Macedonian, following Posidippus.

indicate that the *Iliad* and the *Odyssey* continued to be in demand among Greeks living in Egypt.[70] Homer was believed in antiquity to have been a blind poet from Chios or Smyrna, and whether such a person actually lived and dictated these epics at some point in the eighth or seventh centuries remains controversial. Was Homer, as Albert Lord put it, "an oral poet living in an age of writing,"[71] or are we to understand "Homer" as the embodiment of an archaic tradition of oral poetics that passed from generation to generation of epic singers (*aoidoi*)?[72] While the Homeric Question is unlikely to be resolved to everyone's satisfaction in the absence of new evidence, we do know that by the beginning of the third century the Alexandrian Library housed dozens of Homeric papyri, some of which had been official city texts and others privately owned. Variations in the performances of the *aoidoi* produced inconsistencies in many of these transcripts: lines were missing or added in some and reordered in others. Such transcripts were now being consulted by a new generation of performers, the rhapsodes, who competed in festivals all over the Mediterranean world. Some scholars believe that the contrast between the original *aoidos*, who composed in performance before a local audience, and the itinerant rhapsode (*rhapsoidos*), the professional "song-stitcher," who recited rather than composed from memory, has been exaggerated.[73] In any case, the salient point is that the variations common to all kinds of oral performances, those of *aoidoi* as well as rhapsodes, encouraged a multiform aesthetic that precluded a single definitive textual version.

All this began to change when, at the invitation of Philadelphus, Zenodotus of Ephesus (b. 325), the first head of the Library (*prostates*), became the first "corrector" (*diorthotes*) of Homeric epic,[74] producing an annotated version (*diorthosis*) that served as a standard reference text in the Library. This text did not circulate widely in the modern sense of publication,[75] but despite the lack of what might be properly termed a vulgate edition, the efforts of the Alexandrian scholars, especially the influential

---

[70] Shipley 2000, 247.   [71] Lord 1953, 131.
[72] Amid the vast bibliography on Homeric oral poetics, see esp. Lord 2000; Bakker 1997; Nagy 1996; Foley 1990; Parry 1987.
[73] E.g., Collins 2004, 176–78; Pavese 1998. Nagy 1990, 42: "We must not be too quick to dismiss the importance of the rhapsode, however: he must have been a master of mnemonic techniques directly inherited from oral poets." See also Nagy 1996, 107–52, for his theory of the textual evolution from performance transcripts of Homeric epic to "scripture," Nagy's term for written texts that do not presuppose oral performance.
[74] See Fraser 1972, 1:449; Pfeiffer 1968, 105–6 on Ptolemy's invitation to Zenodotus. For the Byzantine scholar Johannes Tzetzes' description of the founding of the Library (including the acquisition of books and the recruitment of scholars like Zenodotus), see Kaibel 1899, 19–20 (VI. Pb. 19–22). Zenodotus is listed as the first editor (*diorthotes*) of Homer in the *Suda* (*s.v.* Ζηνόδοτος).
[75] The efforts of Zenodotus (b. 325), Aristophanes of Byzantium (257–180), and Aristarchus (216–144) did not lead to the publication of a vulgate edition: Foley 1990, 23 with n. 7.

readings of Aristarchus, seem to have had a unifying effect on Homeric texts, which showed signs of standardization by the middle of the second century BC.[76]

Homer was in fact so revered in Egypt that Euergetes' successor, Ptolemy IV Philopator (ruled 221–205) divinized the poet and honored him with a temple called the Homereum (Ael. *VH* 13.22).[77] But it is harder to ascertain whether new, non-Homeric epics were being written at this time, and as Cameron cautions, "the erection of the Homereum need not mean that Philopator admired or patronized contemporary epic poets."[78] Ancient epic is commonly associated with, to paraphrase Callimachus, lengthy narratives on the deeds of kings and heroes, but in point of fact epic also addressed didactic and panegyric themes and was a vehicle for history, science, philosophy, and regional ethnography. It has been suggested that lengthy epic narrative, particularly historical epic, was the dominant Hellenistic genre, far more representative of popular taste than Callimachus' "slender" (λεπταλέην, *Aet.* fr. 1.24 Pfeiffer i) Muse.[79] This theory, based on a supposed demand for expansive historical epics praising the accomplishments of contemporary dynasts, would certainly account for Callimachus' combative stance in the *Reply to the Telchines*, but the dominance of the genre is hard to prove since we know these epics by title alone and so cannot be certain of either their length or their content.

Cameron has famously questioned the dominance of long epic narratives at this time, arguing that most Hellenistic epic tended to be short, and that specifically historical epic could not have been sufficiently popular to threaten Callimachus.[80] He holds that the *Reply to the Telchines* was directed not against proponents of overly long epic but rather against the *Lyde*, a prolix narrative elegy composed by the fourth-century poet Antimachus.[81] There is some evidence to support this hypothesis: Callimachus wrote an epigram condemning the opacity and expansive girth of the *Lyde*,[82]

---

[76] See West 1967, 15–17 on the diminishing number of so-called eccentric or wild papyri, which are characterized by deviations that appear much less frequently in Roman papyri and medieval manuscripts.
[77] On Homer as a cult figure, see Brink 1972, 549–52.
[78] Cameron 1995, 276. A fair statement, but if Philopator did not, Philadelphus obviously did.
[79] See Ziegler 1966 on the prominence of historical epic; against this and related views see Cameron 1995, 263–302, esp. 265–67, 287–89. On Ziegler see Fantuzzi 1988; for a clear-headed review of Cameron 1995, see Harder 2002b.
[80] Cameron 1995, 295.
[81] Cameron 1995, 337: "For Callimachus, repudiation of Antimachus did not imply repudiation of Homer. Bombast and lack of clarity (παχύ . . . καὶ οὐ τορόν) were *not* characteristic of Homeric style, nor were they to be found only in epic . . . In fact the Homeric commentators regularly praise Homer for the absence of precisely these vices . . . It was not the genre but the poet who was at fault."
[82] Λύδη καὶ παχὺ γράμμα καὶ οὐ τορόν (fr. 398 Pfeiffer i).

which was nonetheless admired by Asclepiades of Samos and Posidippus of Pella. Moreover, both Asclepiades and Posidippus were contemporaries of Callimachus and are listed elsewhere among those who reproached him for his downright "emaciated" (κάτισχνον) verse.[83] Callimachus' elegantly trim *Aetia* would accordingly be an understandable rejoinder to the bombast of the "fat" *Lyde*.

Nevertheless, the possibility remains that *some* kinds of long epic narrative were popular enough to be performed at poetry competitions, which continued well into the second and even third century AD.[84] In the course of challenging the modern characterization of Hellenistic poetry as separate from an authentic civic context and primarily intended for private study by a coterie of scholar-poets,[85] Cameron draws attention to the numerous festivals with agonistic venues for public recitation. While Cameron differentiates historical epic – on his view a short-lived genre for which there is little solid evidence – from full-scale mythological and regional epic, both of which are better attested,[86] he claims that the new epics performed in such contests would rarely have exceeded several hundred lines:

> On the traditional interpretation of the *Aetia* prologue, we have hitherto been asked to believe that short poems were eccentric and provocative, a minority taste without influence till Roman times. The truth is that only short epics can be assigned any plausible social context. By Callimachus's day, the popular significance of the term ἐπῶν ποιητής was someone who wrote short hexametrical poems on local cults and heroes or short hexameter encomia on important people. In this context it is difficult to see why there should have been a "debate" on the "validity" of epic.[87]

Such a debate would indeed have been peculiar under such circumstances, but what is less obvious is whether these circumstances have been properly represented, and whether Cameron is correct in limiting the definition of ἐπῶν ποιητής in this way. This phrase, as he observes, does not connote anything more than a poet composing dactylic hexameters, but if dactylic hexameter need not necessarily entail lengthy epics,[88] by the same token one cannot rule them out.[89]

Although a dearth of long epic narratives is crucial to the argument that the *Lyde* was Callimachus' sole target in the *Reply*, the assumption that

---

[83] See the Florentine Scholia to the Prologue, fr. 1.1–12 Pfeiffer i. Also listed is Praxiphanes of Mytilene, though Apollonius is not.
[84] Collins 2004, 192–202; Fantuzzi and Hunter 2004, 22, n. 84.
[85] See Cameron 1995, 47–53, esp. 50.
[86] On mythological and regional epic, see Cameron 1995, 295–301.
[87] Cameron 1995, 301. On encomia see further Hunter 2003, 8–24.
[88] Cameron 1995, 268.   [89] See Collins 2004, 201–2.

his target could *only* have been the *Lyde* implies a generic specificity that is missing from Callimachus' very general reference to long poems about kings and heroes. Since Callimachus' apparent dislike for the *Lyde* need not preclude dislike for other poems, Cameron's argument requires that almost all varieties of long epic be written off as unsubstantiated conjecture, either because they are to be chronologically disqualified (as later than the date of the *Aetia* prologue – which, however, Cameron dates much earlier than some)[90] – or because they are to be categorically excluded (as ethnographic or regional epic rather than historical, the genre Konrat Ziegler had originally posited as dominant).[91] There is, however, no real reason to assume that a hard line between past and present would have divided historical or ethnographic events from mythological epic (and vice versa), and in any case the self-evident breadth of the performance rubric ἐπῶν ποιητής belies such rigid distinctions.[92] Inscriptional lists of victors and participants show that the same individual might compete as an "epic poet" (ἐπῶν ποιητής) and also as a rhapsode, which indicates that performers of traditional, Homeric epic were being distinguished from the creators of new epic poetry.[93] The third-century poet Rhianus of Crete wrote a number of long epics (now lost), including the *Heracleia* (on the deeds of Heracles) and the *Messeniaca* (on the second Messenian war), but the former did not necessarily exclude historical or regional material, nor did the latter necessarily preclude mythological themes.

Such considerations aside, Cameron's argument that the *Reply to the Telchines* is critical of style (that of a single poem, the *Lyde*) rather than genre (prolonged epic narrative) is surely correct, and has broader implications since, as Annette Harder rightly observes, the *Reply* invites comparative study of style across many genres:

The "message" may well be that a poet should aim for the quality of small-scale, subtle and original poetry, and the reader seems to be invited to read this message against the background of a kaleidoscopic and allusive picture of earlier Greek poetry and earlier literary criticism. This fits in with the character of the *Aetia*, which, in spite of its being basically an elegiac catalogue poem, shows a great deal of generic variety and alludes to many of the predecessors hinted at in the prologue.[94]

---

[90] Cameron 1995, 127–32.   [91] Ziegler 1966.
[92] Cf. Jacoby 1956, 19 on the rationale for including different kinds of prose writing (mythography, biography, ethnography, etc.) in his *Fragments of the Greek Historians (FGrH)*.
[93] *IG* VII.419.14–17; for discussion see Pallone 1984, 161–62.
[94] Harder 2002b, 607–8. See also Harder 2002a, 211.

The same, for that matter, can be said of the *Argonautica* inasmuch as Apollonius draws not only on other epics (Homer, Hesiod), but also on a variety of other genres, from lyric (Pindar) and tragedy (Euripides, Aeschylus) to history and ethnography (Herodotus), not to mention elegy (Callimachus) and pastoral (Theocritus). For Callimachus and Apollonius alike, "[w]hat matters is *techne*, 'poetic craft,' however long the poem."[95]

There are two main points here. First, there were other, more likely targets for Callimachus than the *Argonautica*, as Cameron rightly suggests, and second, as an extended epic narrative the *Argonautica* is not likely to have been an anomaly in the third century, despite Cameron's argument to the contrary. Callimachus himself composed an *epyllion*, or miniature epic, called the *Hecale*, and while it would only have been as long as a single short book of the *Argonautica*,[96] these two works are closer in terms of "poetic craft" than one might initially assume. We possess only fragmentary remains of the *Hecale*, which frames Theseus' well-known slaying of the bull of Marathon with his lesser-known visit to the hut of the impoverished, elderly Hecale.[97] The model for this character is Homer's Eumaeus, the "divine swineherd," who welcomes the disguised Odysseus in *Odyssey* 15. Yet where the *Odyssey* is concerned, as one might expect, with Odysseus, the later epic focuses not on heroic exploits but on the suffering and death of its eponymous heroine, and concludes with Theseus' eulogy and establishment, in her honor, of a new deme, an annual feast, and a sacred precinct for Zeus Hecalius.[98] Theseus may have killed the bull, but Callimachus is more interested in his foundation of a cult celebrating the glory of Hecale's generous hospitality.[99]

This same kind of inversion appears, to comic effect, in the previously mentioned *Victoria Berenices*, the elegy that celebrates the queen's chariot victory at Nemea by recounting not only the origin of the games honoring Heracles' killing of the Nemean lion, but also the origin of the mouse trap. Callimachus tells how Heracles stops at the home of a peasant farmer named Molorchus, who lacks even the wood for a fire and whose meager stores are besieged by mice. Molorchus traps the mice, and the next morning Heracles sets out in pursuit of the lion, returning at some point to spend another night with Molorchus, whom he rewards with a new mule. The focus here, as in the *Hecale*, is on the impoverished host and his

---

[95] Fantuzzi and Hunter 2004, 69.
[96] The estimated length of the *Hecale* is approximately 1,000–1,200 lines; there are about 1,363 lines in *Argon.* 1; 1,285 in 2; 1,405 in 3; and 1,781 in 4; for a total of 5,834.
[97] On the story and background sources of the *Hecale*, see Hollis 1990, 5–10.
[98] On the hospitality theme, Hollis 1990, 341–54.   [99] Zanker 1977.

struggles – in this case to destroy the plague of mice and to satisfy the hero's formidable appetite.[100]

Thus, in both the *Hecale* and the *Victoria Berenices* Callimachus relegates the exploits of the hero to the narrative frame while thematizing tales of domestic poverty (a slender Muse indeed). One might be tempted to conclude that Callimachus' poetic craft as such was more experimental than Apollonius' tale of heroic adventure. However, the *Argonautica* in its turn is much more experimental than Homeric epic.[101] Like Callimachus, Apollonius relegates heroic exploits to the background: battle scenes are infrequent and abbreviated, gesturing in the direction of tradition rather than fully emulating it (e.g., 1.989–1011, 1021–77; 2.1–144; 3.1278–407; 4.482–91). The poem recalls Homer in some ways, such as, for example, the repetition of formulaic phrases or the use of particles, but Apollonius consistently transforms these elements in order to produce a narrative voice that is quite different from its archaic model.[102] And while it is true that the account of the Argonauts' outward voyage is recounted in linear and unbroken fashion, their return to Greece in Book 4 is still marked by chronological omissions, geographical confusion, and a feeling of helplessness that afflicts characters and narrator alike. Both the style and the structure of the *Argonautica* therefore compromise any expectation of a unified heroic world resembling that of Homeric epic.[103] What the poem's "epicizing" tendencies tend to do is to offset its innovative, non-traditional content, and demonstrate the poet's affirmation of the Callimachaean dictum that less equals more.[104]

Along these lines, the constructed and ambivalent character of epic time is clarified by the *Argonautica*'s conflicted temporal schemes. The poem addresses the heroes of the generation before the fall of Troy, but looks far beyond the archaic horizon to the latter-day influence of those heroes, drawing attention to modern gaps in knowledge about them. The narrator starts by temporally distancing himself from his subject ("I will remember the famous deeds of men born long ago," *Argon.* 1.1–2) and yet the poem's recurrent aetiological references collapse the distinction between mythological events set in ancient times and historical events that happened in

---

[100] Ambühl 2004. [101] See Hunter 2001, 105–19.
[102] E.g., on formulae, see Fantuzzi and Hunter 2004, 266–83; Fantuzzi 2001; on the use of particles, Cuypers 2005.
[103] The *Argonautica* steers clear, however, of full-blown epic parody along the lines of the *Batrachomyomachia*, the "Battle of the Frogs and Mice." On epic parody, see Olson and Sens 2000, xxxi–xxxv.
[104] Thus, while Ziegler (1966, 15) argued that the dominant style of Hellenistic poetry was closer to Apollonius than Callimachus, it seems that Apollonius' technique is more akin to that of Callimachus than Ziegler had assumed.

the recent past.[105] Forty years ago Fränkel observed that the aetiological reference to the future cult of the Dioscuri (4.650–53) could be seen as an epic precedent for the living ruler cult of the Ptolemies.[106] Hunter has since described this kind of slippage between the heroic and Hellenistic age as "literary anachronism." Apollonius, that is, created "effects of time disjunction, which strongly suggest that, though the events narrated may have 'happened' long ago, the poet's concerns, like those of Callimachus, are very much of the present."[107]

Space does not permit extensive analysis of the thematic and formal parallels between all Alexandrian poetry and the *Argonautica*, and so the remainder of this section will focus on the portrayal of cult in Callimachus and Apollonius. Callimachus' poetry presupposes what Richard Hunter and Therese Fuhrer have termed a "cultic imagination," meaning an Alexandrian thought-world that was as involved in observing religious activity as it was in being actively observant. In an excellent paper on Callimachus' *Hymns*, they write that "the poems construct an audience interested in rites practised by others, often very remote 'others,' to a far greater degree than the lyric hymns and the major Homeric Hymns; rites, real or imaginary, now exist in a decontextualized space from which they can at any time be drawn into poetic description."[108]

At issue here once more are broader questions of performance context and the authenticity of "literary" hymns. Callimachus' hymns were read and presumably recited, and while recitation constitutes a kind of performance it is highly unlikely that these poems were composed for actual ritual in the manner of an archaic choral hymn.[109] A more likely model would be the Homeric Hymns, a group of approximately thirty poems in dactylic hexameter, believed in antiquity to have been composed by Homer, though they appear to range in date from the eighth to the fifth centuries.[110] However, by the fourth century such hexametrical narrative hymns were no longer limited to rhapsodic competition and were in fact included in formal cult ceremonies. This movement, in which mimetic and essentially aetiological narratives are brought into a ritual context, is the corollary of what is happening in Callimachus' hymns, which dislodge the primacy of hymn-as-ritual-action and realign performative authenticity with hymn-as-literary-experience. This is especially true of the *Hymn to Apollo*, where the

---

[105] For this observation see Fantuzzi and Hunter 2004, 92–93 with n. 16.
[106] Fränkel 1968, 514.   [107] Hunter 1993, 167.   [108] Hunter and Fuhrer 2002, 148.
[109] Hutchinson 1988, 63.
[110] Allen *et al.* 1980, lxiv–lxxix: the evidence does not suggest, however, that Alexandrian scholars considered Homer to be the author (lxxix).

poet is "virtually equating the epiphany of the god with the performance of his poem."[111]

From this perspective Callimachus' experiments with hymnic style are transformed from what some have seen as a technical, fictive, essentially scholastic exercise in traditional forms of religious poetry,[112] to the consecration of poetic craft and its otherworldly capacity to influence and amuse its listeners (both mortal and divine), regardless of external setting. As Hunter and Fuhrer show, in the absence of specifically grounded performance contexts these poems internalize a wider range of "cultic material" as a meditation on the origins of cult experience. Although the break from occasion-bound, ritual performance contexts has been taken as confirmation of the stereotypical inauthenticity and artifice of Hellenistic poetry, their reading suggests that the hymns do not merely allude to the written tradition of cultic experience but also relocate that experience for the audience within the boundaries of a religious text.

The *Argonautica* does not, of course, frame cult activity in the same way that Callimachus' hymns do, but the two poets do share an interest in the story of the Argonauts because they are so often involved in cult foundations – an activity that does not occupy the Homeric heroes to anything like a comparable degree. The Argonauts' water sacrifice in the aition on Anaphe recalls the frugal sacrificial meals that are central to the aetiologies of the *Hecale* and the *Victoria Berenices*. Other common topoi include prophecy and sacrilege: in the *Argonautica* Phineus is punished for revealing the will of Zeus in its entirety (2.311–16), much like Tiresias, who sees far too much of the bathing Athena in Callimachus' fifth hymn (5.75–78 Pfeiffer ii). So, too, Paraebius' father cuts down a sacred oak at *Argon.* 2.468–89, just as Erysichthon destroys a grove sacred to Demeter in Callimachus' sixth hymn (6.31–56 Pfeiffer ii).[113] The Odyssean themes of hospitality, privation, and old age that are featured in the stories of Hecale and Molorchus are also reworked in Apollonius' Lemnian episode. Hypsipyle's aged nurse Polyxo advises the Lemnian women to create a new generation by entertaining the Argonauts in their homes (1.668–99); her selfless social engineering is the inverse of Hecale's self-sacrifice. The

---

[111] Hunter and Fuhrer 2002, 152.
[112] See esp. Depew 2001; 1998; 1993 on the disconnectedness of literary hymns from cult contexts. On the superficial religiosity of the hymns, Haslam 1993, 125 observes: "The *Hymns*, it goes without saying, are literary texts. To call them religious is simply to say that they inscribe themselves within the genre. If we ask, Why hymns?, the best answer might be, Why not? There was much mythological material about gods, and generically contextualizing it as hymnic had multiple poetic advantages over more straightforwardly narrative forms of presentation."
[113] On Ovid's revision of these tree violations, see Murray 2004.

sexual character of Lemnian hospitality sets it apart from its Callimachaean counterparts, but here again individual heroic grandeur is outpaced by communal concerns, and from an aetiological perspective the ultimate consequences of the stay on Lemnos outweigh even the recovery of the Golden Fleece. Like Theseus and the bull or Heracles and the Nemean lion, Jason's quest is merely the heroic frame for what really matters: the establishment of a Greek community in northern Africa.

Other passages suggest that Callimachus and Apollonius not only alluded to each other's work but sought to situate these stories in ways that promote this connection. The second to last aition of *Aetia* 4 (frr. 108–9 Pfeiffer i), for example, refers to the Argonauts' stay on the island Cyzicus, a story that forms the second aition of the epic (1.936–1077).[114] Similarly, in the second aition of *Aetia* 1 the narrator asks about the origin of the insulting sacrifices to Apollo on Anaphe (frr. 7–21 Pfeiffer i), and the same tale then appears as the second to last episode in the *Argonautica* (4.1706–30), before Euphemus' prophetic dream about the clod. Numerous points of correspondence and divergence between these two poems thus make it likely that they were composed during the same period of time, or that at the very least one of the poets was responding to and competing with the completed work of the other.[115]

Finally, it is important to remember that Apollo is as prominent in the *Argonautica* as he is in Callimachus' poems. The narrator not only mentions Apollo in the very first line of the poem, Ἀρχόμενος σέο, Φοῖβε, ("Beginning from you, Apollo," 1.1), but also emphasizes the Delphic oracle's approval of the Argo's voyage (1.209–10, 301–2), which is itself framed in the narrative by Jason's two prayers to the god in Book 1 and Book 4.[116] As has often been observed, the Argonauts, like the narrator, acknowledge Apollo as their guide, and Apollo is the god they most frequently propitiate (see Chapter 5). It is not surprising to find that at the conclusion of his second hymn (2.105–13) Callimachus decides to establish Apollo as his aesthetic spokesman. When Phthonos ("Envy") whispers a complaint about the *aoidos* who fails to sing like the sea (i.e., copiously), the god condemns such poetic flood waters as polluted and praises instead the pure essence

---

[114] The earliest aition is 1.28–31, the explanation for the profusion of wild oaks along the Thracian shore. Noted by Green 1997, 225, nn. 1070–77.
[115] For a structural analysis of the *Aetia* and comparison with the *Argonautica*, see Harder 1993, esp. 103–9; 2002a, 217–23. Harder observes that "Callimachus' brief episode seems to encompass the whole store of the Argonauts, but not in the usual chronological order" (223).
[116] The first prayer is quoted in full by the narrator (1.409–24); the second is reported indirectly and results in the god's revelation of the island Anaphe (4.1701–18). For further discussion of the treatment of Apollo in Callimachus' *Aetia* and in the *Argonautica*, see Harder 1993, 105–7.

of the water that bubbles up from a sacred spring (i.e., rarified poetry). Thinking back to the earlier discussion of the *Reply to the Telchines*, one can understand why Envy's complaint might have suggested that Apollonius, with his "oceanic" epic, was numbered among the Telchines, but Apollonius' affirmation of the god makes it difficult to avoid concluding that the *Argonautica*, too, was drawn from Apollo's sacred spring.

EPIC MODALITIES: ARCHETYPES OF DIVINE JUSTICE

Hellenistic poetry redefined not only the character of religious poetry but also the representation of power, describing gods, kings, and heroes with different emphases and from different perspectives than their literary predecessors. Composed with a royal audience in mind, these works offer an idealized image of kingship, one intended to mirror (or cultivate) a just and peaceful monarchy. As Mary Depew shows in a paper presented at the Groningen 2002 Hellenistic poetry workshop,[117] Callimachus' hymns (to Zeus, Apollo, Artemis, Delos, Athena, and Demeter) were likely intended as a unified group:

> It was accepted practice by the third century to dedicate books and treatises to the Ptolemies: what better gift to the monarchs than six hymns that, when taken together as a collection, construct an image of the dynasty in its first three generations, a construct that represents power, control, authority and mastery of both the great and the complex, the small and intricate?[118]

It should be noted that the Ptolemies were not unique in promoting this kind of politically informed poetry, however. The *Phaenomena*, a didactic epic written by the poet Aratus of Soli, modifies the portrait of Zeus that is familiar from archaic epic with a view to political ends. Aratus studied Stoic philosophy in Athens and accepted an invitation from the king of Macedon, Antigonus II Gonatas (277/6–239),[119] who had also attended lectures given by Zeno, the founder of Stoic philosophy,[120] and sought to cultivate an intellectually sophisticated court at Pella. The *Phaenomena*, Aratus' only extant work, is a verse description of weather signs and the

---

[117] Depew 2004.
[118] Depew 2004, 134. Cf. Hutchinson 1988, 63–64, who comments that while Callimachus' hymns may well have been conceived of as a set by the author, they would not form a unified entity in the manner of the *Aetia* or the *Iambi*: "the six poems show greater differences from each other even than the large Homeric Hymns."
[119] This visit is attested in three of the four Latin *Vitae* of Aratus (I, III, IV) as well as the *Suda* entry (*s.v.* Ἄρατος): for the texts see Martin 1956. For additional biographical information and biography, see Kidd 1997, 3–5.
[120] Shipley 2000, 127–28.

relative positions of the constellations. Callimachus,[121] who may have met Aratus, admired the *Phaenomena*, and so did Apollonius, apparently, since the *Argonautica* shows signs of its influence.[122] The poem's content is based on Eudoxus' prose work of the same name, though Aratus' *Phaenomena* is stylistically modeled on Hesiod's two epics, the *Theogony* and the *Works and Days*.[123] There are differences here too, however, for the *Works and Days* begins with a ten-line hymn celebrating Zeus's power over mortals, whereas the *Phaenomena* hails Zeus as the supreme benefactor of humanity, he who watches over travels by land and sea. For Hesiod, Zeus is quick to anger and a severe judge of human shortcomings (*Op.* 1–10), but for Aratus he is the gentle (*epios*) father of humankind who unfailingly communicates his will through the stars.

The *Phaenomena* also revises Hesiod's Myth of Ages, building on the latter's account of the Golden, Silver, Bronze, Heroic, and Iron Ages (*Op.* 106–201) with the story of Dike, the "Maiden." Aratus identifies Dike, the astral personification of justice, as the daughter of Astraeus, the father of the constellations (*Phaen.* 99), but notes that she is also said to be the daughter of "another," alluding to her descent from Zeus and Themis in Hesiod's *Theogony* (901–2). During the Golden Age Dike enjoyed an idyllic existence on earth, but human society began to deteriorate during the Silver Age, and she eventually retreated to the heavens at the beginning of the Bronze Age (*Phaen.* 96–136). Aratus does more, however, than simply restructure Hesiod. As Alessandro Schiesaro explains:

The Myth, as Aratus molds it, explains why we can no longer enjoy the presence of gods on Earth, why we have to cope with evil and pain; something happened in the past, a fault has been committed. But there is a positive side to this version of the tale, i.e., that we can and must still follow Dike, who is now up in the sky and looks upon us and our deeds, a source of permanent moral admonition.[124]

The tale of Dike's catasterism thus amplifies the Stoic message of the opening hymn to Zeus and expands the moral and political connotations of the entire *Phaenomena*.[125] On Schiesaro's view, the revised myth offers the present generation a choice of two alternatives: live a

---

[121] *Anth. Pal.* 9.507 (= 56 Gow and Page 1968; 27 Pfeiffer ii). For an English translation, see Nisetich 2001, 183, no. 56. On the life of Aratus, see Kidd 1997, 3–5.

[122] Compare, for example, *Argon.* 1.1 with *Phaen.* 1 (cf. Theocr. *Id.* 17.1), and *Phaen.* 15 with *Argon.* 4.444. The constellation Argo is also described (*Phaen.* 342–52) as backing water following the Dog Star Sirius. Jason is compared to the blazing, destructive Sirius when he meets Medea at the temple of Hecate (*Argon.* 3.957).

[123] On Hesiodic influence see Fakas 2001 and Kidd 1997. See Kidd 1997, 36–41 on the evidence for Aratus' interaction with contemporaries.

[124] Schiesaro 1996, 13. [125] Schiesaro 1996, 18.

just, moderate, and peaceful life, or succumb to immorality, violence, and anarchy.

Essential to a well-ordered society is the wisdom of a just king, one who respects the mandates of law and guards the rights of citizens and of subject peoples alike. As the intended audience of the *Phaenomena*, Antigonus Gonatas was presumably flattered by this equation, and indeed he is generally regarded as a moderate ruler, especially in comparison to the brief reign of his son and successor, Demetrius II.[126] Unlike the Ptolemies and other Hellenistic rulers,[127] Antigonus did not institute ruler cult,[128] although he was honored as a god by the Attic deme of Rhamnous.[129] Then, too, he himself dedicated twenty bronze statues of his ancestors, including one thought to be Heracles, in the *temenos* of Apollo on Delos,[130] but this dedication was presumably an expression of filial piety rather than a move toward establishing a dynastic cult. It is not improbable that the Macedonians continued to be as opposed to ruler cult under Antigonus as they were under Philip and Alexander, but what this shows is that piety played a significant role, if not an equally significant role, in royal ideology in monarchies where ruler cults were not established.

More importantly, the *Phaenomena* is an apt model for appreciation of the political relevance of the *Argonautica*, and for two reasons. First, it revises features of archaic epic not simply as a technical exercise in stylistic variation but rather as a conscious response to immanent themes elsewhere within the poem and in other works. Second, its political concerns are not explicit, in the manner of royal encomia, but are clarified by means of mythological tales and moral allegories. Aratus mined the traditions of archaic poetry to fuel a new kind of court epic for an elite, sophisticated, and idealistic audience, an audience versed in Homer and Hesiod but interested, for its own philosophical and political reasons, in updated poetic alternatives to the strife and violent excesses of Homeric warriors and Hesiodic gods.

---

[126] Shipley 2000, 127–28; Schiesaro 1996, 21–22, 25–26.
[127] On Ptolemaic ruler cult, see above. Antiochus I (324–261), ruler of the Seleucid Empire, deified his father, Seleucus Nicator. Phylarchus *ap.* Athen. 6.254–255a; App. *Syr.* 63.
[128] Following Tarn 1913, 250. Cf. the more recent work of Kralli 2003; Mikalson 1998, 160; Habicht 1970, 65–73.
[129] *SEG* 41.75. Gonatas is celebrated as "king and savior of the *demos*" and awarded "honors equal to those of the gods" (*isotheoi timai*). His father, Antigonus the One-Eyed, who preceded him as ruler of Macedonia, was honored as a god at Scepsis in 311 (*OGIS* 1:6).
[130] Only the inscribed plinth now survives; Bohec-Bouhet 2002, 42.

Apollonius' representation of Zeus in the *Argonautica* owes something to Hesiod as well,[131] and like Aratus he avoids parroting his archaic epic model and overhauls the paradigm.[132] Apollonius' narrator refers, rather selectively, to familiar episodes from the *Theogony*: Zeus's hidden childhood on Crete (1.508–11; 3.132–36), his arming by the Cyclopes (1.509–11, 730–31), the killing of Typhon (2.38–40, 1211), and his final rise to power.[133] In contrast to Hesiod, though, Apollonius avoids references to Zeus's extra-marital affairs, in this respect following not only Aratus but also Callimachus, who makes no mention of the loves of Zeus in *Hymn* 1. We hear at 2.1232–35 how Cronos deceived (ἐξαπαφών, 2.1235) Rhea and slept (παρελέξατο, 2.1235) with Philyra, and while two of Zeus's transgressions are briefly noted, neither reference lasts more than two lines,[134] and neither attempt, for that matter, can be counted a success: Sinope tricked Zeus into giving her permanent virginity (2.946–48), and Thetis flatly refused him (4.796–97). Hera admits to Thetis in the latter passage that she knows all about Zeus's philandering (4.794–95), and while this can hardly come as a revelation to anyone, it does bring into relief the difference between Apollonius' portrayal of Zeus in the *Argonautica* and his conventional reputation. I suppose that Apollonius' deemphasis of such erotic *parerga* is somewhat undercut by the narrator's references to Zeus's paternal relation to, for example, Heracles (1.1188), the Dioscuri (1.150; 2.43, 163; 4.651), Aeacus (3.364), Athena (2.547; 3.11), Dionysus (2.905; 4.1134), Artemis (4.334), and the Muse (4.2). But even so, these references are little more than patronymic formulae; generally speaking Apollonius prefers to foreground the deeds of Zeus's children in preference to the manner of their begetting.

The avoidance of this topic may also have something to do with Apollonius' representation of Eros. Eros greedily desires Zeus's power, a power that is symbolized by the golden ball (Zeus's childhood toy) which Aphrodite promises him in return for making Medea fall in love with Jason (3.129–44).

---

[131] Feeney 1991, 58–67.
[132] Apollonius, like Theocritus, emphasizes the role of the king in maintaining order, whereas Hesiod locates Justice among the people: the benefits of living under a good king belong to the past. See Merkelbach 1981, 31–32.
[133] The succession is indirectly reported: in song by Orpheus (1.496–511); in the ecphrasis on Jason's cloak (1.730–34); and in a speech by Argus, one of the sons of Phrixus (2.1211–12). On the multiple sources for Orpheus' hymn (1.496–511), see Clare 2002, 55–58.
[134] Knight 1995, 272. Zeus's admiration for Ganymede is also mentioned (3.115–17). Feeney 1991, 66–67 argues that this and the other references to Zeus's desire indicate a lack of concern for propriety (*to prepon*), yet an allusion to Zeus's "longing for the beauty" of Ganymede is not especially salacious, particularly in comparison with the Homeric description of the *hieros gamos* (*Il.* 14.292–351) or even the veritable catalogue of conquests that Zeus recounts to Hera prior to their love-making (*Il.* 14.313–28).

Epic modalities: Archetypes of divine justice

Whether one thinks of Eros anthropomorphically as a spoiled child or as an overwhelming physical impulse, this scene frames passion as a threat, and an abundance of stories illustrating Zeus's libidinal weakness elsewhere in the poem would only strengthen the impression that the threat to a stable cosmos is rather greater than one could wish (see Chapter 3).

Another reason for the omission of such stories is the fact that Zeus rarely has an active role in the narrative.[135] In keeping with this, certain characters grow uneasy and express doubts about him: Ancaeus, for example, fears that Zeus is unwilling to save them when they are stranded in the Syrtes Gulf (4.1275–76). But to go so far as to scorn the value of Zeus's aid, as Idas does during the feast at Pagasae (1.466–70), is represented as contemptible, and for the most part both the characters and the narrator express confidence in Zeus, referring throughout the poem to his will (*boulē*) and intent (*noos*),[136] his power over the weather,[137] and his role as the god of suppliants.[138] So, for instance, when Jason asks Argus and the sons of Phrixus for help, he comments that "Zeus truly sees everything, and neither the godly nor the unjust can ever escape his attention" (2.1179–80),[139] an observation that echoes Argus' earlier reference to Zeus as Zeus Epopsios, or "Watcher from on High" (2.1123, 1133).[140] Apollonius' Zeus is therefore physically distant from the world of mortals, especially in contrast to Hera, the Argonauts' most active Olympian partisan, but is nevertheless portrayed as upholding justice and interested in mortal affairs.[141] The punishments of Prometheus, Phineus, and the Argonauts are balanced, that is, by his regular intervention as the patron god of fugitives, suppliants, and strangers.

---

[135] The most important examples of his conduct are the three brief references to his reaction to Apsyrtus' death (4.558, 576–77, and 585). Other examples: he punishes Phineus (2.181–93), aids the sons of Boreus (2.275), is angered at the sons of Aeolus (2.1194–95), sends Hermes to help Phrixus (3.587–88), and designates the Dioscuri as patrons of ships (4.653).

[136] References to Zeus's will (*boulē*): for the separation of Polyphemus and Heracles from the Argonauts (1.1315, 1345; 2.154); for punishment of Argonauts (4.576–77). References to Zeus's intent (*noos*): revealed by Phineus (2.181–82, 313); brings the Argonauts together with sons of Phrixus (3.328). Cf. Feeney 1991, 60–61, who notes that the will of Zeus is largely hidden from Apollonius' characters and, oddly, the narrator, who, like Phineus, is less than confident of his story: "The omniscient prophet and the omniscient narrator both appear to have difficulties in communicating the mind of Zeus."

[137] Zeus as sky god: rain storms (2.1098, 1120; 3.1399), winds (2.499, 525), thunder and lightning (1.511, 731; 4.520). The Argonauts also erect an altar to Ikmaios Zeus, the Rain God (2.522).

[138] Zeus as defender of suppliants, strangers, and fugitives: 2.215, 378, 1123, 1133, 1147; 3.193, 986; 4.119, 358–59, 700, 709.

[139] Pietsch 1999, 202 sees this statement as a nod to the god's prominence in archaic Greek religion, but we cannot lose sight of the contemporary significance of Zeus, as he was especially venerated by the Hellenistic kings. See also Bohec-Bouhet 2002.

[140] Cf. Callim. fr. 85.14 Pfeiffer 1.   [141] Rostropowicz 1995, 194.

Apollonius' Zeus has something of Hesiod's punitive deity and something of Aratus' just and kindly overseer, though he is largely consigned in the *Argonautica* to the fourth book and the distant reaches of the heavens. And yet, while the stars may well be a constant source of guidance from Zeus to those who farm the earth and travel by sea, they yield precious little information about the unseasonal dangers (like prodigious monsters or deceptive kings) faced by the Argonauts. In these matters the mind of Zeus is clouded, his purpose veiled, for the narrator as well as the Argonauts themselves, who are quite literally lost in trackless, starless wastes on more than one occasion (4.1245–49, 1694–701). They must try to discern the will of the gods by other means, seeking their aid through portents, omens, prayers, and sacrifice. The divine horizons of epic have receded, as Feeney observes;[142] the gods consort with heroes no more, nor do they dominate the action as they do in Homer and Hesiod.[143] Here, too, Aratus' influence is felt, for it is no accident that the greatest crisis of the poem is Zeus's withdrawal from the Argonauts – like Dike's departure in the Bronze Age – and their utter ignorance of his anger until the revelation of the oak of Dodona. Circe purges Jason and Medea of the miasma of kin-murder, but the Argonauts will not be fully restored to human society until they come under the influence of the Phaeacian king Alcinous, whose wisdom is demonstrated by his unyielding respect for the justice of Zeus (Chapter 5). For Apollonius, though, the ruler who intercedes on behalf of his people is not Antigonus Gonatas but Philadelphus, and it is he who is flattered by the high praise of this epic king.

EPIC INVERSIONS: GREEKS AND BARBARIANS

Such reformulations of heroic and divine ideals have been associated, as noted earlier in this chapter, with the anxiety that attended the Macedonian colonization of North Africa.[144] The *Argonautica* places Greek expansion in a positive light by depicting the Argonauts as peace-loving adventurers, governed, in most cases, by an inborn respect for the gods and customs of all the lands they encounter. Although some of the strangers met by the Argonauts turn out to be aggressively uncooperative, most are well disposed toward them. Stephens has applied to the *Argonautica* Mary Louise Pratt's study of seventeenth- and eighteenth-century travel writing about Africa and South America – such stories typically depict the vulnerability

---

[142] Feeney 1991, 98.   [143] So Hunter 1993, 79–80.
[144] Stephens 2003, 171–237, esp. 183–96; Hunter 1995, and 1993, 153–69.

of invading Europeans and their victimization by fabulous monsters or brutish natives.[145] This initial, "mythic" phase of writing was soon followed by scientific accounts and tales of romance, and the *Argonautica* features plot elements that are comparable to all three phases, from attacks by wild animals and violent men to anthropological accounts of foreign practices and Jason's encounters with royal women. Taken as a whole, these types of narratives work to validate the expansion of the culture of the Greeks, who are depicted as noble, enlightened, and devoted to the cultivation of knowledge. They are accordingly embraced by civilized foreigners, and opposed only by the brutal and unjust.

The Argo is represented as sailing not by imperial design but by the will of the gods, whose benevolent guidance justifies Greek sovereignty. From this perspective Apollonius' Jason, like Callimachus' Theseus in the *Hecale*, is closer to a cult founder than a traditional Greek hero. Pushing this connection somewhat further, it becomes apparent that Jason's behavior in foreign lands has less in common with the reality of Macedonian conquest than with the flattering image intended for a Hellenic audience in Egypt and throughout the Mediterranean.[146] The *Argonautica* accordingly functions as, among other things, an epic amendment to the actual encounters of Greek adventurers with the inhabitants of eastern countries. Hypsipyle, for example, the ruler of the island of Lemnos, not only welcomes Jason as per Polyxo's advice, but is apparently so awed by his innate authority that she immediately invites him to govern Lemnos with her (1.827–29). In the same way the Egyptians, not to mention the Libyans, Persians, and Indians, are imagined to have "welcomed" the pious dominion of the Macedonians. To be sure, the assembly scene shows that Hypsipyle's intentions are self-serving: the Lemnian women have murdered all the men on their island (1.609–10), and now turn to the Argonauts to help them repopulate it (1.675–701). The hospitality of the Lemnians therefore masks a practical political agenda: they must take advantage of the arrival of the Argonauts in order to heal their own fractured society. But even so, Hypsipyle's unscripted and apparently spontaneous offer of joint rule exceeds the original Lemnian plan: the seductive queen is herself seduced and conquered by the civilized Jason, to their mutual advantage. Although the initial Lemnian

---

[145] Stephens finds correspondences with Pratt's three post-colonial narratives in the *Argonautica*: fantastic encounters with monsters; objective scientific analyses; romantic encounters with native women. Where Pratt sees these stages as successive, Stephens suggests that Apollonius simultaneously includes all three, "myth, geographic exploration, and psychological realism" (2003, 185).

[146] Cf., e.g., the popular "Alexander Romance" (Pseudo-Callisthenes), a fictionalized account of Alexander's career, parts of which are thought to date to the third century. See Stoneman 1994, 117–29.

decision to welcome the Argonauts is reached by means of a very democratic (hence Greek) assembly (1.653–66), the mass union between Greek men and Lemnian women is reminiscent of the famed "mass marriage" of Alexander's officers to Asian wives at Susa (Arr. 7.4.4–8). Ostensibly a symbolic wedding of two cultures, Alexander hoped the marriages would thwart Asian revolt by gaining the allegiance of the upper classes.[147] What is interesting is that in the Argonauts' first "foreign" encounter, the plot to engineer a hybrid society is ascribed not to the Greek invaders but to the invaded, as violence, cunning, and natural subordination are projected onto a feminized population. (This formulation is particularly suggestive in the light of Ptolemaic relations with Athens and other mainland Greek states.)[148] The Lemnian assembly maps latent democratic tendencies onto a weakened realm – that is, a realm depleted of its male population by internal strife – whose political security the Argonauts (tellingly characterized as entirely innocent of political ambition) will restore by means of a dynastic monarchy.

Thus, the tale of the Argo is an epic prehistory that justifies the Ptolemies' influence in North Africa, Asia Minor, and elsewhere in the Aegean basin. As Damien Nelis observes:

In the hands of Apollonius, the story of the Argonauts becomes a myth of foundation, the ultimate *ktisis*, an explanation and a history of the Greek cultural presence in North Africa. The reception of Homer in Athens established epic as a public genre, as a poetic form which by its inherent grandeur could lay claim to an important place in the civic sphere, which could indeed define and preserve a cultural identity. It would seem that Apollonios intended his epic to occupy a similar place in the cultural and civic life of Ptolemaic Alexandria.[149]

The *Argonautica* chronicles the travels of a group of heroes who, like Alexander and his army, make an unprecedented voyage, by divine mandate, to distant lands. They are, from time to time, compelled to fight, but never, as the poem is careful to show, without provocation. The Argonauts prefer alliances to battle and, like Callimachus' Theseus, welcome the hospitality of strangers: that of the Lemnian women (1.774–914), as well as that of the Mysians (1.1179–81), the Doliones (1.961–84), the Mariandyni (2.752–

---

[147] Worthington 2004, 180–81. While the empire of the Seleucids was subsequently founded on the marriage of the general Seleucus and the Asian princess Apame I, a daughter of Spitamenes of Bactria, the majority of the Macedonian officers are believed to have abandoned their new wives when they returned home.
[148] On the Ptolemaic support for the freedom of the Greek states, see the discussion of the Chremonidean war in Chapter 4.
[149] Nelis 2001b, 397.

814), and the Phaeacians (4.994–1000).[150] Conflicts arise only from ignorance and accident, as in the case of the misguided attack on the Doliones (1.1018–62) or, more commonly, from foreign provocation, as with the Earthborn giants (1.989–1011), the Bebrycians (2.1–141), Aeëtes (3.401–21, 576–608), the Earthborn men (3.1354–407), and the bronze giant Talus (4.1638–40). Those who willfully resist or oppose the Argonauts are represented as members of ancient, often autochthonous, races: isolated, hostile, prone to anger and pointless aggression, and filled with suspicion verging on paranoia, especially in the case of Aeëtes. The poem implies that ideal societies are open, flexible, and ruled by piety, not passion, and for this reason dominion is rightly given to those who, like the Argonauts, can travel the world more or less peacefully and without prejudice.

Furthermore, since the primary focus of the poem is the voyage out and back rather than a prolonged siege or vengeful attack, the *Argonautica* blunts the martial edge of heroic epic. On a fundamental level, of course, the story of the Golden Fleece invites comparison with the abduction of Helen, and there are numerous other structural parallels with the Trojan cycle. The catalyst for the action in both cases is the loss of a valued "commodity," and many episodes in the *Argonautica*, such as Aeëtes' refusal to relinquish the Fleece and Medea's betrayal of her family, modify or invert plot elements of the Trojan story. Nevertheless, as earlier generations of critics noted, often with displeasure,[151] the general structure of the *Argonautica* differs markedly from that of the *Iliad* and the *Odyssey*. The climax of the poem does not build to a pitched battle, nor is Jason driven to slaughter by loss, grief, or vengeance, like Achilles and Odysseus. For Jason, violence is typically a last resort. During his initial meeting with Aeëtes, he attempts to create an alliance (3.393–95), and while it is true that he and Medea ambush Apsyrtus, they do so because the Argonauts are trapped and outnumbered by the Colchian fleet. Nor, for that matter, can Jason's *aristeia* on the Field of Ares be read as the result of a personal animus against the Earthborn men, creatures who spring to life after Jason sows the teeth of Cadmus' dragon and turn against each other when he hurls a boulder into their midst (3.1355–407). As tasks thrust upon him by an arrogant king, Jason's exploits more closely resemble the labors of Heracles, whom he comes to replace over the course of the poem.[152] We might alternatively regard the harrowing of the Earthborn as a literal enactment of a Homeric agricultural metaphor for war: the ripening of monstrous prodigies born for short lives and swift

---

[150] The remnants of the Colchian fleet also ask formally to be included among the allies of the Phaeacians (4.1210).
[151] See, e.g., Gillies 1928; Wilamowitz-Moellendorf 1924. [152] Clauss 1993, 61–66, 204–211.

harvest, the Earthborn men are as mortal as the Homeric generation of leaves, destroyed by the storm, bringing grief and frustration to Aeëtes. The confrontation with the Earthborn men "packs a whole *Iliad* into the last scene of the book," as Hunter comments,[153] yet their destruction cannot be mistaken for self-absorbed vengeance or senseless brutality on Jason's part.

The Argonauts are not consistently diplomatic, of course. Heracles' killing of the serpent Ladon is a case in point, for it brings terrible suffering (*stygeron achos*, 4.1435) to the nymphs in the Garden of the Hesperides. Yet even this incident may be understood in positive terms, as a form of divine compensation rather than an episode meant to criticize Greek aggression. After shooting the serpent with his bow, Heracles creates a spring that will later save the lives of the Argonauts (4.1443–60).[154] The description of Heracles' desperate search for water in the sands of Libya brings to mind his previous rampage at the Mysian spring (1.1207–72) when Hylas, Heracles' beloved companion, is abducted by an amorous water nymph. Heracles himself is accidentally left behind by the Argonauts, and Eros is chiefly to blame for both losses, but the sea god Glaucus reveals that even this unprincipled god is subordinate to Zeus's cosmic plan (1.1315–25). More importantly, Heracles' futile rampage demonstrates that, while he may verge on divinity in the *Argonautica*, his knowledge is only partial, like that of other mortal characters. In effect, the collocation of the two springs and the two searches offers an answer to the question posed by Hylas' initial disappearance: how can Heracles avenge Hylas when he does not know what has happened to him? Seen from this perspective, Ladon's death is not just an atypical example of unprovoked and incongruous aggression on the part of the Greeks; rather, it echoes and at the same time symbolically resolves and concludes the Hylas episode. For their part, neither Heracles nor the Hesperides nymphs can appreciate Ladon's death as a form of "cosmic" reparation. But as readers of the poem we find ourselves in an intermediate position: we can connect the loss of Hylas with the killing of Ladon by means of a logic that is symbolic rather than causal, divine rather than mortal. The death of Ladon balances the abduction of Hylas as the punishment for the transgression of the Mysian nymph is displaced and transferred to her sisters in the Hesperides. This is the justice of Zeus; this is the balanced cosmos of Apollonius and Aratus.

---

[153] Hunter 1993, 134. See Knight 1995, 106–7 for Homeric parallels.
[154] The nymph Aegle adds that Heracles may have been guided by some god when he struck the rock that created the spring (4.1444–46). The creation of the spring, like the killing of Ladon, is in accord with the will of Zeus.

Mortal access to knowledge is limited in the *Argonautica*, but this limitation is likewise in accordance with Zeus's will, since absolute knowledge is a defining characteristic of the gods, not the narrator, characters, or even the audience.[155] It is Zeus who is responsible for the workings of justice; it is Zeus, we suppose, who urges Heracles to create the spring (4.1445) – not Hesiod's reactionary god, but the benefactor of the later age whose farseeing and compensatory influence is apparent in this episode and elsewhere in the poem. Ladon's death balances the loss of Hylas and the division of the Argonauts: one spring looks ahead to a reunion, of sorts, in the creation of another.

In the end we find that the *Argonautica* tells of the deeds of men born long ago in order to reassure those born in the present day: just as the combination of cult practice and just governance delivers the Argonauts, so it will preserve the Alexandrian Greeks. The Argonauts' return to Greece at the conclusion of Book 4 not only confirms that they have recovered the goodwill of Zeus, it also expresses the desire of the Greeks to secure a homeland here and now in North Africa. In bringing these latter-day heirs of the Argonauts to foreign soil, the gods have brought them home. Argo's safe return, whether to Lake Triton or to Thessaly, is a sign that feelings of exile and isolation are only temporary, and that even the violent transgressions of those who seek divine favor will never exceed the compass of Zeus's plan, no matter how far away he himself may seem. This transcendent interpretation of the *Argonautica*'s conclusion must be weighed, then, against readings of the poem that are burdened by the bleak future that awaits Jason and Medea. The treachery of Eros is manifest in their transient happiness, their broken marriage, and the ruin of their family, but as the *Argonautica* tells us, the true legacy of their union is the birth of a just society on the shores of a bright new land.

---

[155] Phineus, for example, is punished for revealing the mind (*noos*) of Zeus *atrekeos*, "precisely," "in every detail" (2.182). The punishment is appropriately limited, however: the Argonauts stop the visits of the Harpies who soil Phineus' food, although he does remain blind. See Pietsch 1999, 197, who discusses the distinction between will (*boule*), which refers to what Zeus intends, and mind (*noos*), which implies not only intent but the act of cognition that precedes it.

CHAPTER 3

Strife and restraint among the Argonauts

EPIC MODALITIES: EROS AND ERIS

Alexander's notorious differences with his army eventually brought the Macedonian conquest of the east to an end.[1] These protracted tensions offer a useful counterpoint to the Argonauts' various conflicts with Jason, which range from mild criticism to something like mutiny. Sexual desire (*eros*) is linked with strife (*eris*) in the poem, contributing greatly to the religious crisis that jeopardizes the Argonauts' journey home, but on the whole the Argonauts' difficulties are quickly resolved and never disrupt their progress. This chapter explores the political organization and social interactions of the Argonauts, with a particular emphasis on their recovery from factional strife. Historical events or practices, where relevant, afford points of comparison with three episodes: Jason's election (1.317–62), the quarrel between Idas and Idmon (1.460–94), and Telamon's rebellion (1.1286–344). The last episode demonstrates the importance of emotional control aboard the Argo, presenting both a divine justification and a philosophical foundation for the reconciliation between Telamon and Jason. While each episode illustrates a different kind of political tension, all three strengthen the impression that the Argonauts' dominant social register is concord, not strife (*eris*). In particular, it is Jason's behavior – his even temper, self-control, and forgiveness of insults – that revises not only the vengeful extremes of historical figures like Alexander and Cleitus the Black but also heroic characters like Agamemnon and Achilles.

Generally speaking the Argonauts govern themselves by means of group deliberation. They elect Jason as their negotiator, a diplomatic representative rather than a military commander or ruler. Jason's election recalls the combative assemblies of Homeric epic, but certain aspects of the episode

[1] When Alexander's exhausted army refused to cross the Hyphasis River, he was forced to turn back (Diod. 17.94, 108.3; Arr. 5.25–8; Just. 12.8.10–17). See Worthington 2004, 159–61; Bosworth 1993, 133–34; cf. Carney 1996.

look back to Macedonian royal succession. The monarchy was traditionally subject in some degree to the will of an elite segment of society: the Macedones, who served as citizen troops and played a role in the selection and overthrowing of kings.[2] Military acclamation continued to be essential in the Hellenistic period: recognition by the army evidently played a role in the enthronement of Ptolemy I Soter, Antigonus the One-Eyed and his son Demetrius Poliorcetes, and Ptolemy Ceraunus and Arsinoë.[3] The exact details of the election process are known in only three instances, however: the elections of Philip, Alexander, and Philip Arrhidaeus, and each of these varied somewhat from the others.[4] The available evidence does not show whether the process was codified in the form of a constitution, or even to what extent these three elections varied from standard protocol, if indeed there was one.[5] Errington, in fact, has rejected the generally accepted theory of election by acclamation, arguing that neither the Macedonian army nor the People's Assembly would have formally participated in the choice of a new king.[6] While he argues against a rather rigid and narrowly conceived constitutionalist model, he concedes that members of the aristocracy must have exercised some influence on the choice of a royal successor, as was certainly the case with Alexander.[7] Borza sums it up in this way: "Succession appears rather to be the result of a series of political and military decisions made by those in a position to do so, and the manner in which they conducted themselves was a response to the circumstances of the moment."[8]

The election of Jason displays this same kind of flexibility and responsiveness to the circumstances of the moment. Jason calls for an assembly

---

[2] For the definition of the Macedones as citizen troops, see Hammond 1993, 15–19. It is not certain that the group referred to as Macedones should in all instances be equated with the citizen troops, however. See Borza 1993, 25.

[3] Ptolemy I: App. *Syr.* 54; Antigonus and Demetrius: Diod. 19.61–62.1; Ptolemy Ceraunus: Memnon, *FGrH* 434 F 1, 8.3; Arsinoë: Just. 24.3.2. See further Hammond 1993, 16–17.

[4] These differences complicate conclusions about normative or traditional Macedonian practice. In the general discussion following Hammond's 1993 paper on "The Macedonian Imprint," Samuel argues for a minimalist position, noting that it would be dangerous to use information about Alexander (and presumably the other two as well) as evidence for Macedonian institutions because we lack additional supporting evidence (36).

[5] See the discussion of the succession process and the debate about the constitutionalist hypothesis by Borza 1993, 25–29, 31–35.

[6] Errington 1978 rejects the influential work of a number of scholars. Bosworth 1993, 26 acknowledges Errington's article, but adds that the exact means by which a Macedonian king became legitimate are "completely unknown."

[7] Errington 1978, 100–3 argues that the influence typically exerted by the Macedonian elite (*protoi Makedonon*) in the transfer of power can be observed in the successions of Alexander the Great and Antigonus Doson; Lysimachus' defeat of Pyrrhus; Philip V's promotion of his favorite, Antigonus; and the meeting of the Successors after Alexander's death.

[8] Borza 1993, 27.

in order to select a leader, but the Argonauts entrust him with diplomatic authority not through a democratic vote, in the manner of the Athenian democracy, but as a result of the political pressure exerted by Heracles, a hero held in the highest regard and claimed as an ancestor by both Alexander and the Ptolemies (Chapter 2). The Argonauts' political movements are thus composite in nature, much like the portrayal of individual characters, reflecting many different types of polity (Homeric, Athenian, Macedonian, and Ptolemaic) while precisely corresponding to none.

In what follows I examine the politics of the Argonauts from several different perspectives. I reevaluate both the poetic antecedents of Apollonius' representation of strife and the traditional epic models for a number of characters (e.g., Jason, Heracles, Idas) by taking into consideration the historical precedents for the Argonauts' social organization, such as Macedonian royal succession, election by military acclamation, and the recruitment of advisors to the Hellenistic kings. In addition, I consider the contemporary philosophical thinking that likewise informs scenes of conflict and reconciliation. This multivalent approach reveals not only when but why the poem departs, as it often does, from the expectations aroused by traditional epic. My claim is that the Argonauts are rather loosely organized, as a social collective rather than a rigid political hierarchy, although the poem's dramatic focus still remains on individual heroes like Jason, Heracles, and Medea. Jason's characterization in the first book is especially complex, for while he is not treated by the Argonauts as a military commander, his religious responsibilities and diplomatic negotiations with those outside the group still set him apart in the manner of an archaic hero. Though he is isolated from his fellows like Odysseus or Agamemnon, the cooperative spirit of the group, with its tendency toward advice and mild censure – so restrained in comparison with the Achaean feuds – is more in keeping with a third-century model of a well-balanced community.

I begin, then, with a brief review of conflicts in the opening episode of the *Iliad*. When Agamemnon refuses to give up Chryseis, the daughter of Chryses, a Trojan priest of Apollo (1.8–34), Apollo punishes the Achaeans with a plague that eventually compels Agamemnon to return the girl to her father (1.35–52, 430–47). Agamemnon appropriates Achilles' war prize, the girl Briseis, as a replacement for Chryseis (1.318–48). The dispute between Achilles and Agamemnon is resolved only after many losses on the Achaean side, for, after Agamemnon's insult to his honor, Achilles refuses to sacrifice his own life in the battle against Troy. Nestor, the aged councilor, vainly attempts to reconcile the two heroes (1.275–79):

"Μήτε σὺ τόνδ' ἀγαθός περ ἐὼν ἀποαίρεο κούρην,
ἀλλ' ἔα, ὥς οἱ πρῶτα δόσαν γέρας υἷες Ἀχαιῶν·
μήτε σύ, Πηλεΐδη, ἔθελ' ἐριζέμεναι βασιλῆϊ
ἀντιβίην, ἐπεὶ οὔ ποθ' ὁμοίης ἔμμορε τιμῆς
σκηπτοῦχος βασιλεύς, ᾧ τε Ζεὺς κῦδος ἔδωκεν."

"No, [Agamemnon], though you are a true warrior, do not take the girl away,
But leave her as she is, as the sons of the Achaeans first gave the prize,
And you, son of Peleus, do not choose to compete with the king
Face to face: never is honor equally shared with
A sceptered king, one to whom Zeus gave glory."

As Nestor's speech shows, this quarrel is rooted in a heroic code that measures the honor of great warriors through the distribution of trophies, the symbols of a defeated enemy. The public confrontation between Agamemnon and Achilles actually intensifies Briseis' value as a war prize. No longer one of many tokens of glory to be shared out among the Greeks,[9] she becomes a sign of Agamemnon's superiority relative to Achilles alone.[10] Nestor tries to ease the strain by observing that while both men merit the girl – Agamemnon as a king favored by Zeus, Achilles as a champion – both are also acting in ways that are transgressive and destructive. The quarrel could be quickly resolved, of course, if Agamemnon would only, as Nestor advises, respect Achilles' right to his prize, or if Achilles would only concede Agamemnon's prerogative – but the *Iliad* is not concerned with timely reconciliations. This poet sings of Achilles' *menis*, his preternatural wrath, leaving conciliation and swift resolution to a later generation of poets.

The quarrels of Apollonius' Argonauts often allude to Homeric conflicts. As Knight puts it, "the Homeric text is present at every level of Apollonius' [text]."[11] The intertextual tug of Homeric epic is so pervasive and can be so strong that Apollonius' characters appear to compete anachronistically with their Homeric counterparts.[12] Although the voyage of the Argo is set before the Trojan War,[13] the late-born Hellenistic Argonauts have evidently learned

---

[9] Cf. Achilles' even distribution of prizes in the quarrels during the funeral games for Patroclus (*Il.* 23.257–897).
[10] See discussion by Dué 2002, 37–38.
[11] Knight 1995, 8. Fraser 1972, 635 comments that Apollonius "seems frequently to have followed the principle of altering the clothes which he borrowed: most borrowed phrases are altered either in context or in phraseology or both."
[12] See Bing 1988 for a discussion of allusion in Hellenistic poetry.
[13] Chiron the centaur and the infant Achilles, whose father Peleus is an Argonaut (1.90–94), witness the Argo's departure (1.554–58). On the voyage of the Argo as a marker of the evolution of the historical era from a primordial age of monsters, see Clauss 2000.

from their Homeric "past," meaning that they navigate with comparative ease many of the problems that beset the Achaeans. Homer's encoded hierarchy gives way in the *Argonautica* to a social system that places a higher premium on compromise and unanimity; as Hunter observes, "Homer's opening quarrel becomes the opening harmony of the Argonauts."[14] The Greek term for concord, or "together-mindedness," is *homonoia*, a principle that is described by Vian as the quintessential Argonautic virtue.[15] The importance of *homonoia* for the Argonauts is introduced in Book 1 when Jason describes the Argonauts' common interests in preparation for the election (1.336–37), and becomes more explicit later when the Argonauts collectively dedicate a shrine to this divinity (2.717–19).[16] This same political virtue would continue to be popular in Rome, where it was promoted by the name Concordia from the third century until the Augustan era.[17]

Despite this shift of emphasis from the honor of the individual warrior to the harmonious interaction of the group,[18] the *Argonautica* continues to be concerned with the causes and consequences of strife. Hesiod, another signal influence on Apollonius and much of Alexandrian poetry, provides the definitive description of strife in his didactic epic, the *Works and Days*, which announces the existence of two divinities who personify two different types of strife (*eris*). The bad Eris is a cruel abomination (*schetlie*) who causes wars, while the good Eris, a chthonic goddess, rouses men to work and generates healthy competition (*Op.* 11–26). By extension, the Eris that is prominently figured in Agamemnon's quarrel with Achilles (*Il.* 1.8, 177, 210, 319) can only be the bad kind. Both types of strife appear in the *Argonautica*, however: the good Eris stirs the Argonauts to compete with each other in rowing (1.1153), while the bad, warlike Eris is associated with the dangers of love (4.446). For Apollonius, in fact, the true god of discord is Eros. The poem suggests that sexual passion is a prime cause of mortal anguish, and characterizes Eros, the spoiled and flighty child of Aphrodite, as a malevolent and ruinous force (4.445–47):

---

[14] Hunter 1993, 19. See also Carspecken 1952 on the fundamental differences between Apollonius' heroes and those of Homer.
[15] Vian 2002, 1:16–17.
[16] See Thériault 1996, 27–28; and esp. 29–34: Thériault considers it probable that, given the fifty years of political unrest that preceded the death of Lysimachus and the return of Heraclea to democracy, a shrine to Homonoia existed in this region.
[17] See Cairns 1988, 89–92.
[18] Carspecken 1952, 108–10 viewed all the Argonauts as the main "character" of the poem: sacrificing dramatic emphasis on a single hero prevented them from becoming as anonymous as the crew of Odysseus.

"Σχέτλι' Ἔρως, μέγα πῆμα, μέγα στύγος ἀνθρώποισιν,
ἐκ σέθεν οὐλόμεναί τ' ἔριδες στοναχαί τε πόνοι τε,
ἄλγεά τ'ἄλλ' ἐπὶ τοῖσιν ἀπείρονα τετρήχασι·"

"Cruel Eros, monstrous affliction, monstrous abomination for mortals,
From you come destructive wars and suffering and lamentation,
And other agonies heaped upon these come endlessly rioting."

Addressing Eros in line 445 as cruel (*schetlie*), Apollonius employs the word used by Hesiod to describe the bad Eris in the *Works and Days*.[19] As one of few instances of direct address, or apostrophe, by the narrator to a character in the poem, the term *schetlie* rhetorically underscores the thematic importance of erotic strife.[20] The kinship between *eros* and *erides* is further reinforced by their linguistic similarity: for Apollonius, sexual desire is the aetiological foundation of strife.

The association of love with strife is also the theme of several important passages early in the poem. Jason's cloak is decorated with seven scenes; the third one represents the love goddess Aphrodite gazing at her reflection in the shield of the war god Ares (1.742–46).[21] In the *Odyssey* the Phaeacian bard Demodocus sings about their adulterous affair and their ambush by Hephaestus, who captures them in a golden net before an amused crowd of Olympians (*Od.* 8.266–366). This passage was read by later audiences as an allegorical illustration of the "bonds" between the two abstract principles of love and strife, and this interpretation accords well with Apollonius' Empedoclean portrayal of cosmogonic strife (Neikos) earlier in the poem (1.496–511).[22] Like Hesiod's Eris, the Empedoclean Neikos has a mythical origin and multiple aspects: Empedocles contrasts Neikos with the principle of Love (Philotes), but the term is also generally used to refer to the quarrels (*neikea*) of mortals.[23] When Orpheus ends the quarrel (*neikos*, 1.492) between Idas and the prophet Idmon, he diffuses the tension with a song that describes how Neikos (1.498) articulated the cosmos by dividing *chaos* into earth, sky, and ocean. The story of the Neikos that brought the world into being is here conjoined with the first appearance of *neikos* among the

---

[19] Cf. *Argon.* 4.445: Σχέτλι' Ἔρως and *Op.* 15: Σχετλίη. Apollonius places the word in the same position as Hesiod does, at the beginning of the line, but changes the case from the nominative to the vocative. Cf. also σχέτλιος Callim. *Hymn* 6.68 Pfeiffer ii.

[20] Vian 2002, 3:166, n. 4.449; Fränkel 1968, 493–96.

[21] See Shapiro 1980 for a discussion of the ecphrasis as a showcase for Alexandrian aesthetic theory; on the cloak, see Chapter 4.

[22] Clare 2002, 53–59; Clauss 2000, 12–13; Nelis 1992. For more on Orpheus see the section below on the quarrel between Idas and Idmon.

[23] On the relation between cosmic Love and Strife and their material counterparts, see Kirk and Raven 1957, 327–32.

Argonauts, and the juxtaposition of the two points to Hesiod's two types of *eris*, contrasting the power of a productive, cosmological strife with the power of a bad *eris* that destroys human lives.

All but one of the remaining examples of the term *neikos* in the *Argonautica* are presented in a negative light,[24] as a social evil rather than a divine abstraction. Apart from the description of the generative function of the cosmological Neikos, the poem does not explicitly link Eros with *neikea* in the way that it links it with *erides*. However, a symbolic association is apparent in the connection between the childhood of Zeus and the perpetual immaturity of Eros. To persuade her son Eros to make Medea desire Jason, Aphrodite promises him an elaborately worked golden sphere (3.129–44), in an episode noted earlier in Chapter 2. This sphere, representing cosmic power, was once the toy of omnipotent Zeus, and the passage suggests not only that strife-inducing Eros is eager to inherit universal dominion, but also that Zeus's orderly cosmos, first engendered by Neikos, is not entirely free from risk.[25] Any assault made by the impatient Eros is unlikely to be sustained for long, of course, but whatever we make of Eros' chances, it seems that sexual and social divisions sprout from the same root.

Jason, it turns out, was wary of erotic discord even before the Argo sailed. In Book 1 the narrator observes that Atalanta wished to join the Argonauts, but Jason turned her down because he feared the harsh strife (*argaleas eridas*) caused by love (*philotetos*).[26] His apprehension is then borne out by later events. The aid offered first by the enamored Lemnian women, and later by Medea, calls the masculine self-sufficiency of the Argonauts into question,[27] and the heroes Heracles (1.861–78) and Idas (3.556–65) are particularly sensitive to the appearance of weakness in this regard. Once again, however, the Argonauts' respect for *homonoia* keeps their tempers in check. When Heracles criticizes them for wasting time on Lemnos, no one is willing to oppose him (1.876), and when Idas vigorously protests the Argonauts'

---

[24] The teasing of the Argonauts by Medea's handmaids (4.1727) is the single example of a lighthearted *neikos* in the poem. Other examples: Jason describes the responsibility of the leader for resolving quarrels (*neikea*) with strangers (1.340); Heracles berates (*neikessen*) the Argonauts for lingering on Lemnos (1.875); Medea considers the *neikos* between Aeëtes and the Argonauts over the Golden Fleece (3.627, 739); the narrator notes that the Argonauts would have been defeated in a *neikos* with the Colchian army (4.340); Alcinous intends to resolve the *neikos* between the Colchians and the Argonauts (4.1010); Alcinous recognizes that Aeëtes' *neikos* could escalate (4.1103).
[25] Clauss 2000, 29; Campbell 1994, 123–25; Hunter 1989, 113.
[26] *Argon.* 1.773: δεῖσεν δ' ἀργαλέας ἔριδας φιλότητος ἕκητι.
[27] Heracles himself will eventually be left behind in search of Hylas, who is stolen away by the amorous Mysian water nymph. More troubling is the role played by Eros in the ambush of Apsyrtus, which rouses the anger of Zeus against the Argonauts.

tactical reliance on Aphrodite, the others murmur but will neither support nor correct his complaint (3.565). Later, Medea's love compounds the *neikos* between the Colchians and the Argonauts. Eros is explicitly blamed for the murder of Apsyrtus (4.448–49), the event that precipitates a religious crisis for Jason by driving him into conflict with Zeus (Chapter 6). It is thus the root cause of Argonauts' conflicts with the Colchians and with Zeus, and it threatens to divide the Argonauts themselves.

Eros and *eris* are finally brought into balance at the end of the poem by means of a flirtatious *neikos* (4.1727). During their stay on Anaphe, Medea's Phaeacian handmaids tease the Argonauts, who are so reduced by the hardships of the voyage that they can offer only libations of water to Apollo (4.1719–30). As the narrator reports, their gentle mockery is destined to be reenacted thereafter by the men and women of the island in a cult dedicated to Apollo Aegletes ("The Gleamer"). The Argonauts' offering may be poor in contrast to the rich sacrifices of Alcinous, but the offering dearest to Apollo, as Callimachus tells us in *Hymn* 2, is the "slender, pure, and unmixed spring water distilled from a holy fountain, most high, most fair."[28] The offering to Apollo Aegletes takes Callimachus' aesthetic metaphor at its word: the "slender Muse" is here embodied as a water libation. In a badly damaged fragment from the *Aetia*, Callimachus also mentions the Argonauts' stay on Anaphe, speaking from the point of view of Aeëtes who reviles the "deeds of his daughter" (*erga thygatros*), by which he means, most probably, the recent murder of Apsyrtus.[29] Thus, while Callimachus links Anaphe with the Argonauts' blood guilt, Apollonius combines the stay on Anaphe with water libations for Apollo in order to symbolize the purification of the Argonauts. Strictly speaking, the pollution from Apsyrtus' death was purged by Circe's blood sacrifice (4.704–9), but the erotic strife that brought about his death is finally purified in the wake of a new cult practice.

In contrast to the Homeric heroes, then, the Argonauts' behavior shows that they are generally aware of the dangers posed by strife and are successful, by and large, at avoiding or alleviating conflict. The *homonoia* that characterizes social relations within the circle of the Argonauts themselves is shattered twice only, and on both occasions peace is swiftly recovered: when Idas and Idmon quarrel prior to the embarkation (1.462, 492), and when Telamon openly challenges Jason for leaving Heracles behind in Mysia

---

[28] Callim. *Hymn* 2.111–12 Pfeiffer ii: καθαρή τε καὶ ἀχράαντος ἀνέρπει, πίδακος ἐξ ἱερῆς ὀλίγη λιβὰς ἄκρον ἄωτον.
[29] Callim. fr. 7.19–29 Pfeiffer i; for English translation see Nisetich 2001, 68–69.

(1.1284). I will take up these disputes and their consequences after first analyzing the political tensions of the election on the headland of Pagasae.

HERACLES: CONFRONTATION AND SUPPORT

The diplomatic Jason and the violent Heracles represent different heroic types (e.g., 3.185–90),[30] and initially appear to be political rivals. However, Heracles is soon revealed as supportive of Jason, at least to a limited extent, and his impulsive temperament serves as a counterweight rather than a threat. Like Heracles, Idas also represents a traditional heroism that is founded on physical strength, but the telling differences between them are critical to the central themes of the poem. Heracles' worthy ambition is motivated by the good or healthy *eris* that drives men to compete for glory (*kleos*), but Idas' suspicious insults are little more than pointlessly disruptive (see the following section). The Argonauts quickly learn to ignore Idas' bluster, but the loss of Heracles in Mysia will generate the first real crisis faced by the Argonauts.

From the beginning of the poem Heracles' pride, ambition, and preference for action over debate are emphasized. In service to King Eurystheus in Argos, he promptly abandons his responsibilities to join the group (1.122–23):

> Οὐδὲ μὲν οὐδὲ βίην κρατερόφρονος Ἡρακλῆος
> πευθόμεθ' Αἰσονίδαο λιλαιομένου ἀθερίξαι.

> No, nor even do we hear that the power of stout-hearted Heracles
> Slighted Jason, the son of Aeson, in his yearning entreaty.

Apollonius plays with the Homeric epithets for the great hero (e.g., *Il.* 2.658, 666; 14.324; *Od.* 11.601), but varies the syntax and inverts the word order, so that Heracles' Homeric might (βίην) and strong will (κρατερόφρονος) literally precede him. If the narrator assures us that not even he made light of Jason's call, the phrasing hints that he might have done so. As it happens, it is the rumor that a group of heroes are gathering that attracts Heracles' attention (1.124). He drops the Erymanthian boar at the threshold of the palace and strikes out for Iolcus in defiance of Eurystheus' will (παρὲκ νόον Εὐρυσθῆος, 1.130). From the beginning Heracles is shown to be competitive, spurred on by *eris* to abandon his solitary labors in exchange for a voyage that promises renown for others.

---

[30] See DeForest 1994; Clauss 1993; Beye 1969; Lawall 1966.

Heracles: Confrontation and support

Heracles' impulsive departure contrasts with Jason's sad leave-taking. Jason tells his anguished mother Alcimede to have faith in Athena and Apollo, and to remain at home instead of making a public scene of ill-omen (1.295–305).[31] He begins his speech with a gentle rebuke (1.295–97):

> "Μή μοι λευγαλέας ἐνιβάλλεο, μῆτερ, ἀνίας
> ὧδε λίην, ἐπεὶ οὐ μὲν ἐρητύσεις κακότητος
> δάκρυσιν, ἀλλ' ἔτι κεν καὶ ἐπ' ἄλγεσιν ἄλγος ἄροιο."

> "Do not hurl wretched pains at me, mother, pains
> Too great as it is, since you will not stave off evil
> With tears, only sow sorrow upon still more sorrows."

The Homeric model for these lines is Telemachus' rebuke to Penelope (*Od.* 17.45–56),[32] when he asks her not to burden him emotionally as he prepares to meet the Suitors (17.46–47):

> "Μῆτερ ἐμή, μή μοι γόον ὄρνυθι μηδέ μοι ἦτορ
> ἐν στήθεσσιν ὄρινε φυγόντι περ αἰπὺν ὄλεθρον."

> "My mother, do not rouse sorrow in me nor stir the heart
> In my breast, even though I have escaped sheer destruction."

Both speeches repudiate maternal authority and announce a rite of passage from adolescence to adult responsibility and independence.[33] Telemachus' anxiety sets the tone for Jason's situation: both are young, relatively inexperienced, and about to encounter an intimidating group of older warriors. The Suitors have been plotting to kill Telemachus, and nearly succeeded in ambushing him (15.28–35; 17.65–66). Jason is not the youngest member of the Argo's crew, but his age still puts him at a disadvantage.[34] Like Telemachus, he has inherited a politically troubled house, and the instability of the monarchy of Iolcus is one of the main reasons for the Argo's voyage.

---

[31] Jason tells her not to follow him like a "bird of ill-omen" (ὄρνις ἀεικελίη) to the ship (1.304); cf. Priam telling Hecabe not to be an "evil bird omen" for his hall (ὄρνις ἐνὶ μεγάροισι κακός) when she protests his attempt to recover Hector's body from Achilles (*Il.* 24.219).

[32] Beye 1982, 32. See also Clauss 1993, 48–52 for parallels with Achilles, Hector, and Priam; Clauss also notes that both Telemachus and Jason are personally guided by the gods (76–77).

[33] As part of their maturation both heroes have also traveled through Greece: Jason to the oracle of Delphi, and through Greece to enlist the other Argonauts; Telemachus has just returned to Ithaca from Pylos and Sparta.

[34] Hylas is still a boy (1.132) and Meleager does not yet have a downy beard (3.519–20). On the other hand, Cyzicus, the king of the Doliones, is roughly Jason's age and is considered old enough to rule (1.972).

Three justifications for the trip to the Black Sea are given in the poem. King Pelias hopes to be rid of Jason because of a prophecy that he will be destroyed by a man wearing a single sandal, as Jason is when he first comes to Iolcus (1.1–17). In the second book we learn that Zeus's curse on the house of Aeolus can only be lifted by the recovery of the Golden Fleece (2.1194–95; cf. 3.336–39), and in the third Hera explains that she plans to use Jason in order to punish Pelias for neglecting her sacrifice (3.64–65, 74–75).

The differences between these explanations demonstrate the complex political history of Iolcus.[35] The house of Aeolus was cursed years before when King Athamas, at the request of his second wife Ino, attempted to sacrifice Phrixus, his son by his first wife Nephele. Phrixus and his sister Helle escaped on the back of a winged golden ram; Helle fell off the back of the ram into the waters of the eponymous Hellespont, while Phrixus arrived safely at Aia in the land of Colchis on the Black Sea. Aeëtes, the ruler of the Colchians, gave his daughter Chalciope in marriage to Phrixus, who then sacrificed the magic ram to Zeus. Its fleece was suspended from an oak tree and guarded by a dragon in a grove sacred to Ares.[36] Back in Iolcus, the crown passed from Athamas to his brother Cretheus. One would have expected Cretheus' son Aeson to inherit the throne, but it fell instead to Pelias, Aeson's half-brother, the son of Poseidon. Though Apollonius does not call Pelias a usurper,[37] he is so described by Pindar (*Pyth.* 4.109–10),[38] while Jason's childhood follows the heroic pattern: he is hidden away in the mountains like the infant Zeus, and raised, like Achilles, by the centaur Chiron.

At the beginning of the poem Jason has just returned to Iolcus wearing one sandal, having lost the other while helping Hera, disguised as an elderly woman,[39] across the torrential Anaurus River (see Chapter 1). For this act of kindness he becomes her favorite (3.66–74). Pelias, on the other hand, has insulted Hera by excluding her from a general sacrifice to all the gods.

---

[35] Campbell 1994, 301 *ad* 336–39 (first entry) suggests that Jason fabricates this story of the curse, Odysseus-like, to win over the sons of Phrixus; it is not mentioned elsewhere in the poem and it is possible that "the motif of Zeus' wrath is pulled to the forefront for effect."
[36] This version of the story of Phrixus and Helle, which does not appear in the *Argonautica*, is based on Apollod. *Bibl.* 1 9; cf. Pind. *Pyth.* 4.159–62.
[37] Alcimede, for example, does not mention the loss of the throne in her lament (1.278–91).
[38] One version of the myth evidently depicts Pelias as the lawful king; Gantz 1993, 342 suggests that this is so in Hesiod's *Theogony*, where he is called *megas basileus*. For full discussion of the mythic background, see Mackie 2001, Dräger 1993, and Hunter 1989, 12–21.
[39] Cf. the discussion of Theseus and Hecale in Chapter 2.

Heracles: Confrontation and support

Since piety is the foundation of good leadership in the *Argonautica*,[40] Pelias' lack of respect for Hera evokes his failure as a ruler. The three explanations for the voyage of the Argo therefore share a common political focus: the throne, tainted by attempted murder, has come to Pelias, who now attempts to banish Jason to the ends of the earth, a voyage whose success will not only lift the curse on the house of Aeolus but also, ironically, bring about the destruction of the impious king.

Apollonius alludes only briefly to the recent political history of Iolcus, beginning the poem instead with the "Catalogue of Heroes": a list that briefly describes each of the fifty-odd Argonauts and their own individual backgrounds.[41] The structural correspondence between this section and the Homeric "Catalogue of Ships" has long been recognized,[42] but the description of all the Argonauts so early in the poem is also programmatically significant: this is an epic that privileges the group over the lone individual. Within the first twenty-two lines of Book 1, then, the poet has introduced a number of central themes: the interconnection of religious and political leadership (1.12–14); the malice of suspicious rulers (1.5–6, 15–17); and the deeds of a collective, the group of heroes who must come together both physically and mentally in order to win *kleos* and to return home (1.20–22).

Jason appeals to this ideal of collective unity as he calls upon the Argonauts to choose the man best suited to be their leader (*orchamos*). In the speech that he gives shortly after he meets all the Argonauts, he clarifies the diplomatic character of this office, for which the chief responsibility is negotiation with other communities (1.336–40):

> "Ἀλλά, φίλοι, ξυνὸς γὰρ ἐς Ἑλλάδα νόστος ὀπίσσω,
> ξυναὶ δ' ἄμμι πέλονται ἐς Αἰήταο κέλευθοι,
> τούνεκα νῦν τὸν ἄριστον ἀφειδήσαντες ἕλεσθε
> ὄρχαμον ὑμείων,[43] ᾧ κεν τὰ ἕκαστα μέλοιτο,
> νείκεα συνθεσίας τε μετὰ ξείνοισι βαλέσθαι."

> "Come, then, friends, since we are united in our return to Greece,
> And our paths to the land of Aeëtes are united,
> Therefore now without prejudice choose the best man
> As your leader, one who would be responsible for every detail,
> To handle disputes and settlements with strangers."

---

[40] See Chapter 2 on the importance of piety for the construction of political authority in the Hellenistic period, and Chapter 5 on religion as an index of good leadership in the *Argonautica*.
[41] See the description of Heracles above.   [42] See Clauss 1993, 27, for the history of this connection.
[43] Reading ὑμείων with Vian 2002 instead of ἡμείων (Fränkel 1968). On the use of the term *orchamos*, see Sandridge 2004.

The terms of Jason's speech and his reference to disputes (*neikea*) and settlements further emphasize the thematic centrality of leadership and diplomacy in this work. Though he has organized the gathering, he does not assume that he is automatically entitled to lead the group. Still, in some ways this appears to be a counter-intuitive, even irrational, move on Jason's part. The aforementioned parallel with Telemachus suggests Jason's youth and that he might be intimidated by the crowd, yet it does not explain his motivation in calling for a vote. Critics have tended, perhaps as a response to Jason's opaque state of mind here, to focus on the scene's model, the quarrel between Achilles and Agamemnon in *Iliad* 1.[44] Jason's motivation in calling for an election is not made clear, but dramatically speaking the episode seems to set up a rivalry with Heracles, the Argonauts' first choice in the election. Heracles' reputation leads the Argonauts, as many critics have noted,[45] to choose wrongly, for the great hero is much less concerned as a rule with details and diplomatic settlements than with abbreviated bouts of violence. In declining the honor, Heracles does his best to avoid a political rivalry, and yet the sense of conflict lingers, looking back to the quarrel in *Iliad* 1. The comparison raises a number of questions: has Jason's rightful authority been obscured by Heracles, who now plays the role, as Clare comments, "of a disaffected Achilles lurking in the wings"?[46] Does it reveal a hidden antipathy that ironically undercuts the poem's rhetorical flourishes in the direction of Argonautic *homonoia*? Clare well expresses the problem: "A reader who is alive to such allusion is not altogether sure whether the Argonauts are quite as harmonious as they seem, whether a potential quarrel has indeed been avoided, or whether the issue of leadership will become a source of trouble in the future."[47]

The Homeric inflection of this scene generates complex ambiguities that cannot, and in all likelihood probably should not, be resolved. And yet, by looking more closely at the scene we discern another external impetus for Jason's decision to call for an election, namely, the unexpected arrival of Acastus, Jason's cousin, the son of King Pelias. We are told that Pelias did not wish Acastus to sail with the Argonauts (1.323), presumably because of his hope that the venture would founder.[48] Acastus and Argus, the builder

---

[44] For analysis of the various critical perspectives involved, see Clare 2002, 42–53.
[45] Fantuzzi and Hunter 2004, 128; Clauss 1993, 63; Pike 1993, 31 and n. 24; Beye 1982, 83, 98; Fränkel 1968 *ad* 1.338–50. On Heracles' ambivalent characterization, see Hunter 1993, 25–36; Feeney 1991, 95–98.
[46] Clare 2002, 46. See also Hunter 1993, 18–19.   [47] Clare 2002, 47.
[48] Pelias presumably does not want Acastus to join them because of the dangers of foreigners and sea travel (1.17). Clauss 1993, 61 suggests that the Argonauts suspect Pelias' motives, citing Demagetus,

Heracles: Confrontation and support

of the Argo under Athena's guidance, are the last of the heroes to reach the shore, arriving just after Jason (1.321–23):

> Ἐς δ' ἐνόησαν Ἄκαστον ὁμῶς Ἄργον τε πόληος
> νόσφι καταβλώσκοντας, ἐθάμβησαν δ' ἐσιδόντες
> πασσυδίῃ Πελίαο παρὲκ νόον ἰθύοντας·
>
> They saw Acastus and Argus moving down
> Away from the city, and they were astounded to see them,
> Eagerly, in defiance of Pelias, pressing ahead.

As the son of the king, Acastus enjoys a higher status than Jason, and his royal prerogative is signaled and reinforced by the beautiful cloak he wears (1.325–26). Acastus is a reasonable choice for *orchamos*: he could act on his cousin's behalf like Agamemnon, who leads the Argives on behalf of his brother Menelaus.[49] Acastus, moreover, is accompanied by Argus, the builder of the Argo;[50] an association that increases his authority here. He has disobeyed Pelias in order to join the group (Πελίαο παρὲκ νόον, 1.323), an act of filial defiance in keeping with Jason's earlier rebuke of Alcimede. The same phrase is used to describe Heracles, who left Argos contrary to Eurystheus' will (παρὲκ νόον Εὐρυσθῆος, 1.130), as we noted earlier. The use of these words here marks Acastus as a strong-willed hero much like Heracles. There is only one other occurrence of this phrase: when Jason and Medea plot to take the Fleece in defiance of Aeëtes (παρὲκ νόον Αἰήταο, 4.102). It is consistently applied in the poem to untrustworthy rulers whose *noos* probably ought to be ignored, in contrast to the *noos* ("plan," "intention") of Zeus, which may not be fully known, but in any event cannot be thwarted.[51]

Jason's behavior suggests that the dramatic effect of Acastus' arrival is by no means lost on him. The narrator notes that he refrains from asking the two latecomers any questions (1.327–28), as such an action would make him appear subordinate. Instead, he takes charge, and invites everyone to be seated in assembly. It has been suggested that Jason regards Heracles as a political threat, and that he chooses to gamble on an election in

---

according to whom Pelias ordered Argus to use slender nails to weaken the vessel. They would now be reassured: if the builder of the ship is willing to sail in it, the ship must be well constructed. However, Athena was known to have supervised the building of the vessel, which ought to have been sufficiently reassuring in itself (1.19, 226).

[49] Beye 1982, 24, notes that Jason is upstaged by the late arrival of Argus and Acastus.

[50] The *naupegos*, "ship's carpenter," was customarily aboard later Greek vessels (Casson 1971, 302, 308).

[51] At 2.313 Phineus explains that he was punished for revealing in full the *noos* of Zeus; at 3.328 Argus explains to Aeëtes that they must have encountered the Argonauts because of the *noos* of a compassionate Zeus. Cf. 1.242, where a citizen of Iolcus prays to Zeus, asking what the *noos* of Pelias could be for sending Jason to recover the Fleece.

order to settle matters as quickly as possible.[52] But it is Acastus' impressive arrival that triggers the call for election, and by taking charge, Jason draws attention away from him: indeed, Acastus is quickly forgotten and plays a negligible role in the poem thereafter (1.1041, 1082). All eyes turn to Heracles,[53] and it is at this moment that the impulsive hero surprises everyone.

Remaining seated, he raises his right hand, refuses the nomination, and insists that Jason alone be responsible for the expedition,[54] reasoning that he has already taken the leading role in bringing them together (1.345–47):

> "Μή τις ἐμοὶ τόδε κῦδος ὀπαζέτω· οὐ γὰρ ἔγωγε
> πείσομαι ὥς τε καὶ ἄλλον ἀναστήσεσθαι ἐρύξω.
> Αὐτὸς ὅ τις ξυνάγειρε καὶ ἀρχεύοι ὁμάδοιο."
>
> "Let no one press this honor upon me, for I shall not
> Be persuaded and I will also stop any other from standing.
> Let him lead the company who gathered it himself."

Heracles is again portrayed as quick to act, and he is apparently as undismayed at overruling the other Argonauts as he is at defying Eurystheus. In choosing Jason he shows small regard for the royal privilege of Acastus, or of anyone else for that matter, perhaps because as a hero indentured to an unworthy king he identifies with Jason's predicament.[55] Once again, however, the narrator does not explain the reasons for the characters' behavior; he notes only that Jason jumps up and eagerly accepts the nomination,

---

[52] Vian suggests that Jason recognizes his inferiority to Heracles but takes a chance "in the hope that Heracles will refuse it." Vian 1978, 1029, cited in Hunter 1993, 18, n. 40.

[53] Apollodorus notes that Dionysius Skytobrachion (fl. second to first century BC) has Heracles as the leader of the expedition (1.9.19). Heracles arrives in Pagasae after capturing the Erymanthean boar alive (1.122–23). This is traditionally only the third or fourth labor, whereas for Apollonius it occurs later. When the Argonauts encounter the birds of Ares (2.1047–67), Amphidamas recalls Heracles' fifth (or sixth) labor against the Stymphalian birds. Amphidamas says that he witnessed this labor prior to the voyage of the Argo (2.1054). Lycus states that he himself met Heracles after he acquired the belt of Hippolyta (2.778–79).

[54] Fränkel 1968, 69 comments that even in his refusal to act as leader Heracles displays his authority. See also Levin 1971a, 46 and Beye 1982, 31, who suggests that "Heracles' perhaps coy insistence that they choose Jason is of course the perfect ironic revelation of his own authority and Jason's lack of it." Clauss 1993, 64–66 argues that Heracles' refusal to accept the nomination restores Jason's honor and therefore avoids a conflict like that which divided Achilles and Agamemnon. Clare 2002, 45–47 sees the situation as more complex, and regards Heracles' refusal as an Achillean refusal to submit to the authority of another.

[55] Heracles' motivation in refusing the nomination is curious. The narrator describes him as *mega phroneon* (1.348), a phrase suggesting high-mindedness and courage. LSJ cite *Il.* 11.296 ("high-spirited Trojans") and 13.156 ("high-minded Deiphobus"), as well as 16.758 and 11.325 for the use of the phrase in connection with the courage of noble lions or boars, a compelling parallel given Heracles' physical strength. The phrase could connote haughty presumption, although that sense seems unlikely here.

Heracles: Confrontation and support

"delighted" (*gethosynos* 1.350) to secure Heracles' endorsement. Jason's exultation has struck many as peculiar: why, after all, should he be happy that the Argonauts so obviously prefer Heracles?[56] There is no description of Jason's conscious thought in this scene, only his youth, inexperience, and political vulnerability are suggested. Had Heracles not been present, the election might well have turned out differently. Byre, following Fränkel, comments:

> If the other Argonauts think that Heracles is "the best" (τὸν ἄριστον, 1.338) and make him their first choice as leader, no less a man than Heracles himself thinks that Jason, who assembled the group, is the proper one to lead it (1.345–47); sufficient reason, surely, for Jason to accept election as captain with joy and alacrity (1.349–50).[57]

The election has secured Jason's position, but Heracles' forceful intervention renders problematic a reading of the scene in democratic terms. Influence and timing, rather than numbers, have proved crucial to the result. The selection of the Argonauts' leader is closer to military acclamation, in keeping with the traditions of Macedonian succession, than the Athenian institution we might initially associate with it. Although it is doubtful that such acclamation, whether by a group of nobles or by elite members of the army, was constitutionally established as a formal means of election, informal versions of the process were associated with the assumption of power both in Macedonia and among the Successors.

The Macedonian government was traditionally composed of the king, an advisory group of Companions, and an Assembly of nobles. The king was probably not formally constrained by the decisions of either the Council or the Assembly, although the exact scope and definition of their authority are not known.[58] They undoubtedly exercised considerable power in practical terms, however, especially with regard to succession. In 360 Philip II, the father of Alexander the Great, was acclaimed king by the elite over the heir apparent, Amyntas, the young son of Philip's elder brother, Perdiccas III, who had just been killed in battle.[59] Alexander himself came to power in 336, at the age of only twenty, during the political turmoil that immediately

---

[56] Pike 1993, 31 comments that "Apollonius notes (with almost excessive irony, surely?) that 'warlike Jason was delighted' (349–50). Whatever for? His delight, after this farcical election, suggests that he is either very stupid, very vain and/or very naïve (like a child being 'king of the castle')." Pike attributes Jason's delight to his youth, as was first noted by Fränkel.
[57] Byre 2002, 5 with n. 13.
[58] Borza 1990, 241. Cf. Hammond and Griffith 1979. See also the discussions by Borza 1993 and Hammond 1993.
[59] Worthington 2004, 10–11.

followed Philip's assassination. Like Jason, he secured his position largely through the influence of a powerful ally, in this case Antipater, who orchestrated a general acclamation at court for the young king.[60] Alexander's rivals for the throne included his older cousin Amyntas, the same Amyntas who had in his youth lost the throne to Philip. Amyntas was later executed by Alexander on a charge of treason, along with several sons of Aeropus who posed similar political threats.[61]

Macedonian succession entailed factional support, public confirmation, and the elimination of rivals, all of which are elements, to a greater or lesser extent, of the Argonauts' assembly at Pagasae, whether we prefer to label it an election or an acclamation. In effect, Apollonius has Jason call for an assembly at Pagasae because it was an appropriate gesture at the outset of a military expedition in the third century, even if it was anachronistic in terms of the epic itself. Public acclamation was the means by which Macedonians traditionally secured power, bringing to bear whatever political influence they happened to have. Jason does not become king *strictu sensu*, but he has become the leader of a mobile band of nobles whose journey to the east is obviously reminiscent of Alexander's conquest. What is more, what he essentially requests in his address to the assembly is the right to make treaties with foreign powers, and such a right was exercised exclusively by the Macedonian king.[62] Jason may not be king, but he will need to act like one.

One concern with this mode of interpretation might be that the successions of Macedonian kings like Philip and Alexander were too far removed from third-century Alexandria to serve as analogues. There were, however, other examples of military acclamation that occurred after the death of Alexander. At this time there was a "shift away from the Macedonian 'national' monarchy to a characteristically post-Alexander style of personal monarchy based on a mercenary army."[63] In 323 the Macedonian army reached a compromise by acclaiming as joint rulers Philip Arrhidaeus, Alexander's elder half-brother, who was backed by the infantry and one noble (Meleager), and the infant Alexander IV, who was backed by the cavalry and the rest of the commanders – although neither "king" would ever exercise royal authority.[64] Other examples include Antigonus the One-Eyed and his son Demetrius Poliorcetes, both of whom were acclaimed as kings by the Macedonian army, evidently after the news of Alexander IV's

---

[60] Bosworth 1993, 26–27.   [61] Diod. 17.2.1.   [62] See Borza 1993, 24.   [63] Borza 1993, 24.
[64] Arrhidaeus: Curt. 10.7.2ff.; Arr. *Succ.* 1.1a; Just. 13.3.1–3; Diod. 18.2.4. Alexander IV: Curt. 10.6–9, 16–18, 21ff. See Bosworth 1993, 174–75; Errington 1970, 49–53.

death was made public in 306.[65] In the same year Ptolemy I Soter was acclaimed king by his troops (App. *Syr.* 54), and later, in 281, after murdering the general Seleucus, Ptolemy Ceraunus (a half-brother of Ptolemy Philadelphus) was proclaimed king by Seleucus' own army, which also recognized as his queen Arsinoë, Philadelphus' sister (and future wife).[66] While the public recognition of rulers by their troops cannot be construed as a constitutional desideratum for kingship, it served a practical political purpose.[67] The army was integral to the success of the Hellenistic kings and commanders as they struggled to defend their territories. The numerical strength of the troops was critical, but was so their loyalty, as is illustrated by the death of Perdiccas, killed by his own officers during a failed invasion of Egypt (Diod. 18.35.1–36.5).

Heracles' support of Jason in the election is thus in keeping with this model of military acclamation. The Argonauts' acceptance of Jason is predicated on the influence of Heracles, who serves in the capacity of a senior general like a Parmenion or an Antipater. His prestige is due in part to his famous exploits, with which the Argonauts are very familiar (e.g., 2.783–84, 913, 966–69, 1052–57), but it is also derived anachronistically from his political significance in the Hellenistic period. As we saw in Chapter 2, one of the ways in which the Successors legitimated their authority over their "spear-won" kingdoms was to claim a connection with Heracles.[68] The hero's association with Alexander and Macedonia meant that an alliance with him was ideologically powerful both for the Argonauts and for the poem's contemporary audience. Jason's preference for talk over action is at odds with Heracles' characteristic physicality,[69] but it does not detract from the import of Heracles' endorsement – nothing short of a political victory for Jason.[70] Far from ridiculous, Jason's delight at the outcome of the assembly is entirely justified. The Argonauts have more in common with Homeric warriors than with Hellenistic mercenaries, it is true, but this episode indicates that the tenor of the confrontations between Jason and the

---

[65] According to Diod. 19.105.2, Cassander, the son of Antipater, had ordered the execution of Roxane and Alexander IV in 311.
[66] Just. 24.3.2. For discussion of these examples of military acclamation among the Successors, see Hammond 1993, 16–17.
[67] The Macedonian army rejected Eumenes' bid for rule, for example, in 320.
[68] See Chapter 2 on Heracles' political importance.
[69] For a survey of recent scholarship on the contrast between Heracles and Jason, see Glei 2001, 7–10. The bibliographical essay in Beye 1982, 169–75 is also helpful.
[70] Historical parallels also make for the possibility of a darker reading: one might see Heracles in the role of regent, as a Perdiccas figure who expected to maintain control over the nominal leader. Such a reading would account for Heracles' anger and subsequent murder of the Boreads for preventing his rescue on Mysia (1.1300–8).

Argonauts can be fully understood only by comparison with contemporary hegemonic practices.

After the assembly on Pagasae, Heracles continues to enjoy a dominant position among the Argonauts, but his speech on Lemnos indicates an increase in the tension between his desire for independent glory and Jason's interest in political alliance. Heracles does not celebrate on Lemnos but chooses to remain aboard the Argo with a few companions (1.855–56). We know that Jason has told Hypsipyle that he will eventually leave,[71] but the narrator observes that the Argonauts might have stayed indefinitely on Lemnos, were it not for Heracles' frustration (1.861–64). He is Jason's ally, but he reserves the right to speak his mind (1.865–74):

> "Δαιμόνιοι, πάτρης ἐμφύλιον αἷμ᾽ ἀποέργει
> ἡμέας; Ἦε γάμων ἐπιδευέες ἐνθάδ᾽ ἔβημεν
> κεῖθεν, ὀνοσσάμενοι πολιήτιδας; Αὖθι δ᾽ ἕαδε
> ναίοντας λιπαρὴν ἄροσιν Λήμνοιο ταμέσθαι;
> Οὐ μὰν εὐκλειεῖς γε σὺν ὀθνείῃσι γυναιξὶν
> ἐσσόμεθ᾽ ὧδ᾽ ἐπὶ δηρὸν ἐελμένοι· οὐδέ τι κῶας
> αὐτόματον δώσει τις ἑλὼν θεὸς εὐξαμένοισιν.
> Ἴομεν αὖτις ἕκαστοι ἐπὶ σφεά· τὸν δ᾽ ἐνὶ
> λέκτροις
> Ὑψιπύλης εἰᾶτε πανήμερον, εἰσόκε Λῆμνον
> παισὶν ἐπανδρώσῃ μεγάλη τέ ἑ βάξις ἵκηται."

> "You fools, does the murder of kinfolk drive
> Us from our homeland? Or did we come here
>   from there
> In need of wives, scorning our own citizen
>   women? Does it please you to live here
> And divide the rich farmlands of Lemnos?
> No, we shall certainly not become famous
> If we drag on like this for a long time with
>   foreign women.
> Nor will some god give us the fleece
>   automatically just because we ask for it.
> Let each of us pursue his own ends, and leave
>   this one upon the couches
> Of Hypsipyle all day, until the time when he has
>   manned Lemnos
> With sons and great renown comes to him."

---

[71] Jason had already told Hypsipyle that he could not remain on Lemnos because grievous trials urged him on (1.841). As epic sojourns go, the Lemnian delay is not excessive (cf. Odysseus' year-long visit with Circe and eight years with Calypso).

Heracles: Confrontation and support

If the Argonauts continue to waste time on Lemnos, Heracles argues, they will never become famous (*eukleieis*, 1.869),[72] and since many of them, like Heracles himself, joined the voyage for this very reason, the point is well taken.[73]

Heracles takes aim at Jason in particular by suggesting that they leave him to find fame through his sons.[74] His sarcasm finds a confirmation of sorts in the *Iliad*, where he is mentioned only in connection with his son, Euneos, who does not sail to Troy from Lemnos but instead sends 1,000 measures of wine as a gift to Agamemnon and Menelaus (*Il.* 7.468). Heracles' criticism also alludes to the opposition of Eurylochus, Odysseus' second-in-command (*Od.* 10.205).[75] In contrast to the division brought about by Eurylochos, however, the Argonauts maintain their *homonoia*. Heracles rebukes (*neikessen*) the Argonauts,[76] yet no discord ensues. The competitive *eris* that drives Heracles to seek glory does not disturb the Argonauts, who simply take the hint and prepare immediately to depart (1.877–78). And despite the criticism directed specifically at him, Jason is the first to board the Argo (1.910), mindful, perhaps, of his earlier apprehension regarding the divisive *eris* provoked by Eros.

Jason's authority is far from autocratic, with Heracles stepping into the role played by the elite retinue of kings and military leaders in the fourth and third centuries.[77] Both Philip and Alexander relied on their *Hetairoi* ("Companions"), men who drank with them, rode side by side with them into battle, gave them advice, and at times disagreed with them. The

---

[72] Hunter 1993, 34 rightly observes that "it is the delay to the expedition, not the fact of casual love-making, which upsets Heracles; the expedition itself represents for him an interruption to his Labours and to the *kleos* which accrues from them." Heracles sailed without Eurystheus' approval (1.130) and is anxious to continue the voyage so that he may return to finish his Labours.

[73] Alcon sends his son Phalerus to stand out among the heroes (1.100); Idmon, who knows he is fated to die before he returns, takes part in order that his people do not begrudge him glory (1.141); and Palaemonius is said to be included in their number in order to win fame for Jason (1.206).

[74] The irony is, as Hunter 1993, 34 has observed, that "No Greek hero was more fertile than Heracles." DeForest 1994 takes a hard line against both Jason and Heracles, arguing that Heracles destroys Jason's authority, and at the same time suggesting that Heracles' interest in Jason's sexual pursuits is similar to that of Thersites (58–59). Jason's authority does not appear to be diminished among the Argonauts, however, and Thersites' rebuke is condemned, whereas Heracles' is persuasive.

[75] Clauss 1993, 138: Apollonius makes the audience question Heracles' credibility "by casting him in a role that, although sharply contrasting with it, nevertheless provocatively recalls that of the cowardly Eurylochus." See also Knight 1995, 168: "The parallel with Eurylochus here may show Jason's comparative lack of authority over Heracles, or that exacting obedience is less important for him than it is for Odysseus."

[76] Idas also quarrels with Jason at 1.462. These are the only two instances of the verb in the poem.

[77] Pietsch 1999, 130.

Companions did not constitute a formal council, but were a kind of symposium or drinking club.[78]

After the death of Alexander, the *Philoi* ("Friends") of the Ptolemaic kings held an analogous position in the courts of the Hellenistic period.[79] *Philoi* were specialists in various fields who were recruited from among elite groups in many Greek cities,[80] much like the Argonauts themselves. Three of fifteen Ptolemaic envoys recorded at Delos hailed from Alexandria, but the rest came from Athens, Boeotia, Aegae, Cnidus, Cyzicus, Cos, Mylasa (in Caria), Samos, and Sidon, with two of unknown origin.[81] As Fraser observes, "Alexandrians, though the most numerous group, have no absolute majority, and the Ptolemies evidently took the best talent available."[82] In the third century the title "Friend of the King" was used of an official on good terms with the king who was a member of his council (*synedrion*).[83] "Friend of the King" was the court title of numerous officials close to the Ptolemies, a list that included Sostratus of Cnidus, who represented Philadelphus as an envoy at Delos in the 270s,[84] and the nauarch Callicrates, known for founding a cult devoted to Arsinoë-Aphrodite.[85] A *philos* not only advised the king, but could also act as an informal mediator on behalf of his own city of origin, as a highly placed advocate.[86]

The image of the Macedonian leader at the center of a group of allies bears a resemblance to Jason and the Argonauts, whom the narrator refers to, in fact, as "fellow-counselors gathered for Jason" (1.228).[87] Jason most frequently addresses the Argonauts as *philoi* (1.336; 2.641; 3.171, 492; 4.190,

---

[78] The Argonauts number approximately fifty-five, a group comparable in number with Alexander's Companions. Berve 1926 counted sixty-five Companions; another name was added by Hamilton 1969: both cited in Borza 1990, 241–42.

[79] Borza 1990, 227. *Philoi* were Greeks and Macedonians selected by Hellenistic kings to give council and act as military officers, governors, priests, ambassadors. See also Walbank 1984, 68–71 for discussion of the role of *philoi* at court.

[80] On the recruitment of *philoi* see Herman 1987, 155: "Studies of the epigraphical evidence from the Hellenistic period show conclusively that the *philoi* of the rulers were not imposed from above, from within the narrow circle of Macedonian dynasts, but were recruited from below, from among the élites of the Greek cities." Herman 1980–81, 115 states that, although elites of Macedonia, Persia, and Greek city states were defined by birth, "The *philoi* of the early monarchies were, on the contrary, co-opted by the rulers on criteria of achievement, skill, and loyalty."

[81] Fraser 1972, 1:101.   [82] Fraser 1972, 1:101.

[83] The titular system would later become much more elaborate. See Samuel 1993, 185–87; Fraser 1972, 1:102–3.

[84] Fraser 1972, 1:19–20, 102. Misidentified by Pliny as the architect of the famed Pharos lighthouse, he was most likely, as Fraser observes, a "wealthy and influential courtier," who was responsible for its dedication as a gift to the Ptolemies.

[85] Mooren 1975, 58–61.

[86] E.g., the Athenian Philippides of Cephale, *Philos* of Lysimachus: see Shipley 2000, 48, 76–77.

[87] Rostropowicz 1983, 17–18 accordingly sees a connection between the counsel accepted by Hellenistic kings and the behavior of Hypsipyle (1.665–66) and Jason in assembly (or Alcinous, counseled

1347), though he is not alone in this practice. Phineus addresses them as *philoi* at 2.423, as does Paraebius at 2.468, Lycus at 2.774, Argus at 2.1200 and 3.523, Mopsus at 3.545 and 553, Medea at 4.83, and the sea god Triton at 4.1554. And, of course, the vocative *philoi* also appears regularly in Homeric epic. In the *Iliad* it is often used in formulaic expressions such as "ὦ φίλοι, Ἀργείων ἡγήτορες ἠδὲ μέδοντες" ("Friends, leaders and lords of the Argives," *Il.* 2.79; 9.17; 10.533; 11.276, 587; 17.248; 22.378; 23.457) or "ὦ φίλοι, ἥρωες Δαναοί, θεράποντες Ἄρηος" ("Friends, Danaan warriors, attendants of Ares," *Il.* 2.110; 6.67; 15.733; 19.78). These formulae do not occur in the *Odyssey*, where the term is used more variously, as for example when Telemachus addresses the Suitors (*Od.* 2.70). For the most part, however, the term is used not of false friends like the Suitors but of relations and true allies: as when Odysseus addresses his crew (10.174; 12.154, 208, 320; cf. 22.262), or when the Suitors address each other, or when Polyphemus cries out to his friends, the other Cyclopes, that *Outis* ("Nobody," the false name Odysseus gives) is killing him by guile and not by force (*Od.* 9.408).[88] So, in terms of formulaic epic speech, the term is obviously appropriate for Jason and the Argonauts to use, but such an address nevertheless had additional significance for a Ptolemaic audience. Just as the Achaean conquest of Troy is evoked by the Argonauts' cooperative venture, so the Ptolemaic recruitment of individual *philoi* is implicit in Jason's active search for companions from all over Greece.

In the end, Heracles' caustic advice to Jason on Lemnos is more reminiscent of the sparring of Alexander's Companions than of the judicious advice of royal *philoi*. His offhand comment that the Argonauts ought to split up (1.872) inverts Jason's earlier insistence on the unity of their goals and interests. More importantly, it emphasizes Heracles' characteristic independence. The breaking of the oar off the coast of Mysia has often been interpreted as a sign that Heracles' exceptional strength has been misplaced in such a cooperative venture.[89] During a lull, the heroes commence an informal rowing competition under the influence of the good *eris*. Later, when the wind picks up, the sea grows rough, and everyone but Heracles relaxes his efforts. At that moment, he breaks his oar (1.1168–71):

---

by Arete). Jason, she argues, does not give orders but rather listens to advice before determining an appropriate course of action.

[88] Eurymachus (16.346; 22.70); Amphinomus (16.400; 18.414; 20.245); Antinous (18.36, 52); Agelaus (20.322; 22.132); Leodes (21.152).

[89] Clauss 1993, 196–97: "Heracles' godlike strength and self-sufficiency are completely inappropriate for a group of highly talented, but interdependent, heroes engaged in a nautical *aethlos*."

Μεσσόθεν ἆξεν ἐρετμόν· ἀτὰρ τρύφος ἄλλο μὲν αὐτὸς
ἄμφω χερσὶν ἔχων πέσε δόχμιος, ἄλλο δὲ πόντος
κλύζε παλιρροθίοισι φέρων. Ἀνὰ δ' ἕζετο σιγῇ
παπταίνων· χεῖρες γὰρ ἀήθεσον ἠρεμέουσαι.

He splintered his oar in the middle. He himself fell off balance
Holding one part with both hands, the other the sea washed away
And bore off in the backwater. He sat up in silence,
Glancing around, for his hands were unaccustomed to repose.

This episode shows how Heracles' competitive love of action exceeds the constraints of the Argonauts' communal enterprise:[90] the broken oar on this reading is emblematic of his outsized, even inappropriate strength.[91] Heracles dominates the others from his first appearance, and while his power is the catalyst that ensures Jason's election and dislodges the Argonauts from the Lemnian idyll, it is not equal to the spoils of Eros.[92] The splintered oar thus foreshadows the Argonauts' inevitable separation as Heracles, Hylas, and Polyphemus are left behind in the wake of the Argo's passage.

IDAS AND THE HYMN OF ORPHEUS

A fresh challenge to Jason's newly elected authority comes only hours after the assembly at Pagasae. After building an altar to Apollo Embasios ("Apollo of Embarkation"), the Argonauts sacrifice two steers (1.402–459), feasting late into the night. As a group of young men relaxing, telling stories, and drinking heavily, the Argonauts, Jason's "fellow-counselors," can readily "be compared collectively to νέοι at a symposium."[93] But Jason is self-absorbed and sits apart (1.460–61):[94]

---

[90] Knight 1995, 131 comments that Heracles is a "misfit among the crew." Ancient sources vary with respect to Heracles' presence on the voyage. Aristotle (*Pol.* 3.1284a22–5) says the Argo refused to take him because the others would be outmatched. The Scholiast (Wendel 1958 *ad* 1.1289–91a) reports differing views: Herodotus (7.193) says he was left after the Argonauts sent him for water; Dionysius of Miletus has him sail all the way to Colchis; he says that he did not sail with the rest; Antimachus, Pherecydes, and Posidippus all agree that he was forced to disembark because the Argo was overburdened, while according to Ephorus he voluntarily stayed with Omphale – a direct contrast with his behavior on Lemnos (*Argon.* 1.861–76).

[91] E.g., Clauss 1993, 183, for whom the scene implies that Heracles is in arrogant competition with Poseidon; DeForest 1994, 64: "Heracles' reckless energy renders him ridiculous, an oversized hero thwarted by a dainty oar"; Galinsky 1972, 109: "before Herakles can row the boat out of contemporary reality, the oar snaps in the middle, and primitive heroic will and strength are defeated."

[92] Heracles searches for Hylas on Mysia, after Hylas is abducted by an amorous water nymph (1.1207–72).

[93] See Campbell 1994, 173 on 1.458.

[94] See Fantuzzi and Hunter 2004, 112–13 on the inappropriateness of such reserve in a symposiastic context.

Ἔνθ' αὖτ' Αἰσονίδης μὲν ἀμήχανος εἷν ἑοῖ αὐτῷ
πορφύρεσκεν ἕκαστα, κατηφιόωντι ἐοικώς.

But here the son of Aeson, fixed in himself,
Mulled over everything, like a man grieving in silence.

Jason is preoccupied with the details (τὰ ἕκαστα) of the voyage, or rather he is overwhelmed by them, as the adjective *amechanos* suggests. This term has provoked much scholarly debate. In Homeric usage *amechanie* suggests the intractability of a character,[95] whereas in the *Argonautica* it typically describes someone who is stunned, speechless, or paralyzed by anxiety.[96] Since linguistic cognates of *amechanos* appear frequently in connection with Jason,[97] the quality of helplessness (*amechanie*) may seem essential to his character in the same way that resourcefulness (*polymechanie*) is for Odysseus.[98] But while *amechanie* is often appropriate for Jason, it is by no means restricted to him: similar phrases are frequently applied both to other individuals and to the Argonauts as a group.[99] Then, too, despair and self-doubt are common to characters in other epic poems.[100] Glaucus and

---

[95] The term *amechanos* is typically applied to gods and varies in meaning from "impossible" to "indomitable" or "incapable." Zeus calls Hera *amechane* ("impossible," *Il*. 15.14) in connection with the destruction of Hector; Penelope uses the term for dreams that are hard to figure out (*Od*. 19.560); Sleep says Hera asks him to perform an "impossible" task (*Il*. 14.262); Diomedes calls Nestor "indomitable" because he is still active (*Il*. 10.167); Polydamas says Hector is "impossible" to persuade (*Il*. 13.726); and Patrocles says Achilles is "incapable" of being cured of enmity (*Il*. 16.29). Cf. *Il*. 19.273; *Od*. 19.363.

[96] The term *amechanos* is often used to describe Medea's love-pangs and suffering (3.772, 951, 1157; 4.107, 1049); it also describes Ganymede in his game with Eros (3.126). It appears in its Homeric sense when the poet describes the discovery of Cyzicus' accidental death and inexorable fate (1.1053), the proximity of the Argonauts to the "inescapable doom" (2.578) of the Clashing Rocks ("Symplegades"), and the impossibility of the voyage as conceived by Pelias (3.336).

[97] Cognates of *amechanos* are used by the narrator or other characters to describe Jason's reactions to the loss of Heracles (1.1286), to Phineus' description of the trip to Colchis (2.410), to Aeëtes' ultimatum (3.423), to Tiphys' death (2.885), and to Aeëtes' challenge (3.432). The term *amechanie* also occurs when the Libyan nymphs ask Jason why he and the other Argonauts are so downhearted (4.1308, 1318), and when Jason tests the Argonauts by saying the voyage was a mistake (2.623). See Pietsch 1999, 138–58 for a survey of references to Jason's *amechanie*: Pietsch balances Jason's weakness in these episodes against his strengths as a leader, concluding that, while Jason is not portrayed as an irreproachable superman ("einen Übermenschen ohne Fehl und Tadel"), he is nonetheless realized in human terms, given his youth and the enormity of the task that confronts him (158).

[98] For discussion, see Glei 2001, 7–9.

[99] Individuals: Hylas' water nymph (1.1233); Phrixus' son Argus (2.1140); Circe (4.692); Ancaeus (4.1259), Peleus (4.880), and Mopsus, who is literally paralyzed by a poisonous snake (4.1527). Cognates are also used for the fear inspired by the Argonauts on Lemnos (1.638) and in Colchis (3.893). Argonauts as a group: 2.681, 860; 3.504; 4.825, 1308, 1701. On the collective apathy of the Argonauts, see Fränkel 1968 *ad* 1.458–61 with n. 131; 1957, 14 (where he notes Heracles as an exception).

[100] Cf. Clauss 1993, 83, who observes that "Jason is often depicted as a man in the grip of depression and helplessness," without noting that all the Argonauts and many other characters are described in the same terms.

Hector in the *Iliad* as well as Aeneas in the *Aeneid* are marked by moments of indecision and hesitation.[101] As Bulloch writes, "Jason is often diffident, but so are Agamemnon and Menelaus in the *Iliad*; Jason sometimes despairs and loses momentum, but so does Agamemnon".[102]

Be that as it may, Jason's silence arouses the suspicions of Idas, a character of extremes and very nearly a parody of heroic wrath and bluster (1.462–71):[103]

> Τὸν δ' ἄρ' ὑποφρασθεὶς μεγάλῃ ὀπὶ νείκεσεν Ἴδας·
> "Αἰσονίδη, τίνα τήνδε μετὰ φρεσὶ μῆτιν ἑλίσσεις;
> Αὔδα ἐνὶ μέσσοισι τεὸν νόον. Ἠέ σε δαμνᾷ
> τάρβος ἐπιπλόμενον, τό τ' ἀνάλκιδας ἄνδρας ἀτύζει;
> Ἴστω νῦν δόρυ θοῦρον, ὅτῳ περιώσιον ἄλλων
> κῦδος ἐνὶ πτολέμοισιν ἀείρομαι, οὐδέ μ' ὀφέλλει
> Ζεὺς τόσον ὁσσάτιόν περ ἐμὸν δόρυ, μή νύ τι πῆμα
> λοίγιον ἔσσεσθαι μηδ' ἀκράαντον ἄεθλον
> Ἴδεω ἑσπομένοιο, καὶ εἰ θεὸς ἀντιόῳτο·
> τοῖόν μ' Ἀρήνηθεν ἀοσσητῆρα κομίζεις."

Idas observed him and rebuked him loudly:
"Son of Aeson, what is this plot you are mulling over?
Speak out your plan openly. Or has fear attacked and beaten you,
The kind that strikes terror among cowardly men?
Be witness, my bold spear, by which I win greater
Glory in wars than others, and not even Zeus aids me as much as my spear,
There will be no kind of evil ruin, nor vain contest,
While Idas is in your service, even if a god should confront us,
That's how great an ally you bring from Arene in me!"

At this blasphemy, the Argonauts are horrified; Idmon the prophet then speaks, criticizing Idas for his inappropriate speech (1.476–80)

> "Δαιμόνιε, φρονέεις ὀλοφώια καὶ πάρος αὐτῷ,
> ἦέ τοι εἰς ἄτην ζωρὸν μέθυ θαρσαλέον κῆρ
> οἰδάνει ἐν στήθεσσι, θεοὺς δ' ἀνέηκεν ἀτίζειν;
> Ἄλλοι μῦθοι ἔασι παρήγοροι οἷσί περ ἀνὴρ
> θαρσύνοι ἕταρον· σὺ δ' ἀτάσθαλα πάμπαν ἔειπας."

---

[101] Holoka 1999.
[102] Bulloch 1985b, 591. In this connection it is helpful to remember that Isocrates praised Agamemnon in his Panathenaic Speech (74–89) as a model king who preferred rational persuasion to violence, qualities recognizable in Apollonius' Jason. See de Romilly 1988, 36–37, who analyzes the greater insecurity of Agamemnon in tragedy as compared with his Homeric portrait, noting that after the fifth century Agamemnon was seen as an ideal king.
[103] Fantuzzi and Hunter 2004, 113–14. See Fränkel 1960 for discussion of the contrast between Jason and Idas; Glei 2001, 6 argues that the contrast between Jason and Heracles is more natural.

"Fool, have you been mulling over malicious thoughts even before,
Or to your doom does unmixed wine swell
A brash heart in your chest, and drive you to disrespect the gods?
There are other comforting words with which a man
Might encourage his companion, but you spoke thoughtlessly."

Idmon goes on to remember how his father Apollo destroyed the two sons of Aloeus for challenging the gods, to which Idas responds with yet another challenge, threatening to kill Idmon if he prophesies falsely (1.487–91).[104] Idas' speech, disrespectful to Jason and downright insulting to Zeus, thus infects a festive occasion with the worst kind of *eris* and casts a pall over the voyage before it has begun. While it is possible that Apollonius invented this quarrel between Idas and Idmon,[105] there is nothing new about the outlines of the quarrel:[106] the conflict between a warrior and a religious figure recalls Agamemnon's quarrel with Chryses in *Iliad* 1. Apollonius, however, makes a significant change by realigning the factions, uniting the political leader, the prophet, and all the company against a single disruptive influence. Instead of tearing the group apart, Idas' blasphemy unites it by turning everyone against him.

Idas' inappropriate behavior alludes to the intemperate rant of the Homeric Thersites, who takes Achilles' part in the quarrel with Agamemnon (*Il.* 2.211–77). Thersites is more often compared with Heracles, particularly during his tirade on Lemnos,[107] but the parallel with Idas is, I suggest, more appropriate. Thersites' insolence is attributed to his low birth and ill-favored looks; of all the men who went to Troy, he is singled out as the most disgraceful and least well behaved in public (*aischistos* 2.216). Idas, it is true, is well born, but he too is choleric, boastful, and crudely provocative. Both Idas and Thersites are humiliated in various ways: Odysseus publicly beats Thersites with a golden scepter (*Il.* 2.265–77), while Idas' outbursts are ignored and overlooked by the rest of the Argonauts for the remainder of the voyage.[108] Neither man has any followers; both do little to benefit

---

[104] Idmon evidently chooses not to reveal that Idas is fated to be destroyed by Zeus's thunderbolt. On this point see, e.g., Hunter 1993, 177; Nelis 1992, 161; Fränkel 1968 *ad* 1.(496–)511(1).

[105] See the Scholiast at 1.475: οἰκείως τὸν Ἴδμονα ὡς μάντιν ὄντα ποιεῖ ἐναντιούμενον τῷ Ἴδᾳ ἐχθρῷ ὄντι Ἀπόλλωνι.

[106] Cf. Tydeus vs. Amphiaraus; Hector vs. Polydamas.

[107] Clare 2002, 63; Knight 1995, 115, n. 149; DeForest 1994, 58–59; Clauss 1993, 139–40; Hunter 1993, 35–36.

[108] Idas is enraged at the willingness of the other Argonauts to accept Medea's help (3.556–63); he angrily tests Jason's enchanted weapons (3.1252–55). Dräger 2001, following Fränkel 1960, observes that Idas' impious rage is a foil to the justified anger of the gods (121–23, 102–3). Hunter 1993, 58 comments that Idas exemplifies "'brawn' without 'brain.'" Fränkel 1968 *ad* 1.462–94, sees Idas as an old-style hero whose bluster is a foil for Jason's modern practicality ("einen vernünftigen

their companions. The high-minded (*mega phroneon Argon.* 1.348) Heracles, by contrast, continues to aid the Argonauts (though he does not know it) even after his disappearance (2.1047–67, 1432–60).[109] Idas is the closest thing to a villain among the Argonauts, and serves as a model for several dangerous types in Virgil's *Aeneid*. Idas' claim that he values his spear more than Zeus looks ahead to the blasphemous Mezentius, who regards his right hand as a god (*dextra mihi deus, Aen.* 10.773), or even Turnus, who asks his spear to rend the corselet of that "effeminate Phrygian," Aeneas (*semiviri Phrygis, Aen.* 12.94–100).

Idas' motivation in this scene may not be as clearly drawn as those of Mezentius or Turnus, but as Idmon notes (*Argon.* 1.477), he has been drinking unmixed wine (1.472–74):

> Ἦ καὶ ἐπισχόμενος πλεῖον δέπας ἀμφοτέρῃσι
> πῖνε χαλίκρητον λαρὸν μέθυ, δεύετο δ' οἴνῳ
> χείλεα κυάνεαί τε γενειάδες.

> He spoke, and as he grasped a full cup with both hands,
> He drank the sweet, unmixed wine, and drenched with wine
> His lips and dark beard.

The reference is telling because of the notoriety of unmixed wine in the ancient Greek world.[110] Whereas Athenians traditionally diluted their wine with water, the Macedonians had a reputation for enjoying unmixed wine to excess.[111] Theopompus claimed that Philip drank regularly, had lengthy

---

und praktischen Führer modernen Schlages, der vordenkt und vorplant"); Goldhill 1991, 314 notes that Heracles and Idas are often lumped together as "old style" heroes, but notes the important distinction between the crude Idas and the exemplary, if "deeply polyvalent" Heracles.

[109] Griffiths 1990, 32 notes that Heracles "lives on as a powerful symbol" even after his departure. Feeney 1991, 97 interprets the vision of Heracles in the Libyan desert at 4.1477–80 as a farewell prior to his passage into the world of the gods: "He has gone virtually all the way down the path towards becoming a god, and that is the extraordinary interstitial point which Apollonius captures in that beautiful moment when Lynceus sees him in the far distance, or thinks he sees him." Feeney's analysis is compelling, although it should be noted that the apotheosis of Heracles was not supposed to occur until much later, after his enslavement to Omphale, the capture of Troy, Elis, Pylos, and Ephyra, and the defeat of the Dryopians and the Oichalians (Apollod. *Bibl.* 2.6–7).

[110] See Fantuzzi and Hunter 2004, 78–80 on concerns about excessive drinking in Alexandrian symposia.

[111] Villard 1988, 457 observes that all the ancient historians who studied Philip or Alexander commented on their tendency to drink. Some sources, however, were hostile to Macedonia, such as Demosthenes, who compared Philip to a sponge, and Ephippus, who alleged that Macedonians knew no restraint (Plut. *Dem.* 16; *FGrH* 126 F 1). For that matter, as part of the state celebration of Dionysus, wine was said to flow through the streets during the Grand Procession of Ptolemy Philadelphus (Callixenus *ap.* Athen. 199a–b). For discussion of the drinking pavilion built by Ptolemy Philadelphus, see Studniczka 1915.

dinner parties, and was drunk during battle.[112] Alexander reportedly scorned Philip's drunkenness, mocking him for his clumsiness during the feast at his wedding to Cleopatra.[113] Citing Aristobulus, who had first-hand experience of the expedition to Asia, Arrian claims that Alexander generally exercised restraint, and used lavish symposia to promote goodwill,[114] much as Jason attempts to do in this episode. His withdrawal from the Argonauts' drinking party, then, is reminiscent of Alexander's characteristic restraint, while Idas' behavior underscores the threat that intoxication posed to collective equanimity.

Alexander himself is said to have been inebriated at a feast – and with fatal consequences.[115] The feast took place on a day sacred to Dionysus, though Alexander ill-advisedly chose to sacrifice to the Dioscuri instead. The drunken celebrants praised Alexander and compared him favorably with Castor, Pollux, and Heracles. Cleitus, however, who had previously complained about Alexander's adoption of Persian customs, especially the ritual greeting (*proskynesis*) that implied his divinity,[116] now stood up for the traditional Macedonian gods. He belittled Alexander, raising his right hand and reminding the king that he had saved his life in the battle by the Granicus River: "This hand, Alexander, saved you then!"[117] Alexander was incensed. Although a number of other Companions, including Ptolemy, sought to restrain him, he ambushed Cleitus in a doorway, running him through with a pike.

This incident is interesting in two respects: first, because of the thematic similarities of Cleitus' speech to that of Idas, and second, because of the differences in the behavior of Alexander and Jason. To begin with, both Cleitus and Idas traffic in impious bravado. Both boast of their martial success and insult a god: in Cleitus' case the god happens to be Alexander himself. Both also humiliate their leaders by asserting that they are weak and rely on the aid of others: Idas points to his spear, Cleitus to his right hand. Cleitus is more than partly to blame for his own murder, which further damaged Alexander's relations with his men, but Idas is entirely at

---

[112] *FGrH* 115 F 225, F 236, and F 282. Tomlinson 1970, 315 argues for the presence at Vergina of a building devoted to the consumption of alcohol, possibly for religious or symposiastic purposes.
[113] Satyrus *ap.* Athen. 13.557d–e; Plut. *Alex.* 9.3–7; Justin 9.5.9; 9.7.3–4.
[114] Arr. 7.29.4. See also Diod. 17.16.4.
[115] Plut. *Alex.* 51.5–6; Arr. 4.8.8–9. O'Brien 1992 argues that Alexander's drinking was excessive, although this theory has largely been discredited. See also Borza 1983.
[116] *Proskynesis* was a greeting ritual that entailed full prostration before the monarch (Bosworth 1993, 284–85). The Macedonians generally reviled *proskynesis* as a violation of the dignity of freeborn men, but Persian custom dictated that all subjects greet their superiors in this manner, and the failure to do so was a grave insult to the Great King.
[117] Arr. 4.8.7. Worthington 2004, 136–37; Bosworth 1993, 114–15.

fault since Jason neither provokes him nor responds in kind. Of Alexander, Arrian observes that he is to be pitied as the slave of two vices, anger (*orge*) and drunkenness (*paroinia*), whereas Jason avoids both during his confrontations with Heracles, Idas, Telamon, Aeëtes, Medea, and even Apsyrtus. Indeed, Jason's avoidance of anger is one of the characteristics that set him apart from Alexander, although the comparison between the two is inevitable, as Hunter writes: "perceptions of Alexander are one of the 'texts' against which the epic poem can be read, with whatever consequences for that reading."[118] In this case, the point is not that the reticent Jason is a greater leader than Alexander, but rather that one of the benefits of restraint is that it can forestall the kind of *neikos* that actually occurred among the Macedonians, not to mention the Homeric heroes.

The quarrel with Idas thus presents a traditional problem – how to handle a loud and argumentative companion (or Companion) – in terms that flesh out a Hellenistic perspective not only about the causes of strife (alcohol) but also about the value of peaceful resolution. The fight between Idmon and Idas ends with a song from Orpheus, a scene in which the traditional Greek appreciation for music in the restoration and preservation of civic harmony is apparent.[119] Orpheus usually plays the lyre without singing, but he now sings about the succession of the gods (1.494–512),[120] celebrating the history of the creation of the world down to the childhood of Zeus.[121] He privileges rationality over aggression by contrasting the intelligent rule of Zeus with the brutality of the Titans.[122] Using material familiar from Hesiod and Empedocles, he recounts how deadly strife (*neikos*) played a role in the formation and organization of the cosmos (1.498).[123] His

---

[118] Fantuzzi and Hunter 2004, 129.
[119] Terpander, Thaletas, and Stesichorus were all said to have restored civic order through music. See West 1992, 31 with n. 88. See also Clauss 1993, 73 on the power of theogonic music to resolve strife.
[120] Orpheus draws attention to the theme of succession by celebrating the transfer of power from Ophion and Eurynome to Cronus and Rhea, while Zeus is still young and unarmed. Like Aeëtes, Cronus had been warned by his parents to beware of the next generation (cf. Hes. *Theog.* 463–65 and *Argon.* 3.599–600). On Orpheus' hymn as an adaptation of the theogony of Pherecydes of Syros (fl. 6th century BC), see Gantz 1993, 740 (Appendix A: "Some 'Deviant' Cosmogonies") and West 1983, 127–28.
[121] Orpheus plays the wedding hymn of Jason and Medea (4.1159–60). He sings a song to Artemis while the Argonauts first row away from Pagasae (1.540–41), after the battle with the Bebrycians (2.161), and to drown out the song of the Sirens (4.909). As a consummate artist Orpheus plays the wooden box lyre (*phorminx* or *kithara*) that is associated with Apollo (Arist. *Pol.* 1341a18), in contrast to the tortoise-shell bowl lyre said to have been invented by Hermes. Plato *Leg.* 669e–670a condemns playing the *kithara* unaccompanied by voice or dance, but the style dates back to the sixth century. On "bare lyre playing," see West 1992, 69–70 with nn. 92–94.
[122] See Clauss 1993, 83–85; Nelis 1992, 162.
[123] On the discussion by ancient and modern commentators of the Empedoclean symbolism here and throughout the poem see Kyriakou 1994; Nelis 1992, esp. 157–58, with nn. 17–19.

performance recalls the Homeric *aoidos* Demodocus, who sings during the feast in Phaeacia, resolving Odysseus' quarrel with the Phaeacians Laodamas and Euryalus by recounting the love of Aphrodite and Ares (*Od.* 8.254–55).[124] Orpheus emulates the Empedoclean allegory of this song by Demodocus, for, in Damien Nelis' words, "Apollonios is imitating Homer by lifting the veil of the allegory and presenting the true meaning of the model."[125] But Orpheus' celebration of strife and succession in the evolution of the universe also puts the quarrel between Idmon and Idas into perspective. By describing the overthrow of one generation by the next (Ophion and Eurynome by Cronos and Rhea), Orpheus alludes to the problem of usurpation noted earlier in connection with Iolcan politics, while characterizing strife as natural, unavoidable, and even essential, since the cosmos could not have come into being without a quarrel between earth, sea, and sky. By foregrounding this image of a cosmic Neikos, Orpheus also shifts the blame for the quarrel from Idas to an impersonal and divine abstraction, even as he reminds his audience of the thunderbolt that threatens those who oppose Zeus. In Apollonius' hands, Odysseus' physical abuse of Thersites is transformed into a prophetic warning and a cosmic threat: Idas, like Thersites, will eventually pay for his insolence.

Idas' disputes contrast the dangers of strife with the advantages of cooperation and alliance. His self-centered boasting runs counter to the spirit of alliance on which the voyage depends,[126] and his self-reliant confidence in the strength of his spear contradicts the group's tacit agreement that a common fate obliges cooperation.[127] Idmon's admonition to encourage companions underscores the importance of tactful restraint, a virtue that will prove as crucial when dealing with rivals or enemies as with friends. Apollonius consistently presents bold and angry speeches as counterproductive, even when they are justified, as for example when Aeëtes insults the Argonauts during the interview in Colchis, and Jason quickly

---

[124] Elsewhere the songs of Demodocus and Phemius stir the emotions of the main characters as they celebrate the Trojan War. Demodocus brings Odysseus to tears when he sings of his quarrel with Achilles (*Od.* 8.75–82), and when he sings of Troy at Odysseus' own request (*Od.* 8.499–520). Penelope weeps when Phemius sings of the Achaeans' return from Troy (*Od.* 1.325–36). Two other bards are mentioned only briefly: the bard left by Agamemnon to instruct Clytemnestra and later exiled to a desert island by Aegisthus (*Od.* 3.267–68), and Thamyris, the bard who challenges the Muses and is punished for his insolence (*Il.* 2.594–600).

[125] Nelis 1992, 158. On Empedoclean symbolism, see also Hardie 1986, 62.

[126] So Vian 2002, 1:16–17, who adds that Orpheus concludes the quarrel and expresses one of the most important leitmotifs of the poem: the concord of the Argonauts.

[127] Zeus's victory over the Titans, for example, was due in part to the thunderbolts crafted by the Cyclopes.

checks Telamon's indignation with a careful and well-considered reply (3.382–85).

To say that boasts and quarrels are the cause of grave setbacks in the Homeric epics would be an understatement. Agamemnon's ill-considered treatment of Achilles causes a *neikos* that undermines Argive strength in the attack on Troy. Odysseus' *nostos* is cursed when he taunts Polyphemos, ignoring his companions' attempts to quiet him after the escape from the Cyclops' cave (*Od.* 9.473–535). In the *Argonautica*, such disruptions are condemned, along with the assignment of blame. Not only the narrator but also characters in the poem prefer to shift the guilt for such misunderstandings to the influence of alcohol, or more frequently, capricious deities like Eris or Eros. By redirecting attention away from Idas, Orpheus' song peacefully resolves the quarrel, restores *homonoia*, and assures the success of the voyage.

RECONCILIATION WITH TELAMON

Telamon's reaction to the disappearance of Heracles in Mysia provides the climactic end to Book 1. Although harmony will be restored among the Argonauts after this episode, Telamon's challenge to Jason's authority is more problematic than either confrontation we have previously considered.[128] Telamon is the heroic obverse of Idas, whose Thersites-like insolence is unfavorably portrayed.[129] Telamon, by contrast, has a good reputation and enjoys the respect of the Argonauts: he demonstrates courage in battle (1.1043; 2.121–22), is chosen for two embassies to Aeëtes (3.196, 1172–75), and quickly volunteers to plough the Field of Ares (3.515–16).[130] Telamon is as impulsive as Heracles, however, and his nature likewise gets the better of him on two occasions: during the initial audience with Aeëtes (3.382–85) and, more importantly, after the Argonauts accidentally leave Heracles behind on the coast of Mysia (1.1286–344).

The exchange between Telamon and Jason begins when Telamon accuses Jason of orchestrating a quick departure in order to rid himself of the

---

[128] Valerius Flaccus rewrites the scene so that Telamon does not accuse Jason of treachery. The Argonauts search for Heracles for a week until Tiphys and Jason suggest it is time to leave; Telamon argues that they must continue to search (3.641–45); the poet censures Meleager, *potioribus ille / deteriora fovens*, for persuading them to go (3.646–47). Both poets are concerned to show rivalry between the Argonauts, but Apollonius is specifically interested in Telamon's perception that Jason is threatened by Heracles.

[129] Idas' battle prowess against the Doliones is very briefly noted (1.1044), but his appearances in the poem are, by and large, unflattering.

[130] Peleus volunteers first, then Telamon, then Idas, a sequence that implies the relative superiority of the two sons of Aeacus.

popular hero. The quarrel divides the Argonauts until the sea god Glaucus intervenes and explains that the loss of Heracles accords with the will (*boule*) of Zeus. Jason accepts Telamon's apology and comments that while he was initially offended by the accusation, he knows that Telamon was defending a companion and that he would defend him just as fiercely under similar circumstances. Jason's rational analysis of Telamon's motivation allows him not only to put aside his own anger but also to forestall the division of the Argonauts and the disruption of the voyage.[131]

Apollonius experiments with the theme of epic anger in several episodes of the *Argonautica*. Unlike the wrathful Achilles, Jason is marked by rationalization and the inclination toward compromise,[132] and scholars have long viewed him in a relatively negative light.[133] Although Mooney, for example, recognizes that Jason is "slow to anger," he dismisses him as "tame and insipid" in contrast to the passionate Medea.[134] In evaluating the significance of Jason's moderate temper we should not, however, discount the fact that anger is largely ineffectual in the *Argonautica*: angry characters are typically rebuked, dismissed, or ignored. The Argonauts work together to silence Idas' outbursts, first when he insults Jason and Idmon (1.463–71, 487–91), and later when he objects to their reliance on Medea (3.558–63) and tries to break Jason's enchanted weapons (3.1252–55). Although anger (*cholos*) is justified against an openly hostile enemy, as when Amycus challenges and insults the Argonauts (2.19–20) and is then killed in a boxing

---

[131] Cf. Redfield 1994, 94–98 on the series of errors that follows Agamemnon's refusal to ransom Chryseis, as well as his chapter on heroic error (128–59).

[132] For Jason as a new heroic type in contrast to Idas, see Fränkel 1960; for Jason as anti-hero, Lawall 1966; as love hero, Beye 1969; as contradictory Skeptic hero/anti-hero, Klein 1983; as entirely unheroic, Schwinge 1986; as a morally weak, democratic hero, Natzel 1992; as a realistic, modern hero, Clauss 1993; as a multivalent hero, Hunter 1993. Pietsch 1999 and Rostropowicz 1983 see Jason as representative of the Ptolemaic style of leadership, a point of view that has much to recommend it.

[133] E.g., Moreau 1994, 187, for whom Jason lacks, among other heroic qualities, Idas' "martial impetuosity." See Hunter, 1993, 8–15, 25 for an extensive discussion of epic character and the critical reception of Jason (e.g., Clauss 1993, Jackson 1992, Zanker 1979, Beye 1969, Lawall 1966, Carspecken 1952). Pietsch 1999, 158 suggests that Jason charts a middle course between greatness and weakness: we sympathize with Jason because of his youth and the immensity of the task that he undertakes, yet we cannot accept Jason as superior because of his lack of resourcefulness.

[134] Mooney 1912, 36–7. At *Argon.* 4.394 Jason is frightened (*hypoddeisas*) at Medea's fury: she is boiling with rage and yearns, like Aeëtes (3.581–83), to burn the Argo. The verb *hypodeido* ("feel awe," "tremble") appears only in connection with Aeëtes: at 3.318, Argus fears Aeëtes' reaction to the Argonauts, and at 3.435, Aeëtes threatens Jason should he be afraid to yoke the bulls. Thus Jason's fear at 4.394 does not undermine his heroism but rather reminds us of Medea's supernatural lineage. Similarly, in Homeric usage *hypodeido* refers to the awe one feels at supernatural or unusual power (*Il.* 1.406; *Od.* 2.66; 9.377; 10.296) as well as on the battlefield or in assembly (*Il.* 5.521; 12.413; 18.199; 22.282; 24.265; *Od.* 16.425; 17.564).

match by an angry Polydeuces (2.67–97),[135] the poem consistently condemns the irascible, like Idas, and punishes the belligerent, like Amycus and Aeëtes.[136]

The confrontation between Telamon and Jason, like other episodes in the *Argonautica*, falls in line with Aristotelian observations about the causes and characteristics of anger.[137] As an affection of the soul, anger has a share in the operations of both the mind and the body. Anger is not coextensive with (*meta*) bodily pain: rather, it can only occur on account of (*dia*) the thought of outrage that accompanies the feeling of pain (*Rhet.* 1378a21–22, 30–33).[138] Although anger presents itself physiologically, it is rooted in thoughts and beliefs, and open to persuasion. Aristotle observes that the various perspectives of the four causes are especially helpful in analyzing feelings because of the soul's hybrid nature (*De An.* 403a3–b1). Anger is thus classed formally among the *pathe*, the feelings or passions, which have both mental and physical components.[139] The efficient cause of anger is outrage at a slight (*Rhet.* 1378a30), the final cause is the desire for restitution, and the material cause is the boiling of the blood around the heart that causes the face to flush.[140] The description of Heracles' rage – which is no doubt intensified by the erotic nature of his affection for Hylas – provides us with an especially vivid example of the material cause, as sweat drips from his brows and dark blood boils up in his bowels (*splanchna*).[141] In Homer, by contrast, anger is often described as an external force that seizes men (e.g., *cholos*, *Il.* 1.387; *achos*, 1.188; *kotos*, 8.449), but a reference to blood that boils does not occur.[142] Homeric references to *splanchna*, moreover, are restricted

---

[135] The poet takes care to show that Polydeuces' anger is justified. In this instance he acts on behalf of his comrades against an openly hostile enemy. Note that Polydeuces, in contrast to Homeric warriors, refrains from taunting Amycus, and meets his boasts with a smile (2.60–62). Medea's anger against the ancient bronze giant Talos (4.1671–72) is similarly justified inasmuch as he attacked the Argo without provocation (4.1638–39).

[136] The poet refers to Aeëtes' anger on a number of occasions: he angrily threatens the Colchians as he plots to destroy the Argonauts (3.606–8); Medea fears the dread wrath of her father (3.614); Aeëtes is furious at Jason's success (4.6–10); Aeëtes is enraged and threatens the Colchians with death if they fail to recover Medea (4.230–35). He eventually suffers the loss of his fleet as well as of his son Apsyrtus: the Argonauts ambush Apsyrtus and the crew of his ship (4.468–70, 488–89); the rest of the fleet settles elsewhere rather than return to Colchis (4.507–21, 1209–15). Rose 1985, 121–22 notes that while Amycus is openly hostile, Aeëtes hides his aggression. See also Green 1997 *ad* 3.367–81.

[137] See further Fantuzzi and Hunter 2004, 113–14.

[138] For discussion, see Fortenbaugh 1975, 12–15. On the relation of anger to pain, see also *Top.* 125b30–34.

[139] *Eth. Eud.* 1220b10–15; *Mag. Mor.* 1186a10–13.

[140] *De An.* 403a26–b2; [*Phgn.*] 812a26–30; [*Pr.*] 869a4–5, 947b23–24. Renehan 1963 analyzes the confusion between the pericardial boiling of blood and/or heat (*thermos*) in the textual tradition.

[141] 1.1261–62.

[142] Interestingly, Aristotle does include the phrase ἔζεσεν αἷμα ("blood boiled") in a list of Homeric idioms for anger (*Eth. Nic.* 1116b25–30). Yet, as Rackham notes, it does not appear in the Homeric

to the entrails of sacrificial animals (e.g., *Il.* 1.464; *Od.* 3.9, etc.). We do find references to the flashing eyes and "black rage" of the furious Agamemnon and Antinous,[143] but these descriptions are not as explicitly physiological as that of Apollonius, and do not refer to the heating of blood.

Aristotle observes that unlike hatred, which is unfocused and directed against a class, anger is directed against a particular person in return for an unjust act or personal insult (*Top.* 151a15, *Rhet.* 1378a30–b2). It is especially acute in the case of an unexpected betrayal of a friend or companion (*Pol.* 1328a10–15). While such a general description of the motivation of anger is probably applicable to all the quarrels in epic, the reconciliation is exceptional inasmuch as the characters' speeches display the logical components of anger, its rationale and resolution. This episode therefore differs from Homeric precedent not only in its outcome but also in its careful staging and the contrast between Telamon's anger and Jason's restraint. Telamon's actions, for example, place him in the category of the *orgiloi* – those who display anger quickly but quickly extinguish it (*Eth. Nic.* 1126a12–17) – in contrast to a character like Idas, who exemplifies the *akrocholoi* – those who constantly fly into a rage at the slightest provocation (1126a18–19). Telamon's own explanation of his actions is of equal if not greater significance: he alludes to his anguish at the loss of Heracles, the injury which preceded his erroneous perception of injustice. Jason similarly confides that Telamon's accusation hurt him, but he recognizes that Telamon was not motivated by self-interest: his anger halts at the juncture between the perception of pain and an outraged reaction to a slight or injustice. These speeches convey the characters' awareness of the causes of their own emotions, and, taken as a whole, they offer the audience a subtle but nonetheless effective case study of anger and its effects.

The poem's emphasis on *homonoia* recalls Aristotelian ideas about social interaction inasmuch as Aristotle sees *homonoia*, in the sense of political friendship, as critically important to the prevention of *stasis* within a healthy community.[144] The poem's sensitivity to appropriate displays of anger – when, why, and how long it should be sustained – should come as no surprise. From the Argonautic point of view, strife is counterproductive and should be avoided where possible, but it is generally manageable and even justified under certain circumstances.

---

texts that have come down to us, although it does occur in Theocritus (*Id.* 20.15; see Rackham 1968 *ad loc.*) as well as in Apollonius (ζέεν αἷμα, 1.1262). Either an anachronistic idiom slipped into Aristotle's list, or else he was referring to a Homeric passage that has since been lost.

[143] *Il.* 1.103–4; *Od.* 4.661–62. See Irwin 1974, 135–39.
[144] *Eth. Nic.* 1155a20–31. See discussion by Kalimtzis 2000, 51–86.

Turning to the text, we find that Telamon first challenges Jason as he sits brooding over the loss of their ally (1.1289–95):[145]

> Τελαμῶνα δ' ἕλεν χόλος, ὧδέ τ' ἔειπεν·
> "Ἧσ' αὔτως εὔκηλος, ἐπεί νύ τοι ἄρμενον ἦεν
> Ἡρακλῆα λιπεῖν· σέο δ' ἔκτοθι μῆτις ὄρωρεν,
> ὄφρα τὸ κείνου κῦδος ἀν' Ἑλλάδα μή σε καλύψῃ,
> αἴ κε θεοὶ δώωσιν ὑπότροπον οἴκαδε νόστον.
> Ἀλλὰ τί μύθων ἦδος; Ἐπεὶ καὶ νόσφιν ἑταίρων
> εἶμι τεῶν οἵ τόνδε δόλον συνετεκτήναντο."

> Wrath seized Telamon, and he made the following speech:
> "Go on sitting there, at your ease, since it was certainly better for you
> To leave Heracles behind. From you the crafty plan arose,
> That his fame throughout Greece might not eclipse you,
> Should the gods grant our return back home.
> Oh, what's the good of talking? I will go even without these friends
> Of yours who helped you plot this conspiracy."

The parallel with the political conflict of *Iliad* 1 is clear: Telamon is seized by an Achilles-like wrath (*cholos*), and accuses Jason of harboring a petty, Agamemnon-like jealousy. In contrast to the conflict in the *Iliad*, however, the quarrel does not compromise the safety of the Greeks. Glaucus quickly appears to inform them of Hylas' abduction, and Telamon immediately apologizes to Jason (1.1332–35):

> "Αἰσονίδη, μή μοί τι χολώσεαι, ἀφραδίῃσιν
> εἴ τί περ ἀασάμην· πέρι γάρ μ' ἄχος ἧκεν ἐνισπεῖν
> μῦθον ὑπερφίαλόν τε καὶ ἄσχετον. Ἀλλ' ἀνέμοισι
> δώομεν ἀμπλακίην, ὡς καὶ πάρος εὐμενέοντες."

> "Son of Aeson, do not be angry with me, if in error
> I acted rashly. Grief caused me to speak
> Arrogantly and intolerably. Let us cast my error
> To the winds and recover our friendship."

The contrast with the *Iliad* continues, for unlike Agamemnon, Telamon does not blame *ate* for his error. He admits that *achos* ("grief," "mental anguish") has clouded his reason, and places the blame on his strong

---

[145] "The son of Aeson, with no resources (*amechaniesin*), in failure, said nothing, and sat with his head low in ruin, devouring his spirit" (1.1286–89). Such a response to adversity or the unexpected is typical of Jason, as well as other Argonauts: cf. his behavior at the start of the voyage: "The son of Aeson, without resources (*amechanos*) in himself, was mulling over everything" (1.460–61).

attachment to a dear companion.[146] The speaker locates his logical error not in divine misdirection, but in the irrational sway of emotion.

Telamon's anger may have been based on a misperception, but the damage is done: he has publicly wronged Jason. One might expect Jason to become angry and seek revenge, or at the very least to demand tangible compensation for the insult. Personal honor is not, however, of pivotal importance here: Apollonius is more concerned with the capacity of the heroes to cooperate with each other.[147] As we have seen, Jason adopts a philosophical attitude toward the causes of anger,[148] and as Manakidou has shown, both Jason and Telamon can be thought to display their superiority to Achilles and Agamemnon through their concern for the welfare of a comrade rather than for mere property.[149] The distinction made by Jason between noble and ignoble motivations resembles Aristotle's analysis of the range of appropriate and inappropriate occasions for the display of anger in the fourth book of the *Nicomachean Ethics* (1125b26–1126b10). The even-tempered person is angry for the right reasons, at the right person, to an appropriate degree, and for an appropriate length of time. At one end of the spectrum is deficiency: the person who never gets angry, even when anger is warranted,[150] while at the other end is excess: the person who gets angry too quickly, for the wrong reasons, at the wrong person, to an excessive degree, and for too long.[151] Aristotle thus notes the differences between people who are quick-tempered and those who ignore the circumstances of an injury, bearing a grudge until the desire for vengeance is satisfied.[152] He goes on to observe that it is not always easy to determine whether anger is an appropriate reaction, and that blame for excesses and deficiencies

---

[146] Pietsch 1999, 142–43 emphasizes the importance of Glaucus' speech and the influence of the will of Zeus that necessitates it, contrasting Apollonius' passive Jason with Valerius Flaccus' actively searching Jason, and argues that he is led as usual by his *amechania* in contrast to an atypical mistake by Telamon.

[147] Hunter 1988, 444–45 describes the scene as a display piece for "the Argonautic virtues of loyalty and solidarity rather than the highly personal Iliadic emotions."

[148] Clauss 1993, 210 notes the *amechania* that seizes Jason at the disappearance of Heracles, and accordingly argues for opportunistic passivity as a central characteristic of Jason: "He does not make things happen but waits for the dust to settle before taking advantage of the opportunities that others – mortal and divine – have provided." For an argument opposed to the claim that Jason is primarily characterized by a lack of resourcefulness, see Green 1997, 39 with n. 127.

[149] Manakidou 1998.

[150] Hunter 2002, 145–46. Fantuzzi and Hunter 2004, 111–12 consider Jason's general lack of anger in connection with relevant passages in the *Nicomachean Ethics* (2.1108a4–9; 4.1125b26–1126b10), concluding that he is not absolutely without anger (*aorgetos*).

[151] Aristotle cautions, however, that all these extremes of anger could never exist simultaneously in a single person: the scheme is theoretical rather than practical.

[152] E.g., Heracles will eventually kill the two sons of Boreas for preventing the Argonauts from returning to Mysia to find him (*Argon.* 1.1298–309).

should be tailored according to the seriousness of the deviation from the mean (*Eth. Nic.* 1126a31–b10). In any event, since Telamon's accusation is the spontaneous result of anger and is neither malicious nor premeditated, it fits Aristotle's description of a forgivable offense (*Eth. Nic.* 1135b26–29, 1136a5–9).

By contrast, Jason's sympathy for Telamon's motivation checks his own indignation and ends the conflict among the Argonauts. His thoughtful (*epiphradeos*, 1.1336) response is the opposite of Telamon's senseless (*aphradiesin*, 1.1332) error (1.1336–44):

> Τὸν δ' αὖτ' Αἴσονος υἱὸς ἐπιφραδέως προσέειπεν·
> "Ὦ πέπον, ἦ μάλα δή με κακῷ ἐκυδάσσαο μύθῳ,
> φὰς ἐνὶ τοισίδ' ἅπασιν ἐνηέος ἀνδρὸς ἀλείτην
> ἔμμεναι. Ἀλλ' οὐ θήν τοι ἀδευκέα μῆνιν ἀέξω,
> πρίν περ ἀνιηθείς, ἐπεὶ οὐ περὶ πώεσι μήλων
> οὐδὲ περὶ κτεάτεσσι χαλεψάμενος μενέηνας,
> ἀλλ' ἑτάρου περὶ φωτός. Ἔολπα δέ τοι σὲ καὶ ἄλλῳ
> ἀμφ' ἐμεῦ, εἰ τοιόνδε πέλοι ποτέ, δηρίσασθαι."
> Ἦ ῥα καί, ἀρθμηθέντες ὅπη πάρος, ἑδριόωντο.

> The son of Aeson thoughtfully addressed him in turn:
> "Friend, it's true that you insulted me terribly
> When among all these men you alleged that
> I wronged a good man. Yet by no means do I cherish harsh wrath against you
> Even though I was grieved before, since you were not roused to fury
> Out of anger over flocks of sheep or possessions,
> But for a companion. I hope that you will quarrel in this way
> With another for me, should such a thing ever happen."
> He spoke, and united as before, they were seated.

The use of the word *menis* in line 1339 is atypical for Apollonius, who usually employs the terms *cholos* ("gall," "bitter wrath") or *kotos* ("grudge," "smoldering rage"),[153] reserving *menis* for instances of divine or supernatural anger, in keeping with Homeric usage.[154] Through the use of this word Apollonius takes direct aim at the wrath of Achilles. The contrast could not be more pronounced: unlike Achilles, Jason takes the context of the insult into consideration and places it into perspective. He does not equate his anger, however justified it may be, with the wrath of the gods, nor does he destroy the concord of the Greeks to satisfy his injured pride. Like Achilles

---

[153] See Stanford 1983, 30–31 for discussion of the different varieties of anger.
[154] Campbell 1994 *ad* 337–38. There are only three other instances of *menis* in the poem: Cypris' anger at the Lemnians (1.802), Zeus's anger at the Aeolids (3.337), and the expectation of Aeëtes' anger at Alcinous (4.1205). Apollonius also employs the related verb *menioosin* to describe the anger of all the gods at Phineus (2.247).

at *Iliad* 18.112–13, Jason admits that he has suffered from the insult,[155] yet he is immediately able to distinguish those aspects of Telamon's error that are good (defending a friend) from those that are bad (being angry with the wrong man).[156] Unlike Achilles and Agamemnon, who are unable to let go of their wrath and quarrel (*Il.* 1.304–5, 319), Jason does not prolong the incident. He recognizes not only that Telamon's error is commendable because it is grounded in moral outrage on behalf of a friend,[157] but also that it would be wrong to allow his own morally justified anger to linger beyond an appropriate length of time. It is also telling that Jason admits that he was vexed (*anietheis*, 1340) at Telamon's insult: if he were not, he would be too mild, too deficient in anger, and therefore servile (*andrapododes*) in his temperament (cf. *Eth. Nic.* 1126a6–9).[158]

Friendship proves to be a *pharmakon*, both the initial cause of the error and at the same time an antidote to anger.[159] Telamon's hope that they may regain their friendship signals their recovery from *stasis*, and the two heroes end by sitting together as before (1.1344), united by their respect for each other and their concern for the success of the voyage – a perfect illustration of Aristotelian political friendship.[160] Apollonius' use at 1344 of the verb ἑδριόωντο, which occurs five times in the poem in this same position, is significant. It refers twice to the harmonious arrangement of the Argonauts on their rowing benches (1.330, 530), and it also appears as a participle in a similar context (3.170).[161] By sitting down, Jason and Telamon physically realign themselves with the rest of the rowers and symbolically recover their *homonoia* with respect to their common goal.

---

[155] Achilles announces, "We will leave behind what has happened, though we have been grieved (ἀχνύμενοί περ), conquering the *thymos* within our breast by necessity (ἀνάγκῃ)." Cf. Jason's statement that he "was grieved before" (ἀνιηθείς, 1.1340). Achilles' pain lingers on until he is forced to overcome it by external events, rather than by reasoned argument as is the case with Jason.

[156] Fränkel (1968 *ad* 1.1337–44) observes that Jason's speech becomes increasingly intellectualized ("mehr und mehr intellektualisiert") as it emphasizes the importance of loyalty to comrades. He points out the similarity to Hector's rebuke of Paris at *Il.* 6.325–30, where Hector tells Paris that it is not right (*ou kala*) for him to keep anger (*cholos*) in his *thymos*, and that he would himself fight with anyone he caught hanging back from the fray.

[157] Fillion-Lahille 1970, 54: "Ce n'est pas la colère en elle-même qui est morale ou immorale, mais l'usage que l'on en fait." Fillion-Lahille observes that Aristotle's recognition of meritorious anger distinguishes him from the Stoics, who argued for the absolute suppression of anger (55).

[158] See Harris, 2001, 305 with n. 84 on Philodemus' attitude toward anger ("Whoever does not get angry, gives ample evidence of his baseness").

[159] As noted above, anger is most intense between friends (*Pol.* 1328a1). See Allen 2000, 82–83 on friendship as a cure for anger in tragedy.

[160] Kalimtzis 2000, 72 discusses the differences between personal and political friendships: "Aristotle asserts that the utility of political friendship is the [sic] having a share in shaping the ἐν μεγέθει (*en megethei*), the great matters over which citizens' lives depend."

[161] The only other occurrence of this word appears to be thematically unrelated: at 1.671 it refers to the four white-haired virgins seated at the Lemnian assembly.

There is no room on board the Argo for the inordinate wrath of an Achilles. In order to return to Greece, the Argonauts must reconcile their differences with each other and with the immortals. In this chapter we have seen how concord among the Argonauts is jeopardized by confrontations between bold heroes like Idas and Telamon and skilled heroes like Idmon and Tiphys. Their competitive alliance is held together by Jason's gentle words and by the song of Orpheus, which rationalizes strife as an unfortunate, but at times unavoidable, aspect of a cooperative venture. Like the Zeus-born princes of Hesiod (*Theog.* 95–97), Jason stands out among the Argonauts for his diplomacy and eloquence.[162] His leadership is conspicuous because of the ways in which he organizes and maintains their political support. Jason has recruited the Argonauts, his *philoi*, from all over Greece, but it is public acclamation that clarifies his standing through the vote of confidence by Heracles. Jason consistently reminds the Argonauts that they are unified by their single interest and that they must act as a group. To prevent the dissolution of the alliance, Jason demonstrates self-control even when he is misunderstood and criticized. He displays no resentment of Heracles' criticism nor Idas' insults, but acts as a peacemaker, allowing supporters like Idmon and Orpheus to intervene. Jason meets Telamon's challenge not with wounded pride but with encouragement, praising the hero for his loyalty to a companion. Throughout this poem, images of cooperation, such as the harmonious rowing of the Argonauts (1.536–72), contrast with images of dangerous strife, like the violent Earthborn men who destroy themselves when Jason throws a boulder into their midst (3.1363–76). By eschewing the arrogance of both epic and historical leaders, Jason keeps contention from sinking the Argo. Other members of this group will step forward to make their individual contributions to the recovery of the Fleece, but it is Jason who bears the responsibility for all the disputes and settlements of the Argonauts, taking the lead in Colchis as he does on the shores of Pagasae.

---

[162] Clauss 1993, 205. Clauss argues that Jason's diplomatic strength is intended to be realistic and serves to make the best of a bad situation, since the age of great heroes is over. However, the poem is set in the age prior to the Trojan War, which suggests that the impulse toward alliance is not merely compensatory but rather a positive representation of the advantage of mutual cooperation.

CHAPTER 4

Sexual politics in Lemnos, Colchis, and Drepane

ROYAL WOMEN IN HELLENISTIC POLITICS

Much of *Argonautica* 3 is dedicated to the complexities of Medea's psyche, and the combination of passionate vulnerability and arcane knowledge that makes her not only the most fascinating character of the poem, but probably the most significant as well. As Byre observes, "By giving us intimate access to the inner world of Medea, Apollonius makes us care, and care very deeply, about her and about what happens to her."[1] Modeled in part on Homer's Circe, Medea is a priestess of Hecate and skilled in magic, and her characterization also recalls aspects of Nausicaa, Penelope, and Helen.[2] Book 3 begins as Hera and Athena conspire with Aphrodite to make Medea fall in love with Jason, so that he and the other Argonauts may return home with the Golden Fleece. Jason's reliance on Medea is by no means unparalleled in the *Iliad* and *Odyssey*, but critical events in these poems emphasize the self-reliance of heroes like Achilles and Odysseus, regardless of the help they receive. By contrast, the consequences of female aid are of central concern in several Argonautic episodes, all of which demonstrate that a man who accepts such help is not dishonored, and that the woman who offers it merits public honors and recognition.

Medea's prominence has traditionally been seen as an aetiological prehistory of the events portrayed in Euripides' tragic *Medea*, a work that pits a strong heroine against a weak and treacherous husband. Like Euripides, Apollonius renders Medea's thoughts and emotions more vividly than those of Jason, whose motivations remain implicit for much of the poem. The challenge lies in accounting for the inspiration, conscious or otherwise, behind this new emphasis, which projects an emotionally dynamic female character into the dramatic foreground of the epic. Some hold that the *Argonautica* has been influenced, in one way or another, by classical

[1] Byre 2002; 80. [2] Knight 1995, 27.

tragedy,[3] while others see it as a systematic attempt on the part of the poet to subvert the epic tradition by deemphasizing or even degrading the male hero.[4] These interpretations are surely valuable, but the present chapter seeks to qualify such literary comparisons by considering how Medea and other female characters would have been understood by an Alexandrian audience, whose conceptions of authority were based not only on poetic tradition but also on contemporary images of female political agency.

As the product of a court society that celebrated its queen as benefactor, cult figure, and patron of the arts, the *Argonautica* participates in a gendered ideology that is alien both to Attic tragedy and to Homeric epic, each of which arises out of a distinctly different cultural milieu. While Apollonius' emphasis on women alters the male focus of Homeric epic, women continue to be associated with strife in the *Argonautica*, much as they are throughout Greek literature. In his discussion of the Greek wedding, James Redfield, following Levi-Strauss, explains this association as the culturally transformative power of women – what he refers to as their chromatic character (in contrast to the diatonic male):

This chromaticism is a disordering power, therefore (as in tragedy) women are often to blame when things go wrong, or are what things go wrong about. On the other hand, this chromaticism is also an ordering power, particularly in the complex, modulated order which is a successful marriage.[5]

The difference between the *Argonautica* and Homeric epic, or for that matter Euripides' *Medea*, is the greater emphasis of the former on a positive ordering power that is poetically expressed through the religious and social institutions of cult and marriage. While the bond between Penelope and Odysseus, for example, is profound, the couple is separated for most of the *Odyssey*, and they do not collaborate in the dynamic way that Jason and Medea do. This "heroic" union of Jason and Medea is not as idealized, however, as the marriage of Alcinous and Arete, the Phaeacian rulers who are represented in the *Odyssey* as well as the *Argonautica*. As epic, tragic, and mythic couples go, Alcinous and Arete are exceptionally happy; in the *Argonautica* their rule is the prime example of a just monarchy, and they were ideologically linked with the Ptolemies themselves.[6] The purview of Argonautic *homonoia* thus encompasses not only relations between Jason and his "fellow-counselors," discussed in Chapter 3, but also a hegemonic

---

[3] Byre 2002, Sansone 2000; Nishimura-Jensen 1996.
[4] DeForest 1994; Levin 1971b; Beye 1969; Lawall 1966; Carspecken 1952.
[5] Redfield 1982, 185–86. [6] Mori 2001; Hunter 1993, 161–62 and 1989, 1–9.

binary, a kind of gendered formulation that contrasts with the masculine individualism and fractured marriages that predominate in archaic epic.

This chapter accordingly examines the role played by royal women in Macedonia and Egypt in order to understand the historical framework for the depiction of sexual politics in Lemnos, Colchis, and the island of the Phaeacians. The cultic and cultural prominence of these historical queens is poetically figured in Hypsipyle, Medea, and Arete – not because they dominate the narrative (Attic tragedy teems with dominant female characters, after all, with nary an Athenian queen in sight), but because this dominance is predicated on political marriage. Apollonius explores three progressive stages of such relationships: the unmarried (Hypsipyle), the engaged (Medea), and the married (Arete), as he represents marriage, though it is inextricably linked with the dangers of sexual passion, as a stabilizing force in politics. Just as the good *eris* is counterbalanced by the bad, so marital concord is counterbalanced by erotic chaos.

Comparison between the portrayal of epic characters and the activity of historical figures is especially problematic in this case inasmuch as the authority of Ptolemaic queens is neither clearly nor consistently defined. Among the Macedonian elite, women had served as passive links between powerful families, but the formal political role of the Ptolemaic queens, particularly Arsinoë II, is subject to intense debate. Arsinoë was certainly celebrated as a patron of the arts: one of the fragments of Callimachus refers to Arsinoë as the tenth Muse,[7] and there was also a statue of her as a Muse on display at Mt. Helicon (Paus. 9.31.1). Stephens has recently shown, however, that several poems by Posidippus hint strongly at the queen's political activity.[8] In a dedicatory inscription for a strip of linen (36 AB), the queen appears in a dream-vision to the speaker of the poem, Hegeso, a Macedonian girl. In the dream Arsinoë is addressed as Philadelphus ("Brother-loving") and armed with a spear and shield; she wishes to wipe her "sweet sweat" with a strip of linen cloth (*bussinos*) worn as a headband (*bregma*), the very headband that Hegeso is dedicating to the queen at her request. The sweat, the linen band, and the implements of war are all evocative of military and political matters. "Sweet sweat" is a characteristic of gods, but it is also associated with Alexander (Plut. *Alex.* 4.4–5); moreover, the linen band evokes the royal diadem worn by Alexander and the Ptolemaic kings and queens, and the spear likewise suggests images of Macedonian queens and the "spear-won" character of the Macedonian claim to power in Egypt. The poem points to Arsinoë's importance as a symbol of military power and

---

[7] See Chapter 2, note 56.   [8] Stephens 2005, 236–43.

authority, whether or not she personally wielded it in an official capacity as the wife of Ptolemy II Philadelphus.

Among the dynasts, marriage was a popular, if somewhat unreliable, means to diplomatic ends, producing a complex web of alliances between Alexander's Successors as they fought to maintain and acquire territory.[9] A marriage alliance could be a response to an increase in the unilateral power of a third party, or it could promote a claim to the Macedonian throne by strengthening ties to the surviving relatives of Philip and Alexander. The many children of Antipater, who had served as Alexander's viceroy in Europe, proved most useful in this regard. Three of his daughters were married to Successors (all of whom had been Alexander's Companions), including Lysimachus and Ptolemy I, as well as Craterus and Perdiccas.[10] Since the chronology and historical details of these alliances are complicated, the following discussion will focus on the Ptolemies, whose atypical marital arrangements were of some concern in Alexandria and in many ways set the Egyptian royal house apart from other Hellenistic monarchies.

While the Antigonids in Macedonia and the Seleucids in Asia continued to practice exogamy, the Ptolemies turned inward, concentrating and consolidating their power by marrying within the family. Philadelphus and Arsinoë were the first to do this, and while no royal heir was produced, the union of full siblings was controversial, at least initially. The contested marriage of the *Theoi Adelphoi* is especially relevant, from my perspective, because it sets the stage for the troubled engagement of Jason and Medea. The particulars of these two unions are naturally very different, but what is significant is the fact that both are problematic. The point is not that the royal pair is to be identified with Jason and Medea, but rather that a controversial engagement was historically configured as a likely topos for poetic *eris*.

Both royal marriage and erotic strife were measured out equally in the life of Arsinoë. Like her father, she married three times. The first marriage of Ptolemy I Soter to Artacama, the daughter of Artabazus (Arr. 7.4.6), was one of the short-lived unions orchestrated by Alexander at Susa (Chapter 2). Soter subsequently married Eurydice, one of the daughters of Antipater, to strengthen their alliance after the settlement at Triparadeisus in 321. They

---

[9] On the actual political power of Hellenistic queens, see Carney 1991.
[10] Phila was married first to Craterus and then to Demetrius Poliorcetes; Nicaea to Lysimachus and then to Perdiccas; and Eurydice to Ptolemy I Soter. See the helpful table in Shipley 2000, 42 and the genealogical chart in Green 1990, 732–33. Both Craterus and Perdiccas were killed in 321, relatively soon after Alexander's death. Craterus, allied with Antipater against Perdiccas, died fighting the forces of the Greek commander Eumenes of Cardia (Diod. 18.29.1–30.6). Eumenes was later besieged, defeated, and put to death by Antigonus the One-Eyed in 319 (Diod. 19.44).

had at least four children, but Eurydice's position was weakened in 319 by her father's death. Their marriage was dissolved several years later in the wake of Soter's involvement (Theocr. *Id.* 17.38–40) with Eurydice's niece (or cousin), a widow who eventually became Berenice I, the mother of Arsinoë II (b. 316) and Ptolemy II Philadelphus (b. 308).[11]

In 300/299 Soter formed an alliance against Demetrius Poliorcetes, the son of the recently deceased Antigonus the One-Eyed (d. 301), by marrying Arsinoë to Lysimachus, who by this time was ruler of Thrace. Pausanius prefaces his discussion of this marriage with the observation that many sufferings afflict men because of love, adding that Lysimachus' union with Arsinoë was politically unnecessary because he already had an heir by a previous marriage to Nicaea, another of Antipater's daughters.[12] Arsinoë gave birth to three more sons, and is thought to have plotted against Agathocles, the heir to Lysimachus' throne, either because she wished to safeguard the prospects of her own children or because Agathocles, who was much closer to her in age than her elderly husband, had resisted her advances. Whatever the reason, she was evidently successful, for in 283/2 Agathocles was executed by his father on a charge of treason.[13]

Arsinoë may have been helped in this plot by her half-brother (and second husband) Ptolemy Ceraunus ("The Thunderbolt"). Soter's eldest son from his first marriage to Eurydice, Ceraunus, had been passed over for succession in Egypt and was living with Arsinoë and Lysimachus when Seleucus invaded their territory in Thrace.[14] At the Battle of Corupedium (281), the last conflict between two former officers of Alexander, Lysimachus was killed.[15] Arsinoë escaped with her sons to Macedonia, and Ceraunus was captured by Seleucus, who treated him as a guest rather than a prisoner.[16] But Ceraunus had his eyes on the Macedonian throne, and as soon as they landed in Europe he ambushed his host and stabbed him to death.[17] He was immediately acclaimed king by Seleucus' own army,[18] and married the widowed Arsinoë over the prescient objections of her eldest son, who

---

[11] Hölbl 2001, 24. [12] Paus. 1.10.3; cf. Strabo 13.4.1.
[13] Paus. 1.10.3–4; Just. *Epit.* 17.1.4–6; Memnon, *FGrH* 434 F 1, 5.6. See Hölbl 2001, 24–25, 35; Shipley 2000, 49–50; Green 1990, 131–33.
[14] After Agathocles' death Ceraunus was probably Lysimachus' right-hand man according to Tarn 1913, 125, n. 26, cited by Jacoby, Memnon *FGrH* 434 F 1, 8.3 (comm. p. 274).
[15] Hölbl 2001, 35.
[16] Just. *Epit.* 17.2.4–5; Porphyr. *FGrH* 260 F 3.9; App. *Syr.* 62; Nepos *De Regg.* 3.4.
[17] Green 1990, 133 and 768 with n. 124 notes that Ceraunus' murder of Seleucus was well attested in antiquity. Strabo 13.4.1 = C 623 states that Seleucus was treacherously slain. See also Just. *Epit.* 17.2; Trog. *Prol.* 17; and Paus. 1.16.2; 10.19.7. This murder is generally vilified by the ancient historians because of Seleucus' generosity toward Ceraunus: App. *Syr.* 62 is particularly hostile.
[18] On military acclamation, see Chapter 3.

soon fled.[19] During the wedding feast Ceraunus killed her two remaining children. The murders are depicted in Justin (*Epit.* 24.3.5–9), who claims that Ceraunus disguised his true intentions by embracing the boys until the moment he ordered their execution, and that Arsinoë was wounded trying to protect them. She later made her way to Samothrace and from there to Alexandria in 279, the same year that Ceraunus was decapitated during a Gallic attack.[20]

Arsinoë's return to Alexandria had immediate consequences. She likely had a hand in the exile of Philadelphus' first wife Arsinoë I (see Table 4.1). As the daughter of the late Lysimachus, Arsinoë I was not only politically weak but also inconvenient, from Arsinoë's perspective, since she likely bore a grudge against her former mother-in-law for the death of her brother Agathocles. Whether or not there was friction between them, Arsinoë I was soon repudiated by Philadelphus.[21] Arsinoë's subsequent marriage to her brother lasted until her death in 270 or thereabouts,[22] roughly the time of the composition of the *Argonautica*.[23] This union evidently disturbed the Greek community, for whom marriages between full siblings, like those between parents and children or maternal siblings, were not customary. It is true that in Athens certain kinds of familial endogamy had long been practiced for financial reasons. The *epikleros*, or brotherless heiress, traditionally married a close male relative of her father, such as an uncle or cousin; half-siblings sharing the same father could also marry.[24] Marriage between paternal siblings was also practiced by the pharaohs,[25] and in fact the Great Royal Wife, whose son would succeed to the throne, was preferably the pharaoh's full (or half) sister.[26] Philadelphus and Arsinoë evidently believed that full brother–sister marriages were customary for Egyptian royalty and therefore strategically advantageous for their new dynasty.

The Ptolemies represented the union as a *hieros gamos* ("sacred marriage"), akin to that of Isis and Osiris or Zeus and Hera (Theocr. *Id.* 17.128–34).[27] An additional model (or justification) was the marriage of

---

[19] Just. *Epit.* 24.3.1–8 [20] Just. *Epit.* 17.2; 24.5.1–7; Diod. 22.3.2; Paus. 10.19.7.
[21] See Scholiast's comment, Wendel 1967 *ad* Theocr. *Id.* 17.128. On her exile to Koptos see Hölbl 2001, 36; Ogden 1999, 59–62 and 74 with n. 44.
[22] Several scholars have argued for a later date of 268, see Hazzard 2000; Grzybek 1990.
[23] On the date of the poem, see Chapter 1. See also Hunter 1989, 1–9.
[24] The practice was forbidden in Sparta; Pomeroy 1997, 34–3, 123.
[25] Feucht 1997, 324. See Stephens 2003, 242 on the possibility of Greek hostility toward such Egyptian practices.
[26] Hornung 1997, 295–96. Amenhotep III and Rameses II married their own daughters: Myśliwiec 2004, 145.
[27] On royal Egyptian brother–sister marriage, see Pomeroy 1990, 16. On poetic references to the royal marriage, see Bouché-Leclercq 1903, 163 with n. 2. The marriage took place at some point after the

Table 4.1 *The early Ptolemies*

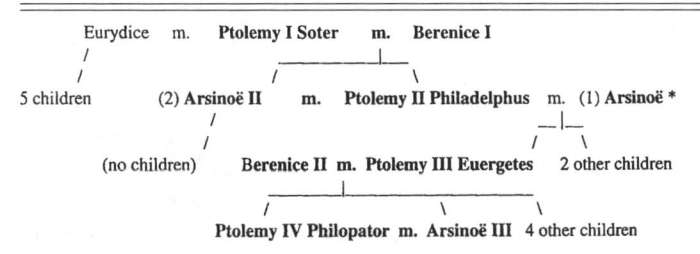

```
    Eurydice   m.   Ptolemy I Soter    m.   Berenice I
       /                        |
       /                 /             \
5 children     (2) Arsinoë II   m.   Ptolemy II Philadelphus   m.   (1) Arsinoë *
                        /                      _|_
                        /                     /     \
              (no children)   Berenice II m. Ptolemy III Euergetes   2 other children
                                         |
                                   /            \
                        Ptolemy IV Philopator m. Arsinoë III   4 other children
```

*Philadelphus' first wife, Arsinoë, was the daughter of Lysimachus, one of Alexander's generals and a rival of Ptolemy I.

---

the epic rulers Alcinous and Arete. Flattering analogies between Arsinoë and other epic characters were implied by Theocritus,[28] as we have seen, but the comparison to the Argonautic Arete was particularly apt because her consanguineous marriage to Alcinous was analogously linked to that of Zeus and Hera.[29] Homer describes Arete as Alcinous' niece (*Od.* 7.53–68), but an Alexandrian scholiast notes, presumably as a response to the royal marriage, that Hesiod identified Arete as the sister of Alcinous. Precedents for the union of Arsinoë and Ptolemy were thus available (or made available) from epic as well as from the Olympian gods and the traditional pharaonic marriage.

The early Ptolemies typically repudiated or divorced a first wife before taking a second, although polygamy was practiced by the Egyptian pharaohs, and had served political purposes in Macedonia.[30] One benefit of monogamy, though, was that it reduced the possibility of multiple heirs to the throne.[31] Alexander is said to have complained about the many children produced by Philip's multiple wives (Plut. *Mor.* 178f.). More to the point, Philadelphus' own succession had been threatened by his many

---

removal of Arsinoë I, in approximately 275 (Stephens 2003, 147; Shipley 2000, 275). Hölbl 2001, dates the marriage to before 274 (see his chronology in Appendix: "*c.* 279: Return of Arsinoe II to Egypt; afterwards (before 274) marriage to Ptolemy II"), while Hazzard 2000, 90 dates the marriage to 273/2. On brother–sister marriage see further Hopkins 1980.

[28] Foster 2006.

[29] Mori 2001; Hunter 1993, 161–62. See Hazzard 2000, 91–92 on the practice of flattering kings by praising Zeus.

[30] On Philip II's marriages see Ogden 1999, 17–29. Pomeroy 1990, 4 notes that the international alliances brought about by Philip's seven marriages would have been undermined had he repudiated any of them in the interest of serial monogamy. In the second century Ptolemy VIII Euergetes II was married simultaneously to his sister, Cleopatra II, and to her daughter (his step-daughter and niece) Cleopatra III from 141 to 116. The three shared rule under the cult title of the *Theoi Euergetae*.

[31] Carney 2000, 231.

half-brothers, so that by marrying Arsinoë, with whom he would have no children, he secured his son Euergetes' claim.[32] To be sure, Philadelphus was sexually active outside the confines of marriage, but while he had at least eleven mistresses, including the famous Bilistiche, any children that resulted from these unions were evidently exposed.[33]

Upon returning to Egypt Arsinoë became not only a queen but also a goddess (Chapter 2). Philadelphus is thought to have founded the cult of the *Theoi Adelphoi* around 271,[34] but Arsinoë also received private cult during her lifetime: in a dedicatory epigram from the Milan papyrus on the temple of Arsinoë-Aphrodite Zephyritis (dedicated to the queen by the *nauarch* Callicrates) Posidippus addresses her as "Queen (*Basileia*) Arsinoë," a title that suggests she was still alive at the time.[35] Arsinoë was also the first of the Ptolemaic queens to be honored posthumously in both Greek and Egyptian temples.[36] Philadelphus introduced statues of her as a guest goddess (*synnaos theos*) beside the image of the main god in every Egyptian temple.[37] She was closely identified by Egyptian worshippers with the goddess Isis, and her cult also had close ties with the temple of Ptah.[38] In addition, Ptolemy dedicated temples exclusively to her (Arsinoeia) as an Egyptian goddess, and she was worshipped all over the Aegean in areas under Ptolemaic influence.[39]

Although the particulars of Arsinoë's cult are relatively well documented, the exact nature and extent of her involvement in internal affairs and international negotiations continues to be debated.[40] There is very little

---

[32] Incest proved to be no obstacle for subsequent rulers, however. Ptolemy V Epiphanes was the son of Ptolemy IV and Arsinoë III, his wife and full sister; Cleopatra II would marry and give birth to the three children of her full brothers, Ptolemy VI Philometor and Ptolemy VIII Euergetes II. Euergetes II, for his part, was married simultaneously to Cleopatra II and to his niece Cleopatra III, daughter of Cleopatra II from her previous marriage.

[33] Ogden 1999, 73–74, 221 (for the names of the mistresses).

[34] Koenen 1993, 51. See above, n. 22 on arguments for the date of Arsinoë's death.

[35] Fraser 1972, 1:239–40 dates Posidippus' dedicatory epigrams (as well as the temple) to Arsinoë's lifetime. On Posidippus' celebration of Arsinoë, see Thompson 2005, 270–74. Hedylus and Callimachus as well as Posidippus dedicated epigrams to Arsinoë-Aphrodite: For poems by Posidippus see 39 AB, 113 AB (= *SH* 978), 116 AB (= 12 GP), Athen. 7.318d (= 13 GP); for Hedylus, Athen. 11.497d–e (= 1843–52 GP); for Callimachus, 5 Pfeiffer ii (= 14 GP; Athen. 7.318b).

[36] On Ptolemy's posthumous deification of Arsinoë as an Egyptian (as well as a Greek) goddess, see Hölbl 2001, 101–4. Rowlandson 2000, no. 4, p. 28, notes the unusual adoption by Greek priestly caste of the Greek names Arsinoë and Berenice. On Arsinoë's iconography, see Koenen 1993, 25–115; see Stanwick 2002, 36–37 on Arsinoë's cult statuary.

[37] Hölbl 2001, 101.   [38] Hölbl 2001, 102–3.

[39] In Cos, Cyprus, Miletus, Lesbos, Samos, Delos, Paros, Ios, Amorgos, Ceus, and Thera. In fact, the cult of Arsinoë was the only Ptolemaic cult established on Cos until the second century. Sherwin-White 1978, 100. See further Hölbl 2001, 96, 101–4.

[40] For an overview of the debate see Hazzard 2000, 82–100, esp. 96–99.

evidence, at least on the Greek side, to prove that Philadelphus shared power with her. Numerous port settlements that served the Ptolemaic fleet were named for her,[41] but such honors do not indicate the parameters of her administrative role. Any official power she had was most likely limited, although this need not necessarily have curtailed her unofficial influence, particularly with respect to foreign policy.[42] The controversial Chremonidean decree, recorded in 268 after Arsinoë's death, states that Philadelphus continued to favor the common freedom of the Greeks "in accordance with the policy of his ancestors and his sister."[43] Arsinoë's interest in the fortunes of mainland Greece is suggested by the street named Arsinoë Chalkioikos, Athena's cult title in Sparta (Chapter 2),[44] but this decree raises the question of whether she herself actually had a distinct and publicly expressed policy. The historian Stanley Burstein has argued against this interpretation, persuasively demonstrating that the reference to Arsinoë's "policy" was purely honorific and cannot be seen as evidence for a real role in foreign diplomacy.[45] Other scholars weigh the Egyptian material more heavily, questioning the limited and largely hostile Greek evidence on the ground that it was prejudiced against female rule.[46] On the Egyptian side, although the queens were generally regarded only as royal consorts, there were instances of queens ruling independently.[47] A number of Great Royal Wives were prominent enough to be mentioned by the king's side,[48] and so it is not inconceivable that Arsinoë had been formally invested with some degree of authority. She was called by the Egyptian throne name, "King of Upper and Lower Egypt," a title that may have been awarded posthumously; still, since it was traditionally reserved for the pharaoh, it too may indicate a higher degree of authority.[49]

---

[41] Cohen 1995.
[42] The strongest proponent of the "weak" Arsinoë thesis is Burstein 1982. Pomeroy 1990: 17–20, argues for Arsinoë's dominance, although she observes that written evidence supports Burstein's view. See also Bevan 1968; Longega 1968; Macurdy 1932; Tarn 1913.
[43] *Syll.* 1:434/35 (= *IG* II 687). See Hölbl 2001, 40: "In the 260s, the Greeks attributed to her a strong influence on Ptolemaic foreign policy which was now strongly anti-Macedonian and eventually led to the Chremonidean war." See further Fantuzzi and Hunter 2004, 380–81; Hauben 1983, 114–19. For English translation of the decree, see Burstein 1985, 77–80 (no. 56).
[44] See Fantuzzi and Hunter 2004, 382–83, on the pivotal role of Sparta in the connection between Arsinoë, Aphrodite, and Athena.
[45] Burstein 1982, 208.   [46] Hazzard 2000, 95–96; Rowlandson 2000, 26; Pomeroy 1990, 17–20.
[47] Sobeknofru, Hatshepsut, and Tauseret ruled in their own right as pharaoh; the rule of unmarried royal women as the wives of the Theban god Ammon (eighth through the sixth centuries) was in lieu of a king, but not regarded as a true kingship. See Hölbl 2001, 85; Hornung 1997, 296.
[48] Feucht 1997, 340.
[49] On the Egyptian evidence, see Quaegebeur 1988, 45; 1971b, 205–9. See also Hauben 1983, esp. 114–19 and 126 on her ties with Greek freedom; Fraser 1972, 1:239–40. Hauben 1970, 35–41, 63–67 addresses Arsinoë's well-known ties with Callicrates, commander of the Ptolemaic navy.

Another influential queen was Berenice II, the daughter of Magas of Cyrene, a son of Berenice I with her first husband. Berenice II married Ptolemy III Euergetes (Philadelphus' son with the exile Arsinoë I), who was her blood relative (though not her brother) through their paternal grandmother Berenice, who was mother both to Magas and to Philadelphus: Berenice II was married to Euergetes from 246 until his death in 221, and the Egyptian evidence also suggests that she too may have wielded real power. She was the first spouse of an Egyptian king with a royal titulary drawn from the Horus name and her birth name; she was also portrayed in temple reliefs in ceremonial contexts as equivalent in rank with Euergetes, and is even described in demotic texts as "Lady Pharaoh Berenice."[50]

As suggestive as the Egyptian evidence is regarding Berenice's office, it must be weighed against the semiotics of *basilissa*, the feminized form of *basileus* ("king").[51] *Basilissa* was adopted as an official title between 306 and 300 by Berenice I, by Phila, the wife of Demetrius Poliorcetes, and by Apame, the Bactrian wife of Seleucus, at a time when their husbands had also assumed royal titles.[52] But, as Elizabeth Carney has shown, *basilissa* functioned differently than *basileus*: it was both the queen's formal title and also an informal signifier of royal blood, referring to "a status that one might acquire by birth or marriage, rather than to a position."[53] The term *basilissa* thus resembles its counterpart *basileia*, which was suitable for the daughter of a king (e.g., Nausicaa, *Od.* 6.115) as well as his wife (Penelope, e.g., *Od.* 4.697; Arete, *Od.* 7.241). In short, all Ptolemaic daughters would have automatically inherited the title *basilissa*, whether or not they ruled or married a king: in itself the title did not convey ruling status in the way that the term *basileus* did. The broad application of *basilissa* argues against the presumption that a queen's public titles necessarily signified political control. That Arsinoë II and Berenice II were honored with unusual titles does not definitively prove that they enjoyed practical powers of a corresponding

---

[50] Hölbl 2001, 85; Quaegebeur 1978, 254–55. Even the famous Cleopatra VII was awarded only a partial set of titles, owing presumably to the reluctance of priests to invest a woman with the theological prerogatives of the male pharaoh. See Chauveau 2000, 46. The traditional pharaonic titulature comprised five names: (1) the Horus name, which identified the king with Horus, the falcon sky god; (2) the Nebty name, which identified the king with the "two ladies" of Upper and Lower Egypt; (3) the golden name, associating the king with Horus again, in connection with the precious metal used for statues of the gods; (4) the throne name, which invoked the sun god Re and the king's rule over both Upper and Lower Egypt; and (5) the birth name, which was linked with Re.
[51] Arsinoë II is referred to as *basilissa* by one of Theocritus' characters (Theocr. *Id.* 15.24). Characters in the *Argonautica* employ only the Homeric term *basileia*, as for example when Medea addresses Arete (4.1014).
[52] For discussion and references, see Carney 2000, 225.
[53] Carney 2000, 227; see also Thompson 2005, 276.

magnitude. Nevertheless, it is apparent that the role of the Ptolemaic queen had taken on new associations and enjoyed greater political renown than their counterparts in either Macedonia or Egypt. Under the Ptolemies the social and functional roles of the queen had evolved as the charisma and destructive power of Alexander's mother, the redoubtable Olympias, were replaced by the iconic status and cult identity of the Ptolemaic *basilissa*.

The ideological role played by early Ptolemaic queens established a positive, even corrective model for the traditional epic representation of women. With respect to the *Argonautica*, the political role of female characters must be understood in the context of the prominence of these royal women, whether or not they had the authority to make official policy. Practically speaking, the figurative space dedicated to the Ptolemaic queen in no way detracted from the authority of the Ptolemaic king; on the contrary, it was believed to enhance it inasmuch as the royal couple was understood as an analogue of Zeus and Hera. Tellingly, those kings who are unflatteringly portrayed in the poem (Pelias, Amycus, Aeëtes) are independent tyrants: their wives, if they are mentioned at all, recede into the background. The hegemonic pairing of Alcinous and Arete (as well as Jason and Medea and even Jason and Hypsipyle) draws on the authority of this gendered hegemonic binary, which sometimes exceeded the confines of legal marriage. Philadelphus honored his Macedonian mistress Bilistiche with the distinguished office of eponymous canephore ("basket-bearer") in the cult of Arsinoë – an exceptional dispensation inasmuch as she could not have been a virgin at the time.[54] He dedicated many shrines and temples where Bilistiche continued to receive cult for several hundred years, down to the time of Plutarch (Plut. *Mor.* 753 F), offering other mistresses comparable honors, a practice that should be understood in connection with the worship of Aphrodite as the divine patroness of courtesans.[55]

Again, the religious prominence of these consorts should not be confused with absolute political power. Philadelphus' relation to them comes closer to a form of conspicuous consumption, since such extravagance was primarily a reflection of the king's great wealth. But the Ptolemaic practice of honoring both queens and courtesans provides a contemporary model for the respect for women in the *Argonautica*, especially Jason's solicitude for Medea and his public acknowledgment of her aid (4.190–97). The Argonauts' reliance on the support of Hypsipyle also expresses this new attitude toward the

---

[54] Bilistiche's origin and the spelling of her name are a matter of debate: see most recently (and definitively) Ogden 1999, 251.
[55] Ogden 1999, 262–63.

public celebration of female political patrons.[56] Seen from this perspective, Idas' irritation at the Argonauts' willingness to accept help from women (3.556–65, 1252–55) is thoroughly in keeping with his initial blasphemy at Pagasae (1.462–71); his overweening confidence in his own sword leads him to affront not just gods like Zeus and prophets like Idmon but also royal priestesses like Medea and queens like Arete, not to mention goddesses like Hera, Athena, Aphrodite, Thetis, the Herossae, and the Hesperides.[57] The *Argonautica*, then, like the Ptolemaic court, places a premium on the public honors, especially in religious contexts, for politically powerful women. This is one of the reasons, presumably, that Jason's reverence for the disguised Hera is prominently introduced at the very start of the poem as the antithesis of Pelias' disrespect – a telling point since Arsinoë herself was identified at times with Hera. This blurring of lines between mortal and immortal, familiar from royal cult, is further expressed in the poem's focus on royal women who are either related to or have close associations with the gods: Medea is the granddaughter of Helios, Hypsipyle is the granddaughter of Dionysus and Ariadne, and Arete is influenced by Hera.[58]

The following section shows how the Lemnian episode establishes the political agency of women while illustrating the preference for shared rule that recurs throughout the poem. Pelias' neglect of Hera's cult is tantamount to a lack of respect for her sphere of influence (1.14), and the failure of the Lemnian women to honor Aphrodite is a related form of impiety regarding sacred matrimonial rites. Their violent revenge against their husbands is not so much a warning against the inherent dangers of the female sex as it is a parable of piety and cooperative rule. With the visit of the Argonauts the Lemnians choose to restore their community, as the loss of their autonomy is outweighed by biological necessity.

A PUBLIC APPEARANCE ON LEMNOS

Shortly after setting out from Pagasae, the Argonauts enjoy a sojourn on Lemnos, but their interactions with the Lemnian women differ markedly from the mad confusion typically ignited by erotic desire. As the reader quickly learns, the Lemnians have already experienced the destruction of Eros, and owe their independence and social isolation to an episode of sexual violence.[59] Eros seems to represent a punitively disruptive version of the sexual drive that would, under ideal circumstances, be channeled

---

[56] Cf. Callicrates' dedication of the temple on Cape Zephyrion to Arsinoë noted above.
[57] On Idas, see Chapter 3.
[58] Such divine lineages are not unusual for characters in epic poetry, of course.
[59] Apollod. *Bibl.* 1.9.17 states specifically that the women are punished for failing to honor Aphrodite.

into socially productive marriage.⁶⁰ The narrator explains that because the Lemnian women failed to honor Aphrodite, their husbands conceived a "savage passion" (τρηχὺν ἔρον, 1.613) for their captured Thracian slave girls. The wives then retaliated by murdering the captive slaves as well as all the men on the island. Lemnian society is thus devastated by Eros, the manifestation of lawless desire and bitter jealousy.

The Argo's subsequent arrival on the island resembles several episodes in the *Odyssey* inasmuch as the Argonauts have landed in the midst of an unfamiliar and potentially dangerous community. However, the narrative perspective of this story differs considerably from its Homeric models.⁶¹ In introducing the Cyclopes or the Laestrygonians to his Phaeacian audience, Odysseus limits himself to various details about their fertile lands, herding practices, and the particulars of the harbor (*Od.* 9.105–51; 10.80–94). Both the Phaeacians and the audience of the poem are drawn into his point of view and are shocked at the destruction of the men. Each new land brings with it, in Odysseus' telling, fresh suspense as safe harbors breed unexpected horrors. By the time Odysseus reaches Circe's island, the audience well knows why his crew is already weeping as the search party sets out to investigate smoke rising from the interior (10.201–2, 209).⁶² The Argonautic narrator, by contrast, lays bare the turbulent history of the Lemnians at the moment the Argonauts make landfall (*Argon.* 1.607–8).⁶³ He recounts both the sexual preference of the Lemnian men for their captive Thracian slave girls and their slaughter at the hands of their wives (1.609–32). He then reverses the Odyssean perspective so that the reader views the arrival of the Argonauts through the eyes of the Lemnian women, who initially mistake them for Thracian raiders bent on revenge (1.633–39). The narrator rescripts the Odyssean formula (in which unsuspecting, civilized Greeks are ambushed by lawless barbarians) and recasts the Argonauts as invaders – well-meaning invaders to be sure, but invaders nonetheless. Nor do the Lemnians lie in wait, like Odysseus' preternatural adversaries, but

---

⁶⁰ This distinction between a malevolent Eros and a benign Aphrodite is not consistently maintained. Eros is consistently portrayed as destructive, but Cypris may also be said to addle the wits of her victims (see the discussion of Hylas' abduction above). On the connection between *eros* and *eris* (strife), see Chapter 3.
⁶¹ Knight 1995, 162–64 contrasts the Argonauts' visit to Lemnos with the Odyssean Circe.
⁶² After this encounter the narrative structure changes as Odysseus is instructed by Circe (about the Underworld, the Sirens, the Planctae, Scylla and Charybdis, and the Cattle of the Sun), just as the Argonauts are instructed by Phineus (about the Symplegades at the entrance to the Black Sea and all the inhabitants of the coast).
⁶³ The narrator also describes the giants and Doliones of Cyzicus, the vagaries of the arrogant king Amycus, and the suffering of the prophet Phineus, all before the Argonauts encounter them. The one exception to this pattern is the Mysian episode, for the narrator describes the Mysians as the Argonauts meet them (1.1179–81), and does not hint of the nymph who will abduct Hylas, presumably so that the audience will share in Heracles' shock.

openly swarm along the shore in confusion. They are armed, the narrator observes, in the manner of savage maenads (Θύασιν ὠμοβόροις, 1.636), but they are also terrified: "Incapacitated, they thronged together, speechless, such was the fear that threatened them" (1.638–39). The Lemnians' wild confusion gives way to an assembly scene that recalls the Phaeacians' hesitant greeting of Odysseus. A warm reception is initiated in both cases by an elderly advisor (Echineus, *Od.* 7.155–66; Polyxo, *Argon.* 1.668–96). By the time Jason and Hypsipyle meet, the Lemnians have already decided to entrust everything – their homes, their cattle, and their city – to the Argonauts (1.694–98).[64] The suspenseful dread provoked by comparable passages of the *Odyssey* is missing here, and any anticipation of violence has been put to rest as the result of the Lemnian assembly (1.653–707), Jason's entrance into the city (1.708–86), and the meeting with Hypsipyle (1.786–860).

The encounter with the Lemnian women constitutes Jason's first diplomatic assignment – the very purpose for which he was chosen as leader (1.336–40). Although the episode is structured differently from Odyssean encounters with the unknown, Jason's preparation to meet Hypsipyle, like his preparation to meet Medea, has been read as an amorous revision of preparations for an Iliadic duel.[65] The Lemnian episode is dominated by the ecphrasis of Jason's cloak: the seven illustrations adorning it are described in a passage modeled on the description of Achilles' shield in *Iliad* 18.[66] This cloak has been understood as the symbol of a distinctly new, erotic kind of heroism that originates in Homer's martial ethos.[67] As Beye puts it, "Dressed in his cloak, the proper amatory warrior, Jason advances in all his beauty upon the city, the palace, and finally, Hypsipyle."[68] It is true that the cloak is the key not only to the Lemnian episode but also to Jason's character within the larger framework of the aesthetic and political concerns of the *Argonautica*. But to characterize it as a symbol of Jason's "loss of male initiative," as one scholar puts it, is to overstate the case.[69] Its erotic

---

[64] Rostropowicz 1983, 17–18, sees the Lemnian assembly as an ideal: the queen is open to the advice and suggestions of others. Lemnian society thus constitutes "une démocratie utopique" (115, from the French resume by K. Ciuk).

[65] Hunter 1993, 48 and 52. For a different interpretation, see Knight 1995, 165–67, who reads references to Thebes and Tityus in the scenes on the cloak as links to the *nekuia* of *Od.* 11.

[66] For verbal parallels between the shield and the cloak, see Knight 1995, p. 108, n. 126. See Goldhill 1991, 308–9 for a survey of interpretations of the ecphrasis.

[67] The view of Jason as an unheroic love hero was first introduced by Beye 1969. See further Pietsch 1999, 110–11; Clauss 1993, 128. Green 1997 *ad* 1.721–68, observes that "Jason, surely . . . exemplifies the new-style leader, whose virtues . . . are irremediably unheroic, *bürgerlich*, middle-class, and rooted in reality."

[68] Beye 1982, 92.   [69] DeForest 1994.

or sinister connotations have been exaggerated,[70] while its positive associations have for the most part been overlooked, as will be shown below. My interpretation of the cloak addresses two central points: first, its historical verisimilitude, and second, the mythical parallels, allusive significance, and poetic resonance of the scenes portrayed on it. While the content of these scenes is undoubtedly tied to themes and events of greater thematic importance in the poem,[71] I am chiefly interested here in the cloak's historical and mythical parallels and its relation to its principal model, the shield of Achilles.

At the level of verisimilitude the cloak is emblematic of Jason's status as a young itinerant hero, one whom the Argo will bear from one location (or stage in life) to the next.[72] The narrator says that Jason fastens a "double-folded purple" (δίπλακα πορφυρέην, 1.722) around his shoulders.[73] There are two references to such garments in the *Iliad*: Helen depicts the Trojans fighting the Achaeans on her δίπλακα πορφυρέην (3.126), while Andromache, awaiting Hector's return, embroiders hers with colorful flowers (θρόνα ποικίλα), whose ephemeral loveliness evokes this fleeting, innocent moment before she learns of Hector's fate (22.441). Both references connect the cloak with battle, and in fact Jason puts on some kind of buckled cloak, an *ephaptis* or *pharos*, a wide cloak worn by men or women, or perhaps a *lope*, a military cloak worn by soldiers in third-century Egypt. Apollonius has Jason pin (περονήσατο, 1.722) his cloak around his shoulder, employing the same verb that Theocritus uses when Thyonichus pins (περονᾶσθαι, *Id.* 14.66) a *lope* on his right shoulder in preparation for military service.[74] Another type of military cloak is the *chlamys*, which was worn by horsemen and associated with Thessaly and Macedonia.[75] Oblong in shape, it was worn over the left shoulder and fastened, like the *lope*, with a buckle on the right. It was associated with itinerant heroes like Odysseus or

---

[70] The cloak was woven by Athena and is dyed *porphyreos*, like the *peplos* used to entrap Apsyrtus (4.423–34) and the *peplos* worn by Medea when she works magic against Talos (4.1661–63). For interpretations of the cloak as a symbol of betrayal and deceit, see Bulloch 1985b; cf. Rose 1985.

[71] Hunter 1993, 52–59; Beye 1982, 91–92.

[72] For iconographic depictions of other traveling heroes wearing the *chlamys*, see, e.g., Perseus in a *chlamys* of ornate design, Apulian red-figure kalyx krater, *LIMC* VII.2, p. 277, no. 34 (Taranto, Mus. Naz. 124007); Odysseus, statue with pleated *chlamys* c. early first century AD, *LIMC* VI.2, p. 624, no. 14 (Boston, I. S. Gardner Mus.); Odysseus, Apulian red-figure volute krater c. 350 BC, *LIMC* VI.2, p. 325, no. 47 (Berlin Staate. Mus. V.1.3157).

[73] Vase painters typically depict Jason with a woven cloak, although in Pindar he wears a leopard skin (παρδαλέα) around his shoulders (*Pyth.* 4.81).

[74] Dover 1971 *ad* 14.65f. In this scene the pinning of the cloak has the idiomatic force of a phrase like "girding one's loins": the cloak is not an effeminate replacement for a shield but rather an intrinsic part of a military outfit.

[75] Guhl and Koner 1872, 167; see also LSJ *s.v.*

Perseus;[76] soldiers; horsemen; and *ephebes*, youths of approximately sixteen to twenty years of age.[77]

Apollonius uses neither *chlamys* nor *lope* to refer to this cloak,[78] emphasizing instead the parallel with Homer with the phrase δίπλακα πορφυρέην. In working elaborate scenes into their respective "double-folded purples," Helen and Andromache offer epic precedents for cloaks, like Achilles' shield, as bearers of symbolic information. The Scholiast states that Apollonius uses the images on the cloak to express the cosmic order and the deeds of men.[79] This interpretation follows contemporary views of the device on Achilles' shield: a marvel that depicts not only the cosmos – sky, sun, sea, moon, and constellations – but also the world of mortals, the city at peace and the city at war. In addition, Hephaestus' elaborate design evokes and probably exceeds the beauty of actual shields whose designs were intended to enhance their power in battle. The apotropaic power of such an image was believed to be symbolically or psychologically appropriated by the warrior,[80] as in the case of the shields in Aeschylus' *Seven Against Thebes*.[81] As Hunter has pointed out, the general Alcibiades carried a shield that showed Eros armed with a thunderbolt, equating Eros with Zeus in order to evoke the sexual core of his military dynamism.[82] The images displayed on both mythical and historical shields were accordingly thought to evoke the essential character of the men who carried them.

The "ecphrastic hermeneutic" of Jason's cloak calls for a synchronic analysis of the type described by Stewart in his analysis of the portraiture of Alexander the Great:[83]

Works of art are neither mere links in a formal or iconographic chain nor simple reflections of a historical reality constituted elsewhere and by other means, but

---

[76] See Guhl and Koner 1872, 192–93.
[77] Hunter 1988, 450: "Recent scholarship has recognised in these myths and the tragedies based on them a recurrent pattern which reflects the generational passage of a young man into adulthood." Guhl and Koner 1872, 192 observe that the *chlamys* was associated in Athens with the male coming of age.
[78] Tarbell 1906, 289 suggests that rectangular robes would not have been recognized as the *chlamys*, which was shaped like a symmetrical triangle, with a curved lower edge and either a flat or curved upper edge. Tarbell observes that unfortunately "[w]e are in the habit of applying the name 'chlamys' with a great deal of confidence to all small brooch-fastened outer garments represented in Greek art" (283).
[79] Wendel 1958 *ad* 1.763–64a.   [80] Hardie 1985, 12.
[81] For example, the Argive Hippomadon, bearing a shield wrought with an image of the dragon Typhon, confronts the Theban Hyperbius, whose shield depicts Zeus with the thunderbolt. Just as Zeus defeated Typhon, so Hippomadon is defeated by Hyperbius.
[82] Plut. *Alcib*. 16.1–2; Athen. 12.534c–e. Hunter 1993, 56: in "Alcibiades, as in Jason, erotic and political power were fatefully combined."
[83] Stewart 1993, xxxiv.

actively comment upon people, events, and situations. They are embedded in the culture of their own time, in what Clifford Geertz . . . has called the "webs of signification" that man spins around himself . . . As active ingredients of the social matrix, they are socially formative products in their own right, making statements that can both change perceptions and mold ideas.

The "web of signification" in which Jason's cloak is embedded comprises not only the ecphrasis of Achilles' shield but also images of Alexander and, as shown below, the aegis of Zeus. Like military shields, ceremonial cloaks were utilized in both military and festival contexts as a semantic locus for the enunciation and symbolic projection of the power of a warrior or a leader, as part of a tradition that extended from the Archaic period down to third-century Alexandria. According to several sources Alexander the Great typically wore a short and informal purple *chlamys*,[84] but adopted a longer, more ornate mantle called an *epiporpoma* for battle and other public occasions.[85] His formal costume customarily included an ornate robe, and he was imitated in this regard by the Successors.[86] Duris of Samos reports that Demetrius Poliorcetes was inspired to commission a famous and fantastic ceremonial cloak decorated with golden stars and the signs of the zodiac, although it was apparently never finished.[87] Closer to home, during the Grand Procession of Ptolemy II Philadelphus (see Chapter 2), the king's pavilion was decorated with cloth of gold and the military tunics, or *ephaptides*, that bore the images of kings and mythological subjects.[88] What is more, Egyptian reliefs both before and after the Ptolemies depict the pharaoh wearing a fringed drape or mantle, a garment that is symbolic of his right to rule.[89] Like Achilles' shield, crafted in the fires of Hephaestus, Jason's cloak originates among the gods: it is a gift of Athena that invests him with the authority of the Argo itself (1.721–24):

> Αὐτὰρ ὅ γ' ἀμφ' ὤμοισι, θεᾶς Ἰτωνίδος ἔργον,
> δίπλακα πορφυρέην περονήσατο, τήν οἱ ὄπασσε
> Παλλάς, ὅτε πρῶτον δρυόχους ἐπεβάλλετο νηὸς
> Ἀργοῦς καὶ κανόνεσσι δάε ζυγὰ μετρήσασθαι.

[84] Ephippus, c. 320 BC *FGrH* 126 F 5 (= Athen. 12.574e); tr. Stewart 1993, 352, T 33.
[85] Plut. *Alex.* 32.8–11.   [86] Plut. *Pyrrh.* 8.1; *Demetr.* 41.3.
[87] Duris *FGrH* 76 F 14 (= Athen. 12.535e–536a). Cf. also Plut. *Demetr.* 41.5. Fränkel 1968, 101 argues that Demetrius' unfinished cloak was too overweening to be worn even by later Macedonian kings. In support of the reading that the wearer of such a cloak implies that he is the focal point of the universe, Fränkel cites the last line of the Duris fragment.
[88] Athen. 5.196e–f.
[89] Stanwick 2002, 37, who notes the relief of a draped Ptolemy III and Berenice II from a gateway at Karnak: the royal couple "stand before the god Khonsu-Thoth, who records the decree bestowing the right to rule." On the Ptolemaic appropriation of the Egyptian fringed mantle in reliefs, see Bianchi 1978, 100–2.

Around his shoulders, he fastened the work of the Itonian goddess,
A double-folded mantle of purple, which Pallas
Gave to him, when she first laid the props for the frame
Of Argo, and taught them to measure the timbers with a canon.

Athena's gift of a cloak to her favorite is thus in keeping with another military convention: Eumenes of Cardia, for example, bestowed cloaks upon his Macedonian troops as a reward for their loyalty (Plut. *Eum.* 8.7).

In addition to the cloak, Jason arms himself with another gift, in this case the spear presented to him by Atalanta (1.769–71):

Δεξιτερῇ δ' ἕλεν ἔγχος ἑκηβόλον. ὅ ῥ' Ἀταλάντη
Μαινάλῳ ἔν ποτέ οἱ ζεινήιον ἐγγυάλιξε,
πρόφρων ἀντομένη.

In his right hand he took a far-darting spear, which Atalanta
Once on Maenalos gave him as a guest gift
In her eagerness to meet him.

This scene is often interpreted as an amorous revision of the arming of Agamemnon in Book 11 or Achilles in Book 19, a gendered recasting of masculine conflict much like Odysseus' initial confrontation with Circe.[90] Although the "battle" was already over before Jason even entered the city, the spear reinforces a romantic subtext inasmuch as it was the gift of a woman, Atalanta, whom Jason regarded as a threat to the *homonoia* of the Argonauts (Chapter 3). But Jason's ceremonial display of the spear and cloak was primarily invested with political, not amatory, meaning. The public costume of authority figures demonstrates that the cloak symbolized his heroism and his claim to hegemony – rather than martial weakness or erotic strength – both to the Lemnian women and, more importantly, to Apollonius' Alexandrian audience.[91]

Like Jason's youth and clean-shaven good looks, the spear and cloak are common in visual representations of kings at the beginning of the third century.[92] A brief survey of the evidence for the iconographic representations of the third-century kings indicates that the cloak and spear were the

---

[90] Agamemnon, *Il.* 11.16–46; Achilles, 19.364–91. See Clauss 1993, 122–23; Hunter 1993, 48; Zanker 1987, 76; Shapiro 1980; Elvira 1977–78, 42, n. 39; Beye 1969, 43; Fränkel 1968.
[91] Cf. Levin 1971a, 17, who sees the cloak as a symbol of Jason's diplomacy in contrast to the martial heroism of Heracles; and Rose 1985 for whom the cloak initially symbolizes diplomacy but comes to represent treachery with the ambush of Apsyrtus.
[92] Smith 1991, 23. See also Ridgway 1990, 114, who observes that beardlessness is seen as a sign of youth, and often associated with Alexander, who himself may have been emulating clean-shaven mythological heroes like Achilles. The youthful, beardless, long-haired image was common in portraiture at the end of the fourth century and beginning of the third; she cautions against always associating these features with Alexander, and suggests Alcibiades as another possible model (134).

marks of leadership peculiar to Hellenistic kings. The cloak and spear were widely associated with representations of the heroic and idealized ruler,[93] a type that is not attested prior to the fourth century and that was particularly associated with statues of Alexander.[94] To promote his connection with the king, Ptolemy I Soter established a cult of Alexander the Founder,[95] and produced a cult statuette, a standing figure of the king holding a spear and wearing the aegis like a short cloak (see Frontispiece).[96] The aegis symbolized Alexander's descent from Homer's "aegis-bearing Zeus," an association that may likewise have included the cloak-shaped Alexandria itself.[97] When Alexander drew the outlines of Alexandria, he is said to have been pleased to see that the city resembled an outspread cloak (*chlamys*).[98] From the aegis of Zeus the cloak derives the symbolic force of divine power and dominion over both the natural and human world. Just as Achilles' shield represented the whole cosmos, so Jason's cloak can be understood as a representation of the *chlamys*-shaped Alexandria.

By weaving together associations from traditional epic with those of contemporary politics, the cloak becomes a symbol of a new type of heroism, but the recent emphasis on Jason's "erotic heroism" does not attend sufficiently to the political motivation of the meeting with Hypsipyle. While

---

[93] E.g., the Baltimore ruler who stands holding a spear with a *chlamys* thrown over his shoulder. Ruler with spear, bronze, third/second century, Walters Art Gallery (Baltimore). Smith 1991, 19–20: "The spear referred loosely to the military aspect of kingship and more specifically to the stated legal basis of the Hellenistic kingdoms as 'land won by the spear', that is, by right of conquest." See also Stewart 1993, 248.

[94] Stewart 1993, 243–52 identifies four types of freestanding representations of Alexander in Alexandria. See Smith 1993, 209 and 210: "The kings are naked and godlike; they may wear a *chlamys* but never a *himation*; and they are clean-shaven." The so-called Fouquet Alexander and the Stanford Alexander also depict the king as a heroic nude with an arm elevated to hold a spear (Fouquet Alexander, Hellenistic/Roman bronze, original 330 BC Paris; Stanford Alexander, original 330 BC Stanford).

[95] See Chapter 2; also Stewart 1993, 247; Fraser 1972, 1:215.

[96] "Alexander Aigiochos": London, British Museum 1922.7–11.1; BMC – 3188. See Ridgway 1990, 135: "Among the copies, the 'Alexander with the Aigis' as the founder of Alexandria, is probably the safest bet for an early third-century prototype." The likeness of the snake-fringed aegis to a Macedonian military *chlamys* has been recognized by both Stewart and Ridgway (Stewart 1993, 246; Ridgway 1990, 116.)

[97] "Carrying the city's emblem like a personal badge, Alexander strides energetically forward under its invulnerable aegis, extending the services of the war goddess both to Ptolemy and to his subjects" (Stewart 1993, 250). See also Ridgway 1990, 116–17.

[98] Plut. *Alex.* 26.5; cf. Strabo 17.1.8; Diod. 17.52.3. Arrian 3.1.5–2.2, however, does not mention the shape of the city, which leads Zimmerman 2002, 34 to conclude that the idea of a *chlamys*-shaped Alexandria had nothing to do with Alexander but was instead modeled by later authors on Eratosthenes' image of a *chlamys*-shaped *oikoumene* ("inhabited world"). Zimmerman shows that the curved upper and lower edges of a *chlamys* were well suited to being mapped by Eratosthenes onto the "inhabited" area of a three-dimensional, spherical earth. Yet whether or not Alexander himself considered Alexandria to be shaped like a *chlamys*, the structural (ecphrastic) parallelism between Achilles' shield and Jason's cloak in itself argues for the programmatic, cosmic significance of the latter.

Jason's encounter with her certainly recalls an Iliadic duel, just as it recalls Odysseus' confrontation with Circe, it does so by reconfiguring its models in Hellenistic terms. Hypsipyle owes as much to royal women of the third century as she does to her epic antecedents; her willingness to welcome the Argonauts is pragmatic, not erotic, and her rather utilitarian interest in Jason is patriotic at heart. And although her blushing cheeks (1.791) suggest that this adherence to duty is hardly disagreeable to her, the narrator comments that she still manages to keep her head (1.791–92), something that those stricken by Eros are incapable of doing, as the subsequent section on Medea will demonstrate.

On Lemnos as elsewhere in the poem, characters are quick to attribute virtue to other members of the elite based on their sophisticated dress and speech,[99] and more often than not such assumptions are confirmed.[100] Hypsipyle welcomes Jason by immediately presenting him with her father's throne (1.827–31):

> Εἰ δέ κεν αὖθι
> ναιετάειν ἐθέλοις καί τοι ἅδοι, ἦ τ' ἂν ἔπειτα
> πατρὸς ἐμεῖο Θόαντος ἔχοις <u>γέρας</u>. Οὐδέ σ' ὀΐω
> γαῖαν ὀνόσσεσθαι· περὶ γὰρ βαθυλήϊος ἄλλων
> νήσων Αἰγαίη ὅσαι εἰν ἁλὶ ναιετάουσιν.
>
> If you should wish
> To live here and it pleases you, then certainly
> You would possess the <u>privilege</u> of my father Thoas, and I also think
> You would not fault our land, for our soil exceeds the fertility of the other
> Islands, as many as there are in the Aegean sea.

The offer of sovereignty is implicit in Hypsipyle's reference to Thoas' *geras*, "privilege" or "royal prerogative," as are the nuptial implications of the agricultural metaphor.[101] Since Hypsipyle does not know Jason, her sudden offer of kingship can only be cued by his noble bearing and regalia.[102] The narrative emphasis on the origins of the spear and the cloak helps to underscore Jason's authority as the leader of the Argonauts and the possible

---

[99] See the discussion of good and bad kings in Chapter 5.
[100] Exceptions (or perhaps "variations" would be a better word) include the accidental battle with the Cyzicans, Aeëtes' reception of the Argonauts, and the ambush of Apsyrtus.
[101] Cf. Menander, *Perikeiromene* 1013–14: ταύτην γν [ησίων / παίδων ἐπ' ἀρότρῳ σοι δίδωμι ("This girl I give to you for the harvest of children"). For further references see Carson 1990, 149, and in general duBois 1988.
[102] The episode certainly recalls the Homeric Alcinous' observation that he would have made Odysseus his son-in-law (γαμβρός) had he wished to remain among the Phaeacians (*Od.* 7.313). For other associations with this scene see further below.

ruler of a "spear-won" land. The term "spear-won" was used by Alexander when he crossed the Hellespont, set foot on Asian soil, and hurled his spear, claiming dominion over Asia as "spear-won" territory given to him by the gods (Diod. 17.17.2). For his part, Jason states that although he is honored he must decline because of the grievous trials (ἄεθλοι, 1.841) that press him. An adventurer by default, he travels only out of necessity, compelled to journey to faraway lands which neither tempt nor interest him. The scene implies by analogy that Greeks and Macedonians have been forced to travel to countries where they were awarded power by virtue of their natural authority.[103] The Macedonian presence in "spear-won" lands was, the audience is encouraged to imagine, a natural result not only of the will of the gods but also of the practical requirements of those communities, and any who think otherwise would be as mistaken as Aeëtes, who wrongly assumes that the Argonauts are plotting to seize his throne (3.375–76).

With respect to this idea of natural authority, the standard "Greek heterology," as Cartledge terms it,[104] traditionally privileged masculinity over femininity. The gendered contrast between the Argonauts and the Lemnians enacts, to some degree, the familiar opposition of "male" Greeks to feminized – read, inferior – foreigners. Yet again the *Argonautica* departs from its models, for when they are not in thrall to Eros the Lemnian women conduct themselves in a politically sophisticated fashion – in contrast, for example, to the male Bebrycians and especially their arrogant king Amycus, who confronts the Argonauts at the beginning of Book 2. Nor, for that matter, is Hypsipyle's offer construed as the result of female weakness in matters of state. She, like the entire assembly of women, is motivated by her recognition of the biological foundations of society (1.675–97), not to mention the necessity of a successor for a hereditary monarchy. Jason, too, is aware that the *aethloi* he faces may well end his family line, for he asks Hypsipyle to send his son, should she have one, to care for his parents, should he fail to return (1.904–9). The possibility of death without glory (*kleos*) may have troubled the sleep of Homeric heroes, but for the characters of the *Argonautica* it is the fear of the loss or absence of progeny. The hopes of Hypsipyle, and for that matter, of Jason, coincide with those of the ruling elite in Apollonius' day: to marry and produce an heir. In the end, it is their children, or rather, the descendants of the Argonauts and

---

[103] See Stephens 2003, 211: "The erotic response of a foreign woman to the arrival of the adventuring male is of course a projection of colonial discourse which functions to legitimate the intruder (and his desires for acquisition) within this alien territory."
[104] Cartledge 1993, 12.

the Lemnian women, who will come to North Africa: after leaving Lemnos for Sparta, they will go on to colonize Thera, the island that is created when Euphemus throws the clod of earth given to him by Triton in Book 4 (4.1755–64). The island, here called Calliste ("Fairest"), is to be renamed for Theras, the group leader, and will serve in the future as a waypoint for the Greek colonization of Cyrene.[105] Divine sanction for the Greek presence in North Africa is thus encoded in the story of the Argonauts' encounter with the Lemnian women.

The poem's pronounced interest in the fruits of political unions like that between the Argonauts and the Lemnian women compromises its psychological realism in certain respects. Jason, for example, accepts without question Hypsipyle's explanation for the disappearance of the male population,[106] and his lack of curiosity could be interpreted as a sign of naïveté and inexperience. But in a comparable situation Alcinous also offers aid, defending the Argonauts against the Colchians in ignorance of the earlier murder of Apsyrtus (4.1011–28). It is Alcinous who sets the diplomatic standard for the poem, and to judge by his behavior it appears that such acceptance is portrayed as an inevitable contingency for the reconciliation of divided societies. The audience realizes that the Lemnian women are not likely to attack the Argonauts as they did their husbands: the murders were not the result, as the narrator is careful to show, of a natural inclination toward violence, but rather the influence of a particular god whose effect on mortal life is inescapably disruptive. On the one hand, like Hypsipyle's account of the disappearance of the Lemnian men, the *Argonautica* whitewashes the military ambition that spurred Macedonian incursions into Asia and Egypt. But on the other hand it also implies that no political entity is entirely free from enemies or unmarred by accidents of fate. If nothing else, the vicissitudes of third-century *Realpolitik* suggest that for groups which share no history, and even for those who do, it may be best to overlook a tarnished past in order to accommodate present considerations. Hypsipyle is not completely truthful with Jason, but she nevertheless confesses that she needs to rebuild Lemnos, and he meets her halfway by trusting her hospitality (1.836–37). The political alliance between the Argonauts and the Lemnians is accordingly rooted on the mutual and immediate needs of both.

---

[105] On the colonization of Libya from Calliste, see Pindar, *Pyth.* 4.256–62; Hdt. 4.145–61. On the connections between the Euphemus' episode, Pindar's fourth Pythian, and the colonization of Cyrene, see Green 1997, *ad* 4.1732–64; Hunter 1993, 152–53, 167–68.

[106] She claims that their husbands abandoned them and took their male children with them to Thrace (1.824–26).

To recapitulate: by framing a specific narrative context (a formal meeting with a foreign queen) with the hegemonic connotations of spears and cloaks (symbols of royal entitlement), the episode invites a political interpretation. In its justification of the Greco-Macedonian presence in Egypt and elsewhere, the Lemnian episode both participates in and promotes Ptolemaic ideology. At the same time, however, it reveals the treacherous sexual ground of contemporary political power: the private lives of monarchs are ruled by a biological mandate to produce a successor, though civilized societies cannot help but founder where Eros reigns unchecked. Jason's pragmatic interaction with Hypsipyle thus puts into proper perspective the risks of his erotic liaison with Medea.

MEDEA: CONFUSION, GUILT, DOUBT, AND DECEPTION

From a diplomatic perspective, the Argonauts' visit to Colchis is far less successful than their stay on Lemnos, although nearly all the blame must rest with the Colchian king Aeëtes. During the embassy, Jason offers the Argonauts' help against the Sarmatians, hoping to win the king's favor by forging a new alliance (3.386–95). But Aeëtes immediately mistrusts the Greeks, wrongly suspecting the Argonauts of piracy, and though he agrees to hand over the Golden Fleece, he certainly has no intention of doing so – mainly because he expects Jason to perish during the labors he has unwillingly agreed to undertake (3.579–93). Disappointed in these expectations, Jason finally hopes that Aeëtes may relent for his daughter Medea's sake (3.1100–1), but he will have to abandon this hope as well, since their anomic relationship will win him no political leverage. Even if Aeëtes' doubts about the Argonauts were initially ill-founded, they are ultimately confirmed by Medea's betrayal (3.594–605). For it is she who not only helps Jason to plough, sow, and harvest the Field of Ares – a metaphor for war if ever there was one – but also charms the dragon that guards the Golden Fleece, and ambushes Apsyrtus so that the Argonauts may escape the Colchian fleet. A Paris-like Jason has essentially stolen the Fleece and the girl, provoking a *neikos* that threatens Greece itself (4.1102–3).

The solution of the Phaeacian king Alcinous to this *neikos* is a marriage, though it is not a dynastic union capable of uniting the political interests of the two royal houses. There is no marriage agreement between the father and the bridegroom and no wedding gifts are exchanged: indeed, Medea's flight from home has more in common with the socially disruptive phenomenon known as abduction marriage. Although mythological abductions like that of Helen generally had disastrous consequences, "bridal theft" was a long-standing practice in the ancient world that allowed the prospective husband, together with his male companions and sometimes the bride herself, to usurp the authority of those properly responsible for such arrangements.[107] As Evans-Grubbs notes, "There is a thin line between an abduction in which the girl, though she was not aware beforehand of plans for her kidnapping, anticipates some sort of action and is willing to be 'stolen,' and an act of elopement planned by the two young people together."[108]

Medea is certainly confused about Jason's motives: she dreams in Colchis that Jason has actually come to marry her (3.619–23), but her dream logic has inverted the order of events, making the Golden Fleece rather than the marriage the means to an end. In a way she is right, of course, though this is entirely by accident since she cannot know that Hera intends to use her magic against Pelias. In her subconscious mind Medea is, truly, the daughter of her father, who fears that the Argonauts have come not for the Golden Fleece but for his crown. Like him, she mistakes the Argonauts' purpose by projecting onto them her own ideas. In her waking hours, however, she realizes that marriage is not Jason's goal but rather the price he is willing to pay, and she therefore promises to acquire the Golden Fleece in exchange for his public oath of betrothal (4.87–91).

Medea's enchantment of the dragon gives Jason time to remove the Golden Fleece from the tree, a deed that has generally been regarded by critics as the opposite of traditional epic heroism.[109] That Jason does not slay the dragon, however, may be less a comment on his lack of valor than a nod to Philadelphus' interest in elephants and other unusual creatures, such as, according to the Alexandrian historian Agatharchides (?b. 215), an enormous snake displayed as a tourist attraction in Alexandria after being captured alive and tamed by hunters – who were, it should be noted, richly rewarded by Ptolemy for the prize. Aeëtes' refusal to reward Jason for his labors certainly contrasts with Ptolemy's generosity in this episode.[110] In any case, because the Golden Fleece is so closely tied to Jason's offer of

---

[107] For a description of bridal theft and discussion of its social impact, see Evans-Grubbs 1989, 61–64.
[108] Evans-Grubbs 1989, 62.
[109] Byre 2002, 114: "Jason's taking of the Fleece and his return with it to the ship is thoroughly unheroic." Hutchinson 1988, 123: "there is no manly action here; Jason does not even kill the serpent that guards the Fleece. All depends on Medea." Beye 1982, 33: "It is not the winning, not the success that animates Jason here, but rather the sensual pleasures of the fleece . . . In terms of epic propriety, Apollonius has perverted a hero's natural instincts." Hutchinson also notes that Apollonius has adopted Antimachus' version (fr. 63 Wyss 1936) in contrast to the heroic versions of Pindar *Pyth.* 4.249, Pherecydes *FGrH* 3 F 31, and Herodorus *FGrH* 31 F 52 (1988, 123, n. 63).
[110] As recorded in Diod. 3.36.3–37.9. Fraser 1972, 2:782, n. 200 does not think that Agatharchides is the source for Diodorus' account of this snake; cf. Burstein 1989, 126, n. 2 for a well-considered response. Aelian *NA* 16.23 reports the capture of five similarly enormous snakes, which were kept in the temple of Aesclepius at Alexandria in the third century.

marriage, the episode is better understood as Medea's auto-*engyesis*, her independent arrangement of the terms of her betrothal.[111] Insofar as such an unusual action would normally occur only after the death of the father, the bride's proper guardian, the social implications of Medea's behavior are extreme.[112] The abduction of Medea, like the theft of the Golden Fleece and the murder of Apsyrtus, is politically expedient, but socially and morally subversive. Taken as a whole, these actions simulate the transgressive side of contemporary politics, the secret plots and internecine strife that plagued the houses of Ptolemy, Antigonus, and Seleucus. What is interesting is the way that the narrator resists assigning blame to Jason or Medea or, for that matter, to Aeëtes. The real culprit, once again, is Eros, the force unleashed by Hera to assail Medea and make of her heart an epic battleground, rent by a passion that will eventually lead to the destruction of her family.

It is tempting to infer a political impetus behind this emphasis on the culpability of an overwhelming, unpredictable, and malevolent deity.[113] As a *ktisis* or foundation epic, the *Argonautica* "mythologizes" the origin of Greek colonization of North Africa.[114] An amalgam of political truth and cosmic figuration, Medea's erotic crimes (betraying her father and murdering her half-brother) are cast, like the murder of the Lemnian men, as an integral and inevitable component of the conflicted prehistory of Ptolemaic Egypt. Apollonius was in a position to know his royal patrons well, and to flatter their interests not only with apposite references to the cults of the Cabiri on Samothrace or Cybele on Mt. Dindymon,[115] but also in the manipulation of politically sensitive material that might bring to mind the tragic past of Arsinoë II. Like Orpheus' song about the abstraction Neikos, which helps to deflect guilt away from individual Argonauts,[116] the narrator's condemnation of the general devastation wrought by Eros on humanity exonerates not only Medea but also, by extension, the queen herself. By shifting the cause of the murder from mortal agents to a cruel god, the reproachful apostrophe encourages sympathy and helps to absolve the beleaguered heroine – and anyone else caught in similar straits.

---

[111] On the Athenian *engye*, see Oakley and Sinos 1993, 9–10.
[112] For Berenice II's initiative in arranging her marriage to Ptolemy III, see Vatin 1970, 70. On marriage practices in Hellenistic Egypt, see further below.
[113] E.g., 4.445–47, 4.62–65; see Chapter 2.
[114] See, e.g., allusions to the foundation of Cyrene: 4.1547–61, 1731–64; for discussion see Green 1997, *ad* 4.1547–61; Hunter 1993, 152–53. For a general discussion of Apollonius' foundation poems, see Krevans 2000.
[115] Green 1997 *ad* 1.1093–94, notes that the description of the ritual celebration of Rhea on Dindymon suggests that the Ptolemies may have been involved in Cybele's worship as well as that of the Cabiri on Samothrace.
[116] On the quarrel between Idas and Idmon, see Chapter 3.

That the Alexandrians might have made such an inference about Arsinoë is probable. As Pomeroy says, "The episodes of her life sound like a pastiche of mythology,"[117] referring to the execution of her stepson Agathocles, the ambush of her first husband Lysimachus, the murder of her sons during the celebration of her marriage to Ptolemy Ceraunus, and her desperate escape afterwards to Samothrace and Egypt (see above). The players may be somewhat altered in the *Argonautica*, but the plot elements are recognizable. Like Medea, Arsinoë was implicated in murder, compelled by political circumstance to marry in haste and in a foreign land, and robbed of her children during a conflict with her own husband.[118] Arsinoë was neither a witch nor a priestess of Hecate, of course, but other aspects of her life were close enough to invite comparison and even censure by an audience familiar with her past. Theocritus' observation that a virgin eclipses a "thrice-wed woman" (τριγάμοιο γυναικός, *Id.* 12.5) – written, presumably, when the poet was no longer in Alexandria – has thus been seen as a dig at Arsinoë.[119] It seems likely that the circumstances of Arsinoë's first two marriages were known, at least in court circles.

We cannot be sure whether Apollonius intended the apostrophe to Eros as an erotic disclaimer for the queen's personal history, nor whether Arsinoë was in point of fact passionately in love with her half-brother. Still, the *epiklesis* Ceraunus ("Thunderbolt"), presumably meant to evoke the precipitous action of an angry Zeus, suggests by way of Alcibiades' famous shield, the armed and dangerous Eros. Moreover, the extremes of their brief marriage were sufficiently vicious to be understood in the kinds of suffering and torment that the narrator blames on Eros (4.445–49). Proceeding slightly further along this admittedly speculative line of inquiry, it seems that such a parallel, intentional or otherwise, ran the risk of backfiring. Medea is a less complementary analogue than, say, the Phaeacian queen Arete, and the comparison could have had an unintended effect. Like "The Murder of Gonzago," the "play-within-a-play" about the king's assassination in Shakespeare's *Hamlet*, certain events of the *Argonautica* might have embarrassed the queen and consequently threatened Apollonius' standing at court. While this interpretation would accord with the story of Apollonius' removal to Rhodes (see Chapter 2), it still seems rather unlikely that he would have accused the queen of intrigue.

---

[117] Pomeroy 1990, 16.
[118] The children are killed in all versions of the myth: either accidentally by Medea or for revenge by friends of Creon. Euripides is generally thought to have invented their premeditated murder by Medea: for discussion and sources see Gantz 1993, 1:368–70.
[119] Macurdy 1932, 123.

Passion and other extreme emotions are shown in an unflattering light throughout the poem. Apollonius represents marriage as a cultural solution (imperfect in some respects) to the strife that is caused by various kinds of emotional excess, from the fiery temper of Aeëtes to the erotic madness that afflicts his daughter. The remainder of this section will accordingly explore the representation of *eros*, paying close attention to its effects on Medea and to the dramatic tension between her psychological turmoil and Jason's efforts to reassure her. Jason's ability to console (and control, to some extent) Medea with "honey-sweet words" (*meilichioisi epeessi*) is the verbal corollary of her cunning and knowledge of magical charms. The final section ("A Wedding in Drepane"), reveals how the transgressive formulations considered here – emotional turmoil, bridal theft, and kin murder – are resolved by the Phaeacian rulers Alcinous and Arete, and how their rule expresses the positive ideological formulations of Hellenistic political practice discussed earlier, from the importance of marriage for reconciliation and the foundation of new communities to the wisdom of diplomatic compromise and the social balance brought by an active queen.

Apollonius associates desire with pain, psychic disorder, and, paradoxically, bright ethereal beauty. The suffering caused by love is described by the Moon, who witnesses Medea's furtive escape from her father's palace (4.62–65):

"Νῦν δὲ καὶ αὐτὴ δῆθεν ὁμοίης ἔμμορες ἄτης,
δῶκε δ' ἀνιηρόν τοι Ἰήσονα πῆμα γενέσθαι
δαίμων ἀλγινόεις. Ἀλλ' ἔρχεο, τέτλαθι δ' ἔμπης
καὶ πινυτή περ ἐοῦσα, πολύστονον ἄλγος ἀείρειν."

"So now you too share in a similar delusion, and
The heart-breaking god has given you Jason as a painful affliction.
Come then, prepare all the same, even though you are wise,
To bear grief and endless lamentation."

Regularly stricken with love for Endymion by the charms of Medea,[120] the Moon now exults at the knowledge that her tormentor suffers in turn. Yet the Moon herself was implicated in the desire of the Mysian water nymph for Heracles' squire, Hylas (1.1229–33):

Τὸν δὲ σχεδὸν εἰσενόησε
κάλλεϊ καὶ γλυκερῇσιν ἐρευθόμενον χαρίτεσσι·
πρὸς γάρ οἱ διχόμηνις ἀπ' αἰθέρος αὐγάζουσα

---

[120] 4.57–61: When Medea needs to work in utter darkness she drives the Moon to the cave of Endymion by reminding her of the pangs of desire (4.60).

118 *Sexual politics in Lemnos, Colchis, and Drepane*

βάλλε σεληναίη. Τῆς δὲ φρένας ἐπτοίησε
Κύπρις, ἀμηχανίη δὲ μόγις συναγείρατο θυμόν.

She saw him close by,
Radiant in his beauty and sweet grace;
The full moon casting pure white light from the upper heaven
Struck him. Cypris disordered her mind,
And in confusion she barely managed to collect herself.

This passage draws attention both to the substance and to the effect of desire, here attributed to Cypris rather than her son. Love is associated with a warm reddish glow: the radiance (ἐρευθόμενον) of Hylas, or the flushed cheeks of Ganymede (3.122) and Medea (3.298, 963).[121] The blush may either inspire love, as in the former case, or it may signal the presence of intense emotion, as in the latter. Jason's cloak is dyed a similar shade of red (ἔρευθος, 1.726; ἐρευθήεσσα, 1.727), a hue that enchants the Lemnian women like brides transfixed by the rosy light of a star (ἐρευθόμενος, 1.778).[122] Jason himself takes pleasure in the delicate glow (ἔρευθος, 4.173) of the Golden Fleece on his face, like a girl dazzled by the shimmer of moonlight on her dress.[123]

The lustrous iridescence that is associated with many colors in the ancient Greek aesthetic is especially significant here because it accompanies and reinforces the concept of desire as an external force,[124] both in its divine origins and in its deployment in the visual field. In these passages the reddish color infuses the beams of the luminary; color is understood to be determined not by blushing skin or dyed fabric but rather by the quality of moon or starlight.[125] So too Eros descends to earth like a star, following the path of the rising sun with its first reddish rays (ἐρεύθεται, 3.163); his arrow strikes, ignites a flame, and causes Medea in turn to cast (βάλλεν, 3.288) repeated glances at Jason and to abandon herself to thoughts of him (3.286–90).[126] And just as Medea's *thymos* is overrun and all else forgotten at

---

[121] Similarly, Hypsipyle's cheeks redden (*erythene*) when she speaks with Jason (1.791).
[122] Cf. the purple cloak (*allika*) worn by Hecale's young and handsome husband (Callim *Hec*. frr. 28, 29 Hollis 1990).
[123] For the correspondence between the moon and eroticism, see Hunter 1993, 17; Bremer 1987; Beye 1982, 156–57; Fränkel 1968 *ad* 4.167–73. For further parallels see Campbell 1994 *ad* 3.121–22.
[124] Byre 2002, 79: "When she is struck by the arrow of Eros, Medea becomes subject to an external compulsion – a compulsion that is thereby internalized – that she cannot understand."
[125] In fact, this conception of color as reflected light is more or less accurate, as Newton first demonstrated in 1704. See Irwin 1974, 5. Color is not inherent in an object but is rather revealed as certain wavelengths are reflected off the surface, while the rest are absorbed.
[126] Calame 1992, 20 notes the role of the gaze as the vision of the love object strikes the desiring subject from afar, like an arrow.

Medea: Confusion, guilt, doubt, and deception

the moment she sees Jason, so the wits of the water nymph are confounded when the moonlight strikes (βάλλε) Hylas.

Mental confusion, or more specifically the lack of control over the *thymos* as it is depicted here, is the second significant characteristic of desire in the poetic tradition as well as the *Argonautica*.[127] Erotic confusion recurs in two other important passages: Heracles' rampage (1.1261–72) and Medea's sleepless night of indecision (3.744–824). The disappearance of Hylas elicits an emotional response from Heracles that suggests the passionate quality of his attachment (1.1265–72):[128]

> Ὡς δ' ὅτε τίς τε μύωπι τετυμμένος ἔσσυτο ταῦρος
> πείσεά τε προλιπὼν καὶ ἑλεσπίδας, οὐδὲ νομήων
> οὐδ' ἀγέλης ὄθεται, πρήσσει δ' ὁδὸν ἄλλοτ' ἄπαυστος,
> ἄλλοτε δ' ἱστάμενος καὶ ἀνὰ πλατὺν αὐχέν' ἀείρων
> ἵησιν μύκημα, κακῷ βεβολημένος οἴστρῳ·
> ὣς ὅ γε μαιμώων ὁτὲ μὲν θοὰ γούνατ' ἔπαλλε
> συνεχέως, ὁτὲ δ' αὖτε μεταλλήγων καμάτοιο
> τῆλε διαπρύσιον μεγάλῃ βοάασκεν ἀυτῇ.

> As when a bull struck by a gadfly dashes off
> And abandons its meadows and fields,
> Taking no notice of the herdsmen
> Or the herd – at one time he hurries along without stopping,
> At another halts, rears back his broad neck
> And bellows, wounded by the noxious fly –
> Just so he raged, now racing
> Continuously, now ceasing his labor
> And shouting a piercing cry that traveled far.

The impulsive Heracles has lost control like the water nymph, yet her mind is subject to the more temperate Cypris, whereas his *eros*-driven fury is extreme. His blood boils like a hot spring or geyser in contrast to the spring's cool waters, and he lets his feet carry him without paying attention to where he is going (1.1263–64), a bull driven by a gadfly (*muops*). Since Eros is likened to a gadfly driving a grazing heifer when he shoots the arrow at Medea, this simile is an indication of the erotic quality of Heracles' passion.[129]

---

[127] See Calame 1992, 19 who observes that *eros* affects the emotions (e.g., the *thymos* of Alcaeus' Helen) and overwhelms the rational capacity of its victims: "the power of Eros cancels out all ability to understand or to make decisions."

[128] Hunter 1993, 38–39 and Beye 1982, 94–96 support this reading, while Hutchinson 1988, 193 does not. See Knight 1995, 93 for additional references.

[129] Hunter 1989 *ad* 3.276–77. These are the only two references to the gadfly in the poem.

The symptoms of the love-struck Medea are similar to those of Heracles: she mentally loses her way as fire races down her nerves from her brain to her physical core (3.761–65). Filled with energy she whirls around her room, impelled by desire and unmindful of the consequences of her actions, her riotous thoughts repeating Heracles' rampage through the Mysian forest (3.835–37):

> Αὐτοῦ δὲ δόμοις ἔνι δινεύουσα
> στεῖβε πέδον λήθῃ ἀχέων, τά οἱ ἐν ποσὶν ἦεν
> θεσπέσι᾽, ἄλλα τ᾽ ἔμελλεν ἀεξήσεσθαι ὀπίσσω.

> And there whirling around her room
> She walked a path unmindful of sorrow, unspeakable things
> At her feet, and others destined to grow in the future.

The narrator also draws attention to Medea's loss of reason the following morning. She has no sense of time passing (3.1140–41), and she fails to take notice of her attendants as "her spirit flits about high in the clouds" (3.1151). She climbs into the chariot like an automaton (3.1152), and is too distracted to heed the words of her sister Chalciope (3.1157–58). Only when she is back in her room after the meeting with Jason does she recover herself, weeping with regret as she contemplates what she has done (3.1161–62).

The advent of *eros* kindles pain, uncertainty, and fevered misdirection. It is apparent that in contrast to Medea's erotic frenzy and the wild rage of Heracles, Hypsipyle's love for Jason is made of milder stuff. Hypsipyle weeps at his departure, yet her sad goodbyes are generous and thoughtful (1.886–98); absent are the heated recriminations launched by Medea whenever her confidence in Jason falters (4.355–93, 1031–52). The politically sensible union with Hypsipyle is as reasonable as the erotic union with Medea is unstable and unreliable. *Eros* is not a weapon to be wielded by Jason; it is instead the weapon that he must turn aside with gentle words and reason – and not just Medea's desire, for deadly *eros* (οὖλος ἔρως, 3.1078), the *eros* that breeds the strife (*eris*) of mortal *neikea*, invades his heart as well. To call Jason a "proper amatory warrior," as Beye does, is misleading, for he fights not by means of *eros* but against it, just as he counters the anger of Idas and the rage of Telamon.

Jason's gentle treatment of Medea is therefore of a piece with his handling of political disagreements among the Argonauts (Chapter 3), and his equanimity is maintained by emotional restraint and persuasive speech.[130] From the moment they first meet at the temple of Hecate, Jason realizes that Medea suffers from some malady sent by the gods (3.973–74).

---

[130] On the use of rhetoric in the *Argonautica*, see further Mori 2007.

The tone and substance of his speech is designed to soothe (3.1102), and he addresses her in a flattering manner (3.974) – not to seduce her, but because he perceives that she is suffering from some delusion.[131] The term *hypossainon*, elsewhere employed to describe the behavior of animals like dogs or lions (see LSJ *s.v.*), is used to describe Jason's manner here (3.974) and on two other occasions in the *Argonautica*: his politic response to Aeëtes' angry accusations (3.396) and his response to Medea's furious reproach when the Argonauts are trapped by the Colchian fleet (4.410). Although translations vary from "soothing"[132] to the uncomplimentary "fawning,"[133] "wheedling,"[134] or worse still, "obsequious address,"[135] the general sense of the term would seem to be "in a conciliatory fashion."

Gentle, persuasive speech is more frequently denoted by forms of the verb *meilisso* ("to sweet-talk") or the adjective *meilichios* ("honey-sweet"). While these translations accurately convey the root meaning of these terms, they are overly suggestive of deceit. The Greek words can certainly be used in such a context, as when Jason uses "honey-sweet" words to test Tiphys' resolve (2.621), and Medea says that she will "sweet-talk" Apsyrtus' heralds into leaving him undefended (4.416), but cognates may also refer to words of consolation, as when Jason says goodbye to his distraught mother (1.294) or reassures Medea (3.1102; 4.394). They may even be "charming" in the literal sense of an enchantment, as when Medea tempers fire (3.531) or calls on the spirits of the dead (4.1665). Furthermore, the adjectival form, *meilichioisi*, is used of gracious speeches,[136] and the same expression is employed to describe the words of the divine Herossae (4.1317) and Hesperidae (4.1431), as well as the oracular clod of earth in Euphemus' prophetic dream (4.1740).[137] The verb is primarily used not of deception, but to designate an appeal,[138] or propitiation of the gods.[139] Ironically, as Aphrodite explains to Hera and

---

[131] Byre 2002, 95.
[132] Green 1997: "soothing" (3.396), "with comforting flattery" (3.974); Rieu 1971: "tried to put her at her ease" (3.974), "trying to placate her" (4.410); Tassos 1960: "trying to win him with gentle speech" (3.396), "with a kindly smile" (3.974), and "soothing her" (4.410). Vian 2002: "cherchant à le flatter d'une voix aimable" (3.396), "il lui parla en la flattant doucement" (3.974), and "cherchant à l'adoucir" (4.410).
[133] Green 1997 *ad* 4.410.   [134] Byre 2002, 95.   [135] Rieu 1971 *ad* 3.396.
[136] The Doliones graciously welcome the Argonauts (1.971); Athena's pleasant conversation with Hera (3.31); Phineus' gracious address of the Argonauts (2.467); Medea's gracious answers to Circe's questions (4.732).
[137] Cf. the "sweet speech" of kings beloved by Zeus (Hes. *Theog.* 97).
[138] Aethalides persuades Hypsipyle to receive the Argonauts (1.650); a hamadryad appeals to a man not to cut down her oak tree (2.478); Ancaeus suggests speaking gently to Aeëtes (2.1279); Hera doubts that Aeëtes can be persuaded (3.15); Jason appeases Aeëtes (3.385); Medea appeals to the Argonauts (4.1012); Medea asks Arete to appeal to Alcinous (4.1026); the Colchians appeal to Alcinous (4.1210).
[139] The Lemnians propitiate Aphrodite and Hephaestus (1.860); Orpheus propitiates Apollo (2.692); Mopsus tells the Argonauts to propitiate the ghost of Sthenelos (2.923); Jason agrees to propitiate

Athena, Eros himself is impervious to such flattery: his base nature can only be persuaded by a bribe.[140]

It should, of course, be noted that even if Jason's speech at Hecate's temple is more gracious than duplicitous, Medea is said to delight in his appearance and his "wily words" (αἱμυλίοισι λόγοισι, 3.1141). The term *haimulios* is used in Homer of Calypso when she attempts to persuade Odysseus to forget Ithaca (*Od.* 1.56); of the two other appearances of the word in the *Argonautica*, the first describes Hypsipyle's speech to Jason (1.792) and the second Aphrodite's speech to Hera and Athena. In these instances *haimulios* speech is deceptive and seeks to press its advantage, but it cannot be called malicious. To see Jason here as cruel or deliberately false in concert with the Euripidean conception of his character is to misread the sad irony of his innocent, if spectacularly ill-fated, promise (3.1128–30):

> "Ἡμέτερον δὲ λέχος θαλάμοις ἐνὶ κουριδίοισι
> πορσανέεις· οὐδ᾽ ἄμμε διακρινέει φιλότητος
> ἄλλο, πάρος θάνατόν γε μεμορμένον ἀμφικαλύψαι."

> "You shall share my bed in a bridal chamber,
> And nothing else will separate us from our love
> Until our allotted death shall enfold us."

That he will ironically abandon her in Corinth may not – and probably cannot – be far from the mind of the reader, but neither can Jason's mortal knowledge of the future be anything more than partial, as the poet shows throughout the poem. In any case, the interview at the temple of Hecate is not simply a lovers' tryst but also a formal negotiation, much like the meeting with Hypsipyle. Jason and Medea have not only agreed to marry but have also embarked on a political alliance, and he will remain faithful to the terms of this agreement despite her volatility and the advantages that could have resulted from betraying her to the Colchians later on.

After her flight from the palace, Medea calls on Jason to honor his previous vows in public (4.93–98):

> Αἶψα δέ μιν περὶ γούνασι πεπτηυῖαν
> ἧκ᾽ ἀναειρόμενος, προσπτύξατο θάρσυνέν τε·
> "Δαιμονίη, Ζεὺς αὐτὸς Ὀλύμπιος ὅρκιος ἔστω
> Ἥρη τε Ζυγίη, Διὸς εὐνέτις, ἦ μὲν ἐμοῖσι
> κουριδίην σε δόμοισιν ἐνιστήσεσθαι ἄκοιτιν,
> εὖτ᾽ ἂν ἐς Ἑλλάδα γαῖαν ἱκώμεθα νοστήσαντες."

Hecate (3.985); Aeëtes recalls that Phrixus made better offerings than other foreigners (3.586); Medea tells Jason he should propitiate Hecate with honey libations (3.1035); Circe propitiates Zeus Catharsius (4.708); offerings to native gods (4.1549).
[140] 3.105.

> She had fallen around his knees, but immediately
> He sank down and lifted her up and embraced and encouraged her:
> "My lady, may Olympian Zeus be witness of my oath,
> And Hera of the Marriage Yoke, consort of Zeus,
> That I shall place you in my home as my wedded wife
> When we return to our homeland in the land of Greece."

Jason here confirms their betrothal by taking hold (ἤραρε, 4.99) of her right hand with his own, just as she had grasped his right hand with her own at the temple of Hecate (3.1067–68).[141] Previously he had lightly touched (θίγεν, 1.842) Hypsipyle's hand while gently refusing her offer of rule on Lemnos, a gesture that evoked both the sexual intimacy of their proposed interaction and its brevity.[142] His firmer grasp of Medea's hand is a subtle alteration of gesture, yet it conveys the relative intensity of his commitment to her. He now swears a great oath by Zeus and Hera (his patron goddess, as he learned after the interview with Phineus), an act that formally binds his marriage contract regardless of Aeëtes' hostility and Medea's constant doubts. As if to reinforce the significance of this bond, the narrator points out that when Medea loses heart and becomes *amechanos* (4.107) as they leave the shore, Jason encourages and supports her (4.108), for he had experienced the same overwhelming sorrow upon leaving Pagasae (1.534–35). A rare glimpse into Jason's psyche, his tenderness here recalls Idmon's advice to Idas (1.480); his reaction to Medea's anguish exemplifies not the destructive power of Eros, but the Argonautic virtue of cooperation and sympathy for the suffering of others.

Jason makes no false promises to win the hospitality of Hypsipyle, nor does he now falsely promise to marry Medea. When they return to the Argo, he tells the Argonauts to honor Medea as the one who has saved them (4.190–97):

> "Μηκέτι νῦν χάζεσθε, φίλοι, πάτρην δὲ νέεσθαι·
> ἤδη γὰρ χρειὼ τῆς εἵνεκα τήνδ᾽ ἀλεγεινὴν
> ναυτιλίην ἔτλημεν, ὀιζύι μοχθίζοντες,
> εὐπαλέως κούρης ὑπὸ δήνεσι κεκράανται.
> Τὴν μὲν ἐγὼν ἐθέλουσαν ἀνάξομαι οἴκαδ᾽ ἄκοιτιν
> κουριδίην· ἀτὰρ ὔμμες, Ἀχαιίδος οἷά τε πάσης
> αὐτῶν θ᾽ ὑμείων ἐσθλὴν ἐπαρωγὸν ἐοῦσαν,
> σώετε."

---

[141] Ojennus 2006, 261–62 observes that Medea's grasp of Jason's hand indicates her dominance in this scene; Jason reciprocates with a similar gesture in the later scene (4.99; noted by Ojennus 2006, 260).

[142] Cf. Ojennus 2006, 258–59, who interprets Jason's brief touch as the gesture of an inferior in the act of making a request.

"Now no longer deprive yourselves, my friends, of your homeward journey
For at this moment the reason for which we
Endured this difficult sea voyage, weary with toil,
Has been obtained easily through the counsels of a maiden
Whom I, for my part, shall with her consent lead home as
My wedded wife. For your part, protect her as a faithful supporter
Of all Greece and of you yourselves."

As an affirmation of Jason's intentions, this speech is as straightforward as the call for election at Pagasae. One might be forgiven for suspecting that he only mouthed his initial proposal of marriage in order to obtain the Fleece, but his actions here are unambiguous.[143] Jason then organizes the Argonauts into two groups, instructing the first group to row and the second to raise their shields in defense (4.197–202). After he takes up his battle armor, the Argonauts cry out in excitement, he then cuts the rope and stands united with Medea and Ancaeus at the helm as the others row together (4.209–10). Far from being abandoned, Medea has taken her place with Jason at the head of the Argo.

Despite these initial assurances, Medea succumbs to doubt once more when they are surrounded by the Colchian army in the Brygian islands. The Colchians have agreed to let the Argonauts keep the Fleece, but now call for the return of Medea herself (4.345–49). Even if Jason had not previously intended to betray her, she fears that he may sacrifice her to keep his prize. She calls on him to protect her and reminds him of his oath, accusing him of agreeing to the treaty only because he intends to bargain for his safety with her life. She appeals to his sense of justice by pointing out how much he has gained, whereas she has been forced to sacrifice everything (4.358–65):

"Ποῦ τοι Διὸς Ἱκεσίοιο
ὅρκια, ποῦ δὲ μελιχραὶ ὑποσχεσίαι βεβάασιν;
Ἧις ἐγὼ οὐ κατὰ κόσμον ἀναιδήτῳ ἰότητι
πάτρην τε κλέα τε μεγάρων αὐτούς τε τοκῆας
νοσφισάμην, τά μοι ἦεν ὑπέρτατα, τηλόθι δ' οἴη
λυγρῇσιν κατὰ πόντον ἅμ' ἀλκυόνεσσι φορεῦμαι,
σῶν ἕνεκεν καμάτων, ἵνα μοι σόος ἀμφί τε βουσὶν
ἀμφί τε γηγενέεσσιν ἀναπλήσειας ἀέθλους."

---

[143] It should be added that by announcing his intention to marry Medea, Jason also reduces the likelihood that she will cause friction among the other Argonauts. His previous worry about the danger of including Atalanta in the crew of the Argo is telling in this context.

> "Where, where have your oaths to
> Zeus of Suppliants, your sweet promises gone?
> For these with shameless desire I have rashly forsaken
> My country and my glorious home and my parents themselves,
> The things I valued above all else. Alone and far away
> I am borne across the sea together with the wretched halcyon
> For the sake of your troubles, because I helped you to
> Accomplish in safety the labors of the bulls and the Earthborn Men."

Medea's plea is moving, and her suspicions are likely to raise doubts about Jason's constancy in the reader's mind. Nevertheless, the tenor of this speech recalls the scene in which she debated whether to abandon her family (3.771–801), and shows that she still suffers from erotic confusion. She mistrusts her alliance with Jason, moreover, because she is accustomed to the untrustworthiness of Aeëtes. During the meeting at the temple of Hecate she comments: "In Greece, I suppose, the honoring of agreements is a fine thing, but Aeëtes isn't disposed toward men the way you said Minos the husband of Pasiphae is" (3.1105–7). Aeëtes misjudges Jason's intentions from the start, and Medea is susceptible to the same weakness. She is her father's daughter: she boils with rage, longing to set fire to the Argo (4.392) just as Aeëtes had planned to do (3.582). Jason again responds to her accusations by trying to comfort her. He is shocked and frightened by her vehemence, but he responds in characteristically gentle fashion (μειλίχιοις ἐπέεσιν, 4.394), soothing (ὑποσσαίνων, 4.410) her just as he did at their first meeting (3.974). He explains that the treaty was strategically necessary not so that they could send her away, but because armed conflict would be ill-advised against the numerous Colchians who are already allied with the local inhabitants (4.398–400). Jason's assessment of the danger in which they find themselves is correct. He recognizes that they cannot trust the Colchians to honor their agreement any more than they could trust Aeëtes, but he genuinely intends to protect Medea, and recognizes that cunning must now come into play to guarantee their escape.

It would not, however, be entirely accurate to conclude that Medea becomes increasingly helpless as the poem progresses. Like Jason, she relies on persuasion and "wily words" to obtain what she wants.[144] Other

---

[144] At 4.731 Medea speaks in the Colchian language to Circe about their misfortunes, leaving out the murder; at 4.1012 Medea persuades the Argonauts to protect her; while at 4.1026 Medea asks Arete to persuade Alcinous.

characters in the poem are well spoken,[145] but these two are exceptional in their ability to propitiate the gods, even if they differ in their respective spheres of influence. Jason normally turns to the sun god Apollo: first on the beach at Pagasae (1.409–24) and then again near the island Anaphe (4.1702), but Medea, the priestess of the night-loving Hecate, shows him how to enlist the aid of the chthonian goddess in preparation for the labors in the Field of Ares. Medea's crowning moment comes late in Book 4 with the felling of the giant Talus (4.1636–88). Here she reaches the apex of malevolent potency as she harnesses the dread power of the underworld, using honeyed words to charm (μειλίσσετο, 4.1665) the Keres, the death gods. When Talus falls after scraping his vulnerable ankle on a rock, he is likened to a tree weakened by a woodcutter's axe and finally toppled by a strong gust of wind (4.1682–88). The narrator observes that the giants at Dindymon killed by Heracles are stacked like fallen timbers (1.1003–5), and Jason's killing of the Earthborn Men is similarly described: the giants lie like saplings in an orchard broken by the torrential rains of Zeus. The Talus episode confirms Medea as one of the most powerful members of the crew of the Argo – neither a pawn in political negotiation, nor a hapless bride stolen against her will, but an Argonaut in her own right.

In sum, Medea's characterization pursues two poetic goals. She is a royal priestess and a divine witch possessed of uncanny knowledge, but she is also a young girl subject to the whims of a disruptive god. This paradoxical blend of preternatural skill and physical vulnerability recurs in the portrait of Phineus, whose prophetic gifts are housed within a fragile mortal frame. For all their knowledge, neither Phineus nor Medea is proof against the forces of Zeus and Eros, and even a Heracles may be overwhelmed by the metaphorical sting of a gadfly. Second, although the alliance with Medea may not be as politically effective as Jason had hoped, it is more or less consistent with the strategies that informed the dynastic unions of the Successors, and his fidelity to Medea in the *Argonautica* is certainly at odds with comparable mythic scenarios. The mythic hero's traditional "reward" for a princess who betrays her father is death,[146] yet Jason not only agrees to

---

[145] Other characters: Aethalides persuades Hypsipyle to let them stay (1.650); Cyzicus is told to receive strangers gently, not in a hostile fashion (1.971); Phineus' story of the nymph who tried to persuade Paraebius (2.478); Argos addresses Aeëtes because he is fearful on Jason's behalf (3.319); the Colchians wheedle Alcinous into allowing them to stay as friends (4.1210); Chalciope fears that she will attempt to persuade Medea in vain (3.613); the Argonauts are told they will learn whether they can persuade Aeëtes by some other means (2.1279).

[146] Scylla helps Minos conquer Megara, but afterwards she is branded a traitor. Minos ties her to the prow of the ship so that she drowns, although in some versions she is transformed into a *keiris*, either a bird or, in some versions, a fish, to be pursued eternally by her father Nisus who has become

marry Medea but even publicly esteems her, much as the Ptolemaic kings honored their royal consorts. Since Jason rejects marriage to Hypsipyle because it is inconsistent with the political *aethloi* that press him, one may conclude the central advantage of the "bridal theft" still outweighs the many dangers it entails,[147] dangers that are as clear as Aphrodite's reflection in Ares' shield. The solution to these problems will then emerge in the kingdom of the Phaeacians, as Alcinous and Arete take on the responsibility for Medea's welfare and assume the role of her foster parents, transforming Jason's subversive bridal theft into a celebration of social order.

A WEDDING ON DREPANE

By arranging the marriage between Jason and Medea, the Phaeacian queen Arete brings an end to the *neikos* between the Argonauts and the Colchians, and her influence in this episode touches on the political role of Arsinoë II. Like Hypsipyle and Medea, Arete comes to the aid of the Argonauts, but unlike them, she is married: her intervention in this quarrel is subject to the judgment of her husband Alcinous. As was already seen, the royal union represents the preferred hegemonic paradigm both for characters in the poem and for the Ptolemaic court. Arete's canonical portrait in the *Odyssey* provides a starting point for evaluation of the ideological force behind her characterization in the *Argonautica*.[148] The Homeric Arete is said to intervene in areas typically thought to belong to men, whereas her Argonautic counterpart plays a more traditional female role of advocate. At the same time, the definition of what constitutes tradition – or at least a plausible alternative to it – with respect to marriage practices has changed, for Medea arranges the terms of her engagement (*engyesis*) on her own initiative,[149] while the physical handing over of the bride to the groom (*ekdosis*) is arranged by Arete.

---

a sea eagle (Ps.Verg. *Ciris*; Ov. *Rem. Am.* 68; *Met.* 8.6ff; Paus. 1.19.4; Apollod. *Bibl.* 3.15.8; Hyg. *Fab.* 198). Similarly, Comaetho helps Amphitryon kill her father Pterelaus and take over the island of Taphus; Amphitryon puts her to death for treachery (Apollod. *Bibl.* 2.4.7). Other treacherous women include Arne, who betrayed her home, Siphnus, to Minos and was changed into a crow (Ov. *Met.* 7.465–68). Pisidice falls in love with Achilles when she sees him from the walls of Methymna. She promises him Lesbos; he has her stoned for treachery (περὶ Πεισιδίκης, Meineke 1843, 324–25).

[147] As Stephens 2003, 215 notes in reference to the ploughing of the Field of Ares, "Jason obviously does not become king of Colchis, but he does perform acts that configure him as Aeetes' successor."

[148] For a thorough analysis of both Phaeacian episodes, see Knight 1995, 244–57; Kyriakou 1995, 156–68.

[149] Fathers normally acted as *kyrioi* to their unmarried daughters, but in Ptolemaic Egypt there were also instances of *autoekdosis* while the father was still alive. See further Yiftach-Firanko 2003, 141–44.

Apollonius' revision of the Phaeacian monarchy is significant. Unlike the Homeric Alcinous, who rules with thirteen other *basileis*, Apollonius' Alcinous governs independently as the sole *basileus* of the Phaeacians (4.1177–79): "In his hand he held the golden scepter of justice, with which the people throughout the city were awarded just settlements."[150] Alcinous' political judgments are also based on secret deliberations rather than debate by a council of nobles; they are not proposed in an assembly, but announced before the people. What is more, Apollonius' Arete intercedes only privately on behalf of her favorites and does not engage, as does the Homeric Arete, in public oration. She is the king's trusted advisor, and their private conversation is the dramatic keystone of the episode. Both monarchs are praised for the resolution of the Colchian conflict, but for Apollonius, and perhaps for the Ptolemies as well, the influence of an ideal queen is to be exercised from behind the throne, rather than openly in the manner of the Homeric Arete.

The political force of this parallel between the Ptolemies and the Phaeacian monarchs is not entirely certain. Would it have been seen as flattery or criticism? The fictional monarchy may be a subtle criticism of Arsinoë's excessive display of power, with Arete offered up as a corrective model. If, on the other hand, Arsinoë was celebrated for her tactful mediation, the characterization of Arete would have paid poetic homage to the real queen's discretion. In the absence of additional evidence it is difficult to rule out the possibility of subdued political censure, but, as noted earlier in discussing the more dramatic episodes of Arsinoë's life, it is more likely that Apollonius sought the approval of his royal patrons. Though the precise nature or extent of Arsinoë's power cannot be determined through an examination of epic poetry, Apollonius' portrait of Arete implies at the very least that Arsinoë's policies and recommendations were biased toward those who sought her favor, and it appears that the *Argonautica* enlists a traditional Homeric episode in order to allude to hidden channels of power in the Ptolemaic court. Such a reading accords well with Hazzard's claim that Arsinoë was widely perceived as influential, regardless of her documented activities (or the lack thereof) in the Ptolemaic administration.[151]

I now turn to the royal division of labor in both poems in order to place in perspective Arete's official role in the *Argonautica*. The circumstances of

---

[150] Cf. Hesiod's just king (*Theog.* 84–87).
[151] Hazzard 2000, 99: "the *perception* of Arsinoe's power was common to those persons outside the court during Ptolemy II's reign . . . Arsinoe II had extraordinary status, and men identified that status with power, especially after the king promoted the cult of Arsinoe Philadelphos throughout his realm in 268."

Odysseus' arrival on the island of the Phaeacians, which is called Scheria by Homer,[152] are well known, but let us begin with those aspects that are relevant to the Phaeacian episode in the *Argonautica*. Athena informs Odysseus that Arete is a conspicuous figure among the Phaeacians, who gaze after her as though she were a goddess (*Od.* 7.71–72). It is she who resolves the quarrels of those she favors, even quarrels between men, which would not normally fall within the purview of women (7.73–74). Athena notes also that the Phaeacians are skilled sailors, but hostile to strangers and wary of human contact (7.30–33). Because the appearance of Odysseus is likely to create conflict, Arete's favor and her talents as peacemaker will be critical for persuading the Phaeacians to help him return to Ithaca.

Heeding Athena's advice, Odysseus enters the palace invisibly, appearing to the Phaeacians only after he kneels in supplication before Arete. The elderly counselor Echeneus is the first to recover from the shock of the apparition, and immediately reminds Alcinous of the sanctity of suppliants. This observation seems to be made not simply for Alcinous' benefit, but for all the Phaeacians. Arete recognizes Odysseus' clothes as her own handiwork (7.233–39), yet refrains from questioning him until after the other Phaeacian chiefs have departed. She is a patient and observant strategist; she does not demand a public explanation from her guest, but waits to consult with him later. Odysseus is a stranger (*xeinos*), but he is also Arete's suppliant, and she shields him from the scrutiny of the court, encouraging him to be wary of the arrogant members of her own community,[153] and advising him to guard the gift chest as he sleeps on the return voyage to Ithaca (8.442–45).

Arete not only offers advice privately to Odysseus, but also speaks out on his behalf. In Book 11, when he pauses in his description of his encounter with the queens in the underworld, she turns to the Phaeacians and asks: "How does this man seem to you now, in looks and stature and even temperament?" (11.336–37). Odysseus is her personal guest, she says, but each of them shares in the responsibility for his proper treatment (11.338). Arete claims Odysseus as her *xeinos*, and then calls on all the Phaeacians to emulate her by offering gifts.[154] Alcinous will join Arete in asking the Phaeacians to provide their guest with gifts and an escort home, adding that his own position necessarily entails greater responsibility (11.352–53): "His safe conduct will concern all our men, yet me most of all, for mine is the authority in the demos."

---

[152] On the various names of the island see Knight 1995, 245–46.
[153] On the hostile Phaeacians, see Carnes 1993; Redfield 1983, 240–42; Ross 1969.
[154] In Book 8 Alcinous directs the Phaeacian chiefs to be generous to Odysseus, and Arete here openly voices support of her husband.

The *Argonautica* expands on the Homeric distinction between Arete's private concern for her suppliants and Alcinous' sense of his public responsibility and status.[155] Apollonius portrays them as benevolent rulers whose administrative roles are determined by their respective genders. Yet as Knight observes, "Although [Arete's] authority officially has been transferred to her husband, she has as much actual influence as in the *Odyssey*."[156] Of the two, Alcinous is the more concerned with the resolution of strife (*Argon.* 4.1010), and more attentive than Arete to the complexity of the threat posed by the conflict between the Argonauts and the Colchians. By contrast, Arete is swayed by compassion for Medea, and adopts clandestine means to protect her. She uses her influence in private counsel with her husband, who sympathizes with Medea but is not willing to provoke international conflict on her behalf (4.1073–109).

In both poems Arete is asked to intercede on behalf of her guests.[157] Upon their arrival at Drepane, the Argonauts are threatened not by arrogant Phaeacians, as Odysseus is, but by the Colchian army. Medea implores Arete to protect her (4.1011–13), in a supplication that recalls Odysseus' appeal (*Od.* 7.142).[158] She tries to justify her actions, noting that she left home only through compulsion by *ate*, "divine ruin" (*Argon.* 4.1016–17), and claiming that she did not willingly run away with strange men, but fled out of fear for her life (4.1021). She points out that she is still a virgin, and concludes by begging the queen to pity her and to use her influence over her husband (4.1025–26).

In contrast to Homeric epic, which does not describe private conversations between Alcinous and Arete (*Od.* 7.344–47), Apollonius brings his audience into the royal bedroom as Arete exercises her influence in accordance with Medea's request.[159] The passage might initially appear somewhat voyeuristic inasmuch as the audience visualizes the couple in the darkened bedroom, but the narrator avoids any hint of physical intimacy, and the seductive wiles used, for example, by Hera against Zeus are absent from Arete's speech (4.1073–95).[160] In effect, Apollonius substitutes this

---

[155] Kyriakou 1995, 157–58. [156] Knight 1995, 250.
[157] Odysseus addresses Arete primarily (*Od.* 7.146), though he also addresses her husband and the other guests at the banquet (7.147–48). Odysseus asks all the Phaeacians to help him (7.151), but Medea appeals only to Arete, although she also demands help from all the Argonauts.
[158] Medea's reluctance to trust a third party recalls Odysseus' mistrust of his Phaeacian hosts: see Most 1989.
[159] Hunter 1993, 71: "Apollonius 'writes' this missing scene for us."
[160] Cf. Nelis 2001b, 317, who finds a "distinct hint of eroticism" in this scene, "which the reader is led to believe will end in love-making." If there is a hint, it is rather comically undercut when Alcinous falls asleep and Arete leaves the room to plan someone else's wedding.

conversation for the Homeric Arete's public defense of Odysseus,[161] omitting not only the counselor Echeneus, but also the Homeric assembly and the council of Phaeacian nobles. On the following day the king, flanked by an elite corps of the Phaeacian army (4.1180–81), will simply announce his decision to the crowd of Argonauts, Colchians, and Phaeacians. Theocritus describes Ptolemy in similar terms at *Idyll* 17.93–94: "About him gather horsemen and shielded warriors in hosts, harnessed in flashing bronze" (tr. Gow). The Phaeacian *aristoi* played no role in the royal deliberations, however: their presence serves primarily to remind the Colchians of Alcinous' military strength (Chapter 5).[162]

Arete begins her defense of Medea by reminding Alcinous that they have close ties with the neighboring Haemonians, whereas Aeëtes is far away and they know little about him (4.1073–77). She appeals to her husband's sense of fairness and political expedience, arguing that since they must choose sides in the matter, they ought to take the side of the Argonauts, who represent the interests of their neighbors. The possibility of an alliance between the Phaeacians and the Greeks is a further contrast with Homer's isolationist Phaeacians, probably due to the later identification of Scheria with Corcyra (modern Corfu), which is located in the Adriatic along the coast of Epirus (Thuc. 1.25.4).[163] Arete then recapitulates Medea's earlier speech in order to forestall the possible objection that the girl might be unworthy of their help. She notes Medea's pitiable suffering and shifts the blame for any misdeeds and misfortunes to *ate* and human frailty (4.1077–83). The third portion of Arete's argument rests on pious obligation (4.1083–87): Jason has sworn to marry Medea, so if they allow her to be taken he will be forced to compromise his oath. Finally, she closes with a reminder of the irrational passion to which fathers are particularly susceptible (4.1087–95). They must interfere, she argues, because Aeëtes would mistreat his daughter in the manner of other excessively jealous fathers. Arete concludes that they must intervene on the grounds of sympathy, respect for the gods, and Phaeacian political ties.

Although Arete frames her argument according to what she sees as Phaeacian self-interest, she is quite willing to accept war as the price for Medea's

---

[161] The Council of *basileis* meets and feasts daily in the palace (*Od.* 7.95–99). Alcinous is preparing to meet with it when Nausicaa asks for permission to do the washing (6.53–55).

[162] Alcinous' confidence is due also to the "unbreakable oaths" the Colchians have sworn prior to his judgment (4.1205): see Byre 1997, 147; Fränkel 1968, 577. Green 1997 *ad* 4.1180–81: "Alkinoös expects his authority to be obeyed, but is taking no chances with these Kolchians: hence the strong military guard."

[163] See the Scholiast's note on *Argon.* 4.982–92d.

protection. Alcinous is sympathetic, but he is more concerned for the international consequences of their decision (4.1098–109):

> "Ἀρήτη, καί κεν σὺν τεύχεσιν ἐξελάσαιμι
> Κόλχους, ἡρώεσσι φέρων χάριν, εἵνεκα κούρης.
> Ἀλλὰ Διὸς δείδοικα δίκην ἰθεῖαν ἀτίσσαι·
> οὐδὲ μὲν Αἰήτην ἀθεριζέμεν, ὡς ἀγορεύεις,
> λώϊον· οὐ γάρ τις βασιλεύτερος Αἰήταο,
> καί κ' ἐθέλων, ἕκαθέν περ, ἐφ' Ἑλλάδι νεῖκος ἄγοιτο.
> Τῶ μ' ἐπέοικε δίκην, ἥ τις μετὰ πᾶσιν ἀρίστη
> ἔσσεται ἀνθρώποισι, δικαζέμεν· οὐδέ σε κεύσω·
> παρθενικὴν μὲν ἐοῦσαν, ἑῷ ἀπὸ πατρὶ κομίσσαι
> ἰθύνω· λέκτρον δὲ σὺν ἀνέρι πορσαίνουσαν,
> οὔ μιν ἑοῦ πόσιος νοσφίσσομαι, οὐδὲ γενέθλην
> εἴ τιν' ὑπὸ σπλάγχνοισι φέρει δηΐοισιν ὀπάσσω."

> "Arete, I could even banish by force of arms
> The Colchians, obliging the heroes for the sake of the girl,
> But I am apprehensive of dishonoring the straight judgment of Zeus;
> Nor would it be a good idea to treat Aeëtes lightly, as you suggest.
> No one is more imperious than Aeëtes, and
> Despite the distance he would readily wage war against Greece.
> Therefore it seems right to make a decision that will
> Be best in the opinion of all men. I will not hide it from you:
> If she is still a virgin, I order that they take her back to her father.
> But if she shares the bed with her husband
> I will not separate her from her spouse, nor will I give their enemies
> Her child, should she bear one in her womb."

Rather than planning to side with the Greeks in a conflict, Alcinous wishes to obviate war entirely.[164] While Arete is thinking of her Greek allies, she lacks Alcinous' dedication to peace. This difference is critical inasmuch as it seems to describe (or prescribe) a royal division of labor: the queen may be a strong lobbyist, but she is less concerned than the king to devise diplomatic solutions.[165] If Apollonius is commenting here on the Ptolemaic monarchy, this distinction could imply that Arsinoë's sympathy for her favorites similarly affected her attitudes toward foreign policy.[166]

Shortly after this discussion Alcinous falls asleep (4.1110), and Arete takes advantage of this opportunity to send a herald to advise Jason to marry

---

[164] In a similar move, Ptolemy II claimed friendship with both Carthage and Rome in 252 BC, and offered to mediate between them, no doubt to avoid involvement in a costly war (App. *Sic.* 1). Ptolemy's generous neutrality in the West may have been necessitated by his diplomatic isolation in the East. See Hauben 1983, 107.
[165] Vian 2002, 3:48. [166] Hauben 1983.

Medea that same night (4.1111–20). Despite, or perhaps more accurately, as a result of their conflicting spheres of interest (Medea's safety; political neutrality) the two rulers are able to orchestrate a peaceful resolution. Vian describes this scene as a quotidian revision of the Iliadic "beguiling of Zeus" (*Dios apate*) in an anti-epic register,[167] but the extent to which Arete is deceiving Alcinous is debatable. Unlike Zeus, Alcinous does not appear to have been beguiled, and unlike Hera, Arete does not use sex as a distraction, nor do her plans contravene those of her husband. By all accounts theirs is a more harmonious union than that of the Homeric Zeus and Hera, whether or not one assumes the presence of sexual innuendo in this scene.[168] It is true that Arete makes no mention of her plan for a secret ceremony to Alcinous, but he could hardly fail to be aware of her partisanship given her previous speech. That Alcinous falls asleep immediately after the discussion suggests that he expects her to act, and he certainly gives her ample opportunity to do so. But does Arete intend to deceive Alcinous? Or does Alcinous knowingly collude in the wedding? There are no signs that she has tricked him into revealing his judgment, nor is there any indication later in the poem that he is disturbed by her actions.[169] He presumably knows what she will do and even expects her to act as she does, but it is impossible to be sure. Their intentions, like the *noos* of Zeus, are unavailable to us, either because they are unavailable to the narrator, or because the narrator has purposely chosen, like the prophet Phineus, not to tell the whole story straight through.[170] Either way the audience, like the characters in the poem, has only partial (that is, mortal) knowledge of the events that are taking place. We see more than the Argonauts, and yet less than the gods themselves. In the end Apollonius revises and enriches the canonical Homeric scene of conjugal deception by focusing on the role of intimacy in royal decision-making and on the connection between knowledge and political (or authorial) control: in this case, when, how, by whom, and to whom the king's decision is revealed.

The wedding does not remain secret for long, since Hera quickly starts a rumor in order to spread the good news to all the Phaeacians (4.1184–85). On the following morning the crowd has assembled both to hear the judgment of Alcinous and to take part in the wedding celebration. The poet notes that one brings a ram and another brings a heifer, and that many more bring wine, robes, gold ornaments, and bridal gifts (4.1185–91). This idyllic

---

[167] Vian 2002, 3:185, n. 4.1072.   [168] Hunter 1993, 71.
[169] Cf. Zeus's angry response to Hera's trickery at *Il.* 15.14–33.
[170] On the *noos* ("intent") of Zeus, see Chapter 2. On Phineus and the punishment for revealing Zeus's plans in full, see Chapter 5.

description of the abundant wealth and spontaneous generosity of the Phaeacian people further distinguishes them from the Homeric Phaeacians, who must be told by Arete and Alcinous to provide gifts for Odysseus (*Od.* 11.339–41; 13.7–15).

Arete's role in the wedding is likewise revealed and publicly acknowledged during the marriage celebration. A chorus of nymphs joins Orpheus in singing and dancing and honors Hera for inspiring Arete to disclose the "wise word" (*pykinon epos*) of Alcinous. On the one hand, their praise of Hera might easily be transferred to Arsinoë herself, given her ideological identification with Arete and the Olympian in her marriage as well as her cult titles.[171] But on the other hand, this public acknowledgment of the divine motivation for Arete's actions helps to sanction it, and to dispel any lingering doubts about the propriety of the deception, if that is what it was (4.1197–200):

> ἄλλοτε δ' αὖτε
> οἰόθεν οἶαι ἄειδον ἑλισσόμεναι περὶ κύκλον,
> Ἥρη, σεῖο ἕκητι· σὺ γὰρ καὶ ἐπὶ φρεσὶ θῆκας
> Ἀρήτῃ <u>πυκινὸν</u> φάσθαι <u>ἔπος</u> Ἀλκινόοιο.

> Then sometimes
> They sang without him [Orpheus] swirling about in a circle,
> Hera, honoring you, for you gave Arete the idea
> Of declaring the <u>wise word</u> of Alcinous.

The narrator here refers to the "wise word" that is expressed by Alcinous to Arete during the bedroom council (4.1096–97). The phrase *pykinon epos* signifies a message whose import will profoundly alter the course of events – provided that it is properly transmitted.[172] The narrator uses this same phrase to describe Alcinous' speech as Arete takes it to heart at the conclusion of their conversation (4.1111). Arete's herald thus relays Alcinous' *epos*, which has now become Arete's speech (*mythos*), to the Argonauts (4.1121–23): "His feet bore him swiftly from the hall, so that he might report the *mythos* of Arete to Jason." When the Argonauts finally receive Alcinous' "wise word," they are delighted that the crisis is to be resolved without bloodshed (4.1126–27), since they have vowed to defend Medea by force if necessary (4.1053–57). Without Arete's intervention, Medea would have been taken, provoking an attack by the Argonauts on the Colchians. In order for this *pykinon epos* to have its desired effects, to prevent the escalation of the *neikos* and to be, as Alcinous says, a decision that seems

---

[171] See Fraser 1972, 1:237–38. [172] Foley 1991, 154–56.

best in the opinion of *all* men (4.1104), it also had to become the speech, the *mythos*, of the queen. Not only is Arete closely associated with Hera, but she also assumes a comparable role as a transmitter of information; it is Hera, after all, who animates the oak beam of Dodona on the Argo, which in turn communicates the judgment of Zeus to the Argonauts (Chapter 1).

Like Hera, then, Arete does not speak publicly, but through an intermediary. The political voices of the two monarchs, the one female, private, hidden in darkness, the other male, public, proclaimed in daylight, are the complementary halves of a united whole. This hegemonic dichotomy recurs in the union of Medea, priestess of the chthonic Hecate, with Jason, a hero championed by shining Apollo. Yet Jason and Medea ironically regret the circumstances of their marriage (4.1161–64):

> Οὐ μὲν ἐν Ἀλκινόοιο γάμον μενέαινε τελέσσαι
> ἥρως Αἰσονίδης, μεγάροις δ᾽ ἐνὶ πατρὸς ἑοῖο
> νοστήσας ἐς Ἰωλκὸν ὑπότροπος· ὣς δὲ καὶ αὐτὴ
> Μήδεια φρονέεσκε· τότ᾽ αὖ χρεὼ ἦγε μιγῆναι.

> The hero, son of Aeson, did not want to be married
> In the hall of Alcinous, but in the halls of his father
> After having returned home to Iolcus,[173] and Medea herself
> Felt the same way. Necessity (*chreō*) drove them to marry at that time.

Like their desperate *eros*-driven elopement, marriage is forced upon them, and is no less transgressive in its rejection of Aeëtes' paternal authority and royal privilege. Previously, when he was compelled to perform Aeëtes' labors in the Field of Ares, Jason ruefully observed that there is nothing worse than necessity (*anangkēs*) for humanity (3.429–30). Describing the particulars of the marriage ceremony, the narrator comments philosophically on the bittersweet nature of the human condition (4.1165–69):

> Ἀλλὰ γὰρ οὔ ποτε φῦλα δυηπαθέων ἀνθρώπων
> τερπωλῆς ἐπέβημεν ὅλῳ ποδί· σὺν δέ τις αἰεὶ
> πικρὴ παρμέμβλωκεν ἐυφροσύνῃσιν ἀνίη.
> Τῶ καὶ τούς, γλυκερῇ περ ἰαινομένους φιλότητι,
> δεῖμ᾽ ἔχεν, εἰ τελέοιτο διάκρισις Ἀλκινόοιο.

> Yet never does the long-suffering human race
> Set foot entirely on the path of joy, but ever does
> Some bitter sorrow accompany our happiness;
> Thus, although they delighted in sweet desire, they were
> Apprehensive about the accomplishment of Alcinous' judgment.

---

[173] Jason's regret at marrying far from home recalls Eur. *Phoen.* 337–49, where it is observed that when a son marries abroad the mother sorrows like a mother whose son is dead.

Medea fears that the Colchian fleet may not in fact be pleased by Alcinous' "wise word," for she knows, as Alcinous does not, that Aeëtes has threatened to destroy them should they return without her (4.228–35). Medea is now effectively at war with her family. Although Circe purifies Medea after the ambush (4.662–752), she will not forgive her niece for her shameless flight (*aeikea phyxin*, 4.748). The ill-timed marriage remains their best hope, representing as it does the brighter half of a tragicomic diptych. The consequences of *eros* (the "bridal theft" of Medea and the killing of Apsyrtus) sacrifice cooperative ideals to unilateral interests and only deepen the division between the two communities. Alcinous' diplomatic solution, by contrast, forestalls a protracted conflict involving not only the Colchians and the Argonauts, but also the Phaeacians and the mainland Greeks. Since the Colchian fleet subsequently decides to seek asylum and abandon the pursuit of Medea (4.1209–11), this wedding represents the triumph of political negotiation over the disruptive strife of *eros*.

Through Arete's intervention the Argonauts are saved from the crisis of an "erotic" murder and the prospect of an endless *neikos*, and on Drepane, as on Lemnos, the ravages of *eros* are remedied by diplomatic necessity. Political expedience aside, the wedding ceremony itself remains irregular. Performed in secret in the cave of Dionysus' nurse Macris, it is arguably illegitimate because of Medea's familial estrangement. The elopement leaves her status open to legal challenge, a fact that could have affected the Alexandrian audience's perception of her subsequent fate in Corinth. A further wrinkle is introduced by the intervention of Arete, who effectively supplants Aeëtes, Medea's proper guardian (*kyrios*). It is Arete who plays the decisive role in arranging for the ceremony prior to Alcinous' public announcement (4.1114–27). She initiates the *ekdosis* ("giving in marriage"), a role typically reserved for the father or another man acting on his behalf. As a woman unrelated to the bride, Arete's prominence would seem incongruous in any Greek wedding, even an anomic abduction marriage.

Such legalistic questions might seem to strike an inappropriate note in connection with an epic poem featuring monsters and mythological characters. Yet even characters in a work of the imagination participate in the ethical norms of the poet's own day, adhering more or less to a social code or idiom that is recognizable to the poem's audience. It is therefore reasonable to question whether Arete's assistance ought to be numbered among the unusual aspects of the wedding ceremony. Should we, in other words, see her actions as an extension of the Homeric Arete's intervention in the male domain, or is she playing a relatively conventional role?

A wedding on Drepane

Marriages by abduction, despite their irregularity, were common enough throughout antiquity to be recognized as valid by the larger community, if not the members of the bride's immediate family.[174] Of greater interest in this regard is the fact that legal protocols in Egypt were generally less restrictive than those of mainland Greece (particularly Athens),[175] and allowed not only for the participation of the mother but even that of a surrogate parent. *P. Eleph.* 1 (*c.* 310, from Elephantine), the earliest surviving Greek marriage document from Egypt, lists the mother of the bride as a participant in the *ekdosis* together with the father,[176] while in another document, *P. Oxy.* X 1273 (*c.* 260) the mother performed it alone.[177] The lone example in Greco-Roman Egypt of *autoekdosis*, a marriage in which the bride gives herself away, occurred in 173 in the Fayuum, when the Macedonian Olympias gave herself to the Athenian Antaios. Earlier evidence for such marriages suggests that this was by no means typical of Macedonian practice, and that such marriages were seen in Athens as less than respectable, as in the case of sacred prostitution in Lydia (Herod. 1.93) or the marriage of the *hetaira* Glykera to the Corinthian citizen Polemon in Menander's *Perikeiromene*.[178] While Olympias' marriage was much later than the date of the *Argonautica*, it points to the increasing flexibility of contractual marriages in Hellenistic Egypt, and represents the new developments in Greek family law that occurred as the result of a mobile population.[179] Pomeroy observes: "The Hellenistic time was a period when people moved around a great deal. Not every girl had a male relative close at hand, but some fatherless and brotherless brides did have a mother."[180] Medea, of course, has no male relatives at hand, having fled the one and murdered the other, and yet, while her history is tragically exaggerated it is nonetheless representative of a very real social phenomenon: the dislocation and fragmentation of the family as a result of the Greek diaspora in the fourth and third centuries.

For all its apparent idiosyncrasies, then, the Phaeacian wedding celebration symbolizes Jason and Medea's reintegration into an organized and

---

[174] Evans-Grubbs 1989, 63.
[175] Kanazawa 1989, 483 argues that in the *chora*, both men and women had the option of referring to whichever law, Greek or Egyptian, best suited their needs. The omission of any reference to a *kyrios* in eighteen Demotic contracts suggests that women in debt often relied on the indigenous law because it did not require the participation of a *kyrios*, who was essential in Greek law.
[176] See Rowlandson 1998, no. 125 on p. 167.
[177] Yiftach-Firanko 2003, 141–44. Both parents are reported as performing the *ekdosis* in four cases, while fathers or mothers did so independently in seven cases each (43, n. 13). See also Vatin 1970, 70. Cf. the later (173 BC) evidence of *P. Giss.* I 2 (= Rowlandson 1998, no. 126 on p. 168), a marriage contract in which Olympias, daughter of a Macedonian cavalry-man gives herself in marriage to an Athenian cavalryman named Antaeus.
[178] Modrzejewski 1981, 252–53. [179] Modrzejewski 1981, 252–53. [180] Pomeroy 1990, 89–90.

civilized society.[181] Arete steps in as Medea's advocate and guardian, and while she is not related to Medea, this need not, by Hellenistic Greek standards, preclude her arrangement of the marriage.[182] As the narrator observes, the Phaeacians immediately greet the Argonauts as though they were their own children (ἑοῖς παισί, 4.997). Later, when the Argonauts take their leave of the island, Arete will informally "dower" Medea with a retinue of twelve Phaeacian slave women (δμωὰς Φαιηκίδας, 4.1222) from the palace.[183] These slaves are among the plentiful guest gifts (ξεινήια, 4.1220) given to the Argonauts by both sovereigns, and they, like the Golden Fleece itself, essentially constitute her dowry.[184]

The dowering of Medea is modeled on a similar scene in the *Odyssey* that involves, as one might expect, Alcinous rather than Arete. In Book 7 Alcinous offers to give Odysseus a house and possessions, if he will only remain on Scheria and become his son-in-law (*Od.* 7.311–15):

"Αἲ γὰρ, Ζεῦ τε πάτερ καὶ Ἀθηναίη καὶ Ἀπόλλον,
Τοῖος ἐὼν οἷος ἐσσι, τά τε φρονέων ἅ τ' ἐγώ περ,
παῖδά τ' ἐμὴν ἐχέμεν καὶ ἐμὸς γαμβρὸς καλέεσθαι
αὖθι μένων· οἶκον δέ κ' ἐγὼ καὶ κτήματα δοίην,
εἴ κ' ἐθέλων γε μένοις·"

"How I wish, Father Zeus and Athena and Apollo,
That with you as you are, and with me thinking as I do,
You would marry my daughter and be called my son-in-law
By remaining here. I would give you a home and possessions
If only you would willingly stay."

Alcinous' offer here is reminiscent of Hypsipyle's offer of marriage to Jason, since both Jason and Odysseus are forced to refuse. More importantly, though, both passages show the Phaeacian rulers arranging marriage for their guests. Although they are as yet childless in the *Argonautica*, the arrival of their new "daughter" Medea permits them to celebrate the promise of a wedding that is ever left undone in Homer by the departure of Odysseus.[185]

---

[181] As do weddings in Homeric epic. See Oakley and Sinos 1993, 4.
[182] On adoptive parents, see Yiftach-Firanko 2003, 50.
[183] As Green 1997 *ad* 4.1217–22 notes, the number of Phaeacian handmaids matches the number Medea left behind in Colchis.
[184] The term *pherne* does not appear in the poem, but it would be appropriate. On the *pherne*, the Egyptian equivalent of the Attic *proix*, see Yiftach-Firanko 2003, 123–24. Yiftach-Firanko views it as a "substantial contribution to the future economic life of the family," and rejects the view that the function of the *pherne* was simply to provide for the personal needs of the wife.
[185] The fifth-century mythographer Hellanicus invented a marriage between Nausicaa and Odysseus' son, Telemachus (*FGrH* 4 F 156).

Like Odysseus, Medea also leaves the Phaeacians, yet her countrymen will remain, in a second mediated substitution that also indirectly fulfills the original wishes of the Homeric king. Furthermore, the resettlement of the Colchians ensures the expansion of the entire Phaeacian community. Homer's Phaeacians become a closed society after Odysseus' return to Ithaca. The state is to be diplomatically immobilized, like the stone ship in their harbor, for they will no longer convey mortals to their destinations (*Od.* 13.179–81). After the departure of the Argonauts, by contrast, the descendants of the adopted Colchians will migrate to the mainland (*Argon.* 4.1211–16).[186] Apollonius thus rewrites history for the Phaeacians and assures the succession of future generations, as the Phaeacian capital becomes a mother city to the new colonies of her adopted Colchian heirs. Although marriage is associated with controversy in the *Argonautica*, it continues to be envisioned, despite its contested nature, as a solution to psychic and political disorder, a bridge between kings and nations, and a locus for cultural renewal and transformation.

---

[186] They will join the tribes of the Amantes (in the Ceraunian mountains), and the Nestaeans (on the Illyrian coast), while others will settle in the town called Oricum (in Epirus).

CHAPTER 5

Piety, mediation, and the favor of the gods

CULT MODELS AND POETIC MIRRORS

As the last two chapters have shown, the depiction of character in the *Argonautica* revises Homeric behavioral patterns, largely in response to contemporary historical models, or rather to the ideological implications of those historical models. The resolution of political tension during several episodes promotes a cooperative ideal that reworks both the strife of *Iliad* 1 and the conflicts in Alexander's army, while the foregrounding of influential female characters alludes to Homeric figures like Arete as well as to the political role, official or otherwise, of Ptolemaic queens. Jason's cloak, moreover, is a symbol of political authority that recalls not only the shield of Achilles but also the iconography of Alexander, like the "sweet sweat" and linen band of Posidippus' epigram.[1] But it is the Argonauts' formal contact with the gods, more than any other feature of the *Argonautica*, which brings the poem in line with its contemporary political context. Like their Egyptian predecessors, the Ptolemaic kings acted as intermediaries between their subjects and the gods; so, too, the epic leader is imagined as the principal link between the divine and mortal spheres. Although the poem draws attention to the Argonauts' shared responsibilities,[2] Jason's ritual activity stands out as exceptional.[3] It is Jason who plays the central role in a greater number of important episodes, such as the night sacrifice to Hecate (3.1191–224) and the noon apparition of the Herossae (4.1305–36). Where Homeric epic shows leaders like Agamemnon and Hector disputing the validity of omens and prophecies,[4] impiety among the Argonauts is confined to Idas,

[1] Posidippus, 36AB; see Chapter 4.
[2] Religious activity of other Argonauts: the Dioscuri (4.592–94, 651–53); Orpheus (1.915–18; 2.698–704, 927–29; 4.1547–50); the Boreads (2.490–95); Heracles (1.406–36); Ancaeus (1.406–36); Mopsus (2.922–23); Medea (4.246–52).
[3] Jason's ritual acts: 1.406–36, 1133; 2.490–95, 1271–75; 3.1200–24; 4.1593–1602. It is also he who interprets Euphemus' dream (4.1746–54).
[4] In the first book of the *Iliad* Agamemnon not only refuses to honor the request of the priest Chryses (1.26–32) but also insults the seer Calchas, alleging that his prophecies are uniformly pessimistic and

and Jason is himself an interpreter of portents like Euphemus' dream, as a precursor, at least in this respect, of Virgil's *pius Aeneas* (Chapter 7). Thus, by closely realigning epic leadership with religious activity, the poem evokes an image of state-run cult.

This is not to imply, of course, that religion was entirely removed from practical governance until the Ptolemaic era. To paraphrase Detienne, one could not exercise political power in the ancient Mediterranean apart from ritual sacrifice; any military leader or king would make offerings to ensure that the gods favored his actions, or at least to ensure that his followers believed as much.[5] So, for example, by praising Philadelphus' divine lineage, piety, skill on the battlefield, and generosity in *Idyll* 17, Theocritus uses terms that would have been "applicable to kings far back in Greek tradition, at a time before the emergence of city-states of old Greece, and long before the conquests of Alexander and the wars of the Successors."[6] Inasmuch as *Idyll* 17 represents an early stage of Ptolemaic ideology, these ideas can be dated to an early period in Philadelphus' reign. Theocritus' focus on such traditional attributes of kingship amounts to a reflection of the views of Soter, the elder Ptolemy,[7] who did not seek divine honors for himself in life. It was some years later, under Philadelphus, that the notion of divine kingship was introduced. Thus, while piety was always associated to some degree with political authority, this association came to assume larger importance after the institution of ruler cult. As a consequence of this shift, the disposition of a given leader toward the gods (and conversely their disposition toward him) assumes rather different, and perhaps even greater, significance in the *Argonautica* than it did in archaic epic.

My purpose in this chapter is to consider the effects of the religious idiom on the representation of character in the *Argonautica*. I compare the cult practice of Argonautic leaders with similar scenes in Homeric epic, taking into consideration the political function of religion in the late fourth and early third centuries. While traditional themes, such as the acquisition of individual honor (*time*) and glory (*kleos*), continue to resonate to some

---

ineffectual (1.106–8). Hector dismisses his brother Polydamas' interpretation of a bird omen, claiming that the only council he heeds is that of Zeus (12.231–42). Cf. the disagreement between Halitherses, a renowned interpreter, and the suitor Eurymachus about the meaning of a portent (*Od.* 2.157–86). Here Eurymachus plays the role of Agamemnon in rejecting Halitherses' correct interpretation of a bird sign that signals Odysseus' revenge against the Suitors.

[5] "Any military or political undertaking – a campaign, engagement with the enemy, conclusion of a treaty, works commissioned on a temporary basis, the opening of the assembly, or the assumption of office by the magistrates – each must begin with a sacrifice followed by a meal." Detienne 1989, 3.

[6] Samuel 1993, 181.   [7] Hunter 2003, 3–7.

extent in the *Argonautica*,[8] it will become clear that Apollonius privileges pious, diplomatic, and emotionally restrained leaders to a greater degree than Homer does, and Jason's ritual prominence is better understood, consequently, in the context of this correlation between piety and just leadership, a correlation that emerges very early in the poem. In Book 1 Jason aligns political hegemony with cult activity when he prays for Apollo's divine sanction, sponsoring a sacrifice to the god immediately after he becomes the Argonauts' leader (1.351–62, 402–59). His piety here strongly contrasts with Pelias' neglect of Hera, which is introduced even earlier, at the programmatically significant start of the poem (1.12–14), where it calls to mind the inaugural strife between Agamemnon and Apollo in *Iliad* 1. But Agamemnon's dispute, strictly speaking, is with Chryses, the priest of Apollo, whereas Pelias affronts Hera directly. In this scene, as elsewhere, the *Argonautica* differs from Homeric epic in highlighting the independent responsibility of leaders with respect to religious matters. There are prophets (Idmon and Mopsus) aboard the Argo, but there is no priest aboard the Argo until the arrival of Medea in Book 4, and Jason shares power amicably with her. His rhetorical skill ensures that any personal conflicts between them (in this poem, at least) are soon resolved, and in any case are far less costly to the company than Agamemnon's quarrel with Chryses is to the Achaeans.

It is, paradoxically, Jason and Medea's unanimity, or more precisely their complicity in the *eros*-driven ambush of Apsyrtus, that threatens to do the greatest harm. Angered by the murder, Zeus delays their return to Greece by secretly ordaining that Jason and Medea must first be purified by Circe (4.557–65). When Hera reveals his judgment, Castor and Polydeuces, the Dioscuri ("sons of Zeus"), raise their hands in prayer and supplication to their father (4.592–94), but the others lose hope at the lingering stench of Phaethon's smoldering corpse, a grim reminder that even the children of the gods are subject to divine punishment (4.619–26).[9] The narrator refers to

---

[8] References to *time* in the *Argonautica*: Orpheus sings of Ophion's loss of *time* to Cronos (1.505); honors bestowed by hero cults on Cyzicus (1.1048); Aeëtes suspects the Argonauts of coming to rob him of honor (3.376 and 596); Jason promises Medea great honor among Greek women (3.1123); the Fleece is used to honor the wedding of Jason and Medea (4.1143); Hera speaks of the honor in which she has been held by Thetis (4.809). References to *kleos*: the narrator announces his concern with the famous deeds of ancient heroes (1.1); the narrator notes Lynceus' famed eyesight (1.154); Telamon accuses Jason of trying to sabotage Heracles' fame (1.1292); the Argonauts win fame for the death of Amycus (2.754); Jason promises Medea that the Argonauts will spread her renown in Greece (3.992); Medea charges the Argonauts with allowing her to lose her good reputation in Colchis (4.361).

[9] Zeus struck Phaethon with the thunderbolt when he lost control of the chariot of the Sun.

Zeus's wrath and its possible consequences only briefly,[10] but the point has been made: Apsyrtus' murder is the catalyst for the central crisis of the Argo's return, namely the impairment of Jason and Medea's strategic connection to the gods. Although Jason and Medea enjoy divine favor as part of their elite birthright, as exiles their relations with Zeus quickly deteriorate. But like the prophet-king Phineus, they survive Zeus's wrath, even if they do not enjoy the perfect political balance of the idealized Alcinous and Arete.

Their tribulations are linked, moreover, to another shift that distinguishes Apollonius from Homer. In the *Argonautica*, *kleos* does not fire the imagination of heroes as it does in the *Iliad*. Those who are tempted by its promise, like Heracles, are children of the gods, demi-gods to whom such honors are naturally owed: they need not win it, although they are perfectly capable of doing so. All the Argonauts admire Heracles; even his immoderate wrath at being left behind (for which, as it happens, he kills the Boreads, 1.1300–8) can be taken as the sign of a latent, powerful divinity. Jason does not rival the great hero in martial glory, but then he does not seek to do so. His manner and bearing are enough to establish him as a member of the nobility: I noted in the last chapter that Hypsipyle appreciates his suitability for rule only moments after meeting him. More importantly, however, Jason instantiates a hegemonic model that is founded on an awareness of the honor that is owed not to him, but to the gods.

In strengthening the association between active piety and just leadership, the poem verges, at times, on an explicit connection between the ritual activity of the Argonauts and contemporary cults. This is certainly the case in the passage where the Argonauts erect a shrine to Homonoia (2.686–719). Early in the third century on Cos, the birthplace of Philadelphus, Homonoia was worshipped in connection with Hygeia ("Good Health"), who was popular in Greece and Asia Minor from the fourth century BC to the second century AD.[11] Another contemporary parallel emerges from the reference to the Argonauts' detour, on Orpheus' advice, to the Island of Electra (Samothrace) for initiation into the mysteries of the "Unnamed Gods" to ensure their safety at sea (1.915–18). The narrator comments that it is not *themis* ("right," or "customary," 1.921) to give further information regarding these gods, but further information is nonetheless available: the cult of Cabiri, the "Great Gods," who offered protection for sailors, was celebrated by a number of royals on Samothrace.[12] Philip II and Olympias

---

[10] Zeus's wrath (*cholos*) is mentioned initially at 4.557–61, then again when Hera first intervenes (4.576–77), and when the narrator notes the fear of the Argonauts on hearing the news (4.584–85).
[11] On the cult generally, see Thériault 1996; on the cult in Cos, Thériault 1996, 21–22.
[12] See Green 1997 *ad* 1.916–21.

are reported as initiates,[13] and sources also point to the initiation of Lysimachus, Philadelphus, and Arsinoë.[14] The island would eventually become a possession of the Lagids later in the third century.[15] The Argonauts' visit to Samothrace is particularly suggestive because of the Hellenistic identification of the Dioscuri with the Cabiri: Castor and Polydeuces are essentially initiated into mysteries on the site of their own future cult.[16] The narrator's reticence about the identity of these "Unnamed Gods" paradoxically (and intentionally, one imagines) draws attention to the overlap between the cultic practices of the Argonauts and the Ptolemies, and implies the possibility of other associations elsewhere in the poem.

Such "mirroring" between divine figures in the poem and in Alexandrian cults is not always observed, however. Of the gods whose cults enjoyed Ptolemaic support, like Demeter, Dionysus, and Aphrodite, only Aphrodite has a speaking role in the poem (3.43–154). As far as the Argonauts, and especially Jason, are concerned, Hera, Zeus, Hecate, and Apollo are the most significant of the Olympians (either because of their advocacy or, in the case of Zeus, because of his hostility) although these cults were not heavily promoted by the Ptolemies.[17] This divergence cannot be accounted for by exclusive comparison with the *Iliad* and the *Odyssey*, though the Argonautic portrayal of these gods often looks back to Homer. Hera and Athena, together with Iris, Thetis, and Aeolus, form what Knight calls the "Homeric core" of divine characterization in the *Argonautica*,[18] but here too Apollonius prefers variation to strict consistency for, as Knight observes, "Apollonius both extends the pantheon to include non-Homeric gods and diminishes it by marginalizing some major Olympians."[19]

Apollonius' taste for variety also means that the poem occasionally features divinities of lesser stature that are neither mentioned in Homer nor have cults that were officially encouraged by the throne. For example, a

---

[13] Alexander also sacrificed to them (Arr. 4.8.2; Plut. *Alex.* 50.4).
[14] Cole 1984, 38. Arsinoë II had taken refuge on Samothrace prior to her return to Egypt in 279/8 and the mystery cult was favored by her; see *P. Cair. Zen.* 2.59296.32 cited in Green 1990, 886, n. 31. Hunter 1993, 160–61 notes the importance of Polydeuces' match with Amycus in terms of Ptolemaic ideology.
[15] See Will 1979, 1:160, n. 1; Vian 2002, 1:260–61, n. 918. The Ptolemies are called Lagids after Soter's father, Lagus. See Chapter 2.
[16] On the association of the Dioscuri with the Samothracian gods, see Hunter 1995, 18–19; both the Dioscuri and the Samothracian gods were honored sometime during the middle of the third century in a *temenos* on Thera established by Artemidorus of Perge. Artemidorus was directed in a dream to erect an altar to Homonoia (*IG* XII 3 Suppl. 1333–48 *Artemidori temenos*; 1349–50 *Artemidori arae ad viam*). The Dioscuri had their own temple in Alexandria, and for that matter were favorites of Arsinoë: Callimachus referred to their role in the apotheosis of the deceased queen (Callim. fr. 228 Pfeiffer i).
[17] Fraser 1972, 1.195–97.   [18] Knight 1995, 271.   [19] Knight 1995, 279.

Hellenistic epigram by Nicaenetus suggests that there may have been a cult dedicated to the Herossae, the guardian nymphs of Libya who appear to Jason,[20] although there is only limited evidence that they were sponsored by the Ptolemies either in Alexandria or other Greek settlements.[21] Correspondences between the gods that are portrayed in the *Argonautica* and the gods that are worshipped in third-century Egypt, while apparently deliberate, are at best selective. Caution is warranted here, as always, but when such mirroring does occur, and while it in part represents a shift from the epic tradition to the aetiology of certain practices, like the cult of the "Unnamed Gods," it suggests that the poem equates much of the ritual activity of the Argonauts with contemporary cult, if only in very general terms and primarily to emphasize the symbiosis of political and religious activity. Of greatest importance, for my purposes, is the recognition that, from the perspective of Apollonius' third-century audience, civilized rule entailed cultic activity of one kind or another.[22] The voyage of the Argo thus prefigures the expansion of Greek culture in Asia and Africa, and at the same time announces an antique precedent for the piety of the Ptolemaic monarchy.

The following section addresses the religious responsibilities of Egyptian and Macedonian kings in order to set up a framework for subsequent discussion of political figures in the *Argonautica*. Poetic as well as historical and legal documents emphasize the Ptolemies' participation in cult, fostering the image of the king as a diplomatic peacemaker. Insofar as the poem draws on many parallels, ranging from the religious activity of Homeric heroes to that of Alexander the Great and the early Ptolemies, not to mention a Greek interpretation of Egyptian religious customs, the methodology of this analysis will often be associative rather than denotative, eclectic rather than exhaustive, in keeping with a general assumption that the *Argonautica* is not allegorical but is as nuanced and allusive in its representation of the political role of religious activity as it is in its treatment of its poetic predecessors. So, for example, a backward glance at the career of Alexander in one episode does not preclude sidelong glances at Ptolemaic practice in another, in the same way that an allusion to Homer in one line by no means precludes an allusion to Hesiod in the next. Such an allusive style is liable to generate a number of conceptual inconsistencies, and while we as readers may well be able to isolate such problems, it may not always be

---

[20] *Anth. Pal.* 6.225. Cited by Green 1997 *ad* 4.1309–11, 1322–23, who notes that the epigram is not necessarily derived from the scene in the *Argonautica*. The episode (*Argon.* 4.1305–36) recalls Menelaus' encounter with Idothea in Egypt (*Od.* 4.363–446).
[21] See Hunter 1995, 19–20. [22] Koenen 1993, 80.

possible (or even necessary) to reconcile them. While none of the characters in the poem is a direct and precisely accurate representation of a Hellenistic king, and while no one, least of all Jason, accepts cult in the manner of the Ptolemies, this does not mean that other practical aspects of the ideology of Hellenistic kingship, such as the king's role as mediator, are irrelevant to the poem.

With the goal, then, of seeing how the Ptolemaic construction of piety, in all its hybrid glory, is inscribed in the Argonautic conflation of religious and political authority, the present chapter examines the relation between the representation of ritual action, especially prayer and sacrifice, and the moral polarization of leaders in the *Argonautica*. As a poetic meditation on the relation between hegemony and divine favor, the *Argonautica* introduces a number of authority figures whose individual characterizations are fairly static, at least in comparison with the dynamic portraits of Jason and Medea. Taken as a group, however, these characters demonstrate an array of ethical modulations ranging from fair and rational to arrogant and xenophobic. What is more, the moral standing of authority figures is correlated with the narrative duration (and/or frequency) of descriptions of their ritual activity. With the exception of Amycus, the foreign kings in the poem all engage in various kinds of sacrifice and the particular details of these episodes accordingly reflect their respective political temperaments. The more arrogant a given ruler is, the less likely he is to be associated in the narrative with ritual contexts, while extended references to prayer and sacrifice consistently appear in connection with civilized societies. This correlation between ritual practice and the just exercise of power therefore creates a coded system for the denotation of a leader's ethical temper.[23]

EGYPT AND MACEDONIA: THE KING AS PRIEST

The primary religious function of the Egyptian pharaoh was to intercede with the gods on behalf of his mortal subjects. In maintaining "right order" (*maat*) between the world of the gods and the world of men, the pharaoh both accepted cult as a divinity and also presided over sacrifices as a divine intermediary, if not in person then through a surrogate priest.[24] Temple reliefs typically depict the pharaoh in the act of offering to the gods rather than accepting cult offerings himself.[25] There is, however, some evidence

---

[23] For generosity, justice, and mildness of temper as the political virtues associated with the idealized Hellenistic king, see Alders 1975, 21.
[24] Pernigotti 1997, 132–33. See also Finnestad 1997.
[25] Thompson 1988, 135; Winter 1978, 158.

that the Egyptians also imagined their pharaohs as the recipients of sacrifices.[26] Inasmuch as kings in the *Argonautica* offer cult but do not receive it, they are closer to Homeric chieftains than to either the Egyptian pharaohs or the Ptolemies and other Hellenistic rulers. Then, too, kings in the *Argonautica* are portrayed as mortals, although there are several important exceptions: Aeëtes, the son of Helios, is a demi-god,[27] and the Phaeacians are traditionally described as close to divine themselves (ἀγχίθεοι, *Od.* 5.35; see further the discussion of Alcinous below). In fact, the Argonauts themselves are as likely to be divine as the foreign kings they meet, though as I noted in Chapter 1, this point is not very heavily emphasized. At the top of the Argonautic hierarchy are the sons of Zeus, Heracles and the Dioscuri.[28] These three are distinguished from the rest of the Argonauts, a number of whom are identified as the sons of gods (2.1223).[29] The Dioscuri are unique, however, in that they pray to their father on behalf of all the Argonauts at the Eridanus River, are celebrated as gods in their own right (4.592–94), and are honored by their shipmates for safe landing in the Stoechades islands (4.651–53).[30] Though they are not kings, their divine status recalls the multiple cult roles of Egyptian royalty.

---

[26] E.g., a statue of Rameses II (1279–1213) at the temple of Abu Simbel is exceptional in that he is depicted making offerings to himself as a god. The image is a striking illustration of the dual roles played by the pharaoh in the sacrificial system of exchange. See Pernigotti 1997, 133, who notes that the king is seated beside images of the deities to whom the temple is dedicated. On the king's roles as high priest and divine intermediary, see Silverman 1991, 64–65.

[27] Signs of Aeëtes' divinity include the use of the term *menis* to describe his probable anger at Alcinous (4.1205). As noted in Chapter 3, this term is typically reserved for instances of divine anger: the only other instances in the *Argonautica* are Cypris' anger at the Lemnians (1.802) and Zeus's anger at the Aeolids (3.337).

[28] On the worship of the Dioscuri, see n. 141 below. See also Green 1997 *ad* 4.650–54; Fränkel 1968 *ad* 4.650–53. Both heroes are sons of Leda; Polydeuces is said to be the son of Zeus, but he will share his divinity with Castor, the son of Leda's husband, Tyndareus.

[29] Other exceptional Argonauts include Orpheus the famed musician, son of the muse Calliope (1.23–34); the sons of Hermes, the tricksters Erytus and Echion (1.51–52); the prophets Mopsus (son of Ampyx, Niobe's only surviving son, 1.1083) and Idmon, who is a son of Apollo (1.65–68 and 139–45 respectively); the son of Dionysus, the wealthy Phlias (1.115–17); the helmsmen Tiphys (son of the Boeotian Hagnias, 1.105) and Nauplius, both descended from Poseidon (1.105–114 and 133–38); the shape-shifter Periclymenus, a grandson of Poseidon, who endowed him with exceptional strength (1.156–60); the far-sighted Lycaeus (brother of Idas: both were sons of the Messenian king Aphareus), also exceptionally strong; wealthy Augeas, a son of Helios (1.172–75); Euphemus, another son of Poseidon, whose feet skim the water when he runs (1.182–84); the sons of the North Wind, the Boreads, Zetes and Calais, can fly (1.219–23); Erginus and Ancaeus, two more sons of Poseidon, have exceptional knowledge of war and sailing (1.189).

[30] The Dioscuri were patron gods of sailors, and often confused with the Samothracian Gods (so Diod. 4.43.1–2); see discussion of the "Unnamed Gods" above. See also the so-called "Homeric Hymn to the Dioscuri," and Theocr. *Id.* 22.14–22. Cf. Orpheus' calming of the sea (*Argon.* 4.903–9; Philostr. *Imag.* 2.15.1).

The ancient Egyptians "envisioned in their ruler both a being and an office, the former originally mortal and the latter always divine."[31] The divinity conferred by kingship brought with it not only divine antecedents but also the attendant consecration of sacrifices on behalf of all.[32] This exact formulation – mortal being, divine office – may have been somewhat unfamiliar to the new Macedonian rulers, but they quickly put it to use. As king of Egypt Ptolemy was understood to be the son of Helios (Re) and the image of Zeus (Amon), and was assimilated to specific Greek and Egyptian gods like Dionysus and Horus, just as the queens were assimilated to Aphrodite, Isis, and Agatha Tyche ("Good Fortune").[33] Such identifications were Egyptian in character, and yet, as Koenen comments, "the basic thought pattern was not foreign to the Greeks."[34] After all, Callimachus' affirmation that there is nothing on earth more godly (*theioteron*) than the lords of Zeus (*Hymn* 1.80) echoes Hesiod, who proclaimed Zeus the father of kings (ἐκ δὲ Διὸς βασιλῆες, *Theog.* 96). As a divine intermediary the king performed sacrifices that both maintained good relations with the gods and increased the prosperity of his realm. Although kings were said to be allied with Zeus *ex officio*, it was not the case that all kings were equally favored by the gods (Callim. *Hymn* 1.84–86 Pfeiffer ii):

ἐν δὲ ῥυηφενίην ἔμβαλές σφισιν, ἐν δ' ἅλις ὄλβον·
πᾶσι μέν, οὐ μάλα δ' ἶσον. ἔοικε δὲ τεκμήρασθαι
ἡμετέρῳ μεδέοντι· περιπρὸ γὰρ εὐρὺ βέβηκεν.

[Zeus] poured riches upon them,
And prosperity enough. On all, but not
The same amounts. We can infer as much
From our lord's case, for he outstrips them all by far.[35]

It is Ptolemy's exceptional piety that wins greater favor from the gods. The sacred responsibilities of the king are also described in Theocritus' *Idyll* 17, an encomium that praises Philadelphus' conscientiousness regarding the honors due to his divine parents (17.121–27):

---

[31] Silverman 1991, 67.
[32] Cf. the classic analysis of sacrifice by Hubert and Mauss 1964, 9–10: "In sacrifice . . . the consecration extends beyond the thing consecrated; among other objects, it touches the moral person who bears the expense of the ceremony. The devotee who provides the victim which is the object of the consecration is not, at the completion of the operation, the same as he was at the beginning. He has acquired a religious character which he did not have before, or has rid himself of an unfavourable character with which he was affected; he has raised himself to a state of grace or has emerged from a state of sin. In either case he has been religiously transformed."
[33] Koenen 1993, 70.   [34] Koenen 1993, 70.   [35] Tr. Nisetich 2001, 23, 111–15.

Egypt and Macedonia: The king as priest

μοῦνος ὅδε προτέρων τε καὶ ὧν ἔτι θερμὰ κονία
στειβομένα καθύπερθε ποδῶν ἐκμάσσεται ἴχνη,
ματρὶ φίλαι καὶ πατρὶ θυώδεας εἴσατο ναούς·
ἐν δ' αὐτοὺς χρυσῷ περκαλλέας ἠδ' ἐλέφαντι
ἵδρυται πάντεσσιν ἐπιχθονίοισιν ἀρωγούς.
πολλὰ δὲ πιανθέντα βοῶν ὅγε μηρία καίει
μησὶ περπλομένοισιν ἐρευθομένων ἐπὶ βωμῶν.

This man, alone of men of the past and of those whose
Warm footprints still mark the trodden dust, has established fragrant
Shrines to his loving mother and father; within, he has set them
Glorious in gold and ivory to bring aid to all upon the earth.
Many are the fattened thighs of cattle that he burns upon the
Bloodied altars as the passage of months proceeds.[36]

By sponsoring countless sacrifices, in this case to the deified Soter and Berenice I, the king is said to ensure the prosperity of the people, bringing "aid to all upon the earth."

It may be worth pointing out that this formulation of the relation between the king's piety and the riches of Egypt would be more accurate if it were reversed. It is likely that the royal treasury of grain-rich Egypt had, under the management of Cleomenes of Naucratis, Alexander's financial administrator, reaped enormous profits during an international famine at the end of the fourth century.[37] But the wealth that supported Ptolemaic religious festivals like the Ptolemaieia,[38] which included mass sacrifices in honor of the late Ptolemy Soter, derived primarily from the collection of rents and personal poll taxes, such as the salt tax, that were generally considered onerous by the Egyptian community.[39] A late source, Jerome, reports that Philadelphus' annual income amounted to a staggering 14,800 silver talents (*On Daniel* 11.5). So, although the king's respect for the gods was imagined as responsible for the material increase of the land, realistically speaking it was the fiscal coercion of the population that afforded such extravagant displays of royal piety. Such practices are by no means unusual for a monarchic system, but the Ptolemies were unusual inasmuch as their own family members were prominent among the gods who received those displays.

The reality of the state's financial well-being aside, royal piety was not only ideologically linked with strength of the domestic economy, but also

---

[36] Tr. Hunter 2003, 89 (slightly altered). [37] Garnsey 1988, 152.
[38] For scholarly debate regarding the date of the Ptolemaieia, see Chapter 2.
[39] See Thompson 1997, 245 on the early Ptolemaic levy of personal taxes. Thompson notes that by the reign of Ptolemy III Euergetes the burdensome tax rate had been gradually reduced (246).

offered practical leverage at the international level. The Nikouria decree (c. 280), passed by the League of Islanders, an organization that represented the political interests of the Cycladic islands of the southern Aegean, responded to Philadelphus' request that the Ptolemaieia be recognized as the equivalent of the Olympian games.[40] This recognition meant that participating cities would sponsor the attendance of sacred envoys and would additionally finance a golden wreath to honor Philadelphus himself. The decree cited, among other things, Philadelphus' continuing friendship with the islanders and his desire to honor his divine ancestors with a great festival. The festival offered an opportunity not only to celebrate the gods, the royal dynasty, and the current sovereign, but also to promote international goodwill between Egypt and the island cities – even if the League had in fact been under Ptolemaic influence since approximately 286.[41] The league's political subjection notwithstanding, the Nikouria decree exemplifies the interrelation of Ptolemaic cult and politics: indeed, the nature of the Egyptian monarchy rendered the two inseparable, regardless of the geographical distance between the country's religious and political centers.

Religious activity thus served several political ends in Ptolemaic Egypt, much as it had also done for the Macedonian monarchy. Macedonian kings, including Alexander the Great, personally performed the ceremonial duties of high priest in order to represent the community before the gods. Fredricksmeyer here summarizes the duties of the king:

> In the exercise of his religious functions, Alexander was assisted by his (half) brother Arrhidaeus, son of Philip (Curt. 10.7.2), and a staff of experts in supplicating and thanking the gods, divining their will and intentions, purifying from pollution, conducting funerals, and organizing festivals, processions and contests in honor of the gods. Alexander performed most of these functions in accord with the "ancestral tradition" (*patrios nomos*), both on a daily basis (with the first sacrifice at dawn), and at all special events, such as campaigns, battles, victories, escape from dangers, foundations of cities, crossing of rivers and straits, banquets, and so on. Many sacrifices were part of elaborate services, with dedications, as at Ephesus and Tyre, processions, sometimes with the whole army in battle array, races, and literary and athletic contests, preferably at established fields and sanctuaries, as at Dium and Ephesus, but also in the field.[42]

From this description it is apparent that the association of the Egyptian monarchy with cult was consistent with the Macedonian since both

---

[40] *IG* XII 7.506 (= *Syll.* 1:390). See translation by Burstein 1985, 117, no. 92.
[41] On the organization of the League and its relation to the Ptolemies, see Bagnall 1976, 136–41. See also Price 1984, 28–29 on Ptolemaic influence over subject states.
[42] Fredricksmeyer 2003, 256–57.

Egypt and Macedonia: The king as priest

traditions posited a medial role for the king. The main difference between the two systems was that the Argead kings, unlike the Egyptian pharaohs, were traditionally considered divine in genealogical origin only, not in their person or by virtue of their royal office.

Chapter 2 touched on the practical difficulty that such cultural differences posed for Alexander as he assumed the kingship of Egypt and Persia, but his sacrificial practice in foreign territory is of interest to us here because of its connection with the ritual behavior of the Argonauts. This section accordingly surveys, briefly, the similarities between Alexander's sacrifices and those of the Argonauts. These similarities are partly due to a common cultural heritage, but there is also a logistical commonality since in traveling through foreign lands both the Macedonian army and the Argonauts are understood to appease the local gods: the natural or elemental divinities of sky, earth, and water, as well as dead heroes, who have become the chthonic guardians of the lands in which they are buried. What follows is not meant to be a complete catalogue of Alexander's itinerant sacrifices; rather, it is intended primarily to demonstrate ways in which the rituals of the Argonauts are, structurally speaking, more reminiscent of Alexander than they are of Egyptian or Ptolemaic cult – the simplest explanation for this being that the *Argonautica* is, among other things, an epic redaction of Greco-Macedonian colonial expansion.

As his army moved through Asia and northern Africa, Alexander's ritual activity consisted primarily of sacrificing and founding shrines and temples. Heracles and Zeus Amon were among the deities he regularly worshipped (Arr. 6.3.2; cf. 3.28.4; 4.4.1; 7.11.8–9), but he also made offerings to foreign divinities, at least those who represented natural elements or were recognized as the equivalents of Greek gods under different names. During a near-total eclipse of the moon just before the battle of Gaugamela, he made offerings to the "natural" deities, Selene (Moon), Helius (Sun), and Ge (Earth) (Arr. 3.7.6).[43] Alexander likewise obtained divine sanction for water crossings by sacrificing to marine deities (Curt. 3.8.22; 9.9.27): in the middle of the Hellespont he poured a drink offering from a golden bowl and sacrificed a bull to Poseidon and the Nereids (Arr. 1.11.6), and he also poured a libation from a golden bowl into River Hydaspes (Arr. 6.3.1). On another occasion he sacrificed bulls to Poseidon, casting them into the sea together with a libation, a golden cup, and golden bowls in exchange for

---

[43] It has been suggested that Alexander did not sacrifice to non-Greek deities (Fredricksmeyer 2003, 259), but fifth-century Athenians considered Helios and Selene to be barbarian gods (Ar. *Pax* 406–13).

the safe passage of his fleet under the command of Nearchus (Arr. 6.19.5).[44] Jason likewise pours into River Phasis libations of honey and unmixed wine to Ge, the gods of the country, and its dead heroes (2.1271–74),[45] and sacrifices a sheep on board the Argo to Triton, the son of Poseidon, in exchange for safe return to Greece (4.1593–96). Like the eastward direction of the voyage out, these rites of passage reinforce a general parallel with Alexander – without arguing for an exact allegorical identification.

Both Alexander and the Argonauts also make offerings to fallen heroes. At the Hellespont Alexander sacrifices to Protesilaus, the first Achaean hero to die on the plains of Ilium (Arr. 1.11.5), and at Mallos (Antioch) to the diviner Amphilochus, one of the Argive Epigoni, the sons of the seven Argives who joined Polynices' attack on Thebes (Arr. 2.5.9). Because the voyage of Argo predates the Trojan war, the Argonauts honor an earlier generation of heroes in the course of their travels: they offer sacrifice at the tomb of Dolops, the eponymous progenitor of a Thessalian tribe, on the Magnesian coast at the end of the first day of sailing (1.587–88), and to Sthenelus, a companion of Heracles who appears to them at his barrow along the Black Sea coast, just east of the Callichorus River (2.926). As was the case with the initiation of the Dioscuri on Samothrace, the Argonauts are shown to establish precedent for Alexander's celebration of hero cults, even as their ritual practices anachronistically emulate his own.

Finally, there is the Argonauts' foundation of the shrine to Homonoia (2.686–719), the divine abstraction whose thematic importance for the poem is discussed in Chapter 3. The Argonauts' erection of this shrine recalls Alexander's foundation of numerous altars and sanctuaries, such as the temple of Zeus at Sardis (Arr. 1.17.5–6), and those dedicated to Greek gods and to Isis at Alexandria (Arr. 3.1.5), as well as the twelve altars dedicated to the Twelve Olympians on behalf of the twelve parts of the army (Arr. 5.29.1–2). Both the altars of Alexander and those of the Argonauts, his mythic "predecessors," are left behind to imprint the foreign landscape with the signs of Hellenic piety, claiming the land for their gods and so, by implication, for themselves. Of the shrines and altars left by the Argonauts,[46] roughly half are said by the narrator to be preserved to the present day: the temple of Homonoia on the island of Thynie (2.718–19),

---

[44] Cf. the oath of Agamemnon (to Zeus, Helios, and the Furies) that he has not slept with Briseis, which is sealed by the sacrifice of a boar thrown over the side of a ship (*Il.* 19.267f.). This procedure is unusual for oaths (see Burkert 1985, 250–54) and implies a strong desire for safe passage.

[45] See Malkin 1987, 150–52, who cites Jason's libations at the Phasis river and notes that the Scholiast considered this a general custom (see Wendel 1958 *ad* 2.1273).

[46] 1.403–4: altar to Apollo Actius and Embasius at Pagasae; 1.1119–24: shrine to Rhea at Dindymon; 2.531–32: altar to twelve Olympians in Bithynia at home of Phineus; 2.718–19: temple of Concord

the altar to Hecate on the Halys River (4.250–52), the altars to the Fates and the Nymphs on Drepane (4.1217–19), and the altars to Poseidon and at Lake Triton in Libya (4.1620–22). Like Alexander, the Argonauts acknowledge and appease local deities, even as they confirm the Greek presence from the coast of the Black Sea in the east to Drepane in the west and to Libya in the south.

For mythical and historical adventurers alike, sacrifice was necessary to earn the favor of gods who might otherwise prove hostile. Inasmuch as a sacrifice or the foundation of a shrine is a gift that signals honor to the recipient and the donor's worthiness for future compensation, all such offerings enact a ritual formula: *do ut des* ("I give so that you may give").[47] This simple formula reduces sacrifice to a contract for an exchange of services, but the character of the contract changes when new divinities are honored and recognized as part of the pantheon.

At its core, religion shapes the essential forms of community, as Burkert observes, and membership in such communities, from the family to larger civic bodies, is defined by participation in cult.[48] To make an offering to a foreign god, then, implicitly redefines and diminishes the differences between a foreign community and one's own. In this discussion Burkert is thinking of the community as a group of mortal participants and the bond that is created both by the collective sharing of blood guilt in the ritual slaying and eating of an animal and by the exclusion of others, from those unworthy of participation (the accursed, polluted, alien, or otherwise unfit) to the gods themselves, whose division from men dates back to the first sacrifice offered by Prometheus to Zeus.[49] The substance of sacrifice is thus the separation of immortal gods from mortal men: "as between life and death a group of equals assert solidarity in the face of the immortals."[50]

One of the ways in which the *Argonautica* is exceptional, then, is in its representation of the gods as part of this community. While it is true that, in contrast to their Homeric counterparts, the Argonautic gods are physically removed from the mortal sphere (see below), they are no less absorbed in

---

on island of Phoebus of the Dawn; 2.806–10: temple and *temenos* established for Dioscuri by Lycus among the Mariandyni; 2.927–28: altar to Apollo Neossoos at Sthenelus' tomb; 4.246–50: altar to Hecate at mouth of Halys; 4.651–53: altars and rituals in honor of Dioscuri established in Stoechades; 4.1217–19: altars to Fates and Nymphs, erected by Medea on spot sacred to Apollo Nomios on Drepane; 4.1620–22: altars to Poseidon and Triton at harbor of Tritonian lake; 4.1690–91: shrine to Minoan Athena on Crete.

[47] On sacrifice as a gift, see Tylor 1958, 2:462–86: Tylor notes the slippage between sacrifice as a gift to the gods and sacrifice as a prelude to a feast, a ceremonial homage rather than a genuine gift (481); on Prometheus and the burning of thigh bones, see 485–86. For a discussion of the various types of prayer/sacrificial formulae in Homer, see Pulleyn 1997, 4–7.

[48] Burkert 1985, 254–55.   [49] Hes. *Theog.* 535.   [50] Burkert 1985, 255.

the details of the lives of mortals. They are, as one would expect, concerned about the neglect of their honors and the symbolic threat of alienation entailed by such treatment. It is not unusual for gods in either Apollonius or Homer to be angered by cult neglect, but the *Argonautica* alters the typical representation of mortal obligation by recasting the act of offering as a form of diplomatic exchange. This innovation is evident in the stories of the twin tripods given by Apollo to Jason at Delphi (4.529–36). The Argonauts offer the first tripod to the Hylleans in Illyria (4.526–32), who initially plotted against them but eventually decide to aid them, as Jason had hoped (4.405–7), after the death of Apsyrtus.[51] The second is given to the Libyan gods (4.1547–50). Both tripods are apotropaic and will forestall hostile attacks wherever they are set up (4.532–33); hence the Hylleans, who bury theirs near their city, are permanently protected, as is Libya, since Triton is thought to disappear with his into Lake Triton, although it happens so suddenly that none of the Argonauts is certain (4.1590–91).[52] The positive political implication of this detail is that Libya (and by extension Ptolemaic Egypt) cannot be taken by force.

More important, however, is the fact that when Triton first accepts the tripod he immediately offers in return a sacred clod of earth as a "guest gift" (*xeineion*, 4.1555).[53] That the clod is a *divine* guest gift is repeated several times for emphasis: in the lines before Triton's speech: "after he raised up the clod of earth / in hospitality (*xeinia*, 4.1553) and held it out to the heroes,"[54] and again by Jason, who later repeats that Triton personally handed it to Euphemus: "Triton gave you this guest gift (*xeineion*) of the Libyan mainland."[55] Green observes that Jason's emphasis on this point seems "odd – and on the face of it unnecessary," since the god's identity was already well known, but the focus is not on the god's identity but on the fact that the god has offered a guest gift.[56] The respective fates of the tripods accordingly establish a functional parity between diplomatic gifts between ethnic groups and offerings to the gods. Although the offering to Triton remains, at some level, a sacrificial exchange (*do ut des*), the connection

---

[51] So Vian 2002, 3:93, n. 2, contra Fränkel 1968, 500 *ad* 4.524–27.
[52] On the identification of εἴσατο ("was seen") with εἴδομαι rather than ἵεμαι here, see Vian 2002, 3:202, n. 4.1590.
[53] This sacred clod of earth will be revealed as a child of Triton, the future island Thera (modern Santorini); see Green 1997 *ad* 4.1732–64.
[54] 4.1552–53.   [55] 4.1752–53.
[56] Green 1997, 359. Such terms do not appear in connection with gods elsewhere in the *Argonautica*: see 1.770 (Atalanta's gift to Jason), 846 (Lemnian gifts to the Argonauts); 2.31 (Polydeuces' rich robe, a Lemnian gift), 529 (Thynian gifts to the Argonauts); 4.421 (false guest gifts for Apsyrtus), 428 (the robe of Dionysus, Hypsipyle's guest gift to Jason), and 1220 (Phaeacian guest gifts to the Argonauts). In the *Odyssey*, Polyphemus the Cyclops twice tries to deceive Odysseus with offers of guest gifts (9.356, 517), but gods do not offer guest gifts to mortals in Homer.

Egypt and Macedonia: The king as priest

is more immediate and concrete than such exchanges between gods and mortals are in Homeric epic, and as a result the offering to a local deity in a foreign land is reconfigured as a political protocol that is crucial for the foundation and preservation of a new community.

It should come as no surprise that an epic notionally concerned with contact between geographically distinct groups should also examine the hierarchical contact with numinous orders as well. This is especially true in the case of the *Argonautica*, since the line between gods and kings was traditionally somewhat blurred for the ancient Greeks (Chapter 2), and was still more indistinct by the time of the Successors and their heirs. If it makes sense for the god Triton to give a guest gift in the manner of mortals, then it seems no less incongruous for mortals to receive cult in the manner of gods. The mainland Greeks could show their political support for Egypt by honoring the Ptolemies' personal or dynastic cults, by making offerings to another god in their name, or by recognizing and attending festivals like the Ptolemaieia. The politicization of sacrifice thus intensifies with the divinization of kings, as the favor of foreign gods and rulers alike can be won with a show of pious observance.

Divinity, in other words, was increasingly awarded as a sign of political merit and family connections. The Athenian celebration of Demetrius Poliorcetes in 307/6 nicely illustrates the point. In return for dislodging Cassander's forces from the city, Demetrius and his father Antigonus the One-Eyed were awarded golden statues, honorary crowns, an altar dedicated to them as the Saviors, annual games in their honor, and the addition of two new tribes (Demetrias and Antigonis) to the ten tribes originally established by Cleisthenes (Diod. 20.46.2). As the liberator of Athens, Demetrius soon overshadowed his father and received unprecedented recognition by the people,[57] who proclaimed Demetrius to be a king and a god. The association of divine honors with kingship was becoming expected – the rise of ruler cult meant that such displays were part of the public recognition of a monarch, even in democratic Athens.[58]

At the heart of such honors, whether offered to kings or to gods, is the expectation of continued benefactions. The preservation of peaceful relations with the powerful, both mortal and divine, is a form of *homonoia*, one of the main concerns of characters in the *Argonautica*, like the birth of a successor, or the representation of diplomacy as a preferable alternative to aggression. This preference is less a rejection of a martial ethos than an embrace of an ideology that posits political authority in divine terms (and vice versa). And, finally, if kings and heroes are modeled on the gods, it

---

[57] See Mikalson 1998, 75–104.   [58] Mikalson 1998, 101.

is telling that the gods of the *Argonautica* do not go openly to war: they scheme, like Hera; they ordain, like Zeus; and they ambush, like Eros. The best way to win them over is to offer prayers and sacrifice, for force of arms will not always carry the day. So it is that conciliation, rather than combat, comes to hold pride of place in a heroic epic.

EPIC MODALITIES: SACRIFICE

Thirty sacrifices, libations, and offerings are specifically described in the *Argonautica*, and there are in addition eight implied or possible sacrifices (see Tables 5.1 and 5.2). Most of the thirty explicit sacrifices are performed by one or more of the Argonauts; the others include Pelias' sacrifice to nearly all the Olympians (1.12–14), Circe's purification of Jason and Medea (4.704–17), the wedding celebration on Drepane (4.1185–86), and three hospitality feasts: on Lemnos for the Argonauts (1.858–60), at Aeëtes' palace for the sons of Phrixus (3.270–74), and on Drepane for the Argonauts (4.994–95). Lycus' welcome feast for the Argonauts presumably entailed numerous sacrifices as well, but they are implied rather than explicitly described.[59]

Before I examine more closely the political and diplomatic aspects of sacrifice in the *Argonautica*, a brief comparison with Homeric sacrifice will help to clarify what is innovative in the later work. Apollonius' representations of sacrifice allude to and at the same time differ from those of archaic epic, in terms of scale and occasion as well as of dramatic function and perspective. Whereas cattle sacrifices predominate in both Homeric epics,[60]

---

[59] The remaining implicit or possible sacrifices are performed by the Argonauts: the initiation on Samothrace (1.915–18), the thank-offering to the Dioscuri for safe landing (4.651–53), a meal (4.883), an offering to Poseidon and Triton in Libya (4.1620–22), three of the four funerals (2.854–57; 4.1499–501, 1534–36). See Table 5.2.

[60] Of the sacrifices actually performed, sheep (12) run a close second to cattle sacrifices (17). Performed sacrifices: *Il.* 1.315–16 (bulls and goats); 2.402–29 (ox); 3.271–94 (two lambs); 7.313–22 (ox), 466 (oxen); 8.545–50 (oxen and sheep); 19.250–66 (boar); 23.29–34 (oxen, sheep, goats, pigs); 23.165–77 (cattle, sheep, horses, dogs, Trojans); 24.621–26 (sheep); *Od.* 3.1–66 (bulls), 417–63 (heifer); 8.59–62 (sheep, pigs, oxen); 9.44–45 (sheep and cattle), 154–65 (goats), 231–32 (lambs), 547–55 (sheep); 10.180–84 (stag), 517–37; 11.23–36 (ram to Hades, ewe to Persephone); 12.353–65, 395–96, 396–98 (Cattle of the Sun); 13.24–27 (ox), 181–83 (bulls); 14.26–28 (pigs), 81 (pigs), 414–438 (pigs); 16.453–54 (sow); 17.178–82 (sheep, goats, ox, pigs), 19.420–23 (ox), 20.248–55 (sheep, goats, ox, pigs), 24.214–16 (pigs). Meals without sacrifice mentioned: *Il.* 9.65–92, 206–22; *Od.* 4.1–19; 10.56–57, 180–84, 371–79, 467–68; 11.410–11; 12.30; 15.77, 97–98; 16.49–50.

Remembered sacrifices: *Il.* 2.305–6, 400; 11.726–28 (bulls and cow), 771–75 (ox); *Od.* 4.351–55, 475–80 (Menelaus' hecatombs, incomplete and complete); 13.349–50 (Odysseus' complete hecatombs); 19.420–77 (Autolycus' bull). Promised sacrifices: *Od.* 10.522–25 (ram and cow); 11.131 (= 23.278) (ram, bull, boar).

Libations: *Il.* 9.171–76, 713; 16.225–32; 24.286–316. *Od.* 2.431–34; 3.330–41; 7.164–65, 179–84; 15.149; 18.425–28; 21.263–73.

Line numbers	Offering	Recipient	Type	Location
1.12–14	Pelias' offering	Poseidon and Olympians	Festival	Iolchus
1.406–36	**Jason**'s two bulls: sacrificed by **Heracles, Ancaeus**; **Jason** prays	Apollo Actius and Apollo Embasius	Propitiation for safe embarkation	Shore of Pagasae
1.516–17	Ox tongues (group offering)	Zeus	Propitiation	Shore of Pagasae
1.587–88	Sheep (group offering)	Dolops	Hero cult	Aphetae, coast of Magnesia
1.858–60	Unspecified	Immortals, esp. Hephaestus and Aphrodite	Lemnian welcome	Lemnos Island, N. Aegean
1.966–67	Sheep provided by **Cyzicus** (group offering)	Ecbasian Apollo	Thanks for safe landing; Cyzicus' welcome	Cyzicus Island, Propontis
1.1124, 1140	Unspecified victims offered by group; **Jason** pours libations	Rhea	Propitiation for favorable winds	Mt. Dindymum, Cyzicus Island
1.1186	Unspecified (group offering)	Ecbasian Apollo	Thanks for safe landing	Cyzicus Island
2.156–57	Bebrycian sheep	Immortals	Meal	Gulf of Olbia
2.291–94	Libation of Styx water; Iris swears Harpies will not return	Styx	Oath	Floating/Turning Islands west of Greece or Italy

(*cont.*)

Table 5.1 (cont.)

Line numbers	Offering	Recipient	Type	Location
2.302–3	Bebrycian sheep	Unspecified	Meal	Thynia
2.490–95	Paraebius' two sheep; **Jason** and **Boreads** participate	Manteion Apollo	Meal	Thynia
2.531–33	Unspecified victims (group offering)	Twelve Immortals	Embarkation	Thynia
2.698–704	Wild game offered by group at **Orpheus'** request	Apollo of the Dawn	Thanks for safe landing; song and dance	Thynias Island, Black Sea coast
2.714–19	Libations	Homonoia	Oath of mutual aid and friendship	Thynias Island
2.839–40	Countless sheep	Idmon	Funeral	Lycus' palace
2.925–26	Libations and sheep (group offering)	Sthenelus	Hero cult	Tomb, east of River Lycus
2.927–28	Thigh bones of sheep at **Mopsus'** request; **Orpheus** dedicates lyre	Apollo Neossoos	Propitiation	East of River Lycus; location now known as Lyra
2.1169–70	Sheep (group offering)	Ares	Thanks for safe landing	Ares Island

2.1271–75	Honey and wine libations: **Jason** pours into river	Earth, native gods, souls of local heroes	Propitiation for safe landing and passage	River Phasis
3.270–74	Bull	Not mentioned	Welcome feast for the sons of Phrixus	Aeëtes' palace in Aea
3.1200–24	Ewe: **Jason** offers	Hecate	Propitiation	Colchian meadow
4.246–52	Unspecified: at **Medea**'s request	Hecate	Propitiation	Halys River
4.704–17	Suckling piglet; libations, cakes	Zeus the Cleanser; Erinyes	Purification and propitiation	Aeaea, Tyrrhenian Sea
4.994–95	Unspecified victims	Unspecified gods	Phaeacian welcome	Drepane, coast of Epirus
4.1129	Sheep	Unspecified god	Wedding	Drepane, Cave of Macris
4.1185–86	Ram, heifer, etc. (Phaeician offerings)	Hera, other unspecified gods	Wedding; hospitality	Drepane
4.1547–50; cf. 4.526–32	Second tripod of Apollo: at **Orpheus**' request	Libyan gods, Apollo	Propitiation for safe passage	Lake Triton, Libya
4.1593–602	Sheep: **Jason** prays, sacrifices, throws victim overboard	Triton	Propitiation for safe passage	Lake Triton, Libya
4.1719–20	Water offered by group	Apollo Aegletes	Thanks for safe landing	Anaphe Island, Aegean Sea

Table 5.2 *Implied sacrifices in the* Argonautica

Line numbers	Offering	Recipient	Type	Location
1.915–18	Not mentioned	"Unknown Gods"	Initiation	Samothrace
2.760–61	Not mentioned	Not mentioned	Welcome feast	Lycus' palace
2.854–57	Not mentioned	Tiphys	Funeral	Lycus' palace
4.651–53	Not mentioned	Not mentioned: altars and rites for Dioscuri	Thanks for safe landing	Stoechades Islands
4.883	Not mentioned	Not mentioned	Evening meal	Shore of Aeaea
4.1499–501	Not mentioned	Canthus	Funeral	Lake Triton
4.1534–36	Not mentioned	Mopsus	Funeral	Lake Triton
4.1620–22	Not mentioned; altars still there	Poseidon and Triton	Propitiation for safe passage	Lake Triton

sheep sacrifices are much more frequent in the *Argonautica*,[61] with thirteen sheep sacrifices in contrast to five sacrifices of other animals (three of cattle, one of wild game, and one piglet), five libations, and inanimate offerings.[62] Sheep sacrifices predominate because the Argonauts acquire flocks after

[61] Sheep sacrifices: sheep joints to Dolops (1.587–88); sheep from Cyzicus to Ecbasian Apollo (1.966–67); sheep sacrifice to immortals (2.156–57) with Bebrycian plunder (2.143–44); to unspecified gods (2.302–3); two sheep from Paraebius to Manteion Apollo (2.491–94); countless sheep at the funeral of Idmon (2.839–40); to Sthenelus (2.926); to Apollo Neossoos (2.927–28); to Ares (2.1169–70); ewe (brought by Argus the son of Phrixus) to Hecate (3.1200–24); sheep at entrance to Macris' cave (4.1129); a Phaeacian ram to an unspecified god, probably Hera (4.1185); and to Triton (4.1596).

[62] Two oxen are sacrificed at Pagasae (1.406–36), a bull in Colchis (3.270–74), and a heifer on Drepane (4.1185–86). Wild game are offered to Phoebus Apollo (2.698–704), and a nursing piglet to Zeus the Purifier (4.704–17). Other offerings: Iris pours a libation of Styx water (2.291–94); the Argonauts pour libations to Homonoia (2.714–19); they pour libations to Sthenelus and Orpheus dedicates his lyre (2.925–28); Jason pours a libation of honey and unmixed wine to Gaia, the Colchian gods, and the souls of dead heroes (2.1271–75); they offer a tripod from Delphi to the Libyan gods (4.1547–50);

the defeat of Amycus and as a result of the hospitality of Lycus (2.143–44, 839–40), but sheep are also more realistic since they could be transported on a ship more easily than cattle, and in any event were more common in ancient Greek practice.[63]

A second variation lies in the narrative frequency of sacrifice. Lengthy descriptions of sacrifice bring out dominant themes in both Homeric poems. In *Iliad* 1, the hecatomb sacrifice to Apollo ends the plague caused by Agamemnon's impious arrogance (1.446–76). Similarly, in *Odyssey* 3 the equitable distribution of the hecatomb to Poseidon between the nine settlements of Pylos contrasts strongly with the political imbalance Telemachus has left behind in Ithaca, where the Suitors contribute nothing to their daily feasts. Generally speaking, the *Odyssey* provides a fairly consistent record of the daily sacrifices associated with the meals of the main characters, whereas the *Iliad* tends to omit the sacrifices that would normally precede daily meals, employing descriptions of ritual slaughter to punctuate episodes of dramatic importance.

Books 1 and 2 of the *Argonautica* are therefore closer to the *Odyssey* inasmuch as they follow a more or less realistic pattern. The narrator marks the Argo's progress with a fairly inclusive record of sacrifices at landings and embarkations, funerals, purifications, celebrations of thanksgiving, as well as simple meals. In Book 1, there are eight explicit sacrifices, with one implicit in the initiation in the mystery cult of the "Unknown Gods" of Samothrace (1.915–18). Book 2 has more sacrifices (twelve explicit and two implicit) than the other books, with a reference occurring every hundred lines or so, even more frequently in several cases. These regular reports are largely restricted, however, to stops on the outward voyage, and gaps in the chronology remain, even in Books 1 and 2, since reports of sacrifice diminish during lengthy stays as on Lemnos (five days) or Drepane.[64]

Sacrifices are fewer and farther between, however, in Book 3 and on the return in Book 4. During the three-day sojourn in Colchis there are only two sacrifices, neither of which is connected with the Argonauts' meals: Colchian servants prepare a bull sacrifice upon the return of the

---

cf. the gift of the other tripod to the Hylleans, 4.526–32); and water libations to Apollo (4.1719–20). There are six other blood sacrifices in which the victim is not specified (1.858–60, 1124, 1186; 2.531–33; 4.246–52, 994–95). Of the eight implicit sacrifices, no victims are mentioned (see Table 5.2).

[63] Burkert 1985, 55: "The most noble sacrificial animal is the ox, especially the bull; the most common is the sheep, then the goat and the pig; the cheapest is the piglet." See also Rosivach 1994, 95–99 for various fifth- and fourth-century calendar budgets for sacrificial victims: the price of an ox ranged from 40–90 dr., sheep 10–17 dr., goat 10–12 dr., adult swine 20–40 dr., piglet 3 dr. Incidentally, the Argonauts would have required several sheep for a meal; Sancisi-Weerdenburg 1995, 293 estimates that one sheep would serve approximately ten persons (for a normal meal among Persian workers).

[64] Apollodorus 1.9.26 estimates four months for the entire voyage; see Green 1997 *ad* 1.861–62.

sons of Phrixus (3.270–74), and Jason sacrifices a sheep to propitiate Hecate (3.1201–24). In the first half of Book 4, the chronology of the Argo's landings is sketchy and, after Medea's propitiatory offering to Hecate at the mouth of the Halys (4.246–47), the chronology of sacrifice is equally vague.[65] In fact, explicit references are missing from the trip along the Eridanus River until Circe's purification sacrifice of Jason and Medea (4.704–17), and no sacrifices for communal feasts are described at all until the landing on Drepane.[66] The heroes lose their collective appetite at the Eridanus River (4.619–20), where the corpse of Phaethon casts a pall that apparently lingers even after Circe purifies Jason and Medea (4.704–17). It may be that we are meant to imagine the Argonauts as not eating – or at least not eating meat – during this entire period,[67] which would have lasted for weeks, but in any event the avoidance of descriptions of sacrifice augments the impression of desolation experienced by them at this time.

There is an implied sacrifice in the fourth book, when the Argonauts set up altars to thank the Dioscuri for their safe arrival in the Stoechades islands (4.651–53).[68] That the Argonauts choose to honor the Dioscuri for their safe landing rather than Apollo, to whom they offer thanks in earlier books (1.966–67, 1186; 2.698–704; 4.1719–20; cf. 2.1169–70), is not improbable, given their contemporary cult (see above). But the emphasis on the Dioscuri instead of Apollo at this particular time also effectively conveys the extremity of their psychological isolation from the Olympian gods, which continues until their welcome by the Phaeacians on Drepane. At that point descriptions of communal sacrifices and divine encounters once again begin to proliferate, reaching a peak comparable to the rate of Book 2, with six explicit sacrifices (4.994–95, 1129, 1185–86, 1547–50, 1593–602, 1719–20) and three implicit (4.1499–501, 1534–36, 1620–22). Two of

---

[65] See Green 1997 *ad* 4.629–44; the geography in this section, as elsewhere in Book 4, is unreliable.
[66] The all-night fires burning at the beginning of Book 4 (4.68–69) could suggest a sacrifice of some kind, but because there is no mention of an offering, a feast, or an extant altar, this passage has not been included in the list of implicit sacrifices. Circe sacrifices a piglet to purify Jason and Medea at 4.704–17; altars remain from an implied sacrifice to the Dioscuri in the Stoechades islands (4.651–53). The Argonauts give one of Apollo's tripods to the Hylleans at 4.529–31, but this is a gift of guest friendship rather than an offering to the gods.
[67] The Argonauts leave Colchis on the morning of their fourth day there; they sail for forty-eight hours to the Halys River, where Medea sacrifices to Hecate. The narrator does not indicate how long it took them to sail across the Black Sea or to travel along the Ister between Thrace and Scythia to the Brygeian Islands in the Adriatic (a route that does not, as it happens, actually exist). In short, the Argonauts spend an unspecified amount of time traveling as far as the southern coast of Gaul in the Mediterranean (Marseilles), and the chronology does not become secure again until their landing on Aeaea (4.659).
[68] There is also another possible sacrifice when they prepare their meal after the purification at Aeaea (4.883).

these implied sacrifices are funerals (Canthus and Mopsus), which cannot be reckoned happy events, but even so their occurrence in quick succession (4.1499–1501, 1534–36) recalls the sacrificial pattern established earlier in Book 2 (cf. the funerals for Idmon at 2.839–40 and Tiphus at 2.854–57). That is, the frequency of the Argonauts' sacrifices in the second half of Book 4 connotes a recovery of the good relations with the gods that they enjoyed until the fatal encounter with Apsyrtus.

Another difference between the Argonautic and the Homeric representations of sacrifice that concerns us here is a change in narrative perspective, a shift away from the point of view of Homeric epic, which often reveals the gods' reactions to sacrifice. This omniscient perspective allows the audience to witness the gods' unpredictability and to appreciate by turns both how influential and how futile mortal offerings may be.[69] It is generally true that, as Feeney shows,[70] the Homeric gods are more accessible than those of the *Argonautica*, but at the same time mortals in the Homeric poems tend to mistrust the efficacy of sacrifice. Odysseus, for example, wrongly suspects that Zeus was unmoved by his sacrifice of Polyphemus' ram (*Od.* 9.553–55).[71] Of course, the audience already knows that Odysseus is one of Zeus's favorites, for as he tells Athena early in the poem, he could not forget a man who has offered so many sacrifices to him (1.65–67). But the point is that the loyalties of the gods are occasionally divided, and while human characters know it is a good idea to offer many sacrifices, they are also aware that the gods reserve the right to disregard them.

The *Odyssey* focuses primarily on the problem of misappropriated sacrifice: the offering of animals that belong to someone else, like the herds of Odysseus, the Cattle of the Sun or even, arguably, the flocks of the Cyclops, while the unpredictability of the gods and the related theme of rejected sacrifice receive greater attention in the *Iliad*. The gods are polarized by the war between the Trojans and the Achaeans, and their loyalties are deeply divided by mortal politics. They continue to hear prayers and accept sacrifices,[72] and they are displeased when they do not receive

---

[69] On the one hand, Athena hears Penelope's prayer (*Od.* 4.761–67), and Zeus responds with thunder to Odysseus' prayer for the destruction of the Suitors (*Od.* 20.95–104). On the other hand, Zeus refuses the mutual prayer – Achaean and Trojan – to destroy those who do not honor the oath regarding the duel between Paris and Menelaus (*Il.* 3.302). For more examples of rejected prayers in Homer, see below.

[70] Feeney 1991, 69–80.

[71] Odysseus' misfortunes are actually due to Poseidon, who is enraged at the blinding of his son Polyphemus (*Od.* 1.68–75).

[72] Apollo hears Chryses' prayers twice, *Il.* 1.43 and 474; Apollo hears Pandarus' prayer, 4.119–20; Apollo hears Meriones promise a hecatomb and therefore helps him in the competition, 23.872–81; Zeus sends an eagle as an omen to Priam, 24.306–20.

what they consider their due.[73] But they are also blithely untroubled by their biases: Athena, for example, ignores the Trojan Theano's offer of twelve heifers to defeat the Greek Diomedes, who happens to be one of her favorites (6.304–11).[74] Even when they show their favor, it may be returned in unexpected ways: Hector's many sacrifices will not save his life, but his piety does win the protection of his body after his death.[75] Zeus's sympathy for the Trojans (3.302; 4.48–49), on the other hand, not only puts him at odds with Hera and Athena but also complicates his relations with the Achaeans. He accepts an ox sacrifice from Agamemnon but will not allow the king to kill Hector (2.420), and grants only one of Achilles' two wishes regarding Patroclus' return to battle (16.225–50).

This dysfunctional system of exchange between mortals and gods is a variation on the breakdown in the social hierarchy that has led to Achilles' public dishonor. Just as rich sacrifices cannot ensure the support of the gods, so deeds of valor cannot guarantee *time*: both systems have foundered under the crippling weight of the war. In the *Argonautica* the social distribution of *time* among heroes does not dominate the narrative, nor does the desire for recognition consume the Argonauts as it does the Homeric heroes. Certainly the poem begins with the narrator's announcement that he will relate the famous deeds (*klea*) of heroes who lived long ago (παλαιγενέων κλέα φωτῶν, 1.1), and most of the Argonauts join because they, like Acastus (who was forbidden to sail by his father King Pelias), do not want to miss the greatest adventure of their day.[76] But in the *Argonautica* the Iliadic *kleos* won by individual warriors through slaughter is overshadowed by the *kleos* of Odyssean survival. The Argonauts are bound together by the hope of a safe return (1.336) – not to perish, nameless and obscure (νώνυμνοι καὶ ἄφαντοι, 4.1306), in the wastelands of Libya or the trackless sea (4.1305–7; cf. 2.607–10). As a consequence of this emphasis on the *kleos* of a communal *nostos*, the

---

[73] Most notably, Poseidon is angered at the building of the Achaean wall without a sacrifice (*Il.* 7.449–50); also Artemis remembers that she did not receive the first-fruits sacrifice from Oineus (9.530). During Patroclus' funeral games Teucer fails to promise Apollo a sacrifice of first-born lambs and therefore misses his target, though Apollo's reaction to the omission is not mentioned (23.863–65).

[74] In a disputed passage the gods similarly refuse the sacrifice of the Trojans because Ilium is hateful to them (8.550–52). The passages at *Il.* 8.548 and 550–52 are bracketed because they do not appear in any manuscript of the *Iliad*; they are, however, quoted as being from Homer in [Plato] *Second Alcibiades*. They were evidently added to the text by an early editor, and have been removed by most of his successors. The lines are not in themselves objectionable, except for the uncertainty of their attestation, but whether or not they truly "belong," they clearly illustrate the problem of rejected sacrifice in the *Iliad*.

[75] Zeus laments Hector who burned many thigh pieces for him (22.170–72); Apollo reminds the gods of Hector's many sacrifices (24.33–34); he also observes that Hector was dear to the gods and that he himself loved him because his sacrifices were always pleasing (24.67–70).

[76] On the ambition of Heracles in particular, see Chapter 3.

poem celebrates the peaceful virtues of *homonoia* and the preservation of the social status quo. The disproportionate desire for personal *kleos* that drives a demi-god like Heracles inevitably distances him from the Argonauts, but in the end their social bonds are strong enough to compensate for his loss.

Such stability in the mortal sphere goes hand in hand with predictability in the realm of the divine. The gods may well be unknowable and removed from the world of mortals, but they are not shown to be unreliable in the way that the Homeric gods are. They do not refuse sacrifices or fail to grant requests: the enactment of the ritual is all that is required to obtain their favor. Admittedly, even references to positive divine reactions are comparatively infrequent: a rare example is the offering to Rhea, who shows her acceptance of the Argonauts' sacrifice through a supernatural abundance of fruit, flowers, tamed animals, and a new spring (1.1140–49). But like Triton's acceptance of the tripod and his reciprocal offer of the clod of earth (4.1554–55), Rhea's response is apparent both to the Argonauts and the reader: the narrator does not indicate the reaction of the god without the knowledge of the poem's human characters.[77]

This shift toward divine reliability is arguably related, at least in part, to the ideology of ruler cult. Hellenistic monarchs encouraged ritual offerings because the act of offering was a demonstration of political support and allegiance. At issue is not the gods' response to sacrifice (which is assumed to be favorable), but the act of offering sacrifice in the first place. The *Argonautica* replaces the Iliadic theme of rejected sacrifice with an emphasis on the mortal responsibility for satisfying the demands of *themis*: that which is traditionally expected or customarily understood to belong to the gods. To avoid Hera's enmity Pelias did not need to pay her exceptional honor, but it was certainly incumbent on him to include her in a collective sacrifice dedicated to Poseidon and other Olympians (*Argon*. 1.13–14). Then again, perhaps it was not. I am thinking here of the roster of the Twelve Gods, which was much less stable than one might assume. The canonical Twelve were represented on the Parthenon frieze, but among the many regional variants there is a Thessalian monument found at Pherae (dated *c*. late fourth/early third century) that names six goddesses, Themis, Aphrodite, Athena, Enodia (= Artemis), Demeter, and Histia (= Hestia), presumably

---

[77] As Nelis 2001b, 195–97 points out, Rhea's anger at the Argonauts parallels Zeus's anger in Book 4, although the reaction of the latter to the requisite purification is neither known to the Argonauts nor described to the audience. Nelis compares the miasma incurred by the Argonauts as a result of Cyzicus' death with the pollution caused by Apsyrtus' ambush, and also notes that the unexpected winds that blow the Argo off course after the ambush serve as Virgil's model for the storms that disrupt the Trojan ships in *Aeneid* 5, after the death of Dido.

the counterparts of a set of six male gods.[78] Hera is here replaced by Themis as Zeus's consort (Hes. *Theog.* 901–6), a substitution that, while atypical, nevertheless suggests at the very least that her sensitivity was not without some justification.[79] In any case, Pelias' disrespect provokes a divine wrath akin to that of Achilles, especially in light of the hero's supernatural strength and divine heritage. Yet Hera's anger diverges from Achilles' famous *menis* most importantly because she neither rejects nor calls into question the social hierarchy. On the contrary, she reifies it as an object lesson: honor the gods (*all* of them), or suffer the consequences. In sum, the sacrificial system of exchange works, more or less, in the *Iliad*, the *Odyssey*, and the *Argonautica*, but each epic also draws attention to inherent weaknesses and types of unreliability, either on the part of the gods, who may reject a sacrifice, or on the part of mortals, who may fail to make an offering or misappropriate their victims.

BULLIES, LIARS, ALLIES, AND ARBITERS

This section considers in greater detail the reception of the Argonauts by foreign kings and the strategic and symbolic role of sacrificial rituals during these encounters. In the *Argonautica* the correlation of justice and ritual practice functions as an index of what are posited as the primary political virtues: diplomacy and restraint. Those kings who prefer compromise to confrontation tend to appear in ritual contexts, and are therefore set apart from those who are unjust, aggressive toward strangers, and unconcerned with sacrifice to the gods. To understand this association of cult with civilized, politically stable communities, I draw on the sociological view of sacrifice as a system of exchange that organizes society by erecting a hierarchy of superior gods and inferior mortals.[80] With respect to the *Argonautica*, the inclusion of ritual in a particular episode gives the impression that a given community cultivates the rule of law – in other words, that it defines and sustains social relations, even with outsiders, through the exchange of honors and benefactions.

Conversely, societies in which sacrifice is depicted as imperfect or compromised in some way are implicitly unbalanced, and liable to be governed

---

[78] See Long 1987, 205–6 with fig. 75.
[79] It is worth noting that Hera was evidently included in Alexandrian representations of the Twelve; Long 1987, 224–27.
[80] See William Robertson Smith's influential book, *Lectures on the Religion of the Semites: The Fundamental Institutions*, which was originally published in 1889, as well as the work of Émile Durkheim, best known for *The Elementary Forms of the Religious Life*, published in 1915. For an introduction to the early theoretical schools, see Bell 1997, 1–60.

through coercion, subterfuge, and intimidation. In fact, Pelias' collective sacrifice is characterized as problematic, as I have observed, because Pelias "ignored [*ouk alegizen*] Pelasgian Hera" (1.14). As king, Pelias is held responsible for decisions regarding sacrificial practice, and it is his personal decision to withhold the honors owed to the goddess.[81] From a technical point of view this omission can be seen as a plot device to account for Hera's enmity toward him, but at a deeper level it also characterizes Pelias' rule as unjust. Thus, while righteous kings rely on sacrifice as a socially constructive ritual that promotes and restores harmonious relations between gods, citizens, and foreigners, sacrifice is avoided, neglected, or otherwise deemphasized by rulers understood as unjust and hostile.

Although a number of monarchs are mentioned in the poem, I consider only those whose interaction with the Argonauts is significant:[82] Pelias (Iolcus); Hypsipyle (Lemnos); Cyzicus (who rules the Doliones on the island of Cyzicus); Amycus (who rules the Bebrycians in Bithynia); Phineus (formerly a king in Thrace); Lycus (ruler of the Mariandyni in Bithynia); Aeëtes (Colchis); Alcinous (ruler of the Phaeacians on the island of Drepane). Most of these kings welcome the Argonauts and are more than willing to lend them aid, whereas Pelias, Amycus, and Aeëtes display impiety, aggression, and treachery, respectively. I begin with Alcinous, focusing on his understanding of justice, especially in contrast to the rule of Aeëtes, before going on to examine the Argonauts' interaction with the six remaining kings.

Alcinous and Aeëtes

Analysis of the Phaeacian monarchy in Chapter 4 focused on Arete's private influence on Alcinous; here I attend to the king's role as a public arbiter in the *neikos* (4.1010, 1103) between the Greeks and the Colchians. As Knight points out, Apollonius seems to have intentionally altered the Homeric description of Alcinous from θεοειδής ("god-like," *Od.* 7.231) to θεουδής

---

[81] Cf. Chapter 2, on the tragic misfortunes of those rulers who promoted the cult of the Twelve Gods. From this perspective, the collective nature of Pelias' sacrifice could in itself be problematic.

[82] Other kings mentioned include: Admetus, king of Pherae (1.49); Eurystheus, king of Mycenae and Tiryns (1.130, 1317, 1347); Neleus, king of Pylos (1.156, 158); Thoas, Hypsipyle's father, deposed king of the Lemnians (1.620–25); Antiope and Otrere, queens of Amazons (2.387); Lycaon, a king of Arcadia (2.521); Orchomenus, king of Orchomenus, son of Minyas (2.654, 1093, 1186); Hippolyte, queen of Amazons (2.779, 968, 999); the king of the Mossynoeci (2.1026–29); Cadmus, king of Thebes (3.1179, 1186; 4.517); Minos, king of Crete (3.1000, 1100); Hyllus, son of Heracles and king of the Hylleans on the eastern coast of the Adriatic (4.537–51); Nausithous, predecessor of Alcinous (4.539, 547); Aeolus, king of the winds (4.764, 765, 778, 820); and Nycteus, king of Thebes, father of Antiope (4.1090).

("god-fearing," *Argon.* 4.1123).[83] The latter term appears several times in the *Odyssey* (not in the *Iliad*, see LSJ *s.v.*), often in the formula used in regard to the mores of unfamiliar peoples. Odysseus uses the term as he speculates about the Phaeacians, having just been awakened by the cries of Nausicaa and her handmaids (6.120–21): "Are they arrogant, savage, and unjust, or do they welcome strangers with god-fearing intent?"[84] In the *Argonautica* by contrast, the nature of the Phaeacians is immediately apparent from the moment the Argonauts land on Drepane. Everyone greets them with joyful celebration, and the Argonauts themselves are as delighted as if they had already come home (4.994–1000):

> Οἱ δ' ἀγανῇσιν
> Ἀλκίνοος λαοί τε θυηπολίῃσιν ἰόντας
> δειδέχατ' ἀσπασίως, ἐπὶ δέ σφισι καγχαλάασκε
> πᾶσα πόλις· φαίης κεν ἑοῖς ἐπὶ παισὶ γάνυσθαι.
> Καὶ δ' αὐτοὶ ἥρωες ἀνὰ πληθὺν κεχάροντο,
> τῷ ἴκελοι οἷον τε μεσαιτάτῃ ἐμβεβαῶτες
> Αἱμονίῃ.

> Alcinous and his people gladly welcomed their arrival with
> Propitiatory sacrifices, and the whole city celebrated:
> You would say they were exulting in their own children.
> The heroes themselves were rejoicing in throng,
> As though they had landed in the heart of Thessaly, the land
> Of Haemon.

Unlike the Homeric Phaeacians (whose response to Odysseus' arrival must be carefully managed by Alcinous and Arete as well as by Athena and Nausicaa), the Argonautic Phaeacians are pious and hospitable, spontaneously joining in with the royal celebration. They claim descent from the Titan Uranus (4.991–92), and have inherited an island of ancient fertility that is sacred to the gods, as the narrator explains in an aetiological account of the two theories regarding the origin of the island.[85] Alcinous' prime attribute, his "god-fearing" (θεουδής) nature, is thus a distinguishing characteristic of all the Phaeacians. But because of Alcinous' position as king, his respect for Zeus plays a crucial role. As he explains to Arete, he is unable to protect Medea by forcing the Colchians to leave because he fears the "straight

---

[83] Knight 1995, 247.
[84] 6.120–21 = 9.175–76 = 13.201–2: ἦ ῥ' οἵ γ' ὑβρισταί τε καὶ ἄγριοι οὐδὲ δίκαιοι, / ἦε φιλόξεινοι, καί σφιν νόος ἐστὶ θεουδής;
[85] The narrator explains that the island is said to be sickle-shaped either because of its association with the instrument used by Cronus against Uranus (4.982–86) or because of its association with the reaping hook of chthonian Demeter (4.986–91).

Bullies, liars, allies, and arbiters 169

justice" of Zeus (*diken itheian*, 4.1100). Justice towards mortals (including foreigners) is synonymous with piety towards the gods: in effect, to be "god-fearing" is to be just. The motivation behind Alcinous' peaceful intervention in this *neikos* is the direct result of his pious regard for "straight justice," a concept which I discuss further below.

Alcinous' arbitration in the Colchian *neikos* is framed in idealistic terms, but from a political perspective it is also realistic inasmuch as it mirrors the practice of third-party mediation in international disputes by Hellenistic kings.[86] The ancient Greeks traditionally relied on arbitration in the resolution of conflict.[87] The practice of intervention by third-party mediators became more widespread, however, in the Hellenistic period.[88] Interstate arbitration on mainland Greece, the islands, and in western Asia Minor generally addressed debt, property disputes, or loan and contract settlements, with teams of dicasts or individual judges invited from one city to another, often to handle an overload of cases. In fact, Hellenistic kings themselves also became involved in the mediation of international disputes. For example, one of the Antigonids mediated between the Locrian cities in regard to the lapsed Locrian maiden tribute to Troy.[89] In 287 Lysimachus settled hostilities between Magnesia and Priene,[90] and four years later he intervened in a land dispute between Priene and Samos.[91] Ptolemy Philadelphus likewise engaged in such activities: Appian records that in 252 he offered to mediate between Carthage and Rome in the First Punic War. Claiming friendship with both states, Ptolemy seems to have been anxious to avoid a costly war; in the end he refused to lend 2,000 talents to the Carthaginians, who would have used the money to strengthen their military forces.[92]

Ptolemy's offer of peaceful negotiation illustrates the extent to which social harmony was perceived as politically (and economically)

---

[86] For evidence dealing with the intervention of kings, see Marshall 1980, 640, n. 47. See Ager 1996 on the largely epigraphic evidence for between 150 and 200 examples of arbitration or mediation in the 250 years after Chaeronea. There is evidence for only about 60 cases of third-party mediation during the previous four centuries. See also Magnetto 1997 on mediation from 337 to 196, continuing the work of Piccirilli 1973, who collected instances down to 338.

[87] See Gagarin 1986, 19–50 on dispute settlements in early Greek literature.

[88] Ager 1996, xiii attributes the rise in third-party intervention to the increasing refinement in diplomatic protocol.

[89] Possibly Antigonus I (the One-Eyed) in 305 BC, but neither the date nor the identity of the king is certain. See Ael. *VH* fr. 47; Ager 1996, 57–59 (no. 11).

[90] See fragments from document inscribed on temple of Athena Polias at Priene; Ager 1996, 87–89 (no. 25).

[91] Marble stele on Samos; Ager 1996, 89–93 (no. 26). The final decision is unknown.

[92] *Sikelika* 1; Ager 1996, 109–10 (no. 35).

advantageous during the period in which the *Argonautica* was composed.[93] In the event of a successful arbitration the host city would reward the assigned *epikrites* ("arbiter") for restoring *homonoia*, social harmony. An inscription on a marble stele from Delos expresses the appreciation of the deme of the Syrians for the efforts of Eumedes of Clazomenae (*IG* XI.4.1052). Eumedes, an *epikrites* sent by the king, is to receive a gold crown of 500 drachmae because he "accomplished his task well and justly and beneficially to the *demos* in accordance with the policy of King Antigonus, and reestablished *homonoia* in the city by reconciling differences in the majority of cases and by making judgments in the rest." Alcinous' arbitration thus fits into a pattern of mediation by Hellenistic rulers and other diplomatic emissaries who sought to preserve *homonoia* both within and between cities all over the ancient Mediterranean world.

To appreciate the significance of Alcinous' involvement in the Colchian *neikos*, it is necessary to look more closely at a precedent for his intervention within the poem itself. Alcinous is not, as it happens, the first king called upon to arbitrate in the matter of Medea's status. When the Argonauts first encounter the Colchian fleet in the Brygian isles, they discover that they are outnumbered and readily come to terms rather than face defeat in battle (4.338–40). The Colchians agree to allow the Argonauts to retain the Golden Fleece, since Jason did technically fulfill the terms of Aeëtes' conditions (4.341–44), but Medea's fate is still disputed (*ampheriston*, 4.345). The decision is therefore entrusted to one of the local "kings who uphold justice" (*themistouchon basileon*, 4.347), while she is sequestered on a separate island in the temple of Artemis.

Doubtful that Jason will come to her defense before this king, Medea berates him for abandoning her (4.376–78):

"Σχέτλιε, εἰ <γάρ> κέν με κασιγνήτοιο δικάσσῃ
ἔμμεναι οὗτος ἄναξ τῷ ἐπίσχετε τάσδ᾽ ἀλεγεινὰς
ἄμφω συνθεσίας, πῶς ἵξομαι ὄμματα πατρός;"

"Cruel man, if he judges that I am to be with my brother,
This king to whom the two of you[94] assign this hurtful treaty,
How will I confront my father?"

---

[93] Philadelphus' diplomatic foreign policy continued under Ptolemy IV Philopator, who attempted to resolve differences between Carthage and Rome during the Second Punic War. He also successfully resolved the Social War in Greece in 217. For discussion of relations between Egypt and Rome in the third century, see Gruen 1984, 673–78.

[94] Presumably Jason and Apsyrtus.

Medea's fear is tied to her powerlessness: this treaty (*synthesias*, 4.378) with the Colchians was made without her consent,[95] and she has no more influence over "this king" (*houtos anax*, 4.377), as she dismissively refers to him, than she does over Aeëtes. Of interest here is her concern regarding the *synthesia*. Medea will use the same term again in line 390, where she threatens that if she returns to Colchis the spirits of vengeance will ruin Jason's homecoming regardless of his faith in this agreement (*synthesiaon*). He cannot treat with the Colchians for safe passage by sending her home to face death, she reminds him, because he has publicly sworn a great oath by Olympian Zeus and Hera Zygie ("Of the Marriage Yoke"), to marry her (4.95–96). Later, when the other half of the Colchian fleet catches up with the Argonauts on Drepane, Medea will use a similar argument to persuade the other Argonauts, entreating them first not to return her to her father, then threatening them with divine retribution if they betray her (4.1042–44):

"Δείσατε συνθεσίας τε καὶ ὅρκια,[96] δείσατ' Ἐρινὺν
Ἱκεσίην νέμεσίν τε θεῶν, εἰς χεῖρας ἰούσης
Αἰήτεω λώβῃ πολυπήμονι δῃωθῆναι."

"Fear <u>treaties</u> and <u>oaths</u>, fear the Erinys
Of suppliants and the vengeance of the gods, if into the hands
Of Aeëtes I fall to perish in agony."

Medea's injunction regarding treaties (*synthesias*) and oaths (*horkia*) has a double meaning: such agreements are to be feared not only because Nemesis and the Furies will punish those who violate them, but also because they may be made covertly, to the disadvantage of others. Medea's suspicion sheds light on the use of the term *synthesia* earlier in Book 1, when Jason asks to be elected in order to conduct wars and agreements with foreigners.[97] This passage seemingly contrasts wars (*neikea*) with the peaceful alternatives of *synthesiai*, which do not entail force, but it is obvious, from a tactical standpoint, that they too may end in violence.

Whatever Jason's original disposition toward *synthesiai* may have been, it is evident that Medea, at least, mistrusts them because she herself has made two against her own family: once in defiance of Aeëtes, when she agreed to help Jason with enchanted drugs (*synthesieisi*, 3.821), and once more when she plotted to kill Apsyrtus. The word *synthesia* is heavily emphasized on

---

[95] The narrator observes that Medea reckoned the situation in her own mind (4.350): τὰ ἕκαστα νόῳ πεμπάσσατο κούρη.
[96] In phrasing (if not sentiment) this line echoes Nestor's speech at *Iliad* 2.339: "What will become of our agreements and oaths?"
[97] 1.340: νείκεα συνθεσίας τε μετὰ ξείνοισι βαλέσθαι.

the latter occasion, occurring three times – twice in the same case, number, and line position. In the first instance (4.404–5), Jason persuades Medea that his *synthesie* with the Colchians and the local kings gives them the chance to craft a trick, a *dolos*, to lead Apsyrtus to his ruin.[98] In the second (4.437–39), the narrator explains the nature of this trick: Apsyrtus is told to meet Medea at the temple of Artemis at nightfall "in accordance with their plan" to plot a *dolos* by which she may escape with the Golden Fleece.[99] This second *synthesia* is thus a secret, false agreement with Medea's tragically deceived half-brother and has been made possible, as Jason says, by the first agreement with the Colchians. The true *dolos*, the luring of Apsyrtus to Artemis' temple, is hidden within Medea's pretended desire to return to Colchis. The word *synthesia* is then repeated a third time at line 4.453 (again in the dative case and initial line position, as in line 4.437) when Medea is left at the temple of Artemis, where it ostensibly means "in accordance with the agreement" between the Colchians and the Argonauts, but also, as the audience now knows, "in accordance with the false agreement" that was believed by Apsyrtus.[100]

From Medea's point of view, then, agreements are not to be trusted because they lend themselves so easily to deception. In fact, Medea is unaccustomed to agreements that are honored at all. As she tells Jason at the temple of Hecate: "In Greece I suppose this is a fine thing, to honor agreements [*synemosynas alegynein*],[101] but Aeëtes isn't disposed toward men the way you said Minos the husband of Pasiphae is." (3.1105–7). Hera likewise describes Aeëtes as an arrogant (*hyperphialos*) king (3.15), a sentiment echoed by Arete as she pleads with Alcinous on Medea's behalf (4.1083), and by Argus, the son of Phrixus, who warns the Argonauts that Aeëtes is "horribly armed with deadly cruelty."[102] These assessments of the king's character are borne out by his behavior, although it must be admitted that he is more sophisticated, or at least has a greater regard for appearances, given the power of the gods, than either Amycus or Pelias.

---

[98] 4.404–5: Ἥδε δὲ συνθεσίη κρανέει δόλον ᾧ μιν ἐς ἄτην / βήσομεν.
[99] 4.437–39: συνθεσίῃ νυκτός τε μέλαν κνέφας ἀμφιβάλῃσιν / ἐλθέμεν, ὄφρα δόλον συμφράσσεται / ᾧ κεν ἑλοῦσα / χρύσειον μέγα κῶας.
[100] 4.452–53: Ἦμος ὅτ᾽ Ἀρτέμιδος νηῷ ἔνι τήν γ᾽ ἐλίποντο / συνθεσίῃ.
[101] The use of this particular term for a covenant or agreement (συνημοσύνη) suggests an agreement that is sanctioned by the gods or close kinship. It is somewhat uncommon, occurring when Jason tells his mother to have confidence in Athena's agreements (*Argon*. 1.300): θάρσει δὲ συνημοσύνῃσιν Ἀθήνης. Achilles also uses it when he refuses to treat with Hector regarding the terms of their duel (*Il*. 22.261): "Hector, don't go droning on and on about covenants, you wretch."
[102] 2.1202–3.

Aeëtes attempts to camouflage his intentions with the semblance of civilized behavior.[103] He suspects the sons of Phrixus of returning in order to seize his throne (3.576–605), and openly accuses them of uttering lies against the gods (3.381). Only his "respect for the rules of hospitality" prevents him, he says, from cutting off their tongues and hands (3.377–80). As Campbell observes, Aeëtes does show some respect for the laws of the gods,[104] yet it seems that this respect is little more than a pragmatic concession. Years ago he received the suppliant Phrixus, but only because Zeus forced him to (3.587–88), and afterwards he sacrificed the ram of the Golden Fleece, somewhat grudgingly, one imagines, to Zeus Phyxios ("Patron of Fugitives"). He now puts on an appearance of welcoming the sons of Phrixus, whose attempt to return to Greece, the land of their father, has ended in shipwreck (3.270–74):

> Τὸ δ' αὐτίκα πᾶν ὁμάδοιο
> ἕρκος ἐπεπλήθει· τοὶ μὲν μέγαν ἀμφεπένοντο
> ταῦρον ἅλις δμῶες, τοὶ δὲ ξύλα κάγκανα χαλκῷ
> κόπτον, τοὶ δὲ λοετρὰ πυρὶ ζέον· οὐδέ τις ἦεν
> ὃς καμάτου μεθίεσκεν ὑποδρήσσων βασιλῆι.

> At once the whole courtyard
> Was filled with people: some of the servants attended to
> A great bull, others cut dry wood with a bronze axe,
> And others heated water for bathing. There was no one
> In service to the king who shirked his labor.

These preparations are little more than a masquerade, given Aeëtes' disposition towards his grandsons (3.597–600), and the spare description of the sacrifice does little to correct this inference. There is no reference to any god, no description of the ritual, no mention of a feast, and it can hardly come as a surprise that the Argonauts are not invited (3.448). The narrator draws attention only to the servants' concern to accomplish their duties without delay; the scene illustrates not the respect of the king for the gods, but the servants' fear of the king. While Aeëtes speaks of respect for the immortals, this amounts to little more than an acknowledgment of their superior strength. In Aeëtes' world, the weak struggle in the shadow of the strong (3.420–21): "It is unseemly for a noble [*agathon*] man to yield to

---

[103] Williams 1996, 465 points out that the Argonauts are themselves uncertain what to expect from Aeëtes, since they have received conflicting reports about his disposition earlier in the poem.
[104] Campbell 1994 *ad* 377f.: "We are reminded then in no uncertain terms that Aeetes does indeed, despite the vile talk issuing from his lips at this moment, have regard for the laws of hospitality . . . not that he can bring himself to appeal to Zeus Xenios openly."

one low-born [*kakotero*]."[105] In the end, however, Aeëtes' philosophy will fail him, when he loses not only his daughter but also his son, and the Colchian fleet as well. He has threatened them with death if they return without Medea (4.234–35), and they judiciously decide to remain among the Phaeacians rather than face a tyrant empty-handed.[106] Alcinous calls Aeëtes "most imperious" of kings (*basileuteros*, 4.1102), and it is tempting to find parallels between Aeëtes and the Great King of Persia.[107] Aeëtes' entrance hall is reminiscent of the sumptuous Persian palaces found by Alexander at Susa, Babylon, and Persepolis.[108] The courtyard is filled with galleries and ringed with a bronze wall covered with flowering vines (3.217–37). Hephaestus has forged not only the great plough and the bronze fire-breathing bulls that Jason must use to plough the Field of Ares, but also four fountains that flow with milk, wine, oil, and water, and run hot and cold in conjunction with the setting and rising of the Pleiades.[109] Aeëtes' ties to the Olympian gods are here conspicuous,[110] but the riches of his palace also suggest that the Argonauts have entered the citadel of a barbarian tyrant.[111]

The hostile reception of the Argonauts also brings to mind the mutual mistrust and long-standing enmity between Persians and Greeks. Herodotus observed that the abduction of Medea was seen by the Persians as an early example of Greek provocation, not to mention the Athenian burning of Sardis during the revolts of the Ionian Greeks (Hdt. 1.2–3; 5.28–38, 97–103). From the Persian perspective, the Ionian Greeks deceived the

---

[105] See also 3.437–38.
[106] Some of them settle on the Brygian isles of Artemis; others on the mainland, either near the tomb of Harmonia and Cadmus or in the mountains of Zeus the Thunderer (4.514–21); and still others among the Phaeacians and later the Abantes, the Nestaeans and the town of Oricum (4.1211–16).
[107] According to Xenophon (*Anab.* 5.6.36), Colchian kings claimed descent from Aeëtes; the name was used at least until the sixth century. See Braund 1994, 37, n. 183.
[108] The Colchians were not exactly thought to be Persian, and this area of the Black Sea coast was settled by Greeks in the sixth century. Herodotus 3.97 observes that the Colchians, like the Ethiopians, were not taxed by Darius with tribute, but instead gave him gifts, and that the government was Persian as far north as the Caucasus mountains, though that was the limit of their sovereignty.
[109] This prodigy of nature suggests a parallel with the marvel of the spring flowing with water and oil encountered by Alexander en route to Sogdiana (Arr. 4.15.7–8). Clauss 1997, 156 notes that other parallels include the four fountains of Calypso's cave (*Od.* 5.68–73) and the hot and cold sources of the Scamander River (*Il.* 22.148–52). See also Knight 1995, 227.
[110] However, an altar to Zeus Hercius ("Of Enclosures") is not mentioned in the description of the courtyard; see Campbell 1994 *ad* 215f. C2. See also Burkert 1985, 130, and cf. *Od.* 22.335 for an altar to Zeus "the Enclosure God" in Odysseus' courtyard. The term ἑρκίον is used by Apollonius at 2.1073 in a simile about a dwelling.
[111] A palace said to have belonged to Aeëtes was reported at the River Phasis by Zosimos (1.31) and Strabo (1.2.39); see Braund 1994, 30 with n. 128. On the Greek perception of the estates of Persian kings, see Hirsch 1985, esp. 8–9.

king by turning against him after paying tribute.[112] The king was therefore responsible for punishing the violation of an agreement by another party, as Aeëtes tries to do when he realizes that Jason has been helped to plough the Field of Ares.

Presumably, the agreement regarding the Golden Fleece was never valid, since, in Aeëtes' opinion, the Argonauts were actually pirates scheming to steal his throne (3.579–83, 589–93). But whatever his motivation may have been (and once again, in typical fashion for Apollonius' characters, it is not expressed), Aeëtes breaks his word. Treachery on the part of the Persians was presumably expected by a Greek audience,[113] from the sixth century on, despite or perhaps even because of the Macedonian conquest.[114] And yet at the same time, Aeëtes remains a grand figure, Poseidon-like in his procession (3.1240–45), who stands very much in the tradition of Homeric chieftains, as the arming scene in which the narrator praises his helmet, shield, and spear reveals (3.1225–34).[115] Like Pelias, Aeëtes is an autocrat made paranoid by an oracle that specifies the conditions of his downfall,[116] but his belligerence, like that of Amycus, is out of step with the post-Homeric ideals of this poem.

In his willingness to break agreements, Aeëtes is the opposite of Alcinous, who piously refuses to do so. Like the "kings who uphold justice" in the Brygian isles, Alcinous intends to resolve the Colchian *neikos* to the satisfaction of both parties (4.1009–10). Yet even among the Phaeacians *synthesiai* are strategically, if not quite deceptively, deployed. A secret agreement is carried out by Arete, who works behind the scenes to ensure that Medea will be married before Alcinous' judgment is publicly announced.

[112] Strauss and Ober 1990, 23: "For Persian followers of Zarathustra's teachings the world was conceived as an eternal struggle between Truth and Lie; thus dishonesty was regarded not only as immoral, but as an attack on the good half of a divine order ... It was the king's religious duty to punish his opponents ruthlessly."
[113] See for example Xenophon's *Anabasis* 2.5.27–6.1 for an account of the betrayal of the Greek generals by Tissaphernes ("most godless and wicked of men," 2.5.39). Hirsch 1985, 18: "After the execution of the Greek generals by Tissaphernes and the Persian king, a series of Greek speakers castigates the faithlessness and untrustworthiness of the Persians. This reproach against the barbarian became standard in the panhellenic rhetoric of the fourth century."
[114] Nevertheless, possible connections between Colchis and Greece hamper strict identification of Aeëtes with Persian monarchy. See above, n. 108, and Braund 1994, 35–39.
[115] See Williams 1996 who takes Aeëtes' part, arguing that in contrast to the thieving Argonauts the king behaves like an outraged Homeric warrior demanding justice.
[116] Pelias knows that he will be destroyed by a man wearing one shoe, as Jason does when he arrives in Iolcus (1.5–7); Aeëtes is suspicious of the Argonauts because they are escorted by his grandsons, the children of his elder daughter Chalciope and Phrixus, and he has been warned by Helios about the deception of his own children (3.597–600). Pindar's Aeëtes very much resembles Apollonius' Pelias inasmuch as he tells Jason where the Fleece is, but expects the dragon to kill him before he can recover it (*Pyth.* 4.241–43).

The crucial difference between this agreement and those in the Brygian isles is its conclusion: the secret marriage on Drepane ensures that no one will be harmed, whereas the *dolos* of Jason and Medea leads to the killing not only of Apsyrtus but also of his ship's crew (4.485–89):

> Κόλχον δ' ὄλεκον στόλον, ἠύτε κίρκοι
> φῦλα πελειάων ἠὲ μέγα πῶυ λέοντες
> ἀγρότεροι κλονέουσιν ἐνὶ σταθμοῖσι θορόντες.
> Οὐδ' ἄρα τις κείνων θάνατον φύγε, πάντα δ' ὅμιλον
> πῦρ ἅ τε δηιόωντες ἐπέδραμον.

> They preyed on the Colchian force like hawks
> On a flock of doves, or as wild lions
> Plunder a sheepfold, rushing among the great flock.
> Not one of those men escaped death: the whole crowd
> They overran, killing like fire.

Here are riotous war, pain, and suffering: the fruits of Eros that are condemned by the narrator some lines above in the apostrophe to the cruel god (4.445–47).[117] The slaughter of the Colchians effectively distances the ineffective intervention of the so-called "kings who uphold justice," who neither inspire confidence nor protect either party, from Alcinous' carefully planned arbitration.

So, while Medea is quite familiar with the unpleasant ends to which secret *synthesiai* may be put, experience has hardly prepared her for their honorable use. On the morning after the wedding Alcinous goes forth to reveal his decision "in accordance with their agreement" (*synthesiesin*).[118] As Vian points out, this agreement was alluded to earlier in line 4.1010, which announced Alcinous' desire to resolve the *neikos* without bloodshed.[119] Moreover, Alcinous has taken care to "yoke" both the Colchians and the Argonauts to this agreement with "unbreakable oaths" (4.1205). They are yoked to their agreement much as Jason is yoked by his oath to Hera to marry Medea; such oaths are certainties to which the Colchians, from Aeëtes and Medea to Apsyrtus and the entire fleet, are unaccustomed. Alcinous thus applies treaties and oaths, like those with which Medea threatens the Argonauts (4.1042), to lawful, peaceful ends. The "straight decrees" (*itheias themistas*, 4.1179; cf. 1207) delivered by the just king are quite different from those of Aeëtes, or Amycus, whose decrees (*emas themistas*, 2.17) are

---

[117] Cf. the wolf in the sheepfold simile of the Argonauts' attack on the Bebrycians after the death of Amycus (2.123–29). On the representation of *eros* in the poem, see Chapter 3.
[118] 4.1175–76: Ἀλκίνοος μετεβήσετο συνθεσίῃσιν / ὃν νόον ἐξερέων κούρης ὕπερ.
[119] Vian 2002 *ad* 4.1176. 4.1009–10: λελίητο γὰρ ἀμφοτέροισι / δηιοτῆτος ἄνευθεν ὑπέρβια νείκεα λῦσαι.

simply that all foreigners must elect a champion to fight him to the death.[120] Alcinous' "straight decrees" anticipate a peaceful reconciliation like those of Hesiod's wise king, whose *themistes* are rooted in "straight judgment" (*Theog.* 84–87):[121]

οἱ δέ τε λαοὶ
πάντες ἐς αὐτὸν ὁρῶσι διακρίνοντα θέμιστας
ἰθείῃσι δίκῃσιν· ὃ δ' ἀσφαλέως ἀγορεύων
αἶψά κε καὶ μέγα νεῖκος ἐπισταμένως κατέπαυσεν.

All the people
Look to him as he makes decisions [*themistas*]
With straight judgment [*itheisi dikeisin*]. He addresses the assembly steadfastly
And quickly puts a stop to even a great conflict in his wisdom.

Alcinous similarly relies on the "straight judgment" (*dikes itheies*) of Zeus, by using Medea's marital status in order to ground his decision.[122] That she is but newly married matters little, since these were evidently the terms of the original agreement with the Colchians. His steadfastness is directly opposed to the "crooked judgment" (to use the Hesiodic idiom) of Aeëtes, who breaks his agreement to hand over the Golden Fleece. The reference to Alcinous' just *themistes* alludes not only to Hesiod's wise ruler, but even to the "decrees that favor the people" (*demoteras themistas*) that are encouraged by Dike, the goddess of Judgment herself, as she is portrayed in Aratus' *Phaenomena*.[123]

From a structural point of view, the centrality of piety in Alcinous' "straight justice" is reinforced by the order of events themselves, for the description of the communal sacrifice and celebration literally interrupts Alcinous' public declaration. On the morning of the pronouncement, the king arrives holding his staff of justice and flanked by Phaeacian warriors (4.1176–81). The narrator then describes the arrival of crowds of women who come to see the heroes (4.1182–83), and field laborers who have learned of the gathering through a rumor sent by Hera (4.1183–85), focusing attention on the preparations for sacrifice and the public acknowledgment and celebration of Jason and Medea's midnight nuptials. This is a lengthy passage, but I will include it in order to clarify the elements of the digression (4.1185–200):

---

[120] The truly lawless, like the Amazons, apparently do not even honor such rudimentary *themistes* as that of Amycus (2.987–88).
[121] Clare 2002, 203–4; Vian 2002, 3:120, n. 5.
[122] 4.1201–2: Αὐτὰρ ὅ γ', ὡς τὰ πρῶτα δίκης ἀνὰ πείρατ' ἔειπεν / ἰθείης, ἤδη δὲ γάμου τέλος ἐκλήϊστο.
[123] Arat. *Phaen.* 107: δημοτέρας ἤειδεν ἐπισπέρχουσα θέμιστας.

            Ἆγεν δ' ὁ μὲν ἔκκριτον ἄλλων   1185
         ἀρνειὸν μήλων, ὁ δ' ἀεργηλὴν ἔτι πόρτιν·
         ἄλλοι δ' ἀμφιφορῆας ἐπισχεδὸν ἵστασαν οἴνου
         κίρνασθαι· θυέων δ' ἀπὸ τηλόθι κήκιε λιγνύς.
         Αἱ δὲ πολυκμήτους ἑανοὺς φέρον, οἷα γυναῖκες,
         μείλιά τε χρυσοῖο καὶ ἀλλοίην ἐπὶ τοῖσιν   1190
         ἀγλαΐην, οἵην τε νεόζυγες ἐντύνονται.
         θάμβευν δ' εἰσορόωσαι ἀριπρεπέων ἡρώων
         εἴδεα καὶ μορφάς, ἐν δέ σφισιν Οἰάγροιο
         υἱὸν ὑπαὶ φόρμιγγος ἐυκρέκτου καὶ ἀοιδῆς
         ταρφέα σιγαλόεντι πέδον κρούοντα πεδίλῳ.   1195
         Νύμφαι δ' ἄμμιγα πᾶσαι, ὅτε μνήσαιντο γάμοιο,
         ἱμερόενθ' ὑμέναιον ἀνήπυον· ἄλλοτε δ' αὖτε
         οἰόθεν οἶαι ἄειδον ἑλισσόμεναι περὶ κύκλον.
         Ἥρη, σεῖο ἕκητι· σὺ γὰρ καὶ ἐπὶ φρεσὶ θῆκας
         Ἀρήτῃ πυκινὸν φάσθαι ἔπος Ἀλκινόοιο.   1200

         One led a ram, selected from the rest
Of his flock, another a heifer still untrained,
And others set up wine jars close by for mixing
While the sacrificial smoke billowed up in the distance.
The women brought robes of rich brocade, as they do,
And golden offerings, and other kinds of finery
Worn by those new to the marriage yoke.
They marveled as they looked at the beauty and form
Of the matchless heroes, and among them Orpheus,
The son of Oeagrus, tapping his ornate sandal
In time to the tune of his well-strung lyre.
All the nymphs mingled their voices, the wedding in mind,
Sweetly hymning a bridal melody, but at other times
They sang unaccompanied, dancing around in a circle,
To honor you, Hera, for it was your inspiration that led
Arete to disclose the wise word of Alcinous.

The contrast with the sacrifice in Aeëtes' palace is apparent: here all the people take part of their own volition, out of curiosity and admiration. The passage is not so much a narrative as a tableau of ecphrastic or pictorial images: the preparations for sacrifice, the harvest of gifts for the married couple, the scene of choral singing and dancing – all these events are framed by the public assembly in a ring composition. As a result, the chronological sequence of events in this passage is very loosely defined: it is not clear whether the wedding celebration takes place before, during, or after Alcinous' declaration. Although the general chronology is uncertain, the ring composition (assembly – celebration – assembly) ensures that the communal sacrifice forms the dramatic heart of Alcinous' proclamation, which is neither quoted nor summarized again here. When the description of the assembly resumes after the climactic apostrophe to Hera in line 1201, it reads like a denouement, especially since the judgment and its effects are only briefly summarized (4.1201–10). In the aftermath of the secret nuptials and the public recognition of the wedding, Alcinous' decision seems unassailable, even anti-climactic, to the reader, not to mention to the Colchians themselves, who quickly acquiesce (4.1206–10). The structure of the scene forcefully demonstrates the strength of the Phaeacian king, whose just power is expressed in the strategic admixture of political diplomacy with a public show of piety and military strength.

The representation of the assembly and celebration as a tableau also evokes the image of the Homeric city at peace that is depicted on Achilles' shield (*Il.* 18.491–508). The city at peace is characterized by scenes of a marriage procession, with women admiring the young men as they sing and dance, just as the young women admire Orpheus and the other Argonauts (*thaumazon, Il.* 18.496; cf. *thambeun, Argon.* 4.1192), and by an arbitration over a *neikos* (*Il.* 18.497) regarding the blood price of a homicide. Alcinous is the Argonautic equivalent of the Iliadic judge who will win two talents of gold for the "straightest judgment" (*diken ithuntata*, 18.508). Both these arbitrations emphasize the connection of the just rule of law with the fertility of the people; they are contrasted, moreover, with scenes of conflict, *neikea*, that end in death. The description of the city at war portrays a terrible ambush by the banks of a river (18.509–40): an apt comparison with the ambush of Apsyrtus and the Argonauts' subsequent slaughter of his crew. What separates ambush from arbitration, or murder from marriage, for both Homer and Apollonius, is Zeus's "straight justice," which enforces *synthesiai, themistai,* and *horkia* with unbreakable bonds. But in the *Argonautica*, the justice of Zeus extends far beyond the walls of the peaceful city to honor and diplomatically embrace all those who come from distant lands, the Argonauts and Colchians alike.

Cyzicus, Phineus, and Pelias

A number of the characteristics of an ideal ruler that are displayed in Alcinous are also represented, to varying degrees, in Cyzicus and Phineus. The primary correlation of sacrifice with diplomacy is maintained in these episodes, but the encounters with Cyzicus and Phineus also bring into relief two new themes: the limits of divine anger and the limits of human knowledge. Like Alcinous, the Dolionian king Cyzicus welcomes the Argonauts when they first arrive on his island (1.961–80), generously providing sheep and wine for the Argonauts' sacrifice to Ecbasian Apollo ("Apollo of Landings," 1.966–69). Cyzicus is accordingly marked as one of the good rulers, although his knowledge, like that of all mortals, remains fragmentary, and with tragic consequences. When the Argonauts mistakenly return to their land during the night, the Doliones confuse them with Pelasgian warriors from Ionian Macria, and in the confusion of battle Jason accidentally kills Cyzicus. His death thus confirms the wisdom of the divine oracle that warned the Doliones never to attack a godly army of heroes (1.970).

The story of Phineus complements that of Cyzicus: the sudden death of the young ruler who dies prematurely out of ignorance is opposed to the protracted age of a far-seeing king who long outlives his reign. Formerly the ruler of Thrace (2.236–39), Phineus was known for his wealth and the gift of prophecy given to him by Apollo (2.180–81). Because he did not observe the limits of mortal knowledge set by Zeus, he suffers blindness, the pains of extreme old age, and endless hunger, for Zeus sends Harpies to steal the food prepared for him by his neighbors (2.181–89). Thus, as his punishment for revealing information reserved for the gods, Phineus is apportioned the crippling effects of mortality and a kind of perverted sacrifice that is offered but corrupted and stolen. An ex-king, Phineus is now mocked like an ex-god.

Physically speaking, Phineus is closer to a ghost than either a king or a god (2.197–205). His spectral appearance and prophetic gifts evoke the Homeric Tiresias, who is met by Odysseus in the underworld. Like Tiresias, whose revelations require a draught of sheep's blood (*Od.* 10.95–99), Phineus will predict some, though not all of the things the Argonauts will face (*Argon.* 2.390–91, 425). The Harpies seize the first meal that is prepared by the Boreads, but after they have been driven off the Argonauts treat Phineus to a great feast of Bebrycian sheep (2.306). This episode therefore inverts the structure of the standard hospitality type scene, inasmuch as it is the visiting Argonauts who bathe and provide food for their host, rather than the reverse (2.301–10).

More importantly, the encounter with Phineus reveals the workings of the anger of Zeus. The Argonauts soon learn that the prophet-king was punished for revealing Zeus's plan in full (2.313–16):

"Ἀασάμην καὶ πρόσθε Διὸς νόον ἀφραδίῃσι
χρείων ἑξείης τε καὶ ἐς τέλος· ὧδε γὰρ αὐτὸς
βούλεται ἀνθρώποις ἐπιδευέα θέσφατα φαίνειν
μαντοσύνης, ἵνα καί τι θεῶν χατέωσι νόοιο."

"I went wrong before by rashly revealing the purpose of Zeus
In order and to the end, for he himself
Prefers to reveal only incomplete oracles to mortals
Through divination, that they may yet desire the purpose of the gods."

Phineus tellingly echoes part of Telamon's apology to Jason during the quarrel about the loss of Heracles in Mysia (1.1332–33):

"Αἰσονίδη, μή μοί τι χολώσεαι, ἀφραδίῃσιν
εἴ τι περ ἀασάμην·

"Son of Aeson, do not be angry with me, if in error
I acted rashly."

The repetition of ἀασάμην ("I erred") and ἀφραδίῃσιν ("rashly," or "in ignorance") points to the similarity of these two episodes. Phineus defines the limits of divine anger in the same way that Jason's reconciliation with Telamon illustrates the appropriate boundaries of mortal anger.[124] Both divine wrath and human knowledge must be circumscribed if the hierarchical structure of society, which is founded on the distinction between god and mortal, is to be preserved. Zeus maintains this hierarchy by disclosing his truths through oracles, which it is the purpose of mortals to interpret. Denied full knowledge, men may die, like Cyzicus, yet such mortal confusion is mediated by limitations on divine wrath that may allow them to live, like Phineus. Phineus has provoked Zeus, but his punishment is neither unreasonable nor unlimited. Just as it is *themis*, the will of the gods, for the Boreads to spare the Harpies (2.284–90), so it is Zeus's will for the Argonauts to save Phineus (2.274–77) – and, by extension, for Jason and Medea to return to society after their purification by Circe. Jason and Medea have committed murder, but even in cases of murder, as the story of Paraebius shows, atonement is possible. Paraebius suffers the curse that fell on his father for killing a tree nymph, yet he is able to atone by sacrificing in accordance with Phineus' directions (2.484–86). In return for this help, Paraebius unfailingly brings his benefactor sheep for sacrifice and feasting (2.487–94). Once again, sacrifice is a narrative marker of the recovery of social harmony and the proper exchange of honors in the hierarchical construction of right relations among men, kings, and gods.

While forgiveness is possible, it is not certain, as is shown by the description of Pelias' impiety. Hera has selected Jason as the vehicle of her vengeance

---

[124] See Mori 2005.

against this king, whose failure to sacrifice to the goddess contrasts with Jason's chivalrous treatment.[125] Burkert's comment that "Hera represents the normal order of the polis: the inversion of this order is her anger," is suggestive inasmuch as Pelias is traditionally cast as a usurper of the throne of Iolcus.[126] When Pelias usurps the throne, his disruption of the polis can be understood symbolically as his failure to honor Hera. From Hera's point of view, Pelias' neglect constitutes nothing less than an outrage, a disgrace (3.74) to her honor that is analogous to Agamemnon's affront to Achilles at the beginning of the *Iliad*.[127] Here the poetic association of justice, political stability, and ritual practice is particularly apparent.

The narrator does not condemn Pelias in terms as strong as he uses for Amycus and Aeëtes,[128] but the characters in the poem voice their dislike and disapproval of the king when he uses his power unjustly against his nephew.[129] Jason's mother Alcimede speaks of Pelias' decision to send Jason away as "a king's evil decree" (κακὴν βασιλῆος ἐφετμήν, 1.279), and Phineus similarly describes the act as "a king's cruel decree" (κρυερ, ῇ βασιλῆος ἐφετμῇ, 2.210). In Book 3 Jason caps these references by describing Pelias as "overbearing" (*atasthalou*), an allusion to Pelias in the *Theogony*, where he is described by Hesiod as a wicked, overbearing brute (*Theog.* 996).[130] Jason here explains during his audience with Aeëtes that he has sailed against his will, and would never have risked such a voyage merely to steal from another: "No, it was a god and the cruel decree of an overbearing king that drove me here."[131] The god in question is Zeus: earlier Jason informed the sons of Phrixus that only the recovery of the Fleece can appease Zeus and atone for the attempted sacrifice of Phrixus (2.1194–95).

Both punishment and atonement are therefore at the heart of the Argo's voyage. Pelias will be punished for the affront to Hera, and the recovery of

---

[125] At 1.8–14 the narrator says that Jason was headed to Iolcus for Pelias' sacrifice when he carries Hera across the torrential Anaurus; later in Book 3 Hera tells Aphrodite that Jason was returning from the hunt when he helped her as she tested the righteousness (*eunomia*) of men (3.66–75).
[126] Burkert 1985, 165.
[127] Finley 1991, 126: "exclusion from the feast was a mark of the social outcast." In the traditional mythological explanation for Pelias' ritual neglect of Hera, Sidero, the stepmother of Pelias and Neleus, is said to have sought protection at Hera's altar just before her stepsons murder her (Apollod. *Bibl.* 1.9.8).
[128] Pelias is given the epithet "strong" in his son's patronymic (*iphthimou*, 1.225).
[129] Unlike Pindar in *Pythian* 4, Apollonius does not mention Pelias' usurpation of the throne, apparently because he prefers to present the background material in a different way. So Campbell 1994 *ad* 333f.
[130] *Argon.* 3.390. Eurystheus, the king who sends Heracles on his labors, is also called *atasthalos* ("wicked") by Glaucus (1.1317). On *atasthalos* as a term of condemnation, see Campbell 1994 *ad* 390, citing Pind. fr. 1400a.56–7.
[131] 3.389–90: Ἀλλά με δαίμων / καὶ κρυερὴ βασιλῆος ἀτασθάλου ὦρσεν ἐφετμή.

the Golden Fleece will atone for the impious attempt to sacrifice Phrixus. If there is a limit to Hera's wrath, Pelias does not seek it, but Zeus will forgive the attempt on Phrixus' life, as well as the murder of Apsyrtus. Both Cyzicus and Pelias know that death will come to them from a man like Jason. Yet this knowledge saves neither of them, for oracles reveal the future not to save men from their fates, since all mortals must die, but to ensure that they will continue to recognize and honor the power of the gods.

Hypsipyle, Lycus, and Amycus

I conclude with a brief look at the sacrifices performed by the Lemnians and the Mariandyni. Both the Lemnians and the Mariandyni welcome the Argonauts and immediately accept them as political allies, either through mutual attraction or the defeat of mutual enemies.[132] Jason's embassy to Hypsipyle ends, like the Phaeacian episode, with a public celebration of marriage – or at least something along those lines. By contrast the Mariandyni, like the Doliones, are joined to the Argonauts by rituals of mourning: the funerals held in honor of Idmon and Tiphys both create and illustrate the bonds of cooperation and concord shared by the two groups.

As I observed in the previous chapter, the Lemnians are so fearful of an attack by the Thracians (1.613–14, 631–32), that they initially mistake the Argonauts for them, just as the Doliones mistake the Argonauts for Pelasgian raiders. Unlike the Doliones, however, the Lemnians decide to hold an assembly before they attack, and wisely choose to welcome the Argonauts in the hope of rebuilding their community. Hypsipyle accepts the assembly's decision to invite the Argonauts into the capital (1.700–1), although she edits Lemnian history when she meets with Jason by telling him that the men have gone with the children to Thrace (1.820–23).[133] Apollonius thus depicts Hypsipyle as a ruler capable of balancing prudent self-interest with piety and civility.[134] Like Pelias, she is associated with the neglect of a powerful goddess, and like Aeëtes, she lies to Jason. But her

---

[132] The city of the Lemnians celebrates the arrival of the Argonauts with feasting and sacrifices to all the immortals, particularly Aphrodite and Hephaestus (1.857–60). In actuality the city was the center of the Hephaestus cult (Burkert 1985, 281). The Mariandyni prepare a feast in the palace (2.759–61): sacrifices are therefore only implied in this instance.

[133] Hypsipyle prefers concealment to confrontation. Her first impulse is to provision the Argonauts and send them on their way rather than risk disclosure regarding the fate of the men (1.657–66).

[134] For a less favorable interpretation of the Lemnian episode, cf. Pavlock 1990, 50–51. Pavlock argues that Apollonius "deemphasizes the traditional theme of Hypsipyle's piety and gives no importance to the theme of female solidarity, so that the sex-starved women collectively appear ridiculous when Polyxo rises in their assembly as a Nestor-like figure (668–98) . . . Even though Hypsipyle actually saved Thoas, Apollonius associates only negative effects with the Lemnians."

lies are harmless, meant only to protect the Lemnians, who subsequently celebrate their alliance with the Argonauts with sacrifices to the gods (1.857–60):

Αὐτίκα δ' ἄστυ χοροῖσι καὶ εἰλαπίνῃσι γεγήθει
καπνῷ κνισήεντι περίπλεον· ἔξοχα δ' ἄλλων
ἀθανάτων Ἥρης υἷα κλυτὸν ἠδὲ καὶ αὐτὴν
Κύπριν ἀοιδῇσιν θυέεσσί τε μειλίσσοντο.

At once the city rejoiced in dancing and banquets,
And filled with the savory sacrificial smoke. Beyond the other
Immortals they honored the illustrious son of Hera
And Cypris herself with song and sacrifice.

Unlike the cheerless sacrifice hastily prepared in the Colchian palace, the Lemnian festivities are public and marked by music and choral dances. The event recalls the Phaeacian wedding celebration, and this resemblance is hardly a coincidence, inasmuch as the Lemnians are celebrating a kind of marriage on a grand, if informal, scale. Accordingly, the highest honors in the Lemnian sacrifice are awarded not to Hera, but to Aphrodite, a more appropriate choice not only because of her previous anger but also because of the character of the Lemnian alliance. Once more, atonement is possible: the Argonauts' arrival ends the sexual isolation of the women of Lemnos and brings their punishment to an end.

The Mariandyni have much to thank the Argonauts for even before they meet them, since they have recovered territory as a result of the defeat of the Bebrycians,[135] an arrogant people (*hyperphialous*, 2.129, 758), who had long oppressed the Mariandyni. As Lycus explains, the Bebrycians stole land as far away as the river Hypius (2.795), and are close in temperament to the Amazons, who do not honor just decrees, caring only for hubris and the deeds of Ares (2.987–89). Their king, Amycus, is the most violent and uncivilized of all the kings;[136] the narrator makes no mention of sacrifice in connection with him, and consistently describes him in unflattering terms. A rude son of Poseidon, he most resembles the Cyclops, and like him "must pay the price for his lack of 'social grace' and thereby serve to define and endorse 'Greek' norms."[137] Unlike Triton, another of Poseidon's sons, Amycus is exceedingly arrogant (*hyperopleestaton*, 2.4), and has

---

[135] See Braund 1994 and Burstein 1976, 80–81 on the subordination of native Mariandyni to Greek colonists (Posidonius, Athen. 6.263c–e).
[136] Knight 1995, 127 notes the similarity between the brutish Cyclops of the *Odyssey* and Amycus, Talus, and Aeëtes, none of whom respects strangers.
[137] Hunter 1993, 160.

killed many of his neighbors, habitually forcing strangers to box with him (2.5–7).[138]

The alliance of the Mariandyni with the Argonauts against the Bebrycians illustrates a political principle consistently followed by Hellenistic leaders: "The enemy of my enemy is my friend."[139] Lycus embraces the cause of the Argonauts, mourning the losses of Idmon and Tiphys and commiserating over the disappearance of Heracles, who had visited the Mariandyni after he acquired the girdle of the Amazonian queen Hippolyte (2.775–79). Lycus also sends his son Dascylus with them as an ambassador to help with foreign relations as far as the River Thermodon in Cappadocia (2.800–3),[140] and finally, because Polydeuces has defeated Amycus, Lycus vows to honor the Dioscuri as gods, setting aside rich fields and erecting a temple on the headlands of the Acheron as a landmark for sailors (2.806–10).[141] Lycus' praise of the Dioscuri and Heracles thus anticipates Hellenistic cult,[142] simultaneously reinforcing its ancient standing as well as his own position as one of the good kings encountered by the Argonauts.[143] The foundation of the *temenos*, whose revenues will support the temple, is likewise reminiscent of the public honors typically accorded Hellenistic rulers.[144]

The ideological construction of the Ptolemies as both pious and diplomatic is felt in the *Argonautica*'s emphasis on sacrifice, arbitration, and political alliance in the portrayal of good kings. While these characters should be read with traditional epic precedents in mind, an exclusive comparison with such precedents distorts their function within the poem as a whole. The portrayal of Aeëtes, a potent hybrid of Homeric warrior and

---

[138] Amycus addresses Jason with arrogant words (2.54); Hunter 1993, 23 and n. 56 notes that the word *hyperphialos* is particularly "associated with the arrogance of Amykos and Aeetes." Amycus' speech recalls the boasting of Idas and stands in direct opposition to Jason's speech, characterized in general by gentle words.

[139] Bringmann 1993, 15 discusses the benefactions bestowed on Greek cities by Hellenistic kings in order to secure their allegiance.

[140] Dascylus is left at the mouth of the Halys River before the Argonauts flee across the Black Sea to the Ister (4.298–300).

[141] Castor and Polydeuces are depicted as cultic heroes during their lifetime, but the poem does not refer to the twins as Dioscuri: Lycus calls them the sons of Tyndareus (*Tyndaride* of Polydeuces, the immortal son of Zeus at 2.798, and *Tyndaridais* of both at 2.806). The Dioscuri were worshipped all over Greece, but especially in their native Sparta and as saviors of sailors in distress. They are closely linked in cult with the Curetes, the attendants of Rhea (mentioned in connection with the hiding of the infant Zeus at *Argon.* 2.1234) as well as the Cabiri and the "Unnamed Gods" of the mysteries at Samothrace. At Orpheus' request the Argonauts are initiated into the mysteries at Samothrace for protection on their journey (1.915–18). See Burkert 1985, 212–13 and 281–85.

[142] Hunter 1993, 160. [143] Hunter 1993, 76.

[144] Bringmann 1993, 16. See Herman 1987, 106–11 on grants of landed estates (*doreai*); on the revenue generated by *temene*, see Malkin 1987, 140.

Persian tyrant, is complex, but it is hard to take his religiosity seriously because it is compromised by a disregard for "straight justice." "Straight justice" redefines the king as a mediator, between warring factions, most obviously, but also and more importantly between the people, whom he represents, and the gods, who must be propitiated.

CHAPTER 6

The bones of Apsyrtus

THE INFLUENCE OF TRAGEDY

The murder of Apsyrtus is the central crisis of the voyage of the Argo. The ambush and its consequences, especially the alienation of the Argonauts from Zeus, illustrate the limits of mortal knowledge and divine retribution, both of which have been considered in Chapter 5. But the ambush also raises questions about the representation of Jason and Medea, the central characters of a poem that is in many ways patterned on Homeric epic and is often responsive to the expectations generated by it. Although the relative prominence of Jason and Medea makes them comparable to figures like Achilles, Odysseus, or Penelope, they are, unlike their Homeric counterparts, involved in the treacherous murder of a family member. The narrator is careful to explain the circumstances of the murder in the first section of Book 4: Jason and Medea are under the influence of Eros, and the Argonauts have been surrounded by a much larger Colchian force that seeks to return Medea to Aeëtes. Still, even with these justifications it is difficult to understand how the fatal trap set by Medea for her own half-brother can appear in a favorable, let alone heroic, light. What accounts for such a dramatic shift in the characterization of the epic hero?

The circumstances of the ambush are as follows. When the Colchians blockade the Argonauts on one of the Brygian Isles, Medea fears she will be sent home to Aeëtes and plots the ambush with Jason, who reasons that the Colchians will lose local support and become disorganized after their leader is killed (4.405–9). Medea sets the trap by sending Apsyrtus a message to meet her in secret at the temple of Artemis, explaining that she has been taken against her will and wishes to return with the Golden Fleece to Colchis. As a sign of good faith she sends guest gifts, including a robe that once belonged to Dionysus (4.421–44). After Apsyrtus enters the temple precinct and agrees to Medea's false plan, Jason leaps out from hiding, stabs him, as the narrator says, like a priest striking an ox, and then performs a ritual for protection against the vengeance of the dead. At Medea's torch signal, the Argonauts lay waste to the crew of Apsyrtus' ship; the remaining Colchian ships give up pursuit of the Argo because of thunderstorms sent by Hera (4.507–21).

Readers have generally condemned this episode as unheroic and a departure from Homeric epic as well as other models like Pindar's fourth *Pythian*.[1] The ambush owes much more, as some have argued, to the treatments of familial murder found in Attic tragedy, particularly Euripides' *Medea*, which recounts Medea's subsequent murder of her two young sons to punish Jason's infidelity.[2] On this reading the Apsyrtus episode serves as an early example of Medea's self-interested capacity to destroy her own family.[3] The location of the trap in the sacred temple precinct (*temenos*) of Artemis (4.468–70) is thought to reinforce the impiety of kin-murder, while other religious features of the scene, such as the comparison of Jason to a "ritual ox-slayer" (*boutypos*),[4] recall the tragic representation of murder as a "corrupted sacrifice,"[5] particularly the deaths of Agamemnon and his family.[6] Jason's removal of the extremities (*exargmata*) from the body and his spitting out of the victim's blood are considered barbaric,[7] and the narrator's comment that the *maschalismos* is a customary (*themis*, 4.479) ritual for "murders by stealth" (*doloktasias*, 4.479) is taken as ironic.[8]

These are important connections, and it is reasonable to think that the *Argonautica*'s debt to classical drama is as significant as its debt to Homeric

---

[1] For the murder as unheroic, see Beye 1969, 53, "unheroic, and an evil crime" and Porter 1990, 264, who comments that Apsyrtus is killed "in a most unheroic fashion." Clauss 1993, 24 contrasts Jason's "unheroic outlook and behavior" with "Pindar's noble hero." Sansone 2000 states "On any showing, the murder of Apsyrtus is repugnant, or, as Aristotle would put it, μιαρόν" (167).

[2] See, e.g., the discussions by Clauss 1993, 9, Porter 1990, 262ff. and Hunter 1989, 18–19.

[3] For example, Hutchinson 1988, 128 sees the killing as the source of deterioration in the relationship between Jason and Medea.

[4] 4.468–69: τὸν δ' ὅγε, βουτύπος ὥς τε μέγαν κερεαλκέα ταῦρον, / πλῆξεν. Homer similarly likens the death of Agamemnon to the cutting down of an ox in its stall: ὥς τίς τε κατέκτανε βοῦν ἐπὶ φάτνῃ (*Od.* 4.535; 11.411). On the close proximity of the temple, the simile of Jason as a *boutypos* striking an ox , and the "willingness" of the victim as sacral or ritualistic features of the murder see, e.g., Green 1997 *ad* 4.465–67, 471–74; Hunter 1993, 61, n. 69; Porter 1990, 264; Fränkel 1968 *ad* 4.469f. See also Bremmer 1997, 84–85.

[5] Zeitlin 1968 analyzes the ways in which the idea of Iphigenia's "sacrificial" death resonates symbolically in the acts of violence that follow, although this symbolism is deceptive and allows the proud Agamemnon and the vengeful Clytemnestra to disguise their murders with "sacramental dress."

[6] Of *Argon.* 4.464–81 Porter 1990, 266 writes that it "is a scene of murderous treachery, of kinship outraged and sacred things defiled, that ominously foreshadows the later history of Jason and Medea . . . but does so, in part, by evoking the troubled atmosphere that pervades the murders of Aegisthus and Clytemnestra in Euripides' *Electra*." See also Griffiths 1990, 25 and 26, where he suggests that "Aeschylus mitigates Orestes's crime slightly," while "Apollonius compounds the heinousness."

[7] See Segal 1971, 28–29, who notes that not only active mistreatment of a body but even natural decomposition may be regarded as an outrage. For discussion of ἀεικέα ἔργα, see Adkins 1960, 41–45.

[8] E.g., Goldhill 1991, 331–32.

epic. The argument for the *Medea*'s influence has pervaded scholarship since Duckworth's 1933 analysis of foreshadowing in the *Argonautica*, and for many readers the poem would lose thematic coherence in isolation from its tragic predecessor.[9] But as a consequence, the Argonautic Jason and Medea have been viewed from a relentlessly ironic perspective; their actions are measured less by the standards of their own epic than by events dramatized in the fifth century: he is "always already disloyal," and she is "always already betrayed." Although Euripides deals with these characters at a later point in their lives, many readers find it hard to avoid reading faithlessness into Apollonius' Jason and a vengeful appetite into his Medea. However, Apollonius' inclination toward variation and adaptation suggests that these connections may be better understood as points of contrast and discontinuity.

This is certainly true of the comparison, raised by Jason himself during his first meeting with Medea, between Jason's treatment of Medea and Theseus' treatment of Ariadne. Jason's selective memory during this meeting has struck many as particularly incriminating (3.997–1000, 1096–99).[10] In this scene, set in the temple of Hecate, Jason is trying to persuade Medea to help him to acquire the Golden Fleece. He promises that the Argonauts and their families will celebrate her (3.997–1006):

> Δή ποτε καὶ Θησῆα κακῶν ὑπελύσατ' ἀέθλων
> Παρθενικὴ Μινωὶς ἐυφροέουσ' Ἀριάδνη,
> ἥν ῥά τε Πασιφάη κούρη τέκεν Ἠελίοιο·
> ἀλλ' ἡ μὲν καὶ νηός, ἐπεὶ χόλον εὔνασε Μίνως,
> σὺν τῷ ἐφεζομένη πάτρην λίπε· τὴν δὲ καὶ αὐτοὶ
> ἀθάνατοι φίλαντο, μέσῳ δέ οἱ αἰθέρι τέκμωρ
> ἀστερόεις στέφανος, τόν τε κλείουσ' Ἀριάδνης,
> πάννυχος οὐρανίοισιν ἑλίσσεται εἰδώλοισιν.
> Ὣς καὶ σοὶ θεόθεν χάρις ἔσσεται, εἴ κε σαώσεις
> τόσσον ἀριστήων ἀνδρῶν στόλον.

> Theseus too was once released from harsh trials
> By a daughter of Minos, kind Ariadne,
> Borne by Pasiphae, daughter of Helios,
> But she also left her fatherland, when Minos calmed his anger,
> Seated on a ship with him, and her even the

---

[9] Byre 2002 comments that "since Duckworth's groundbreaking *Foreshadowing and Suspense*, scholars have become increasingly ingenious in finding hints of Euripides' version of events in Corinth in Apollonius' text" (105, n. 54). He questions the "Euripidean hypothesis," arguing instead that Jason's true motivation in the Ariadne scene is purposely left ambiguous (92, 94–95). See also Clare 1997, 61, who observes simply that "an *Argonautica* is not a *Medea*," arguing that Apollonius' epic and Euripides' tragedy "belong to disparate strands of the myth" with differing themes and emphases that need not be taken as a group.

[10] For a list of scholarly discussions of this passage, see Clare 2002, 280, n. 59.

> Immortals themselves loved; for her, a sign in the heavens,
> A crown of stars, which they call Ariadne's,
> Turns throughout the night amidst the constellations.
> So too for you will there be thanks from the gods, if you will save
> Such an expedition of highborn men.

Jason paints a charming picture here, but what he does not mention – although the narrator later does at 4.433–34 – is that before Ariadne enjoyed the company of the gods she was first abandoned by Theseus. Though Medea is Ariadne's cousin,[11] she is evidently unaware that a significant part of the story has been left out. In pitting a manipulative Jason against an uninformed Medea, the poem seems to direct its audience to think of his future disloyalty.[12]

But this scene does more than merely point out Jason's rhetorical license. The selective "spin" that Jason puts on the Ariadne story resembles other instances of verbal ingenuity in the poem, such as Medea's rather sketchy autobiography during her audience with Arete (4.1019–24),[13] or Hypsipyle's artful retelling of the fate of the Lemnian men (1.798–826). All of these may be read as instances of self-serving manipulation, but they are also examples of *variatio* and the intentional avoidance of the Homeric tendency to recount stories at great length or speeches verbatim. Clare compares the gap in Jason's Ariadne story with the narrator's reluctance to plod straight through a tale from beginning to end (*dienekeos*), and suggests that the stylistic concerns of Apollonius' "poetic persona" are evident in the speeches of characters like Jason, Phineus, and the Argonauts' herald, Aethalides.[14] Aethalides' abbreviated speeches in particular work to revise, as Nishimura-Jensen well shows, the formal expectations created by Homeric epic: "The messenger's memory, earlier so significant for oral technique, becomes less important than Hellenistic *poikilia*; this signals a self-conscious selection of variation over repetition."[15]

Even more relevant are the implicit links between the marriages of Ariadne, Medea, and Arsinoë. In glossing over Ariadne's misfortune Jason's speech emphasizes the triumphant conclusion of the story. Ariadne becomes

---

[11] 3.1076; noted by Fränkel 1968 *ad* 3.998f.
[12] See Goldhill 1991, 301–6, who observes that Jason's "seductive rhetoric, playing with what is stated and unstated, works both on the innocence of Medea and on the sophistication of the reader, whose understanding of the allusions to a significantly untold story is a necessary collusion in the humour of the scene" (302).
[13] Knight 1995, 250, observes that in the later scene Medea becomes a suppliant to Arete, who takes up Medea's earlier role.
[14] Clare 2002, 268–80. On continuous and unbroken narratives in the poem, see further Hunter 2001, 108–9 and 1993, 190–95.
[15] Nishimura-Jensen 1998, 469.

The influence of tragedy 191

the bride of Dionysus, a divinity whose ideological significance for the Ptolemies has already been addressed (see Chapter 2). In similar fashion, Medea will go on to marry Achilles in the afterlife, as Hera elsewhere reminds Thetis (4.811–16). In the end, Medea's association with Jason also leads her toward such honor: the Argonautic equivalent of the undying glory (*aphthiton kleos*) of Homeric heroes. For that matter, Ariadne's abandonment by Theseus no more overshadows her celebration as Dionysus' bride than Arsinoë's past overshadowed her rule as queen, for the marriage to Philadelphus was not her first (see Chapter 4). Then, too, the reference to the catasterism of Ariadne's bridal crown likely resonated in a positive way with a Ptolemaic audience inasmuch as it evokes both the apotheosis of Arsinoë at her death and the astral transposition of the lock of Berenice that is celebrated by Callimachus in Book 4 of the *Aetia*.[16] Such a parallel raises the question of chronology, especially since it has often been assumed that Apollonius draws only on Books 1 and 2 of the *Aetia*, with Books 3 and 4 having been written some years later. However, as Köhnken has recently argued, Pfeiffer was likely correct in his observation that the *Argonautica* draws on all four books,[17] which allows for the possibility that Apollonius continued to revise the *Argonautica* until the beginning of Euergetes' reign in 246.[18]

Jason's Ariadne reference (cf. Theocr. *Id.* 2.45–46) also looks back to the abandonment of Heracles on Mysia in Book 1. Heracles, like Ariadne, is destined to dwell with the gods: ναίειν δ' ἀθανάτοισι συνέστιον (1.1319), and Jason, like Theseus, sails off without him. The question of whether Jason (not to mention the rest of the Argonauts) somehow managed to overlook the absence of Heracles on board, like the question of Theseus' "forgetting" of Ariadne, is unanswered in the poem, though the resolution of the scene does imply that such suspicions are ill-founded.[19] The sea god Glaucus informs the Argonauts that Heracles' abandonment was willed by the gods and that they should not miss him (1.1320), advice that can likewise

---

[16] See Chapter 2. Arsinoë's ascension into heaven was publicly recorded on the Mendes Stele (Sethe 1904–16; 2:40, no. 33); see also Callimachus fr. 228 Pfeiffer i (*Ektheosis Arsinoes*), which describes her as already among the stars, "beneath the Wagon" (l. 5), the constellation better known as Ursa Major; for the conflation of the two, see *Il.* 18.487; *Od.* 5.273. For the catasterism of Berenice's lock, see the first three lines of the *Coma Berenices* (fr. 110 Pfeiffer i).

[17] See Köhnken 2001, 77–80.

[18] Hunter 1989, 7–9 discusses the problems associated with establishing the chronology of works that were circulated and revised for years, but notes the presence of parallels between *Aetia* 4 and the Argonauts' outward journey (p. 7); see also Fantuzzi and Hunter 2004, 87 with n. 179 on the similarity between the *Coma* and Medea's cutting of a lock to leave for her mother as a memento of her virginity (*Argon.* 4.37–39).

[19] Cf. the discussion of Telamon in Chapter 3.

be applied to the tale of Ariadne. Heracles and Ariadne, like Medea, are destined to be abandoned and go on to greater glory; Jason, like Theseus, serves as the necessary means to that end.

These signals in the text suggest that the link between the *Medea* and the *Argonautica* has been misrepresented: the *Argonautica* transmutes Euripides' focus on vengeance into a focus on divine expiation and mortal recovery. Human transgression is subject to the "straight justice" of Zeus, but Zeus's punishments are themselves bounded and subject to intervention. The finite character of Zeus's wrath is illustrated by the Boreads' rescue of Phineus, as well as a later passage that alludes to Heracles' rescue of Prometheus. The Argonauts witness Prometheus' torment, his cries echoing across the sea as they approach Colchis (2.1246–50):

> Καὶ δὴ νισομένοισι μυχὸς διεφαίνετο Πόντου,
> καὶ δὴ Καυκασίων ὀρέων ἀνέτελλον ἐρίπναι
> ἠλίβατοι, τόθι γυῖα περὶ στυφελοῖσι πάγοισιν
> ἰλλόμενος χαλκέῃσιν ἀλυκτοπέδῃσι Προμηθεὺς
> αἰετὸν ἥπατι φέρβε παλιμπετὲς ἀΐσσοντα.

> At last the far corner of the Black Sea appeared to them,
> At last sheer peaks of the Caucasus mountains rose up
> Where, limbs bound to a rocky crag by bronze chains,
> Prometheus fed with his liver an eagle, ever sweeping back.

While they cannot know that Heracles will soon save Prometheus from the eagle, the reader does, despite the fact that the narrator does not mention Heracles by name here. Thus, in his commentary on this passage, the Scholiast reports several interpretations of the rescue as an allegory of a natural or sociological phenomenon.[20] The themes of transgression, punishment, and the essential limitations on mortal knowledge and divine wrath are all present in this scene, and will also prove relevant in the aftermath of Apsyrtus' death.

Just as Apollonius expects his audience to look ahead to Prometheus' rescue, so he expects them to look ahead to the future rupture between Jason and Medea, but he also expects them to look through and beyond it, as Hera's prophetic reference to Medea's marriage to Achilles in the Elysian Fields demonstrates (4.811–16). There are signs that Apollonius is working against the expectations generated by this play in much the same way that he reworks the Homeric epics. Apollonius alludes to peripheral tales and other versions of the stories he presents, but what needs to be

---

[20] Wendel 1958 *ad* 2.1248–50a.

The influence of tragedy

distinguished are the times when he reinforces a model and when (and how) he prefers to destabilize it. The assumption that Apollonius translates the ethical polarities of the *Medea* without alteration into the *Argonautica* is undermined both by events in the epic and by other allusions to poetic, historical, and iconographic sources that lead to an alternate interpretation of the ambush's thematic significance and narrative function. Both in this episode and throughout the poem Apollonius is far more interested in staging scenes of reconciliation than in scenes of revenge. Thus, while the ambush may foreshadow aspects of the characters' deterioration in Euripides, in the *Argonautica* it functions as the central crisis that must be resolved in order for the Argonauts to return to Greece.

While it is apparent that the *Argonautica*'s consideration of familial strife, a central theme in Attic tragedy, sets it apart from Homeric (as well as Virgilian) epic, both of which explore open conflicts between unrelated rivals or foreign enemies,[21] the poem is unusual in its avoidance of the *topos* of vengeance. Characters in fifth-century tragedy as well as archaic epic are dramatically projected toward critical scenes of violent retribution: Achilles, Odysseus, Telemachus, Orestes, Clytemnestra, and Medea – and for that matter, Aeneas, in the conflict with Turnus. Episodes of violence in the *Argonautica*, by contrast, tend to be defensive and preemptive rather than retributive.[22] Admittedly, the audience knows from the beginning that Hera intends to punish Pelias, but his death is not narrated, and we are largely concerned with the positive attributes of the goddess as she protects and defends Jason and the other Argonauts. It is also true that the narrator forecasts Heracles' vengeance against the Boreads (1.1304–8), but the import of this reference is primarily aetiological: Heracles' motivation is given less consideration than monuments that are erected to commemorate the fallen heroes (see below). Finally, though Apsyrtus himself acts as an agent of vengeance sent by Aeëtes,[23] Jason and Medea express no personal animosity toward him, and there is no dramatic catharsis associated with his death. He is killed only because he threatens the plan of Medea and Jason, her sworn protector, to sail to Greece (4.395–409). His death is expedient,

---

[21] See Hutchinson 1988, 127, n. 69: "Ambushes on a grander scale were thought courageous in epic (Hom. *Il.* 13.276ff.), but they are all but completely excluded from the heroic action of the *Iliad* (Paris, *Il.* 11.379)."

[22] One exception is Argonauts' revenge for Caphaurus' killing of Canthus in Libya (4.1498–99). However, the reference is brief, only one and a half lines, and is metaphoric rather than explicit in character ("Nor did he [Caphaurus] escape the violent might (χαλεπὰς ἠλεύατο χεῖρας) of the heroes, when they learned what he did").

[23] Clauss 1993, 126, sees the murder of Apsyrtus as a cruel substitute for a more appropriate victim, Aeëtes.

though it solves their problems only temporarily. Still, the complications that arise from his murder as a source of blood guilt are equally temporary, for both the Erinys and the miasma of blood pollution are nullified by the apotropaic and expiatory rituals performed by Jason and Circe.

The narrative of the ambush does not dwell on the satisfactions of vengeance: not for Apsyrtus, who is dead, nor for Aeëtes, who is defeated by proxy, nor even for the Argonauts, who are, as a result of the anger of Zeus, arguably in worse shape after Apsyrtus' death than they were before. At its core, the ambush is an expression of one of the weaknesses inherent in a monarchic system. The inevitable transfer of power from one generation to the next promotes the fear of usurpation in lesser kings. Although Medea has no interest in her father's throne, her role in Apsyrtus' death suggests the bitter fruit of the struggle for succession: the bloody harrowing of dynastic regimes, a theme that the poet revisits throughout the poem. Both Aeëtes and Pelias fret about disloyalty and are in fact more concerned with prophecies that hint at familial betrayal than with possible attacks from the outside. Pelias hopes that his nephew Jason, who wears but one portentous sandal, will perish in the attempt to recover the Golden Fleece (1.15–17); Aeëtes similarly sends his grandsons, the sons of Chalciope and Phrixus, to certain death, outfitting them with a shabby boat that is, as Argus observes, the very worst of the Colchian fleet (3.342–43). Upon their unexpected return, Aeëtes accuses them of plotting to take the throne with the aid of pirates – that is, the Argonauts (3.367–81).

This same concern with the perils of monarchy is expressed in the contrast between these mistrustful kings and the confident Alcinous, who welcomes the Argonauts as though they were Phaeacian natives, and stands as the antithesis of Pelias and Aeëtes, who treat their own kin like foreign enemies. Interestingly, Alcinous' political security appears to be tied, rather paradoxically, to the lack of potential claimants to the Phaeacian throne. At the time of the Argo's voyage Nausicaa, the daughter of Alcinous and Arete, has not yet been born, for the *Argonautica* is set chronologically in the generation prior to the Trojan War.[24] As the female successor to the Phaeacian throne, Nausicaa exists as only a potentiality in the mind of the reader – like the children of Jason and Medea – but she exists nonetheless, and stands, in her singular potentiality, as a contrast to the complicated family trees of other royal houses in the *Argonautica*. A score of ambitious nephews, illegitimate sons, and grandsons born to foreign sons-in-law all appear as

---

[24] The Homeric Alcinous is but one of many Phaeacian kings, of course, and even within his own home greater power evidently lies, as Athena tells Odysseus, with Arete (see Chapter 4 and Mori 2001).

possible successors to the thrones of Iolcus and Colchis – not to mention legitimate but unreliable sons like Acastus, whose departure on the Argo flouts Pelias' order to remain at home.[25] The kingdom of Lemnos, on the other hand, suffers from the opposite extreme, the absolute negation of all heirs, male and female alike. The "latent" heir Nausicaa represents a happy resolution of the problems posed by an excessive number of potential heirs, and a biological void that would annihilate them. The reader knows that Alcinous and Arete will eventually produce at least one possible successor, but in any case they themselves seem undismayed regarding their present childlessness, in what may be another possible nod to the childless rule of Philadelphus and Arsinoë.[26] Whether or not one accepts this parallel, it is clear that the *Argonautica* not only associates secure succession with a just monarchy but also explores the various consanguineous configurations that are likely to trouble a kingdom.

The history of royal succession in Macedonia well illustrates the threats associated with multiple heirs. The treachery, ambush, and kin-murder that racked the houses of Alexander and his successors in Macedonia, Greece, Asia, and Egypt were public knowledge, and the interfamilial intrigues that were endemic to the Macedonian elite are reflected in the suspicions of Pelias and Aeëtes. The perverse dynamics of Aeëtes' family in particular are reminiscent of such internecine struggles, inasmuch as Aeëtes places his illegitimate son, Apsyrtus, at the head of an army to march against his younger half-sister, who then plots to kill him and finally succeeds in doing so. The ambush reveals the dark side of contemporary political machinations as the poem balances praise of the public persona of kings as diplomatic arbiters and pious intermediaries with condemnation of the private violence of assassination.

The next section therefore surveys the history of ambush and kin-killing among figures of authority in the fourth and third centuries, in order to clarify the distinction between ambush as a common political tactic and ambush as a poetic symbol of weakness, depravity, and compromised heroics. In connection with the latter I will also consider the iconographic representations of Achilles' ambush of the Trojan youth, Troilus, one of the stories from the epic cycle that is omitted from Homeric depictions of the siege of Troy. The Iliadic censure, both implicit and explicit, of ambush, has, like its role in classical drama, led to distorted readings not only of

---

[25] Cf. Lycus who sends his son, Dascylus, to accompany the Argonauts in an ambassadorial capacity (2.802–5).
[26] In contrast to Alcinous, of course, the Ptolemaic succession was secured by the male heir from Philadelphus' previous marriage to Arsinoë I (see Chapter 2).

this episode but also of the entire poem. As a consequence of a misplaced emphasis on the Homeric treatment of ambush, the *Argonautica* has often been reduced to a generic amalgam, an epic preamble to Euripides that attempts to compensate for its lack of genuinely heroic figures with the exploits of cowards, buffoons, victims, and antiheroes.

Much depends on an appreciation of the wide range of examples, whether historical or mythical, of *doloktasia* ("murder by stealth"), an act that, while less than commendable, is not a sign of irredeemable cowardice. The narrator condemns Apsyrtus' killing, but is at the same time careful to point out that it was committed under the influence of a malign and unpredictable deity. While this does not exonerate Jason and Medea, it goes some way toward explaining the poem's concern with their purification. Nor, for that matter, does the poem allude to Medea's future filicide or make an explicit connection between Apsyrtus' death and later events depicted in tragedy. One may prefer to regard this silence as yet another intentional variation on rhetorical *praeteritio*, but such a reading does little to offset my claim that the events of this poem work to contravene the expectations raised by fifth-century tragedy. In other words, identification of a model is not the same thing as being identical with it. The poet includes details, such as the reference to the Erinys who witnesses the murder, as part of the requisite entablature that secures an allusion to Attic tragedy, but the Argonautic portrayal of the spirits of retribution diverges nonetheless from those of its fifth-century forerunners. The glance of the Erinys has no real effect on subsequent action in the poem, apart, that is, from necessitating purification. Jason and Medea are neither hounded by the Erinyes nor do they fall ill of some metaphorical contagion; for their part the other Argonauts neither condemn nor even so much as question the ambush: all of them – even apparently Idas, ever sensitive to the depradations of heroic integrity – accept it as the best solution. That is, there is no mention of a discussion or objection to the plan. The narrative moves from the crafting of the *dolos*, which concludes at 4.421–22, straight to the *dolos* itself, the narrator's apostrophe to Eros, the ambush (4.423–81), and then the attack by the rest of the Argonauts on the Colchians anchored nearby (4.482–91). The episode concludes with the Argonauts' decision to lie low until the remaining Colchian forces are divided by strife at the loss of their leader (4.492–506). In short, while the narrator describes the ambush as a vile deed prompted by Eros, a source of much human suffering (4.445–49), this condemnation is best understood within the larger context of a poem that focuses on the proper limits of divine wrath. Zeus's anger (*cholos*) at the fall of Apsyrtus is the counterpart or successor to the conflict between Telamon and Jason at the end of Book 1, an exchange that illustrates the appropriate range of mortal anger.[27] In contrast to an ungovernable god like Eros, Zeus's emotions are measured and orderly, his punishments both just and fair, which explains why Jason and Medea will succeed in regaining his favor in Book 4, as others do elsewhere, by means of tribulation, ritual purification, and the offering of sacrifice.

MACEDONIAN INTRIGUE AND ASSASSINATION

Among the most troubling aspects of the ambush of Apsyrtus are features that were common to political murders among the Macedonian ruling classes before, during, and after Alexander's campaigns. Although the simile that compares the ambush to ritual slaughter invests this passage with a distinguished pedigree (4.468–69), both the brute fact of the murder and the narrative circumstances leading up to it constitute points of comparison with the practices of ancient *Realpolitik*. The mere prevalence of ambush among the Hellenistic dynasts cannot in itself be used to justify Medea's betrayal of her half-brother, yet it must be drawn into this discussion since, as seen in previous chapters, the poem's participation in the ideological representation of Greco-Macedonian power is as integral to its design as its emulation of poetic sources.

Ambushes, sometimes of family members, sometimes in violation of sacred ground or the rules of hospitality, have been attributed to many political figures of the day, from Alexander, Olympias, Perdiccas, Lysimachus, Antigonus the One-Eyed, and Ptolemy I Soter, to Demetrius Poliorcetes, Pyrrhus, Cassander, Agathocles, Ptolemy Ceraunus, and even Ptolemy II Philadelphus.[28] For the purposes of this discussion, the term ambush is used rather generally to include all types of unexpected killings that do not occur on the battlefield; the victim has been caught off-guard either because he is killed by one whom he trusted such as an ally, subordinate officer, or family member, or because he is in a situation, such as a feast or sacrifice, where violence is entirely unexpected.

The concentration of power along hereditary lines and the allegiance of troops to individual officers meant that betrayal was a necessary component of political survival and advancement. Assassinations and executions could almost be called routine with respect to Alexander's family and the veterans who served with him, for the more powerful a political ally became, the greater the threat he (or she) posed to everyone, allies and enemies alike.

---

[27] See Chapter 3; see also Mori 2005.   [28] For references, see discussion below.

Whether or not such murders actually occurred in the way that they have been described by later historians is less important than the fact that treachery and kin-murder were so closely affiliated with political activity at this time. Ambush, like dynastic marriage, was a defining characteristic of the power struggles of Hellenistic leaders. In truth, the expansion of Macedonian influence in Europe, Asia, and Africa was marked by assassination to such an extent that it could almost be described as the cornerstone of a Hellenistic military career.

The circumstances and characteristics of a number of the political murders committed in the years immediately preceding the composition of the *Argonautica* make them relevant to Apsyrtus' death. Two incidents in northern Africa serve to illustrate the strategic utility of eliminating the commander of an army. In both of the following cases, the army was appropriated after the death of the leader. The first incident is recorded by Diodorus, who relates that in 309 Antigonus the One-Eyed entrusted an army to his nephew Ptolemaeus. Ptolemaeus subsequently wrote to inform Ptolemy I Soter that he was changing his allegiance, and sailed together with the army from Chalcis to Cos. Ptolemy initially welcomed him but later became suspicious when Ptolemaeus began offering gifts to other leaders. In the end he had Ptolemaeus arrested, forced him to drink hemlock, and distributed Antigonus' troops among his own divisions (Diod. 20.27.3).

The second incident involves Agathocles, the tyrant of Sicily, who was at war with Carthage at this time. While campaigning in Africa early in the winter of 308, Agathocles made an alliance with Ophellas, a Macedonian who had served under Alexander and was, as Ptolemy's governor in Cyrene, in possession of a very large army (Diod. 20.40–42). In return for his support against the Carthaginians, Agathocles promised Ophellas autonomous rule of Cyrene. Ophellas accepted this offer, effectively ending his allegiance to Ptolemy, and headed west across the desert along the Syrtes Gulf with an army of over 20,000, more than half of whom consisted of non-combatants with their families. After two months of difficult travel they reached Agathocles' camp. Several days later the Cyreneans were overrun by Agathocles' forces, Ophellas was killed, and Agathocles wound up in control of both armies. The ancient sources (e.g., Diod. 20.42.3–5) assume that Agathocles betrayed his ally, whereas modern scholars generally emphasize the role of accident in Ophellas' death.[29] The ancient assumption that Agathocles

---

[29] See B. Niese, *RE* s.v. "Agathokles" 748–57; *Suda* s.v. Δημήτριος ὁ Ἀντιγόνου. For less suspicious interpretations of the murder see Laronde 1987, 358, and Meister 1984, 397. Laronde observes that the historians' suspicion of Agathocles is due to a common source, Timaeus of Tauromenium.

conspired against Ophellas is significant, however, because it shows the degree to which such treachery was expected.

The strategic premium placed on surprise meant that nothing was sacred: from a tactical perspective an invitation to attend a sacrifice offered a perfect opportunity for murder. In 297 Pyrrhus I, joint ruler of Epirus, who was supported by both Ptolemy Philadelphus and Agathocles,[30] learned that his co-regent Neoptolemus was plotting to kill him. Neoptolemus was the younger son of Cleopatra, Alexander's sister, and Alexander I of Epirus, the brother of Olympias (the same pair whose wedding had furnished the opportunity for the murder of Philip II). Neoptolemus was overheard as he plotted with his older sister to poison Pyrrhus; the latter responded by inviting the former to a sacrifice and then killing him at the feast (Plut. *Pyrr.* 5). Many aspects of this intrigue, from the involvement of siblings to the plot, counter plot, and assumed safety of a religious occasion, are comparable, if not precisely identical, to the main elements of the ambush of Apsyrtus. Most interesting is the fact that, whatever the religious fallout from the murder may have been, Pyrrhus' heroic reputation suffered little damage. Indeed, Pyrrhus was said to bear the closest resemblance of all the Successors to Alexander, and he himself went so far as to represent himself in his coinage and official portrait as the reincarnation of the king.[31] Even from Plutarch's point of view a sacrilegious ambush was not incompatible with legendary greatness.[32]

By the same token, the impious elements of Apsyrtus' ambush translate the strategic tactics of the day into a mythical past, firmly locating the event within a realistic and fairly widespread pattern of political intrigue. Of course, the same components that make this ambush a strategic success are also the source of its infamy: its location in a sacred space, the covert manner of attack, and the close kinship of the victim to (one of) the conspirators. While the narrative does not deny that Jason and Medea are in the wrong, it does submit a gentle defense by drawing attention to the lineage of their error, tracing it back to the impious injustice of kings like Pelias and Aeëtes, and the misdirection of malevolent gods like Eros. This "historical" perspective is consistent with the poem's focus on the causes of things, not just the aetiology of cultic practices but also the multiple factors

---

[30] Pyrrhus sealed the alliance with a marriage to Antigone, the stepdaughter of Ptolemy II. He would also marry the daughter of Agathocles as well as the daughter of Illyrian king Bardylis.
[31] Stewart 1993, 284–85, citing also Plut. *Pyrr.* 8.1 and Lucian *Ind.* 21. Pyrrhus also wrote his own autobiography (*FGrH* 229).
[32] On the contrast between Pyrrhus and Demetrius Poliorcetes see Bosworth 2002, 253–54, who notes that Pyrrhus' heroic reputation was largely based on his successful duel, described in Homeric terms by Plutarch (*Demetr.* 41.3–4; *Pyrrh.* 7.3–5).

that affect all actions, which goes some way toward explaining why there are three separate (though not mutually exclusive) explanations for the voyage of the Argo: Pelias' wish to rid himself of Jason (1–17), the recovery of the Golden Fleece to atone for Phrixus' attempted murder (2.1194–95; 3.336–39), and Hera's desire to punish Pelias through Medea (3.64–65, 74–75).

Another example of the poem's concern with causal motivation – and one that is especially apt with regard to the Apsyrtus episode – is the dispute between Jason and Telamon at the loss of Heracles (see Chapter 3). After Telamon apologizes for accusing Jason of conspiracy, Jason makes a point of forgiving him because he recognizes that the mistake was made out of loyalty, and not for the sake of greed or ambition (1.1339–42). The offense is obviously not as serious as that of Apsyrtus' murder, but a similar logic applies. Neither Jason nor Telamon are motivated by revenge, material gain, or an increase in political power; just as Telamon's guilt is mitigated by his concern for a friend, so Jason's guilt is mitigated by divine interference (Eros) and by the fact that he is upholding his sworn oath to marry Medea.

Such distinctions and considerations made a difference in the ancient world just as they do in the modern. Any ruler would do well to consecrate an aggressive campaign as consistent with divine will and imperative for the country. The Ptolemies were no exception inasmuch as they characterized some of their military achievements as crusades for the recovery of temple artifacts (see Chapter 2). The brief of the warrior-king – to honor the gods, protect the people, and vanquish their enemies – is a potent blend of piety and slaughter.[33] Jason and Medea are not kings, but they do lead the Argonauts, and what is interesting about this ambush is the fact that Apsyrtus' blood muddies the hygienic formulation of this nominal triad (piety, fidelity, and conquest) by means of points of contamination and incongruity. As he falls to the ground Apsyrtus' bloody hands stain the veil and gown of Medea (4.471–74), showing that kinship is no guarantee of loyalty or security, that acts inspired by pious oaths may lead to pollution and, worse still, that sacred ground may serve the purposes of violence, rather than the other way around. The *Argonautica* does not present blood guilt and political leadership as mutually exclusive concepts. On the contrary, the likelihood of pollution makes a restorative necessity of piety for kings and heroes alike.

In sum, the murder complicates the poem's usual association of piety with virtue by exposing the possibility that any mortal, even one who is dear to

---

[33] The parallel between Jason's behavior and that of kings is not exact, but his role as the political leader of an armed group of heroes and the arbiter of foreign quarrels and agreements (1.340) puts him in a comparable position.

the gods, may commit a sacrilegious act. In staging the ambush of Apsyrtus, the poem neither condemns nor exonerates the murders committed by political figures of the day: rather, it portrays such acts as the eventual result of mortal vulnerability, royal excess, and divine influence. The crisis created by the ambush puts to work the poem's principal virtues of negotiation and moderation, and shows that while the punishment of the gods is inevitable, the straight justice of Zeus will be satisfied when those responsible for wrongdoing undergo ritual expiation as well as, in some cases, prolonged suffering. The poem is less concerned to reconcile the destiny of individual characters, like Jason and Medea, with their misdeeds, than to reveal the character of Zeus's wrath, which, in contrast to the unpredictable madness of Eros, is bounded, rational, and orderly, even in the case of an ambush of a blood relation in a temple precinct.

TROILUS AND ACHILLES

I now turn to artistic representations of ambush, which also play a significant role in the proper appreciation of this complex episode. If *doloktasia* is stereotypical of the Macedonian elite in this period, it is by no means restricted to it and appears frequently in mythic stories and the epic cycle. One story that was often represented by Attic vase painters was Achilles' ambush of the Trojan youth Troilus near a temple of Apollo. Although this episode is not mentioned in either of the Homeric poems, it was evidently well known, and Achilles' involvement in the ambush suggests that *doloktasiai* were not culturally encoded as low or cowardly acts. The Homeric Achilles, for example, faults Agamemnon for failing to participate in *lochoi*, the small ambushing parties (*Il.* 1.227–28) that were evidently reserved for the elite.[34] In this section I consider how several epic (but non-Homeric) parallels dealing with Achilles' killing of the youths Trambelus and Troilus work to call into question interpretations of Jason's *doloktasia* as intrinsically "unheroic."

In the story of Trambelus, Achilles discovers the former's identity only after he kills him during a raid on Miletus; he then mourns his death and erects a tomb in his honor. Accident and regret figure prominently here, just as they do when Jason mistakenly kills Cyzicus, the Dolionian king in Book 2. Although the death of Trambelus, like the ambush of Troilus, does not appear in Homeric epic, the story was probably known to Apollonius,

---

[34] On the *lochos* as a vehicle for the demonstration of aristocratic *arete*, see the notes by Pulleyn 2000 *ad.* 1.226–27 and Kirk 1985 *ad.* 1.226–27.

for it was recorded by Istrus, one of Callimachus' pupils.[35] Allusions to episodes from the epic cycle, if less popular than Homeric material, were in fact central to Apollonius' Callimachean project of redacting epic themes and events for a learned Alexandrian audience. As Hunter observes, "much of what happens in Apollonius' poem has closer affinities to what modern scholars regard as typically 'cyclic' than to Homeric poetry."[36] Such allusions to Achillean *parerga* flatter the knowledge of the reader, but they also draw attention to other aspects of the heroic paradigm. Given the variety of stories attached to Achilles, one may grant that Jason's behavior can at times be un-Homeric without further conceding that it is also consistently un-Achillean. If Apollonius is looking to the epic cycle (as well as history) for heroic models, it is not surprising to find contradictions in Jason's characterization. One likely possibility is that certain aspects of Apollonius' Jason recall those of Achilles – even an Achilles who may mourn his victim, an unusual counterbalance to the remorseless killer of *Iliad* 22. And, since the poet relies on different comparisons in order to achieve different kinds of effects, the semantics of one allusion need not necessarily be consistent with those of another. The Cyzicus and Trambelus episodes, which converge in their elegiac depiction of the "lamenting hero," are less disruptive and controversial than the stories of Apsyrtus and Troilus, which feature an impious and transgressive hero.

Troilus' ambush was recorded in the *Cypria*,[37] a part of the cycle, no longer extant, that dealt with the events leading up to the Trojan conflict.[38] In Homer there is but one mention of Troilus, who is numbered by Priam among his favorite sons, all of whom have been killed: Mestor, Hector, and Troilus "delighting in horses" (*hippiocharmen*, *Il.* 24.257). This epithet is consistent with vase paintings that typically represent Troilus riding a pair of horses,[39] or alternatively, as one who fights from a chariot.[40] The twelfth-century commentator Eustathius notes (at *Il.* 24.257) that Troilus was one "whom they say was ambushed by Achilles as he exercised his

---

[35] Istrus (*FGrH* 334 F 57). On the surviving fragments of Istrus, see the introduction to Jackson 2000, 7–16. The story is also recorded by the later Hellenistic writer Lycophron (*Alex.* 467).
[36] Hunter 2001, 124.
[37] Τρωΐλον φονεύει, Procl. *Chrest.*, in Monro and Allen 1912, 5:105, l. 12.
[38] For discussion of the history of this myth, see Robertson 1990 and 1970. For discussion of the variations in the iconographic evidence, see A. Kossatz-Deissmann, "Das Troilosabenteuer," *LIMC* I.1, sec. VII, pp. 72–95 nos. 11–84; Gantz 1993, 597–603 ("Troilos and Lykaon").
[39] He is physically seated, however, on only one of the two horses.
[40] Robertson 1990 notes that the epithet *hippiocharmen* seems to mean one who fights from a chariot rather than a horseman. So for example Virgil describes the dying and unarmed Troilus dragged head down from his chariot on the battlefield (*Aen.* 1.474–78). See also Ausonius, *Epitaphia* 18, "Troilo."

Troilus and Achilles 203

horses in the Thymbraeum."[41] A temple of Apollo was also located in this precinct, which was named for the river Thymbrius (from the nearby town called Thymbra), a tributary of the River Scamander on the Trojan plain.

Philostratus' *Heroicus*, a third-century AD dialogue that focuses on the exploits of Protesilaus and Achilles,[42] tells of another ambush at this same location and seems to be related to or even based in part on the Troilus myth. One of the two speakers in the dialogue, a vinedresser, has ostensibly learned much about the Trojan conquest from a revivified Protesilaus, the first Greek to fall at Troy. Achilles, according to Protesilaus, was smitten by the charming Polyxena during negotiations for Hector's ransom, and has agreed as a result to withdraw Achaean forces from Troy in exchange for marriage with her. However, he is preemptively ambushed by Paris (δολοφονηθείς ἔπεσεν, *Her.* 51.2) as he sacrifices at the altar of Thymbraeus Apollo (51.1–6, see also Hyg. *Fab.* 110). Paris and Apollo are connected with the death of Achilles in this story, just as they are in Homer (*Il.* 22.358–60), but the plot has been reconfigured with the substitution of Achilles as the victim instead of Troilus. Philostratus was writing many centuries after Apollonius, but what is important here is the persistent association of Achilles with an ambush in this particular temple precinct, even if his actual part in the ambush has been changed.

Achilles' ambush of Troilus was popular among black-figure vase painters in the sixth century, though it became far less common in fifth-century Attic red-figure. Achilles is typically depicted crouching behind a fountain outside the walls of Troy in wait for Troilus to finish exercising his horses. Other images show him ambushing the unarmed boy as the horses drink, either chasing him to the nearby altar, or seizing him by the hair as he kills him. The black-figure images can be quite violent: on some vases Achilles is hurling Troilus' decapitated head at the approaching Trojans who fight to recover the body.[43]

---

[41] ὃν φασὶν ἵππους ἐν τῷ Θυμβραίῳ γυμνάζοντα λόγχῃ πεσεῖν ὑπ' Ἀχιλλέως. See also Apollod. *Epit.* 3.32.

[42] For an introduction to Philostratus and the only English translation (with facing Greek text), see Maclean and Aitken 2001.

[43] For Achilles in hiding behind the fountain with Troilus and Polyxena, see, e.g., a mid-sixth-century amphora from Chalcis (Rome, Villa Guilia 56069); another amphora from the same period (London, Brit. Mus. 97.7-21.2 = *LIMC* I.1 *s.v.* Achilleus, sec. VII.a 225 = *ABV* 86, 8); a late sixth-century red-figure hydria from Vulci (Leningrad, Ermitage B628 St. 1588 = *LIMC* I.1 *s.v.* Achilleus, sec. VII.a 266); a mid-fourth-century red-figure bell crater from Campania (Sydney, Nicholson Mus. 69.10 = *LIMC* I.1 *s.v.* Achilleus, sec. VII.a 272). For pursuit scenes, see the mid-fourth-century black-figure hydria (Heidelberg = *LIMC* I.1 *s.v.* Achilleus, sec. VII.b 295); a late sixth-century red-figure bowl that shows a cloaked Troilus astride two horses (London, Brit. Mus. E 13 = *LIMC* I.1 *s.v.* Achilleus, sec. VII.b 342); a Siana cup with a very young Troilus (New York, Met. Mus. 1.8.6 = *LIMC* I.1

Polyxena is sometimes represented in the scene as well, evidently escorted by her brother to the fountain in order to fetch water. On an early sixth-century Siana cup a frightened Polyxena turns away as Troilus wheels his horses about with Achilles in hiding; a black-figure painting on an Athenian tripod *pyxis* shows Achilles about to pull Troilus from the back of a horse while a backward-glancing Polyxena runs ahead.[44] She is also included in the Troilus scene that is located directly beneath the Wedding of Peleus on the famous François Vase.[45] In this scene a young girl is running towards Troy ahead of Troilus,[46] who is riding one of a pair of horses and is being pursued by a (badly damaged) male figure, presumably Achilles.

The *Cypria* also linked Polyxena with Troilus by recounting both their deaths, although he died early in the history of the war,[47] while she survived until the end when she was sacrificed or committed suicide beside the grave of Achilles.[48] Martin Robertson suggests that Achilles may have fallen in love with Polyxena during the ambush of her brother:

> Nothing can be proved, but it makes extremely good sense to suppose that the theme was part of the interweaving of the stories of Polyxene and Troilus which is demonstrated in art and literature in the Archaic period. Waiting at the fountain to kill the boy, Achilleus sees and loves his sister, and that is why her death as well as Troilus' was recounted in the *Cypria*.[49]

But regardless of when Achilles may have fallen in love with Polyxena, or when these deaths actually took place, her association with the story deepens the resemblance of Troilus' ambush to that of Apsyrtus because it creates a similar triangle of a sister romantically linked with her brother's killer. The

---

s.v. Achilleus, sec. VII.b 307 = *ABV* 51, 4). For the murder at the altar: see the late seventh-century bronze work on shield bands, Olympia (Olympia B 987 and 988); for the hurling of the decapitated head: see the early sixth-century Tyrrhenian amphora (Florence, Mus. Arch. 70993 = *LIMC* I.1 s.v. Achilleus, sec. VII.c 360 = *ABV* 96, 5; Munich Antikensammlungen 1426 = *LIMC* I.1 s.v. Achilleus, sec. VII.c 364 = *ABV* 95, 5).

[44] Black-figure tripod pyxis, Athens, c. 550 ([West] Berlin 1728); black-figure Siana cup by C painter c. 570 (Louvre CA 6113 = *LIMC* I.1 s.v. Achilleus, sec. VII.b 310).

[45] 570–560 BC (Florence, Mus. Arch. 4209 = *LIMC* I.1 s.v. Achilleus, sec. VII.b 292 = *ABV* 76).

[46] Gantz 1993, 599 identifies this partially obscured female figure as Polyxena, since the last two letters of her name have survived.

[47] Apollod. *Epit.* 3.32.

[48] Polyxena's sacrifice at the tomb of Achilles was mentioned in the *Iliu Persis* (see Procl. *Chrest.*, Monro and Allen 1912, 5:108.6–8). See also Eur. *Hec.* 218–24; see further the Scholiast's comment at Eur. *Hec.* 41 (Schwartz 1887), which states that according to the *Cypriaka* Polyxena died after being wounded during the capture of the city, and that according to others the marriage to Achilles was arranged in the sacred grove of Thymbraeus Apollo. Cf. Philostr. *Her.* 51.6. On the identification of the *Cypriaka* with the *Cypria*, see Burgess 1996, 90–91 with n. 53.

[49] Robertson 1990, 65. Robertson notes that the death of Polyxena – which properly belongs to the *Iliu Persis* – is out of place in the *Cypria*, which deals with events that took place before the war and during its first ten years (64).

similarity is limited, of course, because the characters' motivations differ (i.e., Polyxena is not plotting against her brother), but the two stories still share a number of common elements. Troilus and Apsyrtus are both eastern princes ambushed by Greek heroes who are involved, either before or after the murder, with the sisters of the victims. Most importantly, the corpse is mutilated in both stories. Troilus is, as was noted earlier, decapitated in the archaic sources, and Apsyrtus is also dismembered in earlier versions as well. Troilus is usually depicted as a youth or even a child,[50] and while Apollonius' Apsyrtus is old enough to lead an army, in other versions he too is very young,[51] and is either murdered at home in Colchis or is abducted and subsequently killed by Medea,[52] who cuts his body into pieces and flings them overboard[53] to allow the escape of the Argonauts as Aeëtes stops to collect the body parts.[54] The mutilation is realized by Apollonius as the performance of an apotropaic ritual, the *maschalismos*, which entails cutting off the extremities (*exargmata*, 4.477) of the corpse, licking some of the blood and spitting three times to atone for the *doloktasia*.[55] The phrase

---

[50] Robertson 1990, 67: "Except in his first naming in the *Iliad*, Troilus is always in the Archaic period, whether in literature or art, represented as a boy, not fully grown." However, the Scholiast at *Il.* 24.254 observes that Troilus could not have been a youth if he is counted among the best of the Trojans.

[51] Pherecyd. fr. 73; Ov. *Met.* 7.54.   [52] Soph. *Colch.* fr. 319; Eur. *Med.* 1334.

[53] Body thrown into the Phasis River: Pherecydes *FGrH* 3 F 32b; see further the Scholiast's comments Wendel 1958 *ad* 4.223–30a. Body thrown into the Pontus: Apollod. *Bibl.* 1.9.24. According to the Scholiast on Eur. *Med.* 167 (Schwartz 1887), Medea killed her young brother with poison. Other later sources for dismemberment along the coast include Cic. *De Imp. Cn. Pomp.* 22; Ov. *Tr.* 3.9.2ff.; *Her.* 6.129ff.; 12.113ff. For Tomi as the spot of the murder, see Ov. *Tr.* 3.9.5ff.; Apollod. *Bibl.* 1.9.24. For the murder along the Illyrian coast, see Orph. *Arg.* 1022ff.; Apollod. *Bibl.* 1.9.24. Hyg. *Fab.* 23 describes the death of Apsyrtus at a temple of Minerva after he overtakes the Argonauts twice and Alcinous tries to intercede between the factions. Val. Flacc. *Arg.* 8.261–87, 369–34 follows Apollonius in depicting Apsyrtus as a young man, however the unfinished epic ends before describing the fate of Apsyrtus (8.375–84).

[54] Hunter 1989, 15–16 notes the influence on Apollonius of two archaic epics: Eumelus' *Corinthiaca* and the anonymous catalogue poem *Naupactia* (on the date of the *Naupactia*, see Hunter 1989, 20 with n. 91). In the *Naupactia* Aeëtes treacherously invites the Argonauts to dinner while planning to burn the Argo. Apollonius was also probably influenced by the *Lyde*, a fourth-century elegiac narrative of unhappy loves by Antimachus of Colophon (Hunter 1989, 17–18 with n. 75). In Dionysius Scytobrachion's third-century account of the voyage there is no mention of Apsyrtus: instead Jason kills Aeëtes during their escape (preserved in Diod. 4.40–55: on the date of the *Naupactia* see Hunter 1989, 20 with n. 91). Pind. *Pyth.* 4 omits any reference to Apsyrtus.

[55] For more evidence on ritual spitting, see Muth 1954, 31. On the *maschalismos* (also called the *akroteriasmos*), see Vian 2002, *ad* 4.477 and Garvie 1988 *ad* 439. The hands, feet, nose, and ears of the corpse are removed and sometimes hung around the neck or under the arms of the corpse. The ritual is attested in tragic sources: see, e.g., Aesch. *Cho.* 439; Soph. *El.* 444–45; Aesch. *Perrhaeb.* and *Laeus* fr. 186a Radt 1985; Soph. *Troilus* fr. 623 Pearson 1917, vol. 2. See *Etym. M. s.v.* ἀπάργματα; *Suda s.vv.* μασχαλίσματα, μασχαλισθῆναι. Cf. the related ritual of wiping the blood of the sword on the victim's head, Soph. *El.* 444–45; *Suda s.v.* ἀποτροπιαζόμενοι.

πλήρη μασχαλισμάτων ("full of the extremities of a corpse") also appears, tellingly, in a fragment from Sophocles' lost *Troilus*.[56] The precise context for the phrase is not known, but the reference to the unusual act combined with the other details noted above makes it likely that Apollonius had either the tragic or the iconographic depiction of Achilles' ambush of Troilus in mind as a predecessor of the Apsyrtus episode.

The *Troilus* ambush offers a heroic precedent for Jason's actions in the Apsyrtus episode, and the precedent is crucial since it is the unpalatability of the *maschalismos* in particular that has generated the greatest controversy – no doubt because as epic violence goes, Apsyrtus' killing is itself rather brief and unremarkable. It is hard to resist the impression that Apollonius is intentionally playing with his audience's notion of the heroic because of the way he deploys the term *heros* in this scene. The narrator's reference to Jason as hero (Ἥρως δ' Αἰσονίδης, 4.477) during the *maschalismos* has been regarded as ironic,[57] yet the narrator also refers to Apsyrtus as *heros* when he falls to the ground some lines earlier (4.471). The use of the same term to refer both to the victor and to the vanquished seems not coincidental here and in fact suggests the model provided by Homeric battle scenes. So in *Iliad* 6.61–63, for example, Agamemnon, called *heros* at 6.61, persuades Menelaus not to spare the life of Adrastus (6.63), or when the *heros* Idomeneus (13.384 and 439) kills the *heros* Alcathous (13.428). The fall of Apsyrtus thus looks ahead not only to the ambush of Troilus, but also to the pitiable deaths of all the heroes on the plains of Troy.

Zeus's anger at Apsyrtus' murder likewise alludes to the anger of the gods at Achilles' mistreatment of Hector's corpse. Apollonius alters the Homeric material, once again, by transforming Achilles' abuse of the corpse into an appropriate ritual for murders by stealth, and it is in fact this description of the *maschalismos* as *themis* ("proper" or "customary") for such murders that brings back the question of irony in the poem. Some find ironic the assertion that a ritual like the *maschalismos* could be considered *themis* under any circumstances, and conclude that the narrator is implying that Jason's behavior in this scene is in fact the opposite of what is proper, let alone heroic.[58] But since there can be no doubt that the ritual is morbidly unpleasant, the real question is whether the term *themis* could be straightforwardly (or

---

[56] Soph. fr. 623 Pearson 1917, vol. 2.   [57] See Hutchinson 1988, 127.
[58] Goldhill 1991, 331 sees as ironic the description of the ritual of spitting the blood of the dead man as *themis*. Both Hutchinson 1988, 127 and Green 1997 *ad* 4.477–81 find irony in the reference to Jason as a hero in l. 477. See also Newman 2001, 333–37, who argues that Apollonius so undercut conventional heroism that the "official caretakers" of the Ptolemies' image encouraged his removal to Rhodes, in much the same way as Augustus would later banish Ovid to Tomi.

straight-facedly) applied to it. If, as appears to be the case, Achilles has also performed the same ritual in a tragedy, then the term would indeed be appropriate – metapoetically at least, in the sense of "customary" – that is, "appropriate in scenes like this."[59]

One might still object that the Sophoclean fragment yields little in the way of context: it is not implausible that other characters in the missing play condemn the ritual, a turn of events that would indeed invest the Argonautic reference with a considerable degree of irony. Yet such an assumption is inevitably speculative, and at the very outset comes into conflict with what we can positively observe of Jason's behavior in this poem. For him to observe what is *themis*, even when he has committed *doloktasia*,[60] is consistent with his characteristic fidelity to ritual demands. What is more, the poet's consistently un-ironic use of the term *themis* elsewhere in the *Argonautica* also makes it unlikely that it would be used ironically in just this one instance. Of the poem's twenty-four references to what is *themis*, the term occurs eleven times in the speeches of characters who intend to persuade others or to justify their own behavior.[61] In the other instances (including the reference to the spitting of Apsyrtus' blood at 4.479) the narrator refers to what is according to custom.[62] In none of these could the

---

[59] Another example of an intertextual allusion to similar characters or practices in other, earlier works is Apollonius' reference to Alcinous' nocturnal deliberations with Arete "in time past" (ὡς τὸ πάροιθεν, 4.1068), meaning in the time of the *Odyssey* – which is set chronologically later than events in the *Argonautica*, but is, after all, a much older work. See Mori 2001, 94.

[60] Cf. Agamemnon's reference to the right (*themis*) of the allies to demand the death of Iphigenia (Aesch. *Ag.* 216) and Clytemnestra's usage at *Ag.* 1433. These references to *themis* are rhetorically loaded because the murderers themselves are using the term to justify their acts, whereas the Apollonian narrator simply uses the term to explain why Jason performs the ritual.

[61] Polyxo notes she will be buried according to the dictates of *themis* before evil strikes (1.692); Hypsipyle tells Jason that the Lemnian women had hoped their husbands would begin to think things in accordance with what is *themis* (1.822); Iris tells the sons of Boreas it is not *themis* for them to threaten the Harpies with swords (2.288); Phineus says it is not *themis* for Argonauts to know everything (2.311); Tiphys notes it is not *themis* for the Argo to be caught because Athena built her (2.614); Lycus states that it is *themis* for weaker men to recompense the stronger who help them (2.800); Jason reassures Medea that she will come to no harm since they have met as friends on holy ground where it is not *themis* to sin (3.981); Jason promises to reward Medea as it is *themis* if she helps him (3.991); Medea claims that she and Jason are bound to each other by *dike* and *themis* (4.373); Medea swears it is not *themis* for her curses to fall to earth unaccomplished (4.387); finally, Hera tells Thetis that Zeus left her alone because Themis (here personified as a goddess) revealed that she (Thetis) would give birth to a son greater than his father (4.800).

[62] Narrator's references to *themis*: it is *themis* to pour libations to Zeus (1.517); it is not *themis* to sing of the secret rites of Samothrace (1.921); the anchor stone of the Argo is moved to the temple of Jasonian Athena as a sacred relic, as was *themis* (1.960); in the context of Cyzicus' death: it is not *themis* for people to exceed their allotment of life (1.1035); the narrator praises Apollo saying that it is *themis* for his hair to remain uncut forever (2.709); funeral games for Cyzicus are held in accordance with what is *themis* (1.1061); countless sheep are sacrificed at Idmon's funeral, as is *themis* for the dead (2.840); the things it is *themis* to do publicly, the Mossynici do at home (2.1019); it is not *themis* for

use of the term be construed as ironic: ten of the references indicate proper ritual behavior,[63] while the remaining two are concerned with social protocols.[64] In describing the *maschalismos* as *themis* the narrator is announcing – without, I submit, winking at the audience – that this ritual is customarily done (at least in epic and tragic stories) by murderers who rely on stealth. An ironic reading of this observation leans heavily on inference; it is, interestingly, both derived from and supportive of the tragic view of the ambush that was discussed at the beginning of this chapter. But regardless of whether one sees the performance of the *maschalismos* as *themis* or "*themis*," the similarity between the two ambushes is significant, not because one must absolutely agree that the one is modeled on the other (although that remains a distinct possibility), but rather because it demonstrates the degree to which the *Argonautica* plays with notions of heroism. Yes, the ambush is un-Homeric, yet it is not unheroic because Achilles too was known for attacking a defenseless youth in a sacred precinct.[65] Again, Achilles' motivation may differ from that of Jason, yet even here it is possible to trace a resemblance.

While some sources suggest that Achilles is avenging the rejection of his erotic pursuit of the handsome Troilus,[66] others explain that the Achaeans were fated not to take Troy if Troilus did not die at a young age.[67] The first account has nothing in common with the Apsyrtus story, at least as Apollonius has it, but the second is intriguing for two reasons. First, like Jason and Apsyrtus, both of whom are young and sent out on sea voyages to recover precious objects,[68] Achilles and Troilus are doublets. Not only are their premature deaths prophetically tied to the fall of Troy, but also, as the *Heroicus* material shows, either Troilus or Achilles may be cast as victim of an ambush in the Thymbraeum. In addition, the prophecy establishes Troilus'

Amazons to burn offerings of sheep or oxen on their altar but rather horses (2.1174); it is not *themis* for Colchians to bury male corpses (3.205); spitting of blood three times is *themis* for murderers in expiation of killings by stealth (4.479); Argonauts mixed kraters to the blessed immortals, an act which is *themis* (4.1129); not even Apollo the Healer (if it is *themis* to say so) could have saved Mopsus (4.1511).

[63] 1.517, 921, 960, 1061; 2.709, 840, 1174; 3.205; 4.1129, 1511.   [64] 1.1035; 2.1019.

[65] Unlike Apsyrtus, however, Troilus is often shown to be on horseback, and on one Corinthian amphora is pointing a bow at Achilles (Zurich ETH 4, from the Graphische Sammlung in the Eidgenössische Technische Hochschule, Zurich).

[66] Lyc. 307–13; see also Servius' commentary on *Aen.* 1.474. See Gantz 1993, 2:601–2.

[67] The death of Troilus, together with the loss of the Palladion and the upper lintel of the Phrygian gate, entailed the destruction of Troy (see Plautus *Bacch.* 953–54). Again, see Gantz 1993, 2:602.

[68] Jason and Apsyrtus as well as the young Dolionian king Cyzicus all share similar features. Clauss 1993, 173–74 compares Jason and Cyzicus, both of whom have the first growth of golden down (ἴουλοι, 1.972; cf. Callim. *Hec.* fr. 274 Pfeiffer i) on their cheeks; Hunter 1993, 42–43 notes other similarities between Apsyrtus and Cyzicus.

death as expedient and crucial for a Greek victory, a practical political consideration that has little to do with Homeric vengeance. It also looks ahead to Jason and Medea's tactical attempt to dissolve local support for the Colchians by removing the head, as it were, of the Colchian army. Although the many shifting components of the Troilus story conspire against an absolutely certain interpretation, Achilles' dispassionate elimination of the obstacle to Greek success provides a more fitting precedent for the calculated killing of Apsyrtus than Medea's vengeful and impassioned slaughter of her own children.

KIN-MURDER AND COLONIZATION IN THE *ARGONAUTICA*

The preceding analysis has helped to place the ambush into better perspective by means of widely known comparanda from the epic cycle and classical tragedy. However, the considerable range of Apollonius' allusions means that an understanding of the Apsyrtus episode, like other aspects of this poem, also entails sifting through a number of cultural and artistic influences, from stories found in myth, epic, and tragedy, to iconographic images and matters of historical record. Although these multiple influences do not suggest that the ambush should be seen as anything less than a crime, they do show that its primary dramatic function is to serve as an errant and unlooked-for misfortune, whose consequences will be overcome.

For one thing, the brevity of Apsyrtus' murder, noted by Wilamowitz-Moellendorf,[69] diminishes its dramatic force, as does the audience's lack of familiarity with Apsyrtus himself. In contrast to the dramatic build-up to the deaths of Hector and Turnus, or the killing of Penelope's Suitors, there is little to prepare the audience for this episode. Apsyrtus rarely appears in the poem prior to the ambush, and the reader does not see enough of him to become emotionally engaged with his fate (especially in contrast to the representation of Medea). The narrator notes that Apsyrtus was born to Asterodia, a nymph of the Caucasus, before Aeëtes married Idyia. His peers call him Phaethon ("The Bright One") because he outshines them all (3.241–44), and later in the poem he holds the reins of the chariot of his father, who stands behind him, raging with a flaming pine brand after the Argonauts' escape (4.223–25). These two brief mentions hint at his coming misfortune by suggesting the fiery death of Phaethon, the son of Helius (and therefore Apsyrtus' uncle) felled by the thunderbolt of Zeus and left

---

[69] Wilamowitz-Moellendorf 1924, 195 suggests that description of the murder should have been longer ("Auch der Mord selbst wird nachher kurz und packend erzählt").

to smolder in River Eridanus (τυφομένου Φαέθοντος, 4.623),[70] and the fate of Troilus "delighting in horses," the one who fights from a chariot.

The remaining references to Apsyrtus are similarly brief. He commands the part of the fleet that first overtakes the Argonauts, anticipates them by hurrying upstream, and then surrounds them (4.305–306, 314, 332–33). He is soon tricked with guest gifts (4.421–22) and led into ambush "like a small child" (4.454–62).[71] I will look more closely at his death scene in the next section; for now it suffices to note that it verges on the epigrammatic. Together with other sudden accidents in the poem it forms a series of fatal vignettes: the miniature tragedies of Cyzicus and Clite, and the Argonauts Idmon (boar attack, 2.815–34), Tiphys (rapid illness, 2.854–57), Canthus (slain by Caphaurus, 4.1485–501), and Mopsus (snake bite, 4.1502–36). Such consistent brevity would seem to be intentional on the part of the poet, as a conscious avoidance of epic excess, but in any case there is little dramatic difference between all these incidental deaths. It is true that by likening Apsyrtus to a small child the narrator introduces a note of pathos and reminds the audience of the other version of the story in which Medea herself dismembers him,[72] and yet his murder does not come crashing down in the manner of a grand emotional fugue. Like other incidental deaths in the *Argonautica*, it is soon left behind in the narrative wake of the Argonauts' subsequent adventures.

Thus, although the fall of Apsyrtus is sad, like that of a fair and youthful warrior at Troy, the focus remains on Jason and Medea: Apsyrtus' blood marks her veil (*kaluptren*, 4.473) and gown (*peplos*, 4.474), and the Erinys immediately takes note (4.475–76), though Jason forestalls vengeance, in the customary way, by means of the *maschalismos* (4.477–79). As a result, the ambush is reminiscent of a number of myths about heroic figures guilty of murder. The killer is forced to undergo purification and exile in order to be free from pollution, but the extraordinary nature of the crime, whether murder of a family member or murder by stealth (or both), often makes it difficult to find someone willing to purify them. Inasmuch as these myths hinge on the troubled fate of the hero rather than the victim's misfortune, the narrative addresses the successful removal of the pollution.

A number of canonical heroes are known for committing murders by stealth, often of family members, including Heracles, Ixion, Tydeus, and Theseus – not to mention Achilles, whose ambush of Troilus was discussed

---

[70] On the association between Apsyrtus and Phaethon, see Albis 1996, 58.
[71] This last reference suggests a rationalization on Apollonius' part of the versions in which Medea is said to have killed her brother when he was a child.
[72] See Hunter 1993, 21 with n. 52.

above. In a political dispute over the throne of Athens, Theseus treacherously kills his uncle Pallas and fifty cousins, and is consequently forced to spend the next year in exile at Troezen.[73] Likewise Tydeus, the father of Diomedes and one of the seven against Thebes, travels to Argos from Calydon after shedding kindred blood.[74] Interestingly, although Theseus and Tydeus must go into exile and be purified, the murders do not damage their social positions (except of course where the victims' families are concerned). So it is that Adrastus, for example, welcomes Tydeus after his purification as a suitable husband for his daughter.[75] These myths center on the difficulty of being purified for horrible crimes, but the hero's eventual absolution for the murder is presented as natural and even unremarkable.

The difficulty experienced by Jason and Medea in obtaining purification also recalls what other heroes, namely Heracles and Ixion, face. When Heracles invites Iphitus to dinner, kills him, and keeps his twelve mares,[76] Neleus, king of Pylos, refuses to purify him because of his friendship with Eurytus, Iphitus' father. Even after his eventual purification at Delphi Heracles continues to suffer from a punitive disease and is cured only after three years' enslavement and the compensatory payment to Eurytus of his own purchase price. Ixion, on the other hand, is guilty of hurling his father-in-law Dioneus into a pit of burning coals when he comes to collect the agreed-upon bride price for his daughter Dia. Because Ixion has committed the first known kin-murder, no one is willing to purify him until Zeus finally relents.[77] Ixion unwisely chooses to repay the god by trying to seduce Hera, a crime for which he is then subjected to the eternal torture of being tied to an endlessly rotating wheel.[78] Technically speaking, then, Ixion's infamous punishment is the penalty for a failed seduction, rather than a successful murder, although it is possible that the latter

---

[73] Eur. *Hipp.* 33–37; Paus. 1.22.2.
[74] Tydeus escapes an ambush by killing forty-nine Cadmians: *Il.* 4.382–400; 5.800–808; 10.285–90. See also Eur. *Supp.* 148; *Oeneus* fr. 558.2; Apollod. *Bibl.* 3.6.1. See Apollod. *Bibl.* 1.8.5 for differing accounts: he killed Alcathous, brother of Oineus, or nine cousins according to the author of the *Alcmaeonid*, or his brother Olenias according to the fifth-century Athenian writer Pherecydes.
[75] As a parricide Adrastus may not be an example of the best society, but Athena herself intended to give Tydeus immortality when he was dying from a stomach wound after the attack on Thebes. Athena changed her mind when she witnessed him eating the brains of Melanippus' severed head (Hdt. 1.35–45; Apollod. *Bibl.* 3.6.8).
[76] *Od.* 21.24–30 (the mares are cattle at Apollod. *Bibl.* 2.6.2). In other versions Heracles kills the trusting Iphitus in a fit of madness by suddenly throwing him from the walls of Tiryns (Diod. 4.31.1–5; Apollod. *Bibl.* 2.6.2).
[77] Cf. Apollo's defense of Orestes by asking whether Zeus could have been mistaken in his forgiveness of Ixion, the first to shed blood (Aesch. *Eum.* 719–20).
[78] Ixion: Aesch. frr. *Ixion* and *Perrhaeb.* Nauck 1964; Diod. 4.69.3–5. See also Pind. *Pyth.* 2.21–48 with scholia; Apollod. *Epit.* 1.20.

compounded the severity of the penalty despite his previous expiation.[79] Like the story of Heracles, this myth shows that although the purification of miasma may not be automatic, its accomplishment satisfies the demands of what is *themis*. The unnaturally prolonged suffering of the mad Orestes (with whom Jason has been compared)[80] represents the exception to the rule, for while greater efforts may be required for kin-killers, absolution is invariably attained.[81]

My analysis of the consequences of kin-killing is not limited to external material, however. There are several references to murders committed by heroes traveling aboard the Argo. For example, Telamon and Peleus, the sons of Aeacus, have joined the Argonauts from Salamis and Phthia respectively. Originally from Aegina, they have gone into exile for the murder of their brother Phocus (1.90–93):[82]

> Τοῖσι δ' ἐπ' Αἰακίδαι μετεκίαθον, οὐ μὲν ἄμ' ἄμφω
> οὐδ' ὁμόθεν· νόσφιν γὰρ ἀλευάμενοι κατένασθεν
> Αἰγίνης, ὅτε Φῶκον ἀδελφεὸν ἐξενάριξαν
> ἀφραδίῃ.
>
> The Aeacids came next, but neither together
> Nor from the same place, since they fled and settled far from
> Aegina after they killed their brother Phocus,
> Accidentally.

In other versions the murder of Phocus was premeditated,[83] but Apollonius, rather predictably, describes it as accidental, which again helps shift the focus away from the guilt of the heroes; the reference to this murder is included not to raise questions about the heroes' culpability, but to explain their separate departures from home and independent travels.

Regarding Heracles' double murder of the sons of Boreas, the narrator explains that after the Argonauts return to Greece he will kill them for forestalling the search in Mysia (1.1304–8):

> Ἄθλων γὰρ Πελίαο δεδουπότος ἂψ ἀνιόντας
> Τήνῳ ἐν ἀμφιρύτῃ πέφνεν καὶ ἀμήσατο γαῖαν
> ἀμφ' αὐτοῖς στήλας τε δύω καθύπερθεν ἔτευξεν,

---

[79] Hera notes that she would protect her favorite Jason even if he were to free Ixion (*Argon.* 3.61–63). For Hera Ixion represents what is worst among mortals, while Jason represents what is best, although both commit kin-murder.
[80] Pietsch 1999, 56; Hunter 1993, 15–16 and 1988, 448–50.
[81] As Parker 1983, 129 observes, "When in myth a purification proves ineffective, this is revealed through the killer's renewed madness and not the affliction of his associates."
[82] For the story, see Hes. *Theog.* 1003–5; Apollod. *Bibl.* 3.12.6; Paus. 2.29.2–10; 10.30.4; 10.33.12. The murder is accidental at Diod. 4.72.6. Parker 1983, 388, states that the accidental version was "certainly secondary."
[83] See Vian 2002, 1:54, n. 2.

ὧν ἑτέρη, θάμβος περιώσιον ἀνδράσι λεύσσειν,
κίνυται ἠχήεντος ὑπὸ πνοιῇ βορέαο.

On their return from the funeral games of the fallen Pelias
On sea-girt Tenos he slew them, and he poured earth
Over them and placed two pillars above;
One of the two, a rare wonder for men to behold,
Is stirred by the blast of the roaring North Wind.

There is a degree of situational irony in the fact that the Boreads are returning from funeral games only to be given a funerary monument themselves, but once again, the emphasis falls less on the murder than on its context. The narrator does not mention any exile or purification undergone by Heracles, but rather devotes several lines to the *stelae* erected above the burial mound. The focus of the passage is aetiological: it is principally concerned, not with the moral implications of Heracles' murder, but with the extraordinary monuments that still exist. Like Achilles after the murder of Trambelus, Heracles demonstrates his association with the Boreads by erecting a tomb, though in this case the murder can hardly be called accidental.

Apollonius also notes Heracles' murder of his own children. In Book 4, soon after the ambush of Apsyrtus, the narrator refers to this murder (*phonos*) during the description of the birth of Hyllus (4.539–43):

Ὁ γὰρ οἰκία Ναυσιθόοιο
Μάκριν τ' εἰσαφίκανε, Διωνύσοιο τιθήνην,
ηιψόμενος παίδων ὀλοὸν φόνον· ἔνθ' ὅ γε κούρην
αἰγαίου ἐδάμασσεν ἐρασσάμενος ποταμοῖο,
ηηιάδα Μελίτην· ἡ δὲ σθεναρὸν τέκεν Ὕλλον.

He came to the home
Of Nausithous and to Macris, the nurse of Dionysus,
To be cleansed of the dread murder of his children. There he
Loved and conquered the daughter of the river Aegaeus,
The nymph Melite, and she bore strong Hyllus.[84]

Here, too, the moral problems posed by kin-murder are not the main point of the story. Instead, it is cited simply to account for Heracles' sojourn in Phaeacia and the conception of Hyllus. The narrator acknowledges the horror of the deed with the phrase, the "dread murder" of his children (ὀλοὸν φόνον, 4.541), but its medial placement before the bucolic diaeresis plays with the emotional reaction of the audience. Rather than end the line with the terminal gravity of the slaughter, the narrator briskly proceeds to

---

[84] The purification is performed by Thespius at Apollod. *Bibl.* 2.4.12.

the surprisingly happy resolution of the story: Heracles falls in love with a nymph and fathers another child, who will later become king among the Phaeacians.

The description of the murder of Apsyrtus similarly integrates a violent episode into an aetiological framework. On two occasions the narrator links the murder with the relocation of the two halves of the Colchian fleet. One group will remain among the Phaeacians, later joining the Nestaeans and the inhabitants of Oricum along the Adriatic.[85] The others will settle in the region consecrated by Apsyrtus' remains (4.480–81). Those that live on the two islands of Artemis are called Apsyrtians (4.513–15), while a second group founds a town near the tomb of Harmonia and Cadmus (4.516–18), and a third moves to the Ceraunian mountains (4.518–21). The murder of Apsyrtus, like the marriage of Jason and Medea that it engenders, will eventually lead to the foundation of several settlements.[86]

As these examples show, the *Argonautica* regularly links tales of murder with tales of civic rebirth and expansion, generally in the form of *ktisis* ("foundation") tales. The ethical consequences of violent killing are given only cursory treatment inasmuch as the poem is less concerned, on the one hand, with the cathartic satisfaction of revenge than either Homeric or Virgilian epic, and because it is largely disengaged, on the other, from the horrors of miasma, at least in contrast to the extremes portrayed in Attic tragedy. In fact, violent episodes in the poem tend to be somewhat flat, emotionally speaking, an effect that brings the poem more in line with the paratactic stories of traditional myth and the epic cycle. While brief accounts of accidental death may occasionally inspire in the reader a feeling of regret at the limitations of mortal knowledge, as a rule the poem reserves its emotional fireworks for the description of Medea's erotic suffering in Book 3. Murder typically serves as a structural tool for plot development, as an entree into an aetiological digression, or as an index of political virtue (i.e., the more violent the king, the less worthy he is). In many of the examples noted here, references to murder are little more than narrative signposts for genealogical or aetiological knowledge, which makes it easy to see why Apollonius has a reputation for pedantry. But more importantly, the treatment of murder in the *Argonautica* recalls Parker's observation that genealogical myths tend to rely on killing as a structural device, as a narrative

---

[85] 4.1211–16: see the end of Chapter 4.
[86] On the role of murder in foundation myths, see Dougherty 1993, 31–44. Dougherty notes: "The Greeks conceptualize defilement as the inversion of a positive religious value . . . Although blood and dust can bring pollution, they can also consecrate (39)." A murderer can therefore be a locus of defilement yet be invested with the ability to consecrate sacred ground.

tool or problem rather than an opportunity for moral investigation.[87] In each of these cases, blood pollution is characterized largely as an obstacle to be overcome, since the true focus and substance of the narrative is the description of the hero's purification and subsequent adventures in exile.

AMBUSH AND THE PIOUS IDIOM

This book advances the argument that the *Argonautica* addresses, incorporates, and often reworks not only the traditions of myth, epic, and drama, but also the politics, cult practices, and ideological self-representation of the Ptolemies and of Alexander. Although Alexander's claims to divinity caused friction with his officers during his lifetime, the Ptolemies relied on his influence as an icon of Greco-Macedonian power in positioning themselves as his political heir and adopting the cult status of the Egyptian pharaoh. Callimachus, Theocritus, and the other court poets were supported by the Ptolemies' royal patronage and celebrated in return both their piety and their divinity. While the *Argonautica* does not mention the Ptolemies by name, it associates cult practice with political strength by means of a religious aesthetic that differs markedly from comparable aspects of Homeric epic. The Argonauts consistently prefer a diplomatic course of action to open aggression and martial confrontation, and are attentive to the formal requirements of worship, regularly offering sacrifice to Apollo and other Olympian deities as well as local gods and even their own companions. These traits are especially pronounced in Jason, who normally embraces piety as well as the politically valuable virtues of restraint, moderation, and compromise.

Yet if there is a connection between the contemporary religious and political climate of Alexandria and innovative aspects of the poem, what does this say about the perversion of the sacred that seems to suffuse the ambush? I have argued that the narrator not only blames the murder on Eros but is also careful to show that Medea is distracted with fear and that the Argonauts are driven to this extreme because they are far outnumbered and at a tactical disadvantage. Moreover, ambushes, even those of close kin, are frequently depicted in myth and were in fact regularly relied upon by the ruling elite. Then, too, Apsyrtus is only a minor character, and Jason's motive is political and pragmatic rather than petty or vengeful; his purpose,

---

[87] Parker 1983, 376, where he notes that the "number of myths in which the moral implications of murder are of central importance is by contrast small (although a poet was, of course, free at any time to transform a structural device into a main theme)."

at least, is honorable inasmuch as he is trying to save Medea and uphold his oath to marry her, in contrast to the example set by Theseus, who abandons Ariadne. Finally, the murder scene itself is brief, and is consonant both with the aetiological tenor of incidental deaths in this poem and with the ktistic bloodshed of genealogical myths.

Even taking these points into consideration, one is still left with a conundrum. Why should the poet create a hero whose cult practice recalls the religiosity of the Ptolemies, on the one hand, but who is guilty of a sacrilegious murder, on the other? By mixing piety with slaughter the ambush complicates the hygienic formulation of political authority, but to what end? And if the scene does not rank Apsyrtus' murder with the "corrupt sacrifices" of Attic tragedy, why is the ambush set in a temple precinct and what is the poetic function of the religious images and figures that appear here? By way of answering these questions, I will conclude with a close reading of the scene and a brief consideration of its aftermath.

The description of the physical assault, as I have noted above, is brief, lasting only eleven lines from the moment Jason leaps out with his sword to the moment of Apsyrtus' death (4.464–74):

αὐτίκα δ' Αἰσονίδης πυκινοῦ ἔκπαλτο λόχοιο
γυμνὸν ἀνασχόμενος παλάμῃ ξίφος. Αἶψα δὲ κούρη
ἔμπαλιν ὄμματ' ἔνεικε, καλυψαμένη ὀθόνῃσι,
μὴ φόνον ἀθρήσειε κασιγνήτοιο τυπέντος.
Τὸν δ' ὅ γε, βουτύπος ὥς τε μέγαν κερεαλκέα ταῦρον,
πλῆξεν ὀπιπεύσας νηοῦ σχεδὸν ὅν ποτ' ἔδειμαν
Ἀρτέμιδι βρυγοὶ περιναιέται ἀντιπέρηθεν.
Τοῦ ὅ γ' ἐνὶ προδόμῳ γνὺξ ἤριπε· λοίσθα δ' ἥρως
θυμὸν ἀναπνείων χερσὶν μέλαν ἀμφοτέρῃσιν
αἷμα κατ' ὠτειλὴν ὑποΐσχετο· τῆς δὲ καλύπτρην
ἀργυφέην καὶ πέπλον ἀλευομένης ἐρύθηνεν.

At that moment the son of Aeson sprang forth from the dense thicket
With the naked blade held high in his hand. Quickly the girl
Looked the other way and covered her eyes with a linen veil
So that she would not see the blood of her wounded brother.
And he, as a ritual slaughterer strikes a strong-horned bull,
Struck when he saw him near the temple, which at one time the Bryges,
Neighbors dwelling on the mainland, built for Artemis.
He fell to his knees in the forecourt; the hero
Gasping out his life, with both hands
Caught the dark blood from the wound, and stained red
Her silvery veil and robe as she drew back.

Notice first that the description moves away from Jason at several points. It is disjunctive, shifting the reader's attention rapidly from one character or idea to another. Jason leaps out from hiding in lines 464–65, but the narrator immediately looks to Medea in the next line, and the description of her as she covers her eyes shields the eyes of the audience from the murder as well.[88] By the time the narrator turns back to Jason, he has been figuratively transformed by a simile into the iconic representation of a ritual slaughterer. Just before the critical moment when Jason strikes Apsyrtus (4.469), the narrative is again disrupted, this time by an aetiological point, as the narrator pauses to refer to the origin of the temple. This intrusion softens the dramatic impact of the moment, drawing the reader's attention from the deathblow to the thought of those ancient days when the Thracian Bryges built and consecrated the temple to Artemis. Once again, the reader is shielded from a graphic description of violence; the foundation of the temple stands in the place of an extensive account of the details of the blow such as one would expect to find in Homer.[89] The historical aside is logical inasmuch as it explains the temple's history, but the shift in perspective breaks up the immediacy and tension of the scene: a historical digression is less emotionally intense than a fatal assault; the audience is not invited, as is true of Homeric epic, to exult in the dominance of the hero.[90]

When the narrative resumes, Apsyrtus has already fallen to his knees, staining his sister's clothes with his blood as he implicates her in his death. The naked (*gymnon*, 4.465) blade is held high seconds before the killing blow, but the image of the as-yet-uncontaminated weapon is quickly contrasted with the blood-soaked linen garments of Medea. Jason kills Apsyrtus, but the blood guilt falls, literally and ironically, on his sister, who is stained with his blood despite her efforts to avoid guilt and defilement (cf. 4.466 and 474). At this moment it becomes clear that Medea's involvement is the most problematic aspect of the murder (4.557–61):

Αὐτόν που μεγαλωστὶ δεδουπότος Ἀψύρτοιο
Ζῆνα, θεῶν βασιλῆα, χόλος λάβεν, οἷον ἔρεξαν·

---

[88] Cf. Agamemnon's looking away at the moment of Iphigenia's death (Eur. *IA*). Note the contrast between Iphigenia, who gazes openly at the officiating priests and sheds her saffron robe (Aesch. *Ag.* 239–41), and Medea, who hides behind her robe to avoid witnessing the murder.

[89] Cf. the precise descriptions of Homeric death blows, e.g. *Il.* 11.95–98, where Agamemnon stabs Oeleus in the face with a spear that passes through helmet and bone and scatters the brains; 13.506–8, where Idomeneus strikes Oenomaus in the belly, breaking the armor so that the bronze draws out the intestines; and 13.615–18, where Menelaus smashes the bridge of Pisandrus' nose so that his eyes fall in the dust bleeding next to his feet.

[90] Byre 2002, 131 similarly observes that the narrator is removed from the characters and that the description of the scene is detached and unemotional.

> Αἰαίης δ' ὀλοὸν τεκμήρατο δήνεσι Κίρκης
> αἷμ' ἀπονιψαμένους πρό τε μυρία πημανθέντας
> νοστήσειν. Τὸ μὲν οὔ τις ἀριστήων ἐνόησεν·
>
> When Apsyrtus had fallen, the king of the gods,
> Zeus himself was greatly angered at what they had done,
> And ordained that through the skill of Aeaean Circe
> They be cleansed of the dreadful spilling of blood,
> And that only after countless hardships would they
> Return home. But none of the heroes knew this.

For Zeus the crisis emerges from the ὀλοὸν αἷμα – the dreadful shedding of kindred blood; neither the treacherous manner of death nor the defilement of sacred ground enter into consideration here.[91] The narrative thus focuses less on Jason's strength and more on Medea's guilt, because it is her relation to the murder victim that will provoke divine wrath, rather than the manner in which he is killed or the location of the ambush.

The location is telling for other reasons, however. It is appropriate to compare Jason to a *boutypos* and Apsyrtus to a bull precisely because of their location; indeed, it is the setting that prompts the narrator to notice this. This simile has been generally accepted as an allusion to the Homeric description of Agamemnon's death: "as one would kill an ox at the manger" (ὥς τίς τε κατέκτανε βοῦν ἐπὶ φάτνῃ, *Od.* 4.535; 11.411). Yet there is a crucial difference here. The image of the manger emphasizes the inappropriateness of Agamemnon's death: a murder in the home is unjust, like the killing of an ox while he feeds at the manger. The ox has had no warning of his death and has therefore not "agreed" to the sacrifice in accordance with ritual convention.[92] By contrast, the slaughter of a bull by a *boutypos* in a *temenos* is appropriate, so to take the allusion to Agamemnon's death as a figurative way of deepening Jason's impiety is to overlook the crucial disparity between these killings. Agamemnon's death is shown to be out of place by the ox-slaughter simile, but the Argonautic simile works in the opposite way because it imagines Apsyrtus' death to be like a sacrifice because it takes place in a temple precinct.

In addition, the reference to the *boutypos* resonates with the goddess Artemis, whose *temenos* this is, and who is often represented in the

---

[91] Circe is likewise troubled by Medea's betrayal of her family (4.739–48), though it must be admitted that she does not know the specific details of Apsyrtus' death because Medea avoids talking about it (4.736–37), but she has no more success concealing the murder from her spooky aunt than Jason did from the Erinys.

[92] The ritual sprinkling of the bull with water prior to the sacrifice would cause it to jerk its head in symbolic "acceptance" of its death (Burkert 1985, 56).

Ambush and the pious idiom 219

iconography of bull sacrifice.[93] As *Potnia Theron*, "Mistress of Animals" (*Il.* 21.470–71) she both cherishes the wild and kills the animals that inhabit it.[94] Though she does not play an active role in the poem like Hera or Aphrodite, she is mentioned in several cult contexts. She is identified as the patron goddess of Iolcus,[95] her priestess Iphias kisses Jason's right hand as he leaves the city (1.312),[96] and Orpheus sings a hymn in her honor as the Argo leaves the harbor of Pagasae (1.571). Artemis is the goddess who threatens the lives of adolescent girls when they marry;[97] the "Mistress of Sacrifices"[98] plays a part in stories of the death of Medea's counterpart Ariadne; and in Aeschylus' *Agamemnon* (134–55) she demands the sacrifice of her future priestess and avatar Iphigenia in order to avenge the slaughter of the pregnant hare by Zeus's eagles.

As a priestess of Hecate, Medea is similarly linked with Artemis,[99] with whom she is explicitly compared when she drives her chariot to meet Jason (3.878). An unmarried girl like Iphigenia and Ariadne, she is vulnerable to the goddess' power, and in betraying her half-brother she will be covered in kindred blood that is partly her own. Then, too, her influence over Apsyrtus is cast in terms that recall Artemis' ties to the wild. To set up the ambush Medea misleads Apsyrtus with a false story of her abduction (4.442–44):

---

[93] E.g., Aristotle speaks of a golden bull on the altar of Artemis Orthosia (Farnell 1896, 2:455). Nicander gives Artemis the epithet "Eater of Bulls" (Farnell 1896, 2:454, who notes, however, that there is no evidence of bull sacrifice to Artemis in Attica or Lemnos). See Roscher 1884–1937, 1:567–68 on the confusion of Artemis Tauropolos, the goddess of bulls (or Tauropola, so Soph. *Aj.* 172), with the orgiastic Artemis of Tauris. Roscher cites Eur. *IT* 1457 as an early example of syncretism. On Artemis Tauropolos see *LIMC* II.1 *s.v.* Artémis Tauropolos, sec. IV.6; see especially tetradrachms from Amphipolis, 703 (*c.*158–150 BC) and 704 (third century BC). For iconographic evidence of Artemis Tauropolos: e.g., Athenian terracotta reliefs of Artemis seated on a bull from Brauron 500 BC (Mus. κ 2077a, b + 2503 + 3242 and 2617 = *LIMC* II.1 *s.v.* Artémis Tauropolos, sec. IV.6, 700, 701).
[94] Burkert 1985, 149. She received sacrifices of wild animals such as the hare, wolf, deer, wild boar, or the bear and was only rarely associated with the sacrifice of domesticated animals like the ox, horse, or pig, and in some areas calf or sheep sacrifices to Artemis were forbidden. Farnell 1896, 2:431.
[95] See Clinton 1988, 7 on the rarity of Artemis as a civic patron during the Classical period. For Artemis as civic patron later in the Hellenistic period, see Mikalson 1998.
[96] On Iphias as an allusion to Iphigenia, see Nelis 1991, 96–105. Sansone 2000 notes a connection between Medea and Iphigenia, and observes that both were married or promised marriage with Achilles. For Iphigenia as Artemis, see Roscher 1884–1937, 1:304–5; Burkert 1985, 152: "Just as Apollo is mirrored in Achilles, so Artemis is mirrored in Iphigeneia; Iphigeneia herself becomes a goddess, a second Artemis."
[97] Burkert 1985, 151. On the celebration of Ariadne's sacred marriage to Dionysus in the Attic Anthesteria, see p. 164.
[98] Burkert 1985, 152: "especially of cruel and bloody sacrifices."
[99] For Hecate's identification with Artemis: Hes. fr. 23.26 Merkelbach-West 1967; Paus. 1.43 (Farnell 1896, 2:502–3). On the Rhodian cult of Artemis-Hecate dated to the last two decades of the second century, see Nilsson 1967–74, 1:465 and Christou 1961. For iconographic evidence, see two tentatively identified Rhodian statuettes, *LIMC* II. 1, *s.v.* Artémis Tauropolos, sec. VI. 1. 1, s.v. Artémis-Hekate(?), 875 and 877, with bibliography.

> τοῖα παραιφαμένη, θελκτήρια φάρμακ' ἔπασσεν
> αἰθέρι καὶ πνοιῇσι, τά κεν καὶ ἄπωθεν ἐόντα
> ἄγριον ἠλιβάτοιο κατ' οὔρεος ἤγαγε θῆρα.
>
> She used words so beguiling, sprinkling magic drugs
> In the air and breezes, that even from afar
> They would lead a wild beast down from a high mountain.

Like this wild beast, Apsyrtus will be charmed by Medea's words and brought from afar into ambush. His death in the *temenos* thus resembles that of a wild animal sacrifice offered to Artemis, with Jason acting the role of ritual slaughterer and Medea presiding over the sacrifice as a priestess.

This metaphorical transformation of Apsyrtus into an animal does not go so far, however, as to render his murder the equivalent of a "corrupt sacrifice." What the comparison does is to reshape murder in sacrificial terms; the poet alludes to animal sacrifice without literally identifying Apsyrtus' murder with human sacrifice. Apollonius avoids the term for ritual bloodletting, the cutting of the throat of the sacrificial animal, σφάγειν, here, and in fact this term occurs only twice in the *Argonautica* and on both of these occasions it refers to actual – as opposed to figurative or perverted – sacrifices (1.432; 4.1596). Nor does Jason claim to be sacrificing Apsyrtus, as Clytemnestra does when she stabs Agamemnon: "This man I sacrifice" (τόνδ' ἔσφαξ ἐγώ, Aesch. *Ag.* 1433).[100] Clytemnestra's performative assertion that she is in fact offering Agamemnon as a sacrifice is very different from the comparatively superficial similarity of a murder to a sacrifice because of its location. In contrast to Aeschylus, Apollonius does not employ ritual imagery to compound the horror of the murder; instead the poet uses allusion and aetiological asides to deflect the brutality of the act. The similes contain and transform the ambush in much the same way that ritual sacrifice itself works to contain and transform the guilt associated with bloodshed.[101] Here, as throughout the poem, then, the *Argonautica* is concerned not with the dramatization of force, but with the political – or in this case consciously metapoetical – alternatives to it.

When the description of the murder resumes, the struggle is already over. The narrator does not describe the actual blow, but skips ahead to the pathos of Apsyrtus' fall. At the instant his blood touches Medea's gown, the Erinys takes note of the murder (4.475–76):

---

[100] See also her description of the act using the term ἐπιθύσας at *Ag.* 1503.
[101] See Burkert 1983, 45: "Civilized life endures only by giving a ritual form to the brute force that still lurks in men."

ὀξὺ δὲ πανδαμάτωρ λοξῷ ἴδεν οἷον ἔρεξαν
ὄμματι νηλειὴς ὀλοφώιον[102] ἔργον Ἐρινύς.

Sharply all-conquering, ruthless Erinys looked
Straight at the act of <u>treachery</u> they performed in ambush.

Jason and Medea are victims of the Erinys from the moment Apsyrtus becomes their own. Jason then takes counter measures by performing the apotropaic *maschalismos* and burying the corpse (4.477–81).

Ἥρως δ' Αἰσονίδης ἐξάργματα τάμνε θανόντος.
τρὶς δ' ἀπέλειξε φόνου, τρὶς δ' ἐξ ἄγος ἔπτυσ' ὀδόντων,
ἣ θέμις αὐθέντῃσι δολοκτασίας ἱλάεσθαι.
Ὑγρὸν δ' ἐν γαίῃ κρύψεν νέκυν, ἔνθ' ἔτι νῦν περ
κείαται ὀστέα κεῖνα μετ' ἀνδράσιν Ἀψυρτεῦσιν.

The hero, son of Aeson, cut off the extremities of the corpse,
Three times he licked the blood, and three times he spat the
  pollution from his teeth,
The proper expiation for those who murder by stealth.
Then he covered the wet corpse in earth, where even now
Those bones still lie among the Apsyrtian people.

Although this ritual, unpalatable as it is, will succeed, the attempt to cover the crime will fail. The ambush will be widely known to gods and mortals, for Apsyrtus' bones now consecrate the island, and its inhabitants will henceforth be known as Apsyrtians. The poet thus displays greater interest in how the landscape is permanently marked by the episode – as one of the tracks left by the archaic past, like the Brygian temple – than he is in the transient violence, suffering, and miasma of the murder itself.

My claim in this chapter has been that Apollonius' allusions to tragic models highlight their differences from this ambush. The poet not only represents Jason and Medea as Eros' victims but also, and more importantly, uses certain details of the religious context to set this murder apart, drawing on earlier representations of ambush in the epic cycle. Then, too, the historical frequency and political expedience of kin-murder (typically by ambush) must also be taken into consideration, together with other mythic accounts of such deeds as they are described in the *Argonautica* and other sources. These parallels and contrasts combine to diminish the audience's emotional reaction to the murder (in contrast, however, to the disgust that is generally provoked, intentionally or not, by the *maschalismos*), an aim that is underscored by the narrator's reluctance to represent

---

[102] For ὀλοφώιον see LSJ *s.v.*: "The notion of destruction, necessary in Theoc. and Nic. ll. cc., and assumed by Hsch., is perh. not certain in Hom, where ὀ. may mean simply *deceptive, tricky*."

the killing blow in physical terms. Thus, whereas tragedy dwells on the pollution of kin-murder, the *Argonautica* takes such considerations in its stride en route to a longer aetiological view, identifying the death of Apsyrtus as the foundation of a new community.

I conclude with the observation that the ambush also turns on the contradictions inherent in the use of power. The incongruous duality that is implied with respect to Artemis (she who both hunts and protects animals) becomes more explicit in the representation of Zeus, who represents the interests of victims of all kinds. Zeus's divided loyalties are mirrored in the conflicts experienced by Jason, who violates Zeus's law in order to honor an oath sworn to him. Though Zeus is angered at Apsyrtus' downfall (4.557–58), he is also the god to whom Jason and Medea must appeal as suppliants. Circe becomes a vehicle for this duality: she reveres the injunction of Zeus Hicesius ("Of Suppliants"), "who bears great anger and great aid to the killers of men" (*androphonoisin*, 4.701), and makes offerings to Zeus Catharsius on their behalf (4.713–17):

> ὄφρα χόλοιο
> σμερδαλέας παύσειν Ἐρινύας ἠδὲ καὶ αὐτός
> εὐμειδής τε πέλοιτο καὶ ἤπιος ἀμφοτέροισιν,
> εἴ τ' οὖν ὀθνείῳ μεμιασμένοι αἵματι χεῖρας
> εἴ τε καὶ ἐμφύλῳ προσκηδέες ἀντιόωσιν.

> that she might keep
> The horrifying Furies from their wrath and that Zeus
> Himself might show them both warmth and kindness,
> Whether they make their supplication defiled with the blood
> Of strangers on their hands, or even blood of their own kin.

Zeus's call for purification and a delayed *nostos* is thus mirrored in Circe, who purifies Medea before wrathfully sending her into exile. Whether Circe would have performed the purification *after* learning the identity of the victim is unclear, but it is tempting to speculate that Zeus chooses Circe in particular to perform the purification to ensure that the murder will be known to Aeëtes – perhaps to punish him in turn.

As the arbiter of both vengeance and purification, Zeus establishes the celestial paradigm for the multiple roles played by mortals in positions of authority, who must often choose between what they would privately prefer to do and what they must do here and now. So, too, the implication is, contradiction and compromise inhabit all who lead and rule, including the Ptolemies themselves. Ruler cult, in a manner of speaking, has not only divinized mortals, it has also humanized divinity. Apsyrtus' death points to the divine allowances made in the course of colonial expansion, and if political strife, as Orpheus' Empedoclean song suggests, is inevitable, the idealized Zeus, unlike the retrograde Aeëtes, is neither absolute nor unreasoning in his wrath. Rather, like Alcinous, he is open to negotiation and wishes, like the Zeus of Aratus, to be gentle (*epios*) with all, even those who break his laws (above, 4.715). In Apollonius' view, the judgment of Zeus is straight, but it maintains peace by tempering the private bonds and rights of kinship with the demands of political diplomacy and a god's eye view of history – which, from the ideological perspective of the Ptolemaic court, can only be progressive. In the *Argonautica*, the political excess of the past and the violence of archaic epic and classical tragedy are revised and reborn through the poetic synthesis of Hellenized cult practices with a new dynastic vision as the Greek heroes begin their journey home, joyfully bearing the Argo across the desert, beneath the Libyan sun.

CHAPTER 7

Quid denique restat: Apollonius and Virgil

INTIMATIONS OF THE *AENEID*

In 30 BC during his first and only trip to Alexandria, Octavian is said to have viewed Alexander's sarcophagus, though he scorned an invitation to visit the tombs of the Ptolemies: "I wished to see a king, not corpses."[1] He is also said to have refused, in rather un-Alexander-like fashion, to enter the presence of the Apis bull, saying that he was accustomed to worshipping gods, not cattle.[2] Though he was initiated into the mysteries at Eleusis and generally represented himself as respectful of foreign divinities, Octavian seems to have made an exception in the case of Egypt, a land where, as he observed in an earlier speech, they honor reptiles and other wild beasts as gods.[3]

Octavian's rejection of the Egyptian gods was as politically calculated, of course, as Alexander's generous appreciation had been. As his visit to Alexander's tomb suggests, his quarrel was not with the ancient glories of Ptolemaic rule, but rather with the most recent incarnations of Isis and Dionysus, and he was doing what he could to erode these bonds as well. On the night before Antony committed suicide, while Octavian's legions were camped outside Alexandria, Dionysus was rumored to have abandoned the city with a retinue of Bacchic dancers and musicians (Plut. *Ant.* 75.4–6).[4] Although the story may have been added later, it is possible that Octavian engineered the ritual as a stunt in the manner of a traditional Roman *evocatio*, inviting the god (the particular god of Alexander, it would seem, rather than the Antonine variety) to abandon the defeated city and take up residence elsewhere.[5] In later years the first three Ptolemaic generations would be represented as a kind of Golden Age; both Augustus' *Res Gestae*

---

[1] Suet. *Aug.* 18.1; Dio 51.16.   [2] λέγων θεοὺς ἀλλ' οὐχὶ βοῦς προσκυνεῖν εἰθίσθαι, Dio 51.16.5.
[3] Suet. *Aug.* 93; Dio 50.24.6.   [4] Pelling 1988, 303, n. 4–5.
[5] The latest (fragmentary) evidence for the *evocatio* is, however, dated only to 75 BC; see Beard et al. 1998, 1:132–34. On the ideological problems posed by Dionysus for Octavian, see Hunter 2006, 42–50.

and the encomia of Propertius and Virgil relied on a topos of territorial expansion that had been inherited, at least in part, from them.[6] However, for Octavian to go so far as to recognize the Apis bull at this time would have put him in the position of having to acknowledge, in some unpalatable way or other, the divinity of his late enemies,[7] something he was disinclined to do, and for reasons that are obvious. The conflict with Antony was accordingly depicted as an attack on noble Roman gods by monstrous Egyptian deities. Propertius refers to the barking Anubis (*latratem Anubim*), sent against Jove by the prostitute queen Cleopatra (*meretrix regina*, 3.11.39–42), while Virgil depicts the battle between multiform Egyptian gods and the Roman Neptune, Venus, and Minerva as one of the events on Aeneas' shield.[8] But like Octavian's response to the Apis bull, the treatment of the gods in the *Aeneid* serves as a foil for the definition of political identity, particularly that of the hero Aeneas.

Philip Hardie sees the conflicted Aeneas as "the first clearly defined example of the 'synecdochic hero,' the individual who stands for the totality of his people present and future, part for whole."[9] Accordingly, while the *Aeneid* looks forward to the rise of Augustus as the culmination of the history of Rome, the action of the poem is set in the turbulent prehistory of Italy. On the whole, Virgil is concerned less with the future glory of a settled Rome (still unfolding in 17 BC, the year of his death) than with its troubles in the immediate past.[10] As Michael Putnam writes:

although Virgil, Horace, Propertius, and Tibullus as well as the historian Livy were all at work on their masterpieces in the 20s, the first two poets at least had already produced extraordinary writing in the preceding decade, writing that in the case of Virgil reflects the contemporary ugliness of ongoing civil war. We must also remember that, even when penning the *Aeneid* in the years after Actium, Virgil places in the foreground, as the gist of his narrative, only the rise to omnipotence of one man and his allies. He ends at the moment of ambiguous victory that results from such a movement, not with some glorious aftermath with peace confirmed, an appropriate marriage celebrated, a new city established and the titular hero undergoing apotheosis – all events that by various means the poem predicts in a future beyond its own conclusion.[11]

---

[6] Hunter 2006, 61–62, 143.
[7] On Antony as Dionysus, see, e.g., Plut. *Ant.* 24.4; 60.3.
[8] *Aen.* 8.698–700: *omnigenumque deum monstra et latrator Anubis / contra Neptunum et Venerem contraque Minervam / tela tenent.*
[9] Hardie 1993, 4.
[10] Cairns 1988, 93 sees the second half of the *Aeneid* as a response to the recent civil wars.
[11] Putnam 2005, 454.

Thus, whether or not Virgil's family lands were caught up in the confiscations after Philippi in the late 40s down through the 30s, the personal cost of political victory is a prominent concern of his poetry.

Human suffering is balanced but not outweighed in the *Aeneid*, as it is in the *Argonautica*, by the (ever receding) promise of future political success. There is nothing to compare with the pathos of Dido's anguished death in Apollonius, a poet who does not, as a rule, pay much attention to the tension between the demands of Zeus's greater plan and its consequences in terms of mortal suffering. This is partly because the narrator singles out Eros for blame, and partly because Apollonius places greater emphasis on the justice, piety, and diplomacy of the Greeks as benign authority figures in foreign lands. There are casualties among the Argonauts: the youth Hylas, the seers Idmon and Mopsus, the helmsman Tiphys, and Canthus, who alone of the Argonauts dies in combat. Although these losses are relatively light, like the nicking of the Argo's stern as it passes through the Clashing Rocks (2.601–2), there are more casualties to come: Pelias, the sons of Boreas (killed by Heracles after the funeral of Pelias), and the doomed children of Jason and Medea, and a list of the fallen could also include the young king Cyzicus and many of his countrymen, the Earthborn giants, Amycus, the Earthborn men, the serpent Ladon, Apsyrtus, and the bronze giant Talus. Though the *Argonautica* briefly acknowledges these misfortunes, the theme of mortal suffering is far more extensively and systematically explored in the *Aeneid*, an epic that not only openly proclaims Jupiter's plan for the future of Rome but also directly confronts the cost of this fate in human terms.

If the extent of Virgil's debt to Apollonius has come as something of a revelation in the last few years, the light shed by the *Aeneid* on the historical and political concerns of the *Argonautica* may come as even more of a surprise. That there are parallels between the epics, especially in the representations of Medea and Dido, has long been recognized: the fourth-century AD grammarian Servius, for example, attributes all of *Aeneid* 4 to Apollonius.[12] More recently, Damien Nelis and Richard Hunter have shown that Virgil relied on Apollonius to a greater degree than was previously thought.[13] Nelis' exhaustive analysis of parallels between the *Argonautica* and the *Aeneid* explores Virgil's consistent use of "window reference" or "multi-tier allusion," a technique that references in a single passage both the original Homeric passage and Apollonius' particular interpretation of

---

[12] Servius 4.1. This observation is qualified by Macrobius 5.17.4, who says it was almost entirely based on the *Argonautica*. See Nelis 2001a, 238; Boyle 1993a, 106, n. 33.
[13] Nelis 2001a; 2001b; Hunter 1993, 170–89.

it. In his 1993 *Literary Studies* Hunter explores how Virgil uses Apollonius at times to distance the *Aeneid* from Homeric epic and to introduce magical and other "unepic" elements into his poem. Although Aeneas' trip to the underworld, for instance, is derived in part from Odysseus' meeting with the seer Tiresias, it also varies and expands on the chthonic associations that reveal the Argonauts' voyage to Colchis as a *katabasis*.[14] What is more, both Nelis and Hunter point to the growing scholarly recognition of the political resonance of the *Argonautica*.[15] As Hunter puts it, "The inscription into the *Argonautica* of what – in an unsatisfactory shorthand – we may call 'the Ptolemaic idea,' and perhaps too of the Ptolemies themselves, becomes in Virgil's poem the explicit inscription of Augustus into the epic."[16] Following the insightful work of these scholars, then, I offer a brief discussion of how my own interpretation of the *Argonautica* resonates against the *Aeneid*, paying particular attention to the endings of the two epics.

FATHERS, GODS, AND FOUNDATIONS

Anyone familiar with the *Aeneid* will perceive that Virgil recounts the actions of the gods and their interactions with mortals more fully than Apollonius does,[17] although when Virgil's gods manifest themselves, they tend to do so in disguise.[18] Aeneas has more direct contact with the gods than any other character in either the *Argonautica* or the *Aeneid*. On a number of occasions he sees Venus, and she often aids him by intervening behind the scenes, as Apollonius' Hera helps Jason.[19] She is his mother, of course, but her behavior in this respect, like that of other gods in the *Aeneid*, is largely patterned on divine conduct in Homeric epic rather than in the *Argonautica*.[20]

Virgil also tends to place more narrative emphasis than Apollonius on the positive responses of the gods to mortal prayers. The pattern is set by Jupiter's response to the first prayer of the poem, sending a portent (a comet) in answer to Anchises' prayer (2.689–91). The immediacy of such divine

---

[14] For discussion of the Argonautic *katabasis* in terms of Egyptian cosmology, see Stephens 2003, 218–37.
[15] See Chapter 1.   [16] Hunter 1993, pp. 188–89.   [17] See, e.g., Feeney 1991, 69–80.
[18] Such disguises are rarely successful: Apollo, disguised as Butes, is recognized by the Dardanians: 9.638–60; Pyrgo is able to see through Iris' disguise as Beroe: 5.618–53; Turnus recognizes Juturna disguised as Metiscus: 12.623–49. One exception is Cupid, who is successfully disguised as Ascanius and embraced by Dido: 1.657–722.
[19] Divine appearances to Aeneas include the Penates: 3.147–71; Mercury: 4.259–78, 554–70; River Tiber: 8.26–65; Pines of Ida nymphs: 10.219–48; appearances of Venus: 1.314–417; 2.588–623; 8.608–25; 12.554–56; Venus' aids: 4.90–128; 5.779–826; 10.330–332; 12.786–90.
[20] Cf., e.g., Athena's frequent conversations with Telemachus and Odysseus.

responses, which typically take the form of disembodied voices, divine manifestations, or meteorological events,[21] helps to reinforce the sense of closeness between mortals and the gods.[22] As a general rule the gods tend to favor Dardanian requests,[23] except in the case of Arruns, who asks Apollo to let him kill Camilla and then return home safely: Apollo grants only the former (11.784–98). When there is no mention of the divine reaction to a direct request, the implication in the narrative is that the response is probably not exactly what was hoped for, as happens during the boat race in Anchises' funeral games. Mnestheus calls on Neptune: *sed superent, quibus hoc, Neptune, dedisti* ("Let them conquer, Neptune, to whom you grant it," 5.195). Ironically, this is what actually happens: one of those to whom Neptune grants success (Cloanthus) is indeed victorious. Mnestheus had obviously intended himself as the referent, but Neptune did not grant his prayer, for Cloanthus promised a white bull to all the sea gods and won the race with the help of the Nereids, Phorcus, Panopea, and Portunus (5.235–46).

Generally speaking, then, sacrifices in the *Aeneid* are not rejected outright or misappropriated, as they can be in the *Iliad* and the *Odyssey*, but neither do they "work" in every instance, as they do in the *Argonautica*. Virgil reports the positive reactions of the gods when a request is granted, omitting their reaction to requests that are not – except where the god's response is mixed (Arruns). He uses the Homeric model, in other words, when he wants to emphasize that a character is in good standing with the gods, while he uses the Apollonian model (which never reports the reactions of the gods to prayers) when the gods' response is negative. By avoiding explicit references to divine rejection, Virgil glosses over the fact that sacrifices do not always succeed, yet by omitting the gods' responses he still leaves room for ambiguity, though he is absolutely clear about favorable responses.

Virgil also alludes to the connections drawn by Apollonius between religious activity and political authority. While it is not my purpose here to

---

[21] E.g., Aeneas' appeal to Gradivus and the woodland nymphs about the omen of bleeding tree that leads to the speech of Polydorus: 3.22–48; the voice answers Aeneas' prayer at the temple of Apollo: 3.84–98; the rains come after his appeal to Jupiter to save the burning ships: 5.687–99; his prayer to the gods of Italy, Night, Jupiter of Ida, Venus, Anchises, etc., is answered by thunder and bright cloud: 7.135–43; his prayer to River Tiber and nymphs is answered by appearance of the white sow: 8.68–85.

[22] By contrast, the reactions of gods to sacrifices are not mentioned unless there is a specific request. Sacrifices by Aeneas: 3.19–21, 79, 176–78; 5.61–83, 94–103, 772–76; 6.249–54; 8.81–85; 10.517–20; 11.1–11; 12.176–86, 213–15; sacrifices by Anchises: 3.118–20, 525–29; general offerings: 3.219–24, 278–80; 543–47; 5.762–63; 6.35–41; 8.179–83, 278–79, 280–84.

[23] 9.403–9 Nisus prays to the Moon, Artemis, to guide his weapons in defense of Euryalus (implicit response in the arrow that finds its mark in Sulmo's back).

engage in an extensive study of *pietas* and *auctoritas* in the *Aeneid*, a few examples of Virgil's representation of these concepts will help to illuminate their function in the *Argonautica*. Apollonius, as Chapter 5 explains, contrasts the differing grades of piety and justice in a variety of authoritative figures in order to show how each virtue reinforces the other. The following passage shows how Virgil, by contrast, uses a visual image to create an impression of the functional link between cult and state interests. Consider the narrator's description of the palace of Latinus (7.173–76):

> hic sceptra accipere et primos attollere fasces
> regibus omen erat; hoc illis curia templum
> hae sacris sedes epulis, hic ariete caeso
> perpetuis soliti patres considere mensis.
>
> Here it was propitious for kings to receive their scepters,
> To lift up their fasces for the first time; this temple was their senate,
> These their seats for sacred meals; here, after the slaughter of a ram,
> It was the custom of the elders to sit at long rows of tables.

The proximity of the temple and senate house of the ancient Latini figures the coordination of official respect for the gods with official respect for political justice. This image posits the longevity and stability of civic traditions and state rituals, and is plainly opposed to the breakdown of order that is symbolized by the violent, sacrilegious death of Priam earlier in the poem. In Book 2 Aeneas tells Dido of the final days of Troy, alive with sacrifice and feasting, the Trojans willfully ignoring (or misinterpreting) signs of ill-omen. The strange end of Laocoön and his two sons, struck down by two serpents as he sacrifices a bull (2.201–27), confirms the breakdown of religious authority, and with no one left to object the Trojans are free to welcome and celebrate the deceptive horse (2.248–49). As the Achaeans lay waste to the city, Neoptolemus (also called Pyrrhus) murders the aged monarch on an altar already steeped in the blood of Polites (2.550–58):

>   altaria ad ipsa trementem
> traxit et in multo lapsantem sanguine nati,
> implicuitque comam laeva, dextraque coruscum
> extulit ac lateri capulo tenus abdidit ensem.
> haec finis Priami fatorum; hic exitus illum
> sorte tulit Troiam incensam et prolapsa videntem
> Pergama, tot quondam populis terrisque superbum
> regnatorem Asiae. iacet ingens litore truncus,
> avulsumque umeris caput et sine nomine corpus.

>   to the altar stone itself
> Pyrrhus dragged him, trembling, slipping in a pool of his son's blood.
> He twined his hair in his left hand, and with his right
> Drew out the flashing sword, and into his side
> He plunged it as far as the hilt.
> This was the end of Priam's fortunes, this the finish
> That fell to him by lot, to see Troy burn and
> Pergamus ruined, once an overlord of many lands and peoples,
> Ruler of Asia. A massive trunk, he lies beside the shore,
> Head torn from his shoulders, an unknown corpse.

The slaughter of a powerful ruler is figured unflinchingly here as sacrifice: a variation on the symbolic defeat of Aeëtes through the ambush of his son Apsyrtus in the *temenos* of Artemis (Chapter 6). At the same time the scene introduces the chiastic interplay of paternal and filial relationships (by killing Polites and Priam, Neoptolemus avenges the death of his father Achilles, killed by Paris, a son of Priam) and also recalls the ransom of the body of Hector from Achilles in *Iliad* 24 (and *Aen.* 2.540–43) – even as it looks ahead to the pattern of familial grief and vengeance that occupies the second half of the *Aeneid*, a subject about which I have more to say below.

The only surviving son of Priam and Hecuba is Helenus, who settles in Epirus and there founds Chaonia, a city modeled after Troy. When Aeneas first comes to the plains of the city he meets Andromache, formerly the war-prize of Neoptolemus, now turned over to Helenus' care, as she honors the memory of Hector (3.300–5). Helenus welcomes Aeneas with a banquet and libations (3.353–55), and later, after a sacrifice of steers (3.369), he reveals the portents and dangers that await the Trojans en route to Italy. A king with the gift of prophecy, Helenus recalls the Argonautic Phineus: he can tell Aeneas only part of what he has foreseen because the Fates have limited his knowledge of the future and Juno has forbidden the telling of it (3.379–80; cf. *Argon.* 2.390–91, 425). But the theme of divine punishment that dominates the Phineus episode is missing here: Virgil chooses instead to focus on the rituals that will be required in the new land. Helenus advises Aeneas (and his descendants) to veil their hair with a purple robe when sacrificing (3.405–9), and emphasizes the importance of honoring Juno (3.434–40) and of entreating the Sibyl to reveal the conflicts that are to come (3.453–60).

Virgil's use of Apollonius is therefore variable, at times in harmony and at times diverging from his predecessor, in much the same way that Apollonius relates to Homer, Hesiod, and his other poetic models. As the main male hero of the poem, Aeneas is patterned in part after Jason, and his

Fathers, gods, and foundations 231

authority (both political and religious) increases as the poem progresses. In the first half of the poem Aeneas seeks counsel more frequently than he does in the second half after the death of his father Anchises. Though Putnam sees Anchises' performance prior to 3.527 as that of "a dubious leader at best,"[24] the father regularly advises the son (e.g., 3.57–59, 169–70, 178–91), instantiating the symbolically paternal role that is played by Heracles vis-à-vis Jason. Both Anchises and Heracles (see Chapter 3) are well respected, assume high positions of authority,[25] and continue to exert influence even after they are gone. Distant though he may be, Heracles rescues the Argonauts by creating a spring in the Garden of the Hesperides (*Argon.* 4.1445–60),[26] just as Anchises provides advice to Aeneas in the afterlife (*Aen.* 5.721–45; 6.886–92). Both Heracles and Anchises must depart before the main heroes, Jason and Aeneas, can assume their proper (i.e., unrivaled) authority in their respective poems.

Aeneas' son, Ascanius, likewise becomes more dominant in the second half of the poem as he is groomed for future glory. Destined to be the founder of Alba Longa, Ascanius is marked by several portents: the crown of fire in Troy at 2.680–86, and divine prophecy at 9.638–65, when Apollo hails him as *dis genite et geniture deos* ("son of gods and father of gods to be," 9.642). Ascanius (or rather Cupid disguised as Ascanius) is young enough in Book 1 to be innocently embraced on Dido's lap, and yet old enough by the end of the poem to fight and to send men to war. He promises Jupiter a white bullock in return for guiding an arrow against Remulus (9.621–31),[27] and asserts his authority in Aeneas' absence by promising rewards for Nisus and Euryalus – who is just barely his elder: *mea quem spatiis propioribus aetas / insequitur* (9.275–76) – as well as consideration for Euryalus' mother (9.256–80, 292–302).[28]

In many ways, then, the associations between fathers and sons as well as hegemony and religious activity become stronger and more explicit in the *Aeneid* than they are in the *Argonautica*. These emphases owe something to the character of Augustan politics, to be sure, but Virgil's variations continue to allude to the patterns established by the earlier epic. For Apollonius, who

---

[24] Putnam 1995, 59.
[25] Anchises is the first to pray in the poem (2.689–91) and regularly acts as the Trojans' leader, giving orders to depart (e.g., 3.144–46, 189–91, 472) and counseling Aeneas, together with the other elders (3.57–59).
[26] Heracles, or rather Hercules, is a father in his own right in the *Aeneid* (of Aventinus: 7.655–58). His status as father-figure is reinforced by his cult worship in the kingdom of Evander, whose central role in the *Aeneid*, at least from a dramatic point of view, is to grieve for the loss of his son Pallas.
[27] Cf. Pallas' prayer at 10.420–25 to River Tiber to help him kill Halaesus: the god's immediate response is noted in 424.
[28] Cf. his tearful reaction to the news of Euryalus' death and her lamentations: 9.473–502.

redefines epic heroism as diplomatic moderation and pious reverence in the midst of human uncertainty, some leaders are more devout than others, but for Virgil, who weighs the demands of fate and empire against mortal *dolor*, they all are.[29] In Africa, Dido seeks the favor of the gods by pouring libations, sacrifices, and examining entrails (4.60–65), hoping to keep Aeneas in Carthage,[30] while Iarbas, the king of the Gaetulians and Dido's suitor prior to Aeneas' arrival, is said to pray regularly to Jupiter (4.205–18).[31] In Italy, the longstanding sacrificial practice of Latinus' ancestors is described (7.173–76) as was noted above; likewise, Evander's palace is said to smoke with incense and warm blood (8.104–6), and he lavishly entertains Aeneas with a bull feast (the roasted meat brought by a priest, 8.179–83), followed by many libations and prayers (8.278–84). Even Turnus, the king of the Rutulians and Aeneas' rival for the hand of Lavinia, is shown in prayer. At 10.668–79 he hails Jupiter, and during his final combat with Aeneas his prayer to Faunus is answered, though it cannot save him (12.776–80).

For Virgil, then, there are no degrees of piety: leadership entails religious activity *simpliciter*; the gods favor whom they will regardless. The Etruscan king Mezentius is a lone exception, and represents Virgil's solution to the problem of immoral kings (Amycus, Aeëtes) that is raised in the *Argonautica*.[32] From Virgil's perspective, a ruler as brutal as Apollonius' Amycus would be unworthy and incapable of uniting a nation; thus Mezentius is defeated in combat like Amycus – but only after first suffering a political defeat (8.481–93). Contemptuous of gods and men alike, Mezentius joins Turnus after being driven into exile by his subjects for savage acts that include such atrocities as tying living prisoners to corpses (*mortua quin etiam iungebat corpora vivis*, 8.485). The citizens cut down his followers and set fire to the roof of his palace (*obtruncant socios, ignem ad fastigia iactant*, 8.491), a telling revision of Aeëtes' plan to cut down (ἀναρρήξας) an overhanging wooded hilltop and burn the Argo together with her arrogant (at least in his view) crew (3.579–83). In Virgil's hands the armored Aeëtes, who dazzles like the Sun as it climbs above the ocean and crosses the plain in a chariot like Poseidon (*Argon.* 3.1225–34), becomes Mezentius

---

[29] With the possible exception of the *contemptor divum* Mezentius (see below).
[30] Subsequent sacrifices to chthonic deities like Erebus, Chaos, Artemis, Hecate, and Stygian Jupiter (4.509–21, 638–40) are a direct expression of her suicidal state of mind. The responses of the gods are not mentioned, but they evidently are not fooled, as Anna is, by the offerings of Aeneas' sword and image that are heaped on the funeral pyre. In the end, Juno takes pity on her during her death throes and sends Iris to help her into the afterlife (4.693–705).
[31] The narrator notes that Jove sends Mercury in response to his most recent prayer (4.205–18, 219–22).
[32] Cairns 1988, 72.

as he advances in his massive armor like a whirlwind, towering above men like Orion crossing the ocean on foot (*Aen.* 10.762–68).

One way to understand how Virgil constructs his political and religious hierarchies is to see them as larger and more complicated versions of the primary hierarchy of fathers and sons. Mortals worship gods and subjects are loyal to their king, just as sons owe their allegiance to their fathers, and descendants to their ancestors.[33] And yet while these three paradigms are simultaneously at work in the *Aeneid*, they are not always in sync: the man who rules badly may nevertheless produce good children. Like Aeëtes, Mezentius has a noble son (Lausus), and like Apsyrtus, this noble son will be killed by his father's enemy, the hero of the epic. But Mezentius himself is killed, while Aeëtes is not, which suggests that Virgil is rectifying a disturbing lack of consequences for the treacherous ruler in the earlier epic (apart from the knowledge that his son has been killed, that is). This may well be true, but what Virgil also does is to isolate moral and political weakness from familial loyalty and strength, expanding on the inherent contradictions of the grand yet petty Aeëtes and thereby destabilizing any sense of a moral absolute that might have otherwise arisen. This is the effect of his decision both to show Lausus' mournful reaction to Mezentius' fatal wound (10.789–90), and to linger on the agony of Mezentius at the sight of his son's body, pouring dust on his head (10.844–45) in the high epic style reserved by Homer for tragic heroes: Achilles in mourning for Patroclus (*Il.* 18.22–27) or Priam for Hector (*Il.* 24.163–65). Mezentius is pierced at last by exile, he says, vainly swearing to avenge the death of Lausus (*Aen.* 10.846–66), who has been killed out of love for his father (*cari graviter genitoris amore*, 10.789), as Michael Putnam notes, to perish as an emblem of *pietas*.[34]

The pathos of father–son relations accordingly occupies Virgil to a much greater extent than it does Apollonius, though these ideas and images have their origins in the *Argonautica*'s focus on the connections between piety and political authority. In his consideration of the human *dolor* that is entailed by the fulfillment of Jupiter's divine plan, Virgil dramatizes the erotic torments of Dido, the counterpart of Medea and Hypsipyle,[35] in Book 4, but devotes much of the remainder of the poem to the sorrows of war, particularly parental laments for the untimely death of their children. When Aeëtes loses his son Apsyrtus in the *Argonautica*, Apollonius makes no

---

[33] Such categories become increasingly difficult to differentiate over time (as per Euhemerus): at 7.135–40 Aeneas prays to the spirit of Italy, Earth, as yet unknown river nymphs, Night, rising signs, the Jove of Ida, the Phrygian mother, and his parents.
[34] Putnam 1995, 142.   [35] See Nelis 2001b, 175–82; Hunter 1993, *passim*.

explicit mention of his grief. Virgil, by contrast, explores the interconnected dynamics of Mezentius' and Lausus' deaths at the hands of Aeneas, so strangely foreshadowed by Neoptolemus' slaughter of Priam and Polites on the altar of Troy (noted above). Evander likewise grieves for his son Pallas, killed by Turnus, and Aeneas is himself overwhelmed by the young hero's death (11.24–58). When the body is returned to Evander, the king lays the responsibility for avenging Pallas' death (and his own grief) at Aeneas' feet (11.176–79):

> vadite et haec memores regi mandata referte:
> quod vitam moror invisam Pallante perempto
> dextera causa tua est, Turnum gnatoque patrique
> quam debere vides.
>
> Go, and remember, bear this report to the king:
> If I prolong my spiteful life with Pallas dead
> The cause is your right hand, which you see owes
> Turnus to father and son.

So it is that, in contrast to the crisis of the *Argonautica*, which takes place in the first half of Book 4, the crisis of the *Aeneid* comes at the very end, when Aeneas hesitates, debating whether to kill or accept Turnus' plea for mercy, whether to identify with Turnus' victim Pallas or Turnus' father Daunus, who will grieve like Evander if his son is killed (12.932–36). But when Aeneas sees Pallas' belt, worn in triumph by Turnus, any thought of mercy or pity is lost, and not just for Aeneas. Aeneas' vengeful identification with Pallas (*Pallas te hoc vulnere, Pallas / immolat et poenam scelerato ex sanguine sumit*, 12.948–49) blots out Anchises' programmatic injunction in the underworld to spare the subject and conquer the proud: *parcere subiectis et debellare superbos* (6.853). As Putnam observes, "No custom for peace is established because Aeneas' emotional response to a reminder of his grief at Pallas' death forestalls any remembrance of Anchises' exhortation."[36]

On this reading, at least, the ending of the *Aeneid* is as dark as the future of Rome will be bloody. As with the *Argonautica*, the crisis has been resolved in the wrong way – or rather it is resolved in the way that accounts for generations of civil war in Italy. There are similarities between the ambush of Apsyrtus and the killing of Turnus: Aeneas becomes an *alius Achilles* in avenging the death of Pallas just as Jason does, for the ambush of Apsyrtus recalls Achilles' ambush of Troilus. But the last line of the *Aeneid* is one of despair: Turnus' ghost groans and flees to the shadows – *vitaque cum*

---

[36] Putnam 2005, 465.

gemitu fugit indignata sub umbras (12.952). The song Virgil sings is one of exile and alienation. The Rutulian king is now a corpse, and Aeneas has come home to a land as foreign, in some ways, as Egypt was to Octavian. The *Argonautica*, by contrast, ends in happiness: its heroes are safe, the crisis of Book 4 peaceably resolved. Jason and Medea have had time to find absolution: the pollution of kin-murder is cleansed, the war that threatens Greece is averted, and the wandering of the Argo brings the Greeks home – both to Pagasae in the present and to North Africa in the future. The poem ends as the Argonauts sail easily (ἔκηλοι, 4.1778) along the Greek coast, and as they gladly set foot on the headland of Pagasae (ἀσπασίως ἀκτὰς Παγασηίδας εἰσαπέβητε, 4.1781), the purpose of Zeus is fulfilled.

Bibliography

Adkins, A. W. H. 1960. *Merit and Responsibility*. Oxford.
Ager, S. 1996. *Interstate Arbitrations in the Greek World, 337–90 B.C.* Berkeley and Los Angeles.
Albis, R. V. 1996. *Poet and Audience in the Argonautica of Apollonius*. Lanham.
Alders, G. J. D. 1975. *Political Thought in Hellenistic Times*. Amsterdam.
Allen, D. S. 2000. *The World of Prometheus: The Politics of Punishing in Democratic Athens*. Princeton.
Allen, T. W., W. R. Halliday, and E. E. Sikes (eds.) 1980. *The Homeric Hymns*. Amsterdam.
Ambühl, A. 2004. "Entertaining Theseus and Heracles: The *Hecale* and the *Victoria Berenices* as a Diptych." In Harder *et al.* (eds.) 23–47.
Andrews, N. E. 1989. "The Poetics of the *Argonautica* of Apollonius of Rhodes: A Process of Reorientation (the Libyan Maidens)." Dissertation. Harvard University. Cambridge, MA.
Anson, E. M. 2004. *Eumenes of Cardia: A Greek among Macedonians*. Boston and Leiden.
Assmann, J. 1996/2002. *The Mind of Egypt: Time and Meaning in the Time of the Pharaohs*. Tr. A. Jenkins. New York.
Auerbach, E. 1953. *Mimesis: The Representation of Reality in Western Literature*. Tr. W. Trask. New York.
Badian, E. 1996. "Alexander the Great between Two Thrones and Heaven: Variations on an Old Theme." In A. Small (ed.) *Subject and Ruler: The Cult of the Ruling Power in Classical Antiquity*. Ann Arbor. 11–36.
Bagnall, R. S. 1976. *The Administration of the Ptolemaic Possessions Outside Egypt*. Leiden.
Bagnall, R. S. and P. Derow 2004. *The Hellenistic Period: Historical Sources in Translation*. 2nd edn. Oxford. (First published 1981.)
Bakker, E. J. 1997. *Poetry in Speech: Orality and Homeric Discourse*. Ithaca.
Barnes, M. H. 2003. "Inscribed *Kleos*: Aetiological Contexts in Apollonius of Rhodes." Dissertation. University of Missouri.
Baynham, E. 1998. *Alexander the Great: The Unique History of Quintus Curtius*. Ann Arbor.
Beard, M., J. North, and S. Price. 1998. *Religions of Rome*. 2 vols. Cambridge.

Bell, C. 1997. *Ritual: Perspectives and Dimensions*. Oxford.
Berve, H. 1926. *Das Alexanderreich auf prosopographischer Grundlage* I. Munich.
Bevan, E. 1968. *The House of Ptolemy: A History of Egypt under the Ptolemaic Dynasty*. Chicago.
Beye, C. R. 1982. *Epic and Romance in the Argonautica of Apollonius*. Carbondale and Edwardsville.
— 1969. "Jason as Love-Hero in Apollonios' *Argonautika*." *Greek, Roman, and Byzantine Studies* 10: 31–55.
Bianchi, R. S. 1978. "The Striding Draped Male Figure of Ptolemaic Egypt." In H. Maehler and V. M. Strocka (eds.) *Das ptolemäische Ägypten*. Mainz. 95–102.
Billows, R. A. 1990. *Antigonos the One-Eyed and the Creation of the Hellenistic State*. Berkeley and Los Angeles.
Bing, P. 2005. "The Politics and Poetics of Geography in the Milan Posidippus, Section One: On Stones (AB 1–20)." In Gutzwiller (ed.) 119–40.
— 1988. *The Well-Read Muse: Present and Past in Callimachus and Hellenistic Poets*. Göttingen.
Bingen, J. 1988. "Ptolémée Ier Sôter ou la quête de la légitimité." *Bulletin de la Classe des Lettres et des Sciences Morales et Politiques de l' Académie Royale de Belgique*. 5e série. 74: 34–51.
Blumberg, K. W. 1931. *Untersuchungen zur epischen Technik des Apollonios von Rhodos*. Leipzig.
Bohec-Bouhet, S. le. 2002. "The Kings of Macedon and the Cult of Zeus in the Hellenistic Period." In D. Ogden (ed.) *The Hellenistic World: New Perspectives*. Swansea and London. 41–57.
Borza, E. 1993. Response to Hammond, "The Macedonian Imprint on the Hellenistic World." In Green (ed.) 23–35.
— 1990. *In the Shadow of Olympus: The Emergence of Macedon*. Princeton.
— 1983. "The Symposium at Alexander's Court." *Ancient Macedonia* 3: 44–45.
Bosworth, A. B. 2002. *The Legacy of Alexander: Politics, Warfare, and Propaganda under the Successors*. Oxford.
— 1993. *Conquest and Empire: The Reign of Alexander the Great*. Cambridge.
Bouché-Leclercq, A. 1903. *Histoire des Lagides: Les Cinq premiers Ptolémées (323–181 avant J.-C.)*. Vol. 1. Paris. (Reprint 1963.)
Bowman, A. K. 1986. *Egypt after the Pharoahs*. Berkeley and Los Angeles.
Bowra, C. M. (ed.) 1947. *Pindari Carmina*. 2nd edn. Oxford.
Boyle, A. J. (ed.) 1993a. *Roman Epic*. London and New York.
— 1993b. "Virgil's Aeneid." In Boyle (ed.) 79–107.
Braund, D. 1994. *Georgia in Antiquity*. Oxford.
Bremer, J. M. 1987. "Full Moon and Marriage in Apollonius' *Argonautica*." *Classical Quarterly* 37: 423–26.
— 1981. "Greek Hymns." In H. S. Versnel (ed.) *Faith, Hope, and Worship*. Leiden. 193–215.
Bremmer, J. N. 1997. "Why did Medea Kill her Brother Apsyrtus?" In J. J. Clauss and S. I. Johnston (eds.) *Medea: Essays on Medea in Myth, Literature, Philosophy, and Art*. Princeton. 83–100.

Bringmann, K. 1993. "The King as Benefactor: Some Remarks on Ideal Kingship in the Age of Hellenism." In Bulloch, *et al*. (eds.) 7–24.
Brink, C. O. 1972. "Ennius and the Hellenistic Worship of Homer." *American Journal of Philology* 93: 547–67.
Bulloch, A. W. 1985a. *Callimachus: The Fifth Hymn*. Cambridge Classical Texts and Commentaries 26. Cambridge.
— 1985b. "Hellenistic Poetry." In P. E. Easterling and B. M. W. Knox (eds.) *The Cambridge History of Classical Literature*. Cambridge. 541–621.
— 1984. "The Future of a Hellenistic Illusion: Some Observations on Callimachus and Religion." *Museum Helveticum* 41: 212–14.
Bulloch, A. W., E. S. Gruen, A. A. Long, and A. Stewart (eds.) 1993. *Images and Ideologies: Self-Definition in the Hellenistic World*. Hellenistic Culture and Society 12. Berkeley and Los Angeles.
Burgess, J. S. 1996. "The Non-Homeric Cypria." *Transactions of the American Philological Association* 126: 77–99.
Burkert, W. 1985. *Greek Religion*. Cambridge.
— 1983. *Homo Necans. The Anthropology of Ancient Greek Sacrificial Ritual and Belief*. Berkeley and Los Angeles.
Burstein, S. M. 1996. "Ivory and Ptolemaic Exploration of the Red Sea: The Missing Factor." *Topoi* 6.2: 799–807.
— 1992. "Hecataeus of Abdera's History of Egypt." In J. M. Johnson (ed.) *Life in a Multi-Cultural Society: Egypt from Cambyses to Constantine and Beyond*. Studies in Ancient Oriental Civilization 51. Chicago. 45–50.
— 1991. "Pharaoh Alexander: A Scholarly Myth." *Ancient Society* 22: 139–45.
— (ed.) 1989. *Agatharchides of Cnidus: On the Erythraean Sea*. London.
— 1985. *The Hellenistic Age from the Battle of Ipsos to the Death of Kleopatra III*. Translated Documents of Greece and Rome. Cambridge.
— 1982. "Arsinoë Philadelphos: A Revisionist View." In W. L. Adams and E. N. Borza (eds.) *Philip II, Alexander the Great, and the Macedonian Heritage*. Washington. 197–212.
— 1976. *Outpost of Hellenism: The Emergence of Heraclea on the Black Sea*. Berkeley and Los Angeles.
Burton, J. B. 1995. *Theocritus's Urban Mimes: Mobility, Gender, Patronage*. Berkeley and Los Angeles.
Byre, C. S. 2002. *A Reading of Apollonius Rhodius' Argonautica: The Poetics of Uncertainty*. Lewiston, NY, Queenston, and Lampeter.
— 1997. "Suspense in the Phaeacian Episode of Apollonius' *Argonautica*." *Illinois Classical Studies* 22: 65–73.
— 1996. "The Killing of Apsyrtus in Apollonius Rhodius' *Argonautica*." *Phoenix* 50: 1–16.
Cadell, H. 1998. "À quelle date Arsinoé II Philadelphe est-elle décédée?" In H. Melaerts (ed.) *Le Culte du souverain dans l'Égypte ptolemaïque au IIIe siècle avant notre ère*. Studia Hellenistica 34. Leuven. 1–3.
Cairns, F. 1988. *Virgil's Augustan Epic*. Cambridge.
— 1972. *Generic Composition in Greek and Roman Poetry*. Edinburgh.

Calame, C. 1993. "Legendary Narration and Poetic Procedure in Callimachus' Hymn to Apollo." In M. A. Harder, R. F. Regtuit, and G. C. Wakker (eds.) *Callimachus*. Hellenistica Groningana 1. Groningen. 37–55.
— 1992. *The Poetics of Eros in Ancient Greece*. Princeton, NJ.
Cameron, A. 1995. *Callimachus and his Critics*. Princeton, NJ.
Campbell, M. 1994. *A Commentary on Apollonius Rhodius Argonautica III.1–471*. Leiden.
Carnes, J. S. 1993. "With Friends like These: Understanding the Mythic Background of Homer's Phaiakians." *Ramus* 22: 103–15.
Carney, E. D. 2000. *Women and Monarchy in Macedonia*. Norman, OK.
— 1996. "Macedonians and Mutiny: Discipline and Indiscipline in the Army of Philip and Alexander." *Classical Philology* 91: 19–44.
— 1991. "'What's in Name?' The Emergence of a Title for Royal Women in the Hellenistic Period." In S. Pomeroy (ed.) *Women's History and Ancient History*. Chapel Hill and London. 154–72.
— 1987. "Olympias." *Ancient Society* 19: 43–48.
Carson, A. 1990. "Putting Her in Her Place: Woman, Dirt, and Desire." In D. M. Halperin, J. J. Winkler, and F. I. Zeitlin (eds.) *Before Sexuality: The Construction of Erotic Experience in the Ancient Greek World*. Princeton, NJ. 135–69.
Carspecken, J. F. 1952. "Apollonius Rhodius and the Homeric Epic." *Yale Classical Studies* 13: 22–144.
Cartledge, P. 1993. *The Greeks*. Oxford.
Casson, L. 1971. *Ships and Seamanship in the Ancient World*. Baltimore and London.
Cawkwell, G. L. 1994. "The Deification of Alexander the Great: A Note." In I. Worthington (ed.) *Ventures into Greek History: Essays in Honour of N. G. L. Hammond*. Oxford. 293–306.
Cerfaux, L. and J. Tondriau. 1957. *Le Culte des souverains dans la civilisation grécoromaine*. Bibliothèque de Théologie, Ser. 3. Vol. 5. Tournai.
Černy, J. 1954. "Consanguineous Marriages in Pharaonic Egypt." *Journal of Egyptian Archaeology* 40: 23–29.
Chamoux, F. 2003. *Hellenistic Civilization*. Tr. M. Roussel. Oxford, Malden, and Berlin. French edition first published 1981.
Chauveau, M. 2000. *Egypt in the Age of Cleopatra*. Tr. D. Lorton. Ithaca and London.
Christou, C. 1961. "Ἄρεμτις Ἑκάτη." *Archaiologike Ephemeris* 1953–54.3: 188–200.
Clare, R. J. 2002. *The Path of the Argo*. Cambridge.
— 1997. "Catullus 64 and the *Argonautica* of Apollonius Rhodius: Allusion and Exemplarity." *Proc. Camb. Philolog. Soc.* 42: 60–88.
Clarysse, W. 1992. "Some Greeks in Egypt." In J. M. Johnson (ed.) *Life in a Multi-Cultural Society: Egypt from Cambyses to Constantine and Beyond*. Studies in Ancient Oriental Civilization 51. Chicago. 51–56.
Clauss, J. J. 2000. "Cosmos without Imperium: The *Argonautica*'s Journey through Time." In M. A. Harder, R. F. Regtuit, and G. C. Wakker (eds.) *Apollonius Rhodius*. Hellenistica Groningana 4. Leuven. 11–32.

— 1997. "Conquest of the Mephistophelian Nausicaa: Medea's Role in Apollonius' Redefinition of the Epic Hero." In J. J. Clauss and S. I. Johnston (eds.) *Medea: Essays on Medea in Myth, Literature, Philosophy, and Art*. Princeton, NJ. 149–77.

— 1993. *The Best of the Argonauts: The Redefinition of the Epic Hero in Book One of Apollonius' Argonautica*. Berkeley and Los Angeles.

Clayman, D. 2000. "The Scepticism of Apollonius' *Argonautica*." In M. A. Harder, R. F. Regtuit, and G. C. Wakker (eds.) *Apollonius Rhodius*. Hellenistica Groningana 4. Leuven. 33–53.

Clinton, K. 1988. "Artemis and the Sacrifice of Iphigeneia in Aeschylus' Agamemnon." In P. Pucci (ed.) *Language and the Tragic Hero: Essays on Greek Tragedy in Honor of Gordon M. Kirkwood*. Atlanta. 1–24.

Cohen, G. M. 1995. *The Hellenistic Settlements in Europe, the Islands, and Asia Minor*. Berkeley and Los Angeles.

— 1982. "Colonization and Population Transfer in the Hellenistic World." In Van 'T Dack *et al*. (eds.) 63–74.

Cole, S. G. 1984. *Theoi Megaloi: The Cult of the Great Gods at Samothrace*. Leiden.

Collins, D. 2004. *Master of the Game: Competition and Performance in Greek Poetry*. Washington, DC and Cambridge, MA.

Cuypers, M. 2005. "Interactional Particles and Narrative Voice in Apollonius and Homer." In A. Harder and M. Cuypers (eds.) *Beginning from Apollo*. Leuven, Paris, and Dudley, MA. 35–69.

Davidson, J. N. 1997. *Courtesans and Fishcakes: The Consuming Passions of Classical Athens*. London.

Davies, J. K. 2002. "The Interpenetration of Hellenistic Sovereignties." In D. Ogden (ed.) *The Hellenistic World: New Perspectives*. Swansea and London 1–21.

— 1994. "On the Non-usability of the Concept of Sovereignty in an Ancient Greek Context." In L. A. Foresti, A. Barzanò, C. Bearzot, L. Prandi, and G. Zecchini (eds.) *Federazioni e federalismo nell' Europa antica: Alle radici della case commune europea*. I. Vita e pensiero. Milan. 51–65.

DeForest, M. M. 1994. *Apollonius' Argonautica: A Callimachean Epic*. Mnemosyne 142. Leiden, New York, and Köln.

Delia, D. 1993. Response to Samuel. In P. Green (ed.) 192–204.

Depew, M. 2004. "Gender, Power, and Poetics in Callimachus' Book of Hymns." In Harder *et al*. (eds.) 117–38.

— 2001. "Enacted and Represented Dedications: Genre and Greek Hymn." In M. Depew and D. Obbink (eds.) *Matrices of Genre. Authors, Canons, and Society*. Cambridge, MA and London. 59–79.

— 1998. "Delian Hymns and Callimachean Allusion." *Harvard Studies in Classical Philology* 98: 155–82.

— 1993. "Mimesis and Aetiology in Callimachus' Hymns." In M. A. Harder, R. F. Regtuit, and G. C. Wakker (eds.) *Callimachus*. Hellenistica Groningana 1. Groningen. 57–77.

Detienne, M. 1989. "Culinary Practices and the Spirit of Sacrifice." In M. Detienne and J.-P. Vernant (eds.) *The Cuisine of Sacrifice Among the Greeks*. Tr. P. Wissing. Chicago and London. 1–20.
Diehl, A. 1993. "Response." In Bulloch *et al.* (eds.) 287–95.
Dittenberger, W. (ed.) 1903–5. *Orientis Graeci Inscriptiones selectae*. 2 vols. Leipzig.
Dodds, E. R. 1951. *The Greeks and the Irrational*. Berkeley and Los Angeles.
Dougherty, C. 1994. "Archaic Greek Foundation Poetry: Questions of Genre and Occasion." *Journal of Hellenic Studies* 114: 35–46.
— 1993. *The Poetics of Colonization*. Oxford.
— 1991. "Linguistic Colonization in Aeschylus' *Aetnaeae*." *Greek, Roman, and Byzantine Studies* 32: 119–32.
Dover, K. J. (ed.) 1971. *Theocritus: Select Poems*. Bristol and Oak Park, MI.
Dräger, P. 2001. *Die Argonautika des Apollonios Rhodios: das zweite Zorn-Epos der griechischen Literatur*. Munich.
— 1993. *Argopasimelousa: der Argonautenepos in der griechischen und römischen Literatur*. Stuttgart.
Droysen, J.-G. 1877–78. *Geschichte des Hellenismus*. 2nd edn. 3 vols. Gotha.
duBois, P. 1988. *Sowing the Body: Psychoanalysis and Ancient Representations of Women*. Chicago.
Duckworth, G. E. 1933. *Foreshadowing and Suspense in the Epics of Homer, Apollonius, and Vergil*. Princeton, NJ.
Dué, C. 2002. *Homeric Variations on a Lament by Briseis*. Greek Studies: Interdisciplinary Approaches. Oxford.
Durkheim, E. 1976. *The Elementary Forms of the Religious Life*. Tr. J. W. Swain. London.
Dyck, A. R. 1989. "On the Way from Colchis to Corinth." *Hermes* 117: 455–70.
Easterling, P. E. and B. M. W. Knox (eds.) 1985. *Greek Literature*. Cambridge.
Edson, C. F. 1970. "Early Macedonia." In B. Laourdas and Ch. Makaronas (eds.) *Ancient Macedonia: Papers Read at the First International Symposium Held in Thessaloniki, 26–9 August 1968*. Thessaloniki. 17–44.
Ellis, W. M. 1994. *Ptolemy of Egypt*. London and New York.
— 1976. *Philip III and Macedonian Imperialism*. London.
Elvira, M. A. 1977–78. "Apolonio de Rodas y la pintura del primer Hellenismo." *Archivo español de arqueología* 50–51: 32–46.
Errington, R. M. 1978. "The Nature of the Macedonian State under the Monarchy." *Chiron* 8: 77–133.
— 1970. "From Babylon to Triparadeisos: 323–320 B.C." *Journal of Hellenic Studies* 90: 49–77.
Erskine, A. 2003. *A Companion to the Hellenistic World*. Malden, MA.
— 1995. "Culture and Power in Ptolemaic Egypt: The Museum and Library of Alexandria." *Greece & Rome* n.s. 42: 38–48.
Evans-Grubbs, J. 1989. "Abduction Marriage in Antiquity. A Law of Constantine (CTh IX 24.1) and its Social Context." *Journal of Roman Studies* 79: 59–83.
Faerber, H. 1932. "Zur dichterischen Kunst in Apollonios Rhodios' *Argonautika* (Die Gleichnisse)." Dissertation. Friedrich-Wilhelms-Universität, Berlin.

Fakas, C. 2001. *Der hellenistische Hesiod: Arats Phainomena und die Tradition der antiken Lehrepik.* Wiesbaden.

Fantuzzi, M. 2001. "'Homeric' Formularity in the Argonautica of Apollonius of Rhodes." In Papanghelis and Rengakos (eds.) 171–92.

— 1988. "L'epos ellenistico tradizionale prima e dopo Ziegler"; "Epici ellenistici." In K. Ziegler *L'epos ellenistico.* Tr. G. Aquaro. Bari. xxv–lxxxix.

Fantuzzi, M. and R. Hunter 2004. *Tradition and Innovation in Hellenistic Poetry.* Cambridge.

— 2002. *Muse e Modelli: La poesia ellenistica da Alessandro Magno ad Augusto.* Rome and Bari.

Farnell, L. 1896. *The Cults of the Greek States.* Vol. 2. Oxford.

Feeney, D. C. 1998. *Literature and Religion at Rome: Cultures, Contexts, and Beliefs.* Cambridge.

— 1991. *The Gods in Epic.* Oxford.

Feucht, E. 1997. "Women." In S. Donadoni (ed.) *The Egyptians.* Chicago.

Fillion-Lahille, J. 1970. "La Colère chez Aristote." *Revue des études anciennes* 72: 46–79.

Finley, M. I. 1991. *The World of Odysseus.* London.

— 1983. *Politics in the Ancient World.* Cambridge.

Finnestad, R. 1997. "Temples of the Ptolemaic and Roman Periods." In B. Shafer (ed.) *Temples of Ancient Egypt.* Ithaca. 185–237.

Foley, J. M. 1991. *Immanent Art: From Structure to Meaning in Traditional Oral Epic.* Bloomington, IN.

— 1990. *Traditional Oral Epic: The Odyssey, Beowulf, and Serbo-Croatian Return Song.* Berkeley and Los Angeles.

Fortenbaugh, W. W. 1975. *Aristotle on Emotion.* New York.

Foster, J. A. 2006. "Arsinoe II as Epic Queen: Encomiastic Allusion in Theocritus Idyll 15." *Transactions of the American Philological Association* 136: 133–48.

Fowler, D. P. 1991. "Narrate and Describe: The Problem of Ecphrasis." *Journal of Roman Studies* 81: 25–35.

Fränkel, H. 1968. *Noten zu den Argonautika des Apollonios.* Munich.

— 1960. "Ein Don Quijote unter den Argonauten des Apollonios." *Museum Helveticum* 17: 1–20.

— 1957. "Das Argonautenepos des Apollonios." *Museum Helveticum* 14: 1–19.

— 1952. "Apollonius Rhodius as Narrator in *Argonautica* 2.1–140." *Transactions of the American Philological Association* 83: 144–55.

Fraser, P. M. 1972. *Ptolemaic Alexandria.* 3 vols. Oxford.

Fredricksmeyer, E. 2003. "Alexander's Religion and Divinity." In J. Roisman (ed.) *Brill's Companion to Alexander the Great.* Leiden and Boston. 253–78.

Froidefond, C. 1971. *Le Mirage Égyptien dans la Littérature grecque d'Homère à Aristote.* Aix-en-Provence.

Fuhrer, T. 1993. "Callimachus' Epinician Odes." In M. A. Harder, R. F. Regtuit, and G. C. Wakker (eds.) *Callimachus.* Hellenistica Groningana 1. Groningen. 79–97.

Gagarin, M. 1986. *Early Greek Law.* Berkeley and Los Angeles.

Galinsky, G. K. 1972. *The Herakles Theme*. Oxford.
Gantz, T. 1993. *Early Greek Myth*. 2 vols. Baltimore and London.
Garnsey, P. 1988. *Famine and Food Supply in the Graeco-Roman World: Responses to Risk and Crisis*. Cambridge.
Garvie, A. F. (ed.) 1988. *Aeschylus: Choephori*. Oxford.
Gerhard, E. 1816. *Lectiones Apolloniae*. Leipzig.
Giangrande, G. 1980–81. *Scripta Minora Alexandrina*. Amsterdam.
Gillies, M. M. 1928. *The "Argonautica" of Apollonius Rhodius: Book III*. Cambridge.
Glei, R. F. 2001. "Outlines of Apollonian Scholarship 1955–1999." In Papanghelis and Rengakos (eds.) 1–26.
Glotz, G. 1904. *La Solidarité de la famille dans le droit criminel en Grèce*. Paris.
Gold, B. K. 1987. *Literary Patronage in Greece and Rome*. Chapel Hill, NC and London.
Goldhill, S. 1994. "The Naive and Knowing Eye: Ecphrasis and the Cult of Viewing in the Hellenistic World." In S. Goldhill and R. Osborne (eds.) *Art and Text in Ancient Greek Culture*. Cambridge. 197–223.
— 1991. *The Poet's Voice: Essays on Poetics and Greek Literature*. Cambridge.
Gordon, R. L. 1979. "The Real and the Imaginary: Production and Religion in the Greco-Roman World." *Art History* 2: 5–34.
Gow, A. S. F. and D. L. Page (eds.) 1968. *The Greek Anthology: Hellenistic Epigrams*. 2 vols. Cambridge.
Goyon, J.-C. 1988. "Ptolemaic Egypt: Priests and the Traditional Religion." In R. S. Bianchi *et al.* (eds.) *Cleopatra's Egypt: Age of the Ptolemies*. Brooklyn, NY. 29–3.
Graf, F. 1987. "Orpheus: A Poet Among Men." In J. N. Bremmer (ed.) *Interpretations of Greek Mythology*. London and Sydney. 80–101.
Green, P. 1997. *The Argonautika: Apollonios Rhodios*. Berkeley and Los Angeles.
— (ed.) 1993. *Hellenistic History and Culture*. Berkeley and Los Angeles.
— 1991. *Alexander of Macedon 356–323 B.C.: A Historical Biography*. 2nd edn. Berkeley and Los Angeles.
— 1990. *Alexander to Actium*. Hellenistic Culture and Society 1. Berkeley and Los Angeles.
Griffiths, F. T. 1990. "Murder, Purification, and Cultural Formation in Aeschylus and Apollonius Rhodius." *Helios* 17: 25–39.
— 1979. *Theocritus at Court*. Leiden.
Gruen, E. S. 1984. *The Hellenistic World and the Coming of Rome*. Berkeley and Los Angeles.
Grzybek, E. 1990. *Du calendrier macédonien au calendrier ptolémaïque*. Basle.
Gühl, E. and W. Koner 1872. *Das Leben der Griechen und Römer nach antiken Bildwerken*. Berlin.
Gutzwiller, K. (ed.) 2005. *The New Posidippus: A Hellenistic Poetry Book*. Oxford.
Habicht, C. 1997. *Athens from Alexander to Anthony*. Cambridge, MA.
— 1970. *Gottmenschentum und griechische Städte*. Munich.
— 1958. "Die herrschende Gesellschaft in den hellenistischen Monarchien." *Vierteljahresschrift für Sozial- und Wirtschaftsgeschichte* 45: 1–16.

Hamilton, R. 1969. *Plutarch: Alexander: A Commentary*. Oxford.
Hammond, N. G. L. 1999. "Heroic and Divine Honors in Macedonia before the Successors." *Ancient World* 30: 103–15.
— 1993. "The Macedonian Imprint on the Hellenistic World." In Green (ed.) 12–23.
— 1967a. *Epirus: The Geography, the Ancient Remains, the History and Topography of Epirus and Adjacent Areas*. Oxford.
— 1967b. *A History of Greece to 322 B.C.* 2nd edn. Oxford.
Hammond, N. G. L. and G. T. Griffith. 1979. *A History of Macedonia*. Vol. 2: 550–336 B.C. Oxford.
Harder, M. A. 2002a. "Intertextuality in Callimachus' *Aetia*." In *Callimaque. Sept exposés suivis de discussion*. Entretiens sur l'Antiquité Classique 48. Geneva. 189–223.
— 2002b. Review of A. Cameron. *Callimachus and his Critics*. *Mnemosyne* 55: 599–608.
— 1998. "'Generic Games' in Callimachus' *Aetia*." In M. A. Harder, R. F. Regtuit, and G. C. Wakker (eds.) *Genre in Hellenistic Poetry*. Hellenistica Groningana 3. Groningen. 95–111.
— 1993. "Aspects of the Structure of Callimachus' *Aetia*." In M. A. Harder, R. F. Regtuit, and G. C. Wakker, (eds.) *Callimachus*. Hellenistica Groningana 1. Groningen. 99–110.
— 1992. "Insubstantial Voices: Some Observations on the Hymns of Callimachus." *Classical Quarterly* 42: 384–94.
Harder, M. A., R. F. Regtuit, and G. C. Wakker (eds.) 2004. *Callimachus II*. Hellenistica Groningana 6. Leuven.
Hardie, P. R. 1993. *The Epic Successors of Virgil*. Cambridge.
— 1986. *Virgil's "Aeneid": Cosmos and Imperium*. Oxford.
— 1985. "Imago Mundi: Cosmological and Ideological Aspects of the Shield of Achilles." *Journal of Hellenic Studies* 105: 11–31.
Harris, W. V. 2001. *Restraining Rage: The Ideology of Anger Control in Classical Antiquity*. Cambridge, MA.
Haslam, M. W. 1993. "Callimachus' Hymns." In M. A. Harder, R. F. Regtuit, and G. C. Wakker (eds.) *Callimachus*. Hellenistica Groningana 1. Groningen. 111–25.
Hauben, H. 1983. "Arsinoé II et la politique extérieure de l'Egypte." In Van 'T' Dack *et al.* (eds.) 99–127.
— 1970. *Callicrates of Samos: A Contribution to the Study of the Ptolemaic Admiralty*. Leuven.
Hazzard, R. A. 2000. *Imagination of a Monarchy: Studies in Ptolemaic Propaganda*. Toronto, Buffalo, NY, and London.
— 1992. "Did Ptolemy I Get His Surname from the Rhodians in 304?" *Zeitschrift für Papyrologie und Epigraphik* 93: 52–56.
Herman, G. 1997. "The Court Society of the Hellenistic Age." In P. Cartledge, P. Garnsey, and E. Gruen (eds.) *Hellenistic Constructs: Essays in Culture, History, and Historiography*. Hellenistic Culture and Society 26. Berkeley and Los Angeles. 199–224.

—— 1987. *Ritualised Friendship and the Greek City*. Cambridge.
—— 1980–81. "The 'Friends' of the Early Hellenistic Rulers: Servants or Officials?" *Talanta* 12–13: 103–27.
Hirsch, S. 1985. *The Friendship of the Barbarians: Xenophon and the Persian Empire*. Hanover and London.
Hölbl, G. 2001. *A History of the Ptolemaic Empire*. Tr. T. Saavedra. London and New York.
Hollis, A. S. 1990. *Callimachus: Hecale*. Oxford.
Holoka, J. P. 1999. "*Heroes cunctantes*? Hesitant Heroes: Aeneas and some others." In J. N. Kazazis and A. Rengakos (eds.) *Euphrosyne: Studies in Ancient Epic and its Legacy in Honor of Dimitris N. Maronitis*. Stuttgart. 143–53.
Hopkins, K. 1980. "Brother–sister Marriage in Roman Egypt." *Comparative Studies in Society and History* 20: 303–54.
Hornung, E. 1997. "The Pharaoh." In S. Donadoni (ed.) *The Egyptians*. Tr. R. Bianchi *et al.* Chicago and London. 283–314.
Hubert, H. and M. Mauss. 1964. *Sacrifice: Its Nature and Function*. Tr. W. D. Halls. London.
Hunter, R. 2006. *The Shadow of Callimachus: Studies in the Reception of Hellenistic Poetry at Rome*. Cambridge.
—— (ed. and tr.) 2003. *Theocritus: Encomium of Ptolemy Philadelphus*. Berkeley and Los Angeles.
—— 2001. "The Poetics of Narrative in the *Argonautica*." In Papanghelis and Rengakos (eds.) 93–125.
—— 1995. "The Divine and Human Map of the *Argonautica*." *Syllecta Classica* 6: 13–27.
—— (ed.) 1993. *The "Argonautica" of Apollonius: Literary Studies*. Cambridge.
—— 1992. "Writing the God: Form and Meaning in Callimachus, *Hymn to Athena*." *Materiali e discussioni per l'analisi dei testi classici* 29: 9–34.
—— 1991. "Greek and Non-Greek in the *Argonautica* of Apollonius." In S. Said (ed.) HELLENISMOS: *Quelques jalons pour une histoire de l'identité grecque. Actes du colloque de Strasbourg 25.27 octobre 1989*. Leiden. 81–99.
—— (ed.) 1989. *Apollonius of Rhodes: Argonautica Book III*. Cambridge Greek and Latin Classics Cambridge.
—— 1988. "'Short on Heroics': Jason in the *Argonautica*." *Classical Quarterly* 28: 436–53.
—— 1986. "Apollo and the Argonauts: Two Notes on Ap. Rhod. 2, 669–719." *Museum Helveticum* 43: 50–60.
Hunter, R. and Th. Fuhrer 2002. "Imaginary Gods? Poetic Theology in the Hymns of Callimachus." In *Callimaque. Sept exposés suivis de discussions*. Entretiens sur l'Antiquité Classique 48. Geneva. 143–87.
Hutchinson, G. O. 1988. *Hellenistic Poetry*. Oxford.
Huxley, G. L. 1980. "ΒΟΥΠΟΡΟΣ ΑΡΣΙΝΟΗΣ." *Journal of Hellenic Studies* 100: 189–90.
Irwin, E. 1974. *Colour Terms in Greek Poetry*. Toronto.
Jackson, S. 2000. *Istrus the Callimachean*. Amsterdam.

— 1992. "Apollonius' Jason: Human Being in an Epic Scenario." *Greece & Rome* 39: 155–62.
Jacoby, F. 1956. "Über die Entwicklung der griechischen Historiographie und den Plan einer neuen Sammlung der griechischen Historikerfragmente." In H. Bloch (ed.) *Abhandlungen zur Griechischen Geschichtschreibung*. Leiden. 16–64.
Jebb, R. C. (ed.) 1962. *Sophocles: The Plays and Fragments: Part 6. Electra*. Amsterdam.
Kahane, A. 1994. "Callimachus, Apollonius, and the Poetics of Mud." *Transactions of the American Philological Association* 124: 121–33.
Kaibel, G. (ed.) 1899. *Comicorum Graecorum fragmenta*. Berlin.
Kalimtzis, K. 2000. *Aristotle on Political Enmity and Disease: An Enquiry into Stasis*. Albany, NY.
Kanazawa, Y. 1989. "Observations on either Acculturation or Constancy of the Indigenous Culture and Society in Hellenistic Egypt." In L. Criscuolo and G. Geraci (eds.) *Egitto e Storia dall' Ellenismo all' Eta Araba. Bilancio di un Confronto*. Bologna. 475–89.
Kemp, B. 1991. *Ancient Egypt. Anatomy of a Civilization*. London and New York.
Kidd, D. (ed.) 1997. *Aratus Phaenomena*. Cambridge Classical Texts and Commentaries 34. Cambridge.
Kirk, G. S. (ed.) 1985. *The Iliad: A Commentary*. Vol. 1: Books 1–4. Cambridge.
Kirk, G. S. and J. E. Raven 1957. *The Presocratic Philosophers*. Cambridge.
Klein, T. M. 1983. "Apollonius' Jason: Hero and Scoundrel." *Quaderni Urbinati di Cultura Classica* 42: 115–26.
Knight, V. 1995. *The Renewal of Epic: Responses to Homer in the "Argonautica" of Apollonius*. Leiden.
Koenen, L. 1993. "The Ptolemaic King as a Religious Figure." In Bulloch *et al.* (eds.) 25–115.
— 1977. *Eine agonistische Inschrift aus Ägypten und frühptolemäische Königsfeste*. Meisenheim.
— 1968. "Die Prophezeiungen des "Töpfers."" *Zeitschrift für Papyrologie und Epigraphik* 2: 178–209.
Köhnken, A. 2001. "Hellenistic Chronology: Theocritus, Callimachus, and Apollonius Rhodius." In Papanghelis and Rengakos (eds.) 73–92.
Kralli, I. 2003. "The Date and Context of Divine Honours for Antigonos Gonatas – a Suggestion." In O. Palagia and S. V. Tracy (eds.) *The Macedonians in Athens 322–229 B.C. Proceedings of an International Conference held at the University of Athens, May 24–26, 2001*. 61–66.
Krevans, N. 2000. "On the Margins of Epic: The Foundation-Poems of Apollonius." In M. A. Harder, R. F. Regtuit, and G. C. Wakker (eds.) *Apollonius Rhodius*. Hellenistica Groningana 4. Leuven. 69–84.
Kyriakou, P. 1995. *Homeric Hapax Legomena in the Argonautica of Apollonius Rhodius: A Literary Study*. Stuttgart.
— 1994. "Empedoclean Echoes in Apollonius Rhodius' *Argonautica*." *Hermes* 122: 309–19.

La'da, Csaba A. 2002. *Foreign Ethnics in Hellenistic Egypt.* Prosopographia Ptolemaica 10; Studia Hellenistica 38. Dudley, MA.
Landels, J. G. 1999. *Music in Ancient Greece and Rome.* London and New York.
Lape, S. 2004. *Reproducing Athens: Menander's Comedy, Democratic Culture, and the Hellenistic City.* Princeton, NJ.
Laronde, A. 1987. *Cyréne et la Libye hellénistique.* Paris.
Launey, M. 1945. "Études d'historie hellénistique, II. L'exécution de Sotadès de l'expédition de Patroklos dans la mer Êgée." *Revue des études anciennes* 47: 33–45.
Lawall, G. 1966. "Apollonius' *Argonautica*: Jason as Anti-Hero." *Yale Classical Studies* 19: 119–69.
Lefkowitz, M. R. 2001. "Myth and History in the Biography of Apollonius." In Papanghelis and Regakos (eds.) 51–71.
— 1980. "The Quarrel between Callimachus and Apollonius." *Zeitschrift für Papyrologie und Epigraphik* 40: 1–19.
Levin, D. N. 1971a. *Apollonius' Argonautica Re-examined: The Neglected First and Second Books.* Mnemosyne Supplement 13. Leiden.
— 1971b. "Apollonius' Heracles." *Classical Journal* 67: 22–28.
Lewis, N. 1986. *Greeks in Ptolemaic Egypt: Case Studies in the Social History of the Hellenistic World.* Oxford.
Lincoln, B. 1994. *Authority: Construction and Corrosion.* Chicago and London.
Livrea, E. (tr. and comm.) 1973. *Argonauticon: Liber Quartus.* Florence.
Lloyd, A. 2002. "The Egyptian Elite in the Early Ptolemaic Period: Some Hieroglyphic Evidence." In D. Ogden (ed.) *The Hellenistic World: New Perspectives.* Swansea and London. 117–36.
Lloyd-Jones, H. 1990. "A Hellenistic Miscellany." In H. Lloyd-Jones. *Greek Epic, Lyric, and Tragedy: The Academic Papers of Sir Hugh Lloyd-Jones.* Oxford. 231–49.
Lombardi, M. 1985. "Aspetti del realismo nelle Argonautiche di Apollonio Rhodio." *Orpheus* 6: 250–69.
Long, C. R. 1987. *The Twelve Gods of Greece and Rome.* Leiden.
Longega, G. 1968. *Arsinoë II.* Rome.
Lord, A. B. 2000. *The Singer of Tales.* 2nd edn. Ed. S. Mitchell and G. Nagy. Cambridge and London.
— 1953. "Homer's Originality: Oral Dictated Texts." *Transactions of the American Philological Association* 84: 124–34.
Lund, H. S. 1992. *Lysimachus: A Study in Early Hellenistic Kingship.* London and New York.
Mackie, C. J. 2001. "The Earliest Jason: What's in a Name?" *Greece & Rome* 48: 1–17.
Maclean, J. K. B. and E. B. Aitken (tr.) 2001. *Flavius Philostratus: Heroikos.* Atlanta.
Macurdy, G. H. 1932. *Hellenistic Queens: A Study of Woman-Power in Macedonia, Seleucid Syria, and Ptolemaic Egypt.* Baltimore. (Reprint, 1985.)
Maehler, H. 1988. "Poésie Alexandrine et art hellénistique à Memphis." *Chronique d'Egypte* 63: 113–36.

Magnetto, A. (ed.) 1997. *Gli arbitrati interstatali greci*. Vol. 2. Pisa.
Malamud, M. and D. T. McGuire, Jr. 1993. "Flavian Variant: Myth. Flaccus' *Argonautica*." In Boyle (ed.) 192–217.
Malkin, I. 1987. *Religion and Colonization in Ancient Greece*. Studies in Greek and Roman Religion 3. Leiden, New York, Copenhagen, and Cologne.
Manakidou, F. 1998. "*Cholos, menis, neikos* in den Argonautika des Apollonios Rhodios." *Philologus* 142: 241–60.
Manning, J. G. 2003. *Land and Power in Ptolemaic Egypt*. Cambridge.
Marshall, A. J. 1980. "The Survival and Development of International Jurisdiction in the Greek World under Roman Rule." *Aufstieg und Niedergang der römischen Welt* 2.13: 626–61.
Martin, J. 1956. *Histoire du texte des Phénomènes d'Aratos*. Paris.
McGing, B. C. 1997. "Revolt Egyptian Style: Internal Opposition to Ptolemaic Rule." *Archiv für Papyrusforschung* 43: 273–314.
Meineke, A. (ed.) 1843. *Analecta alexandrina: sive, Commentationes de Euphorione Chaleidensi, Rhiano Cretensi, Alexandro Aetolo, Parthenio Nicaeno*. Hildesheim. (Reprint, 1968.)
Meister, K. 1984. "Agathocles." In *The Cambridge Ancient History*. Vol. 7. 1: The Hellenistic World. 2nd edn. Cambridge. Ch. 10, 384–411.
Merkelbach, R. 1981. "Das Königtum der Ptolemäer und die hellenistiche Dichter." In H. Hinske (ed.) *Alexandrien*. Aegyptiaca Treversnia 1. Mainz. 27–35.
Merkelbach, R. and M. L. West (eds.) 1967. *Fragmenta Hesiodea*. Oxford.
Mikalson, J. 1998. *Religion in Hellenistic Athens*. Berkeley and Los Angeles.
— 1991. *Honor Thy Gods: Popular Religion in Greek Tragedy*. Chapel Hill, NC and London.
— 1983. *Popular Athenian Religion*. Chapel Hill, NC and London.
Mineur, W. H. 1984. *Callimachus: Hymn to Delos*. Leiden.
Modrzejewski, J. 1981. "La Structure juridique du mariage grec." In E. Bresciani, G. Geraci, S. Pernigotti, and G. Susini. *Scritti in onore di Orsolina Montevecchi*. Bologna. 231–68.
Monro, D. B. and T. W. Allen (eds.) 1912. *Homeri Opera*. Vol. 5. Oxford.
Mooney, G. (ed.) 1912. *The Argonautica of Apollonius Rhodius*. Dublin.
Mooren, L. 1982. "The Nature of the Hellenistic Monarchy." In Van 'T Dack et al. (eds.) 205–40.
— 1975. *The Aulic Titulature in Ptolemaic Egypt*. Brussels.
Moreau, A. 1994. *Le Mythe de Jason et Médée. Le va-nu-pied et la sorcière*. Paris.
Mori, A. 2007. "Acts of Persuasion in Hellenistic Epic: Honey-Sweet Words in Apollonius." In I. Worthington (ed.) *A Companion to Greek Rhetoric*. Malden, MA, Oxford, and Victoria. 458–72.
— 2005. "Jason's Reconciliation with Telamon: A Moral Exemplar in Apollonius' *Argonautica* (1.1286–1344)." *American Journal of Philology* 126.2: 209–36.
— 2001. "Personal Favor and Public Influence: Arete, Arsinoë II, and the *Argonautica*." *Oral Tradition* 16.1: 85–106.
Mørkholm, O. 1991. *Early Hellenistic Coinage from the Accession of Alexander to the Peace of Apamea (336–188 B.C.)*. Ed. P. Grierson and U. Westermark. Cambridge.

— 1980. "Cyrene and Ptolemy I: Some Numismatic Comments." *Chiron* 10: 145–59.
Most, G. 1989. "The Structure and Function of Odysseus' *Apologoi*." *Transactions of the American Philological Association* 119: 15–30.
Murray, J. 2004. "The Metamorphosis of Erysichthon: Callimachus, Apollonius, and Ovid." In Harder *et al.* (eds.) 207–41.
Murray, O. 1972. "Herodotus and Hellenistic Culture." *Classical Quarterly* n.s. 22: 200–13.
— 1970. "Hecataeus of Abdera and Pharaonic Kingship." *Journal of Egyptian Archaeology* 56: 141–71.
Muth, R. 1954. *Träger der Lebenskraft; Ausscheidungen des Organismus im Volksglauben der Antike*. Vienna.
Mynors, R. A. B. (ed.) 1960. *P. Vergili Maronis Opera*. Oxford.
Myśliwiec, K. 2004. *Eros on the Nile*. Tr. G. L. Packer. Ithaca, NY.
Nagy, G. 1996. *Poetry as Performance: Homer and Beyond*. Cambridge.
— 1990. *Greek Mythology and Poetics*. Ithaca, NY and London.
Natzel, S. A. 1992. Κλέα γυναικῶν: *Frauen in den "Argonautika" des Apollonios Rhodios*. Trier.
Nauck, A. (ed.) 1964. *Tragicorum Graecorum Fragmenta*. Hildesheim.
Nelis, D. P. 2001a. "Apollonius and Virgil." In Papanghelis and Rengakos (eds.) 239–59.
– 2001b. *Vergil's Aeneid and the "Argonautica" of Apollonius Rhodius*. ARCA Classical and Medieval Texts, Papers and Monographs 39. Leeds.
— 1992. "Demodocus and the Song of Orpheus." *Museum Helveticum* 49: 153–70.
— 1991. "Iphias: Apollonius Rhodius, *Argonautica* 1.311–16." *Classical Quarterly* 41: 96–105.
Newman, J. K. 2001. "The Golden Fleece: Imperial Dream." In Papanghelis and Rengakos (eds.) 309–40.
Nilsson, M. P. 1967–74. *Geschichte der griechischen Religion*. Handbuch der Altertumswissenschaft 5.2. 3rd edn. 2 vols. Munich.
Nisetich, F. 2001. *The Poems of Callimachus*. Oxford.
Nishimura-Jensen, J. M. 1998. "The Poetics of Aethalides: Silence and Poikilia in Apollonius' *Argonautica*." *Classical Quarterly* n.s. 48: 456–69.
— 1996. "Tragic Epic or Epic Tragedy: Narrative and Genre in Apollonius of Rhodes' *Argonautica*." Dissertation. University of Wisconsin at Madison.
Nussbaum, G. B. 1967. *The Ten Thousand: A Study in Social Organization and Action in Xenophon's Anabasis*. Leiden.
Oakley, J. H. and R. H. Sinos 1993. *The Wedding in Ancient Athens*. Madison, WI.
O'Brien, J. M. 1992. *Alexander the Great: The Invisible Enemy*. London and New York.
Ogden, D. 1999. *Polygamy, Prostitutes, and Death: The Hellenistic Dynasts*. London.
O'Higgens, L. 2003. *Women and Humor in Classical Greece*. Cambridge.
Ojennus, P. 2006. "Holding Hands in the *Argonautica*." *Classical Journal* 101: 253–70.
Olson, S. D. and A. Sens 2000. *Archestratos of Gela: Greek Culture and Cuisine in the Fourth Century B.C.* Oxford.

Onians, J. 1979. *Art and Thought in the Hellenistic Age*. London.
Otto, W. 1905. *Priester und Tempel im Hellenistischen Aegypten: Ein Beitrag zur Kulturgeschichte des Hellenismus*. 2 vols. Leipzig and Berlin.
Pallone, M. R. 1984. "L'epica agonale in età ellenistica." *Orpheus* 5: 156–66.
Papanghelis, T. D. and A. Rengakos (eds.) 2001. *A Companion to Apollonius Rhodius*. Mnemosyne, Bibliotheca Classica Batava. Supplementum 217. Leiden, Boston, and Cologne.
Parker, R. 1983. *Miasma: Pollution and Purification in Early Greek Religion*. Oxford.
Parry, M. 1987. *The Making of Homeric Verse: The Collected Papers of Milman Parry*. Ed. A. Parry. New York and Oxford (First published 1971.)
Parsons, P. J. 1993. "Identities in Diversity." In Bulloch *et al.* (eds.) 152–70.
— 1977. "Callimachus: *Victoria Berenices*." *Zeitschrift für Papyrologie und Epigraphik* 25: 1–50.
Pavese, C. O. 1998. "The Rhapsodic Epic Poems as Oral and Independant Poems." *Harvard Studies in Classical Philology* 98: 63–90.
Pavlock, B. 1990. *Eros, Imitation and the Epic Tradition*. Ithaca, NY and London.
Pearson, A. C. (ed.) 1917. *The Fragments of Sophocles*. 3 vols. Cambridge.
Pelling, C. B. R. (ed.) 1988. *Plutarch: Life of Antony*. Cambridge.
Peremans, W. 1962. "Egyptians et étrangers dans l'Egypte ptolemaique." In H. Schwabl (ed.) *Grecs et barbares. Six exposés et discussions*. Entretiens sur l'Antiquité Classique 8. Geneva. 121–66.
Peremans, W. and E. Van 'T Dack. 1950–1981. *Prosopographia Ptolemaica*. Studia Hellenistica. 9 vols. Leuven.
Pernigotti, S. 1997. "Priests." In S. Donadoni (ed.) *The Egyptians*. Tr. R. Bianchi *et al.* Chicago and London. 121–50.
Perrotta, G. 1978. *Poesia ellenistica: Scritti minori*. Vol. 2. Rome.
Pfeiffer, R. 1968. *History of Classical Scholarship: From the Beginning to the End of the Hellenistic Age*. Oxford.
— 1955. "The Future of Studies in the Field of Hellenistic Poetry." *Journal of Hellenic Studies* 75: 69–73.
— 1953. *Callimachus: Hymns and Epigrams*. Vol. 2. Oxford.
— 1949. *Callimachus: Fragments*. Vol. 1. Oxford.
Phinney Jr., E. 1967. "Hellenistic Painting and the Poetic Style of Apollonius," *Classical Journal* 62: 145–49.
Piccirilli, L. 1973. *Gli arbitrati interstatali greci*. Vol. 1. Pisa.
Pietsch, C. 1999. *Die Argonautika des Apollonios von Rhodos*. Hermes Einzelschriften 80. Stuttgart.
Pike, D. 1993. "Jason's Departure: Apollonius Rhodius and Heroism." *Acta Classica* 36: 27–37.
Plantinga, M. 2000. "The Supplication Motif in Apollonius Rhodius' *Argonautica*." In M. A. Harder, R. F. Regtuit, and G. C. Wakker (eds.) *Apollonius Rhodius*. Hellenistica Groningana 4. Leuven. 105–28.
Pollitt, J. J. 1986. *Art in the Hellenistic Age*. Cambridge.
Pomeroy S. B. 1997. *Families in Classical and Hellenistic Greece*. Oxford.
— 1990. *Women in Hellenistic Egypt: From Alexander to Cleopatra*. New York.

Porter, J. R. 1990. "Tiptoeing Through the Corpses: Euripides' *Electra*, Apollonius, and the *Bouphonia*," *Greek, Roman, and Byzantine Studies* 31: 255–80.
Potter, D. 2003. "Hellenistic Religion." In Erskine (ed.) 407–30.
Préaux, C. 1978–92. *Le monde héllenistique*. 2 vols. 3rd edn. Paris.
Price, S. R. F. 1984. *Rituals and Power: The Roman Imperial Cult in Asia Minor*. Cambridge.
Pulleyn, S. (ed.) 2000. *Homer: Iliad I*. Oxford.
— 1997. *Prayer in Greek Religion*. Oxford.
Putnam, M. C. J. 2005. "Virgil's *Aeneid*." In J. M. Foley (ed.) *A Companion to Ancient Epic*. Oxford. 452–75.
— 1995. *Virgil's Aeneid: Interpretation and Influence*. Chapel Hill, NC and London.
Quaegebeur, J. 1988. "Cleopatra VII and the Cults of the Ptolemaic Queens." In R. S. Bianchi *et al.* (eds.) *Cleopatra's Egypt: Age of the Ptolemies*. Brooklyn, NY. 41–54.
— 1978. "Reines ptolémaïques et traditions égyptiennes." In H. Maehler and V. M. Strocka (eds.) *Das ptolemäische Ägypten*. Mainz. 245–62.
— 1971a. "Documents concerning a Cult of Arsinoë Philadelphus in Memphis." *Journal of Near Eastern Studies* 30: 242–44.
— 1971b. "Ptolémée II en adoration devant Arsinoé II divinisée." *Bulletin de l'Institut français d'archéologie orientale* 69: 191–217.
Rackham, H. (ed.) 1968. *Aristotle: The Nicomachean Ethics*. Loeb Classical Library. Cambridge, MA.
— (ed.) 1926. *Aristotle: Nichomachean Ethics*. London.
Radt, S. (ed.) 1985. *Tragicorum Graecorum fragmenta*. Aeschylus. Vol. 3. Göttingen.
Ray, J. 1994. "Literacy in Egypt in the Late and Persian Periods." In A. K. Bowman and G. Woolf (eds.) *Literacy and Power in the Ancient World*. Cambridge. 51–66.
Redfield, J. M. 1994. *Nature and Culture in the "Iliad": The Tragedy of Hector*. 2nd edn. Durham, NC and London.
— 1983. "The Economic Man." In C. A. Rubino and C. W. Shelmerdine (eds.) *Approaches to Homer*. Austin, TX.
— 1982. "Notes on the Greek Wedding." *Arethusa* 15: 181–201.
Redondo, J. 2000. "Non-Epic Features in the Language of Apollonius Rhodius." In M. A. Harder, R. F. Regtuit, and G. C. Wakker (eds.) *Apollonius Rhodius*. Hellenistica Groningana 4. Leuven. 129–54.
Reed, J. D. 2000. "Arsinoe's Adonis and the Poetics of Ptolemaic Imperialism." *Transactions of the American Philological Association* 130: 319–51.
Rehm, A. and G. Kawerau 1914. *Das Delphinion in Milet*. Berlin.
Renehan, R. 1963. "Aristotle's Definition of Anger." *Philologus* 107: 61–74.
Rengakos, A. 1992. "Zur Bibilographie des Apollonios des Rhodos." *Wiener Studien* 105: 39–67.
Rice, E. E. 1983. *The Grand Procession of Ptolemy Philadelphus*. Oxford.
Richter, G. 1987. *A Handbook of Greek Art*. New York.
Ridgway, B. S. 1990. *Hellenistic Sculpture I: The Styles of ca. 331–200 B.C.* Bristol.
Rieu, E. V. 1971. *Apollonius of Rhodius: The Voyage of Argo*. New York.

Rittner, R. K. 2003. "The Satrap Stela." In W. K. Simpson (ed.) *The Literature of Ancient Egypt*. New Haven, CT. 392–97.
Roberts, C. H. 1953. "Literature and Society in the Papyri." *Museum Helveticum* 10: 264–79.
Robertson, M. 1990. "Troilus and Polyxena: Notes on a Changing Legend." In J-P. Descœudres (ed.) *Eymoysia: Ceramic and Iconographic Studies in Honour of Alexander Cambitoglou*. Sydney. 63–70.
— 1970. "Ibycus: Polycrates, Troilus, Polyxena." *Bulletin of the Inst. of Classical Studies* 17: 11–15.
Rohde, E. 1907. *Psyche: Seelencult und Unsterblichkeitsglaube der Griechen*. Vol. 1. 4th edn. Tübingen.
Romilly, J. de 1988. "Agamemnon in Doubt and Hesitation." In P. Pucci (ed.) *Language and the Tragic Hero. Essays on Greek Tragedy in honor of Gordon M. Kirkwood*. Atlanta. 25–37.
Roscher, W. H. (ed.) 1884–1937. *Ausführliches Lexicon der griechischen und römischen Mythologie*. Vol. 1. Leipzig.
Rose, A. 1985. "Clothing Imagery in Apollonios' *Argonautika*." *Quaderni Urbinati di Cultura Classica* 50: 29–44.
Rosivach, V. J. 1994. *The System of Public Sacrifice in Fourth-Century Athens*. APA American Classical Studies 34. Atlanta.
Ross, G. P. 1969. "The Unfriendly Phaeacians." *Transactions of the American Philological Association* 160: 387–406.
Rostovtzeff, M. 1941. *The Social and Economic History of the Hellenistic World*. 3 vols. Oxford.
Rostropowicz, J. 1995. "*Theoi Soteres* in den *Argonautika* des Apollonios Rhodios und Ptolemaios I. Soter." *Listy filologické* 118: 191–201.
— 1990. "Das Heraklesbild in den *Argonautika* des Apollonios Rhodios." *Act. Class. Univ. Sci. Debrec.* 26: 31–34.
— 1983. *Odbicie rzeczywistosci politycznej, spolecznej i gospodarczej w poezji aleksandryjskiej*. Warsaw. (With French resume by K. Ciuk. 113–18.)
Rowlandson, J. 1998. *Women and Society in Greek and Roman Egypt*. Cambridge.
Samuel, A. E. 1993. "The Ptolemies and the Ideology of Kingship." In Green (ed.) 168–92.
Sancisi-Weerdenburg, H. 1995. "Persian Food. Stereotypes and Political Identity. In J. Wilkins, D. Harvey, and M. Dobson (eds.) *Food in Antiquity*. Exeter. 286–302.
Sandridge, N. 2004. "Jason and *Orchamos*: A New Style of Leadership Built on Homeric Models." Presented at the annual meeting of the Classical Association of the Middle West and South Annual Meeting (April 15–17, 2004) in St. Louis, MO.
— 2005. "Jason's Selfless Leadership in the *Argonautica* as an Alternative to Homeric Heroism." Dissertation. University of North Carolina.
Sansone, D. 2000. "Iphigeneia in Colchis." In M. A. Harder, R. F. Regtuit, G. C. Wakker (eds.) *Apollonius Rhodius*. Hellenistica Groningana 4. Leuven. 155–72.
Schiesaro, A. 1996. "Aratus' Myth of Dike." *Materiali e discussioni per l'analisi dei testi classici* 37: 9–26.

Schwartz, E. 1887. *Scholia in Euripidem*. Berlin.
Schwinge, E.-R. 1986. *Künstlichkeit von Kunst: Geschichtlichkeit der alexandrinischen Poesie*. Zetemata 84. Munich.
Segal, C. 1971. "The Theme of the Mutilation of the Corpse in the *Iliad*." Supplements to *Mnemosyne* 17. Leiden.
Selden, D. 1998. "Alibis." *Classical Antiquity* 17.2: 289–420.
Sethe, K. (ed.) 1904–16. *Hieroglyphische Urkunden der griechisch-römischen Zeit*. Vol. II of the series Urkunden des aegyptischen Altertums. Publ. in 3 sections (1: 101–80, 2: 81–158, and 3: 159–230). Leipzig. (Reprint 1977.)
Severin, T. 1985. *The Jason Voyage: The Quest for the Golden Fleece*. New York.
Shapiro, H. A. 1980. "Jason's Cloak." *Transactions of the American Philological Association* 110: 163–86.
Sherwin-White, S. 1978. *Ancient Cos*. Göttingen.
Shipley, G. 2000. *The Greek World after Alexander: 323–30 B.C.* London.
Silverman, D. P. 1991. "Divinity and Deities in Ancient Egypt." In B. E. Shafer (ed.) *Religion in Ancient Egypt: Gods, Myths, and Personal Practice*. London. 7–87.
Simpson, R. S. 1996. *Demotic Grammar in the Ptolemaic Sacerdotal Decrees*. Oxford.
Smith, R. R. R. 1993. "Kings and Philosophers." In Bulloch *et al.* (eds.) 202–11.
— 1991. *Hellenistic Sculpture: A Handbook*. London.
Smith, W. Robertson. 1927. *Lectures on the Religion of the Semites: The Fundamental Institutions*. New York.
Solomon, E. M. 1998. "Jason the Great?: Reminiscences of Alexander in Apollonius' *Argonautica*." MA thesis. University of Georgia.
Stanford, W. B. 1983. *Greek Tragedy and the Emotions*. London.
— 1959. *The Odyssey of Homer*. 2nd edn. London.
Stanwick, P. E. 2002. *Portraits of the Ptolemies: Greek Kings as Egyptian Pharaohs*. Austin, TX.
Stephens, S. A. 2005. "Battle of the Books." In Gutzwiller (ed.) 229–48.
— 2003. *Seeing Double: Intercultural Poetics in Ptolemaic Alexandria*. Berkeley and Los Angeles.
— 2000. "Writing Epic for the Ptolemaic Court." In M. A. Harder, R. F. Regtuit, G. C. Wakker (eds.) *Apollonius Rhodius*. Hellenistica Groningana 4. Leuven. 195–215.
Stewart, A. 1993. *Faces of Power. Alexander's Image and Hellenistic Politics*. Berkeley and Los Angeles.
Stoneman, R. 1994 "The Alexander Romance: From History to Fiction." In J. R. Morgan and R. Stoneman (eds.) *Greek Fiction: The Greek Novel in Context*. London. 117–29.
— (tr.) 1991. Pseudo-Callisthenes. *The Greek Alexander Romance*. London and New York.
Strauss, B. and J. Ober 1990. *The Anatomy of Error*. New York.
Studniczka, F. 1915. "Das Symposion Ptolemaios II." *Abh. Kön. Sächs. Ges. d. Wiss., Phil.-Hist. Cl.* 30: 3f.
Taplin, O. 1980. "The Shield of Achilles within the *Iliad*." *Greece & Rome* 27: 1–21.
Tarbell, F. B. 1906. "The Form of the Chlamys." *Classical Philology* 1: 283–89.

Tarn, W. W. 1930. *Hellenistic Civilization*. London.
— 1913. *Antigonus Gonatas*. London. (Reprint: 1969.)
Tassos, A. (tr.) 1960. *Apollonius Rhodius: Argonautica: Jason and the Golden Fleece*. New York.
Thériault, G. 1996. *Le Culte d'homonoia dans les cités grecques*. Lyon, Quebec.
Thompson, D. J. 2005. "Posidippus, Poet of the Ptolemies." In Gutzwiller (ed.) 269–83.
— 2002. "Families in Early Ptolemaic Egypt." In D. Ogden (ed.) *The Hellenistic World: New Perspectives*. Swansea and London. 137–56.
— 1997. "The Infrastructure of Splendour: Census and Taxes in Ptolemaic Egypt." In P. Cartledge, P. Garnsey, and E. Gruen (eds.) *Hellenistic Constructs: Essays in Culture, History, and Historiography*. Berkeley and Los Angeles.
— 1994. "Literacy and Power in Ptolemaic Egypt." In A. K. Bowman and G. Woolf (eds.) *Literacy and Power in the Ancient World*. Cambridge. 67–83.
— 1990. "The High Priests of Memphis under Ptolemaic Rule." In M. Beard and J. North (eds.) *Pagan Priests*. Ithaca, NY. 95–116.
— 1988. *Memphis under the Ptolemies*. Princeton, NJ.
Tod, M. N. 1948. *A Selection of Greek Historical Inscriptions*. Vol. 2: From 408 to 323 BC. Oxford.
Tomlinson, R. A. 1970. "Ancient Macedonian Symposia." In B. Laourdas and C. Makaronas (eds.) *Archaia Makedonia (anakoinōseis kata to Prōton Diethnes Symposion en Thessalonikē, 26–29 Aug. 1968)*. Thessaloniki. 308–315.
Tondriau, J. 1953. "Quelques problèmes religieux ptolémaïques." *Aegyptus* 33: 125–30.
Tunny, J. A. 2001. "The Health of Ptolemy II Philadelphus." *Bulletin of the American Society of Papyrologists* 38: 119–34.
Turner, E. G. 1984. "Ptolemaic Egypt." In *The Cambridge Ancient History*, Vol. 7.1: The Hellenistic World. 2nd edn. Cambridge. Ch. 5, 118–74.
Tylor, E. B. 1958. *Primitive Culture*. 2 vols. New York.
Valverde Sanchez, M. 1989. *El aition en las Argonauticas de Apolonio de Rodas. Estudio Literario*. Madrid.
Van 'T Dack, E. 1988. *Ptolemaica Selecta. Études sur l'armée et l'administration lagides*. Studia Hellenistica 29. Leuven.
Van 'T Dack, E., E. Van Dessel, and W. Van Gucht (eds.) 1983. *Egypt and the Hellenistic World: Proceedings of the International Colloquium, Leuven, 24–26 May 1982*. Leuven.
Vasunia, P. 2001. *The Gift of the Nile: Hellenizing Egypt from Aeschylus to Alexander*. Berkeley and Los Angeles.
Vatin, C. 1970. *Recherches sur le mariage et la condition de la femme mariée à l'époque hellénistique*. Paris.
Vérilhac, A-M. and C. Vial. 1998. *Le Mariage grec du VIe siècle av. J.-C. à l'époque d'Auguste*. Bulletin de Correspondance Hellénique. Supp. 32. Athens.
Veyne, P. 1983. *Les Grecs ont-ils cru à leurs mythes?* Paris.
Vian, F. (ed.) 2002. *Apollonios de Rhodes, Argonautiques*. 2nd edn. 3 vols. Paris.

— 1978. "ΙΗΣΩΝ ΑΜΗΧΑΝΕΩΝ." In E. Livrea and G. A. Privitera (eds.) *Studi in onore de Anthos Ardizzoni II*. Rome. 1025–41.
— 1974. Review of D. N. Levin. *Apollonius' Argonautica Re-examined: The Neglected First and Second Books. Gnomon* 46: 346–53.
Villard, P. 1988. "Ivresses dans l'antiquité classique," *Histoire, économie, et société* 7: 443–59.
Visser, E. 1938. *Götter und Kulte im ptolemäischen Alexandrien*. Amsterdam.
Walbank, F. W. 1987. "Könige als Götter: Überlegungen zum Herrscherkult von Alexander bis Augustus." *Chiron* 17: 365–82.
— 1984. "Monarchy and Monarchic Ideas." In *The Cambridge Ancient History*. Vol. 7. 1: The Hellenistic World. 2nd edn. Cambridge. Ch. 3, 62–100.
— 1982. *The Hellenistic World*. Cambridge.
Welles, C. B. 1934. *Royal Correspondence in the Hellenistic Period: A Study in Greek Epigraphy*. New Haven, CT.
Wendel, C. (ed.) 1967. *Scholia in Theocritum Vetera*. Stuttgart.
— (ed.) 1958. *Scholia in Apollonium Rhodium Vetera*. 2nd edn. Berlin.
West, M. L. 1992. *Ancient Greek Music*. Oxford.
— 1983. *The Orphic Poems*. Oxford.
West, S. 1967. *The Ptolemaic Papyri of Homer*. Cologne.
White, H. 1980. *Essays in Hellenistic Poetry*. Amsterdam.
Wilamowitz-Moellendorf, U. v. 1924. *Hellenistische Dichtung in der Zeit des Kallimachos*. 2 vols. Berlin.
Will, É. 1979. *Histoire politique du monde hellénistique (323–30 av. J.-C.)*. 2 vols. Nancy.
Williams, M. F. 1996. "The Character of Aeëtes in the '*Argonautica*' of Apollonius Rhodius." *Hermes* 124: 463–79.
Winter, E. 1978. "Der Herrskult in den ägyptischen Ptolemäertempeln." In H. Maehler and V. M. Strocka (eds.) *Das ptolemäische Ägypten*. Mainz. 147–60.
Worthington, I. 2004. *Alexander the Great: Man and God*. London.
— 2003. *Alexander the Great: A Reader*. London.
Wyss, B. (ed.) 1936. *Antimachi Colophonii Reliquiae*. Berlin.
Yiftach-Firanko, U. 2003. *Marriage and Marital Arrangements: A History of the Greek Marriage Document in Egypt. 4th Century BCE–4th Century CE*. Munich.
Zanker, G. 1987. *Realism in Alexandrian Poetry: A Literature and its Audience*. London.
— 1979. "The Love Theme in Apollonius Rhodius' *Argonautica*." *Wiener Studien* 13: 52–75.
— 1977. "Callimachus' Hecale: A New Kind of Epic Hero?" *Antichthon* 11: 68–77.
Zeitlin, F. 1968. "The Motif of the Corrupted Sacrifice." *Transactions of the American Philological Association* 96: 463–508.
Ziegler, K. 1966. *Das hellenistische Epos: ein vergessenes Kapitel griechischer Dichtung*. 2nd edn. Leipzig.
Zimmerman, K. 2002. "Eratosthenes' *Chlamys*-Shaped World: A Misunderstood Metaphor." In D. Ogden (ed.) *The Hellenistic World: New Perspectives*. Swansea and London. 23–40.

Index

Acastus 64–6, 164
Achilles
   Agamemnon and 54–6, 64, 86–7, 142, 182
   arming 108
   grief 3, 49, 202, 203
   Hector and 164, 172
   self-reliance 91
   shield 106, 107, 140, 179
   Troilus, killing of 201–9
   wrath (*menis*) 1, 88–90, 166
Adulis inscription 25
Aeëtes
   demi-god 147
   Homeric 175
   hostility 49, 81–4, 113, 115, 194, 232–3
   injustice of 65, 177, 199, 232
   instability of rule 195
   Persian 174–5
   punishment of 222, 230, 233
   religious activity 12, 185–6
Aeneas 4, 13, 75–6, 141
   characterization 225–6, 230–1
   shield 225
Aeschylus 219
aetiologies 16, 30, 37–8, 56–7, 152–3, 213, 214–15, 216, 221–2
Agamemnon
   conflicts, religious 77, 140, 142
   hero, as 108, 206
   king, as ideal 76
   murder of 218, 220
   quarrel (*see also* Achilles)
Agathocles
   son of Lysimachus 95
   tyrant of Sicily 198–9
akroteriasmos (see *maschalismos*)
Alcibiades 106, 108, 116
Alcimede 61
Alcinous
   arbiter 169
   Arete, meeting with 131–2, 133
   diplomacy of 112, 129–30, 138–9, 179
   father-in-law, prospective 110, 138–9
   idealized 92, 117, 143, 223
   pykinon epos ("wise word") 134
   religious activity of 12, 168
   security of rule 194–5
   Zeus, respect for 46, 168–9
Alexander
   Argonauts, compared with 18, 19, 52, 151–3
   Cleitus "the Black," murder of 79–80
   conquest, idealized 47, 48
   coronation 21
   death 5, 10
   Dionysus-like 26
   divinity 109, 215
   Egypt, arrival in 12, 20–1
   election of 52–3, 67–8
   founder cult 23–5, 126–7
   funeral cortege 24–5
   mass wedding 48
   military and 140
   mythic heroes, emulation of 18
   proskynesis 79
   Ptolemaic ideology and 19–20
   religious activity 12, 21, 145–6, 150, 151–3
   sibling rivalry 97
   "sweet sweat" 93
   visit to Siwah 13–14, 15, 17, 21
   wonders and 174
Alexandria
   foundation 23, 104
   Library 6, 27, 30, 32
   poetry 5–6, 8–9
Amazons 177
ambush 193, 197–9, 215
amechania ("lack of resources") 75–6
   Homeric usage 75–6
Amon-Re 14, 27
Amycus 145–6, 184, 232
Anchises 227

256

anger
    Aristotelian, views on 84–5, 87–8
    Homeric, representation of 84–5, 88–90
    Philodemus, views on 89
    see also Hera, Zeus
Antigonus Gonatas 46, 170
    Ruler cult 43
Antigonus the One-Eyed 198
Antimachus 114
    Lyde 33–5, 205
aoidoi ("singers") 32, 80
Apollo 26, 40–1, 59, 162
Apollonius Rhodius 7–8, 9
    foundation poetry 4, 214
    life 4, 5–6, 9–10, 31, 206
Apsyrtus 187–223
    characterization 209–10
    murder of 12, 154, 163, 171–2, 216–17, 230, 233
    trick (*dolos*) 105
Aratus 41, 223
    Phaenomena 41–3, 177
        Hesiod, influence of 42–3
        Stoicism, influence of 41, 42
arbitration 169–70
Arete 190
    deception (see also Hera, *Dios apate*) 133
    Homeric 127–8
    idealized 92, 117, 143
    influence, political 117, 127–39, 140, 194
    marriage, consanguineous 97
    Medea, defense 131
    mythos ("speech") 134–6
Argo
    portage of 2–4, 13–18, 27
    primordial age and 55
    Syrtes Gulf, in 1–2
    voyage of 1, 62–3, 200
Argonautica
    Aratus, influence of 42, 43, 46
    Callimachus, influence of 37–8, 39–41, 59
    central themes 61, 145, 155–6, 166–7, 215
    characterization 4–5, 11–12, 13–18, 37–8, 63, 145–6, 185–6
    foundation myth, as 48, 115, 145, 214
    gods in 144, 153–5
    heroism in 231–2
    Homeric epic, compared to 49
    publication 31, 115
    religious activity, emphasis on 13–18, 19–20, 63, 145–6
    Virgil, influence on 76
Argonauts
    characterization 53–4, 140–1, 145–6, 210, 215
    conflicts 48–50, 55–6, 59–60, 81–2
    divine heritage 15, 145, 147

number of 72
religious activity 140–1, 156
Ariadne 189–90, 192, 219
Aristotle
    De Anima 84
    Eth. Eud. 84
    Eth. Nic. 84, 85, 87–8, 89
    Mag. Mor. 84
    Politics 80, 85
    Rhetoric 84, 85
    Topics 85
Arsinoë I 96
Arsinoë II 2–12, 69, 127, 134
    death 96
    divinity 28–9, 98, 101, 102, 190–1
    encomia 27–9
    influence of 48, 51, 93–4, 98–9, 100, 128, 132
    life 94–6, 138–9
    marriage 96–8, 195
Artemis 218–20, 222
    appropriate sacrifices 219
    Hecate 219–20
Ascanius 231
assassination 197–8
ate ("divinely wrought ruin") 86, 130, 131
Atalanta 108
Athena 107–8
Ausonius 202

basilissa (royal title for women) 100–1
Bebrycians 184
Berenice I 100, 148–9
Berenice II 12, 115, 190–1
    encomia 29–30
    influence 100
Boreads 212–13
boutypos ("ritual ox-slayer") 188, 217, 218, 220
Bracidae 22
bridal theft 113–14, 127, 137

Cabiri, *see* Dioscuri, Unnamed Gods
Callicrates 72, 99, 102
Callimachus 7–8, 9, 41–3, 93, 202, 215
    Aetia 12, 29, 40, 59, 191
    Aetia Prologue (*Reply to the Telchines*) 30–1, 35–6, 41
    Coma Berenices 29–30
    "cultic imagination" 38
    deification of Arsinoë 28–9
    dislike of lengthy (or "heavy") poetry 30–1, 33–4
    Hecale 36, 37, 39–40, 208
    Hymn to Zeus 27, 44, 148
    Hymn to Apollo 10, 59
    Hymn to Delos 26–7

Callimachus (*cont.*)
  Hymn to Athena 39
  Hymn to Demeter 39
  performance contexts 38–9, 41
  quarrel with Apollonius 30–1
  Victoria Berenices 29, 36–7, 39–40
Calypso 174
"Catalogue of Heroes" 63
Chremonidean decree 99
Circe 162, 218, 222
Cleopatra 225
cloaks *see also* Jason 105, 106–7, 140
Clytemnestra 220
Curetes 185
Cybele 115
Cyrene
  foundation of 2, 14, 111–12, 115
Cyzicus 165, 172, 179–80, 201, 208, 210

Demodocus 57, 80–1
Demotic Chronicle 10
Diadochs, *see* Successors
Dido 165, 172, 226, 229, 232, 233
Dionysius Scytobrachion 66, 205
Dionysus 191, 224
  Grand Procession, in 26
  Ptolemaic ancestor 26
Dioscuri 8, 142, 143–4, 145, 147, 162–3, 185
doloktasia ("murder by stealth") 196–7, 201, 205, 207
dolos ("trickery") 105, 171–2, 176, 196, 219
dream vision 2

Earthborn men 50, 126
ecphrasis 104, 107
Egypt
  attitude to Alexander 21
  attitude to Ptolemies 10, 149
  Colchis, links to 17
  gods, theriomorphic 224–5
epic
  Alexandrian scholarship on 31–3
  Cypria 202, 203, 204–5
  epic cycle 202, 204
  Hellenistic 31, 33–8
  Homeric 31–3
  Homeric Hymns 38
  oral poetics 32
  parodic 37
  Proclus 202
  violence, Iliadic 217
Erinys 194, 196, 210, 220–1
Eris ("Strife") 56–60, 81–2, 136, 140
Eros 44–5, 50, 51, 116, 117, 196–7, 199, 200
  bright color and 117–19

  condemnation of 56–7, 81–2, 115, 176, 215, 226
  effects of 110, 118
  Eris, source of 56–9, 71, 94, 102–3, 115
  gadfly 119
  golden sphere of 58
Eumelus
  Corinthiaca 205
Euphemus 40, 112, 121, 141, 154
Euripides 91–2, 116, 122, 188–9, 192–3, 196, 204, 217
Eurylochus 71
Eurystheus 182
evocatio 224

geras ("privilege") 110
gifts 154–5, 210
Golden Age 224
Golden Fleece 62–3, 114–15, 117–18, 183, 187, 189, 194
Greece
  Egypt, attitudes to 17
Greek
  divine honors 22–3

Hecate 219–20
Hector 1, 140, 164, 165, 172, 203, 206, 209
Helenus 230
Hellenistic poetry
  approaches to 7–8, 9
  defined 5–6, 7
  variety 30
Hera 15, 62, 102
  Dios apate 133
  favors Jason 15, 62, 123, 227
  intervention 133–5, 142
  wrath 166, 179, 181–3, 187
Heracles 60–74, 147
  ambition 60–71, 74, 143, 165
  Boreads and 193, 212–14
  divine 25–6, 167–85, 191–2
  election, role in 66–7
  god, as 151
  impulsiveness 60, 119
  Iphitus, murder of 211–12
  Jason, rivalry with 64
  Labors 40, 230–1
  left behind (*see also* Hylas) 181, 200
  Prometheus and 192
  self-sufficiency 58, 73–4
  violence 50–1
hero cult 22–3
Herodotus 2–3, 17
Herossae (guardian nymphs of Libya) 1–2, 16, 18, 121, 140, 144–5

Hesiod (poet) 42, 44, 58, 147–8
  Theogony 42, 45, 90, 121, 128, 147–8, 166, 176
  Works and Days 42, 56, 58
Hetairoi ("Companions") 71–2, 73
Homer (poet) 32, 33
homonoia ("like-mindedness")
  Argonautic 18, 52, 56, 58, 59–60, 64, 71, 81–2, 85, 89–90, 92, 108, 155–6, 165
  arbitration and 170
  Aristotelian 85
  cult of 8, 56, 143, 152
hospitality 48–9, 112, 173
Hylas 50, 117–18, 119
Hyllus 213–14
Hypsipyle 12, 47–8, 101, 102, 109–12, 120, 122, 123, 183, 190

Idas 12, 58, 76–7, 78, 79–82, 102, 140, 185
  comparison with Cleitus "the Black" 79–80
ideology
  Augustan 224–5
  Ptolemaic
    Alexander and 20–1
    Argonautica and 4, 7, 9, 113, 145–6, 215, 222–3
    Callimachus and 8–9
    coinage and 24
    cult and 10–11, 19–20, 145, 149–50, 155–6, 200
    formation of monuments and 23–4, 200
Idmon 76–7, 142, 183, 210
Iphigenia 217, 219
irony 188–9, 206–8, 213
Istrus 202
Ixion 211–12

Jason 180
  Alexander, compared with 4, 18, 19, 52, 68, 72, 79–80
  amechania ("lack of resources") 75–6
  Apollo-like 19
  Apsyrtus, killing of 216–17
  aristeia ("deed of valor") 49, 135, 175
  characterization 4–5, 19, 49–50, 52, 53–4, 187–93, 215
  cloak 57, 104–8, 140
  election of 63–7, 69–70
  eloquence 90, 117, 120–2, 125, 185, 190–2
  love hero 104, 109, 120
  loyalty 122–4, 125, 190–2, 216
  Ptolemy-like 18, 19
  ritual activity 142
  self-control 79–80, 215
  unheroic 114, 188, 206–8
justice
  Dike ("Justice") 42–3, 46, 177
  see also Zeus

katabasis ("path below") 227
kings, representation of 13–18, 41–3, 145–6, 167
kin-murder 210–15
kleos ("glory") 63, 141, 143, 164–5, 191
knowledge, limits of 46, 49, 50, 51, 179, 180–1, 187

Lemnos 39–40, 47–8, 102–4, 113, 183–4
Libya 154
Lycophron 202
Lycus 184
Lysander 22

Macedonian
  election 52–3, 67–9
  language 11
  ruler cult, opposition to 21–2, 43
Mariandyni 183, 184–5
marriage
  anomic 113–14, 135, 136–7
  Athenian 96, 137
  consanguineous 96–8
  Egypt, in
    Greek 137–8
    royal 96, 99
  Jason and Medea 114, 115, 135–7
  polygamous 97
  representation of 93
maschalismos (ritual mutilation) 188, 205–8, 210, 221
Medea 2–12
  blood guilt 217
  characterization 91–2, 126–7, 187–93, 214
  doubts 124–5, 170–2
  erotic suffering 120
  temper 125
Menander 6, 110, 137
Menelaus 145, 147
Mezentius 232–4

Naupactia 205
Nausicaa 194–5
neikos ("quarrel") 64, 177
  Achilles' shield, on 179
  Empedoclean 57–8, 80–1
  Greek vs. Colchian 113, 127, 134, 136, 167, 169
  Macedonian 80

Neoptolemus
co-regent of Epirus 199
son of Achilles 229–30
Nikouria decree 150
nostos ("return") 82, 164, 222

oaths (*horkia*) 122–4, 163–70, 175, 176, 200, 216
Agamemnon 152
Octavian 5, 224–5
Odysseus
cloak 105
disguised 36
marriage 92
Phaeacians and 1, 110, 128–9, 133–4, 138–9, 168
religious activity 163
self-reliance 91
Suitors and 1, 49
underworld, in 180, 227
wanderings (in *Odyssey*) 103–4, 108, 122, 154
Ophellas 198–9
Orestes 211, 212
Orpheus 80–1, 115, 134, 143, 219, 223
Ovid 206

Pallas (son of Evander) 234–5
Paraebius 181
Peleus 2, 13, 17, 212
Pelias 62–3, 102, 142, 165–6, 167, 181–3, 193, 199
heroic defiance, object of 65
king, lawful 62
Penates ("gods of the home") 16–18
Penelope 92, 209
Phaeacians 127–34, 138–9, 147–8, 168
Pharaoh 107, 146–8
divinity of 19, 25, 150, 215
titulature 100
Philip II 67, 143–4, 199
divine honors 22
drunkenness 78–9
Philoi ("Friends") 72
(*Iliad*, in) 73
(*Odyssey*, in) 73
Philostratus 203, 208
Phineus 39, 48, 51, 179, 183, 230
Phrixus 62
Pindar
Pythian 2–3, 114, 188, 205
Polyxena 203, 204–5
Polyxo 39
Posidippus 28, 98, 140
post-colonial narrative 16, 40, 46–51, 139
Priam 229–30
Prometheus 45, 153, 192
Propertius 225
prophecy 39, 180, 230

Protesilaus 203, 204
Ptolemaieia 26, 149, 150
Ptolemies 4, 10, 12, 97
acclamation, military 68–9
Alexander, ties to 9
coronation 21
cult politics 10–11, 23–4, 148
divine ancestry 25–6
Philoi, recruitment of 72
religious activity 11, 12, 143–4, 145–6
strength, military 23
wealth 23, 26, 101, 149
Ptolemy I (Soter) 11, 94–5, 198–9
Alexander, successor to 24–5
coinage 24
Egyptians, treatment of 23–4
encomia 26, 141, 215
religious activity 23–5, 109
Ptolemy II (Philadelphus) 9, 11, 32, 92, 101, 114, 115, 143, 199
mediation 169–70
divine ancestry 25–7
encomia 26–7, 46, 215
Grand Procession 26, 107
Greece, support of 48, 51
marriage 96–8, 195
mediator 132
religious activity 25, 26, 101, 141, 148–50
Ptolemy III (Euergetes) 9, 10, 19–25, 29, 98, 100, 191
Ptolemy IV (Philopator) 33, 163–70
Ptolemy Ceraunus 95–6, 116
purification 210–15
Pyrrhus
son of Achilles (*see* Neoptolemus)
Successor 197
resemblance to Alexander 199

reconciliation 82–90, 192–3
religious activity
defined 4
revenge 187, 193–4, 208, 210, 222
rhapsodes 32, 35
Rhea 165
Rhianus (epic poet) 35
ruler cult 9, 141, 148, 155–6, 165

sacrifices 156–60, 166–7
animals, types of 156–61
corrupted 188, 220
efficacy of 163–4, 165
frequency 13–14, 161, 162
Homeric 156, 161, 163–4
implied 162–3
misappropriated 163

rejected 163–4, 165
sociological function of 148, 153, 166–7
Virgilian 227–8
sacrilege 39, 48, 51, 76–7, 200–1, 215–16, 220, 229
Samothracian gods, *see* Unnamed Gods
Sarapis 18, 24
Sesostris 8, 17
similes 2
Siwah Oasis 13–14
solar boat 14
Sophocles 206, 207
"spear-won" 69, 110–11
speech 120–2, 135, 196
succession 194–5
Successors 10, 24, 25, 26, 69, 107, 169–70
    assassinations 197–8, 199
    elections 52–3
    marriages 94–6, 100
    rule, recognition of 68–9, 155–6
suffering 214, 217, 226
symposium 74
synthesiai ("treaties") 171–2, 176
Syrtes Gulf 1, 198

Talus 105, 126
Telamon 12, 82, 90, 181, 191, 200, 212
Telemachus 61, 64, 73, 138
themis ("customary," "correct") 143, 165–6, 188, 206–8, 212
Theocritus 7–8, 9, 215
    Idyll 2, 191
    Idyll 12, 116
    Idyll 15, 27–8
    Idyll 17, 25, 26, 95, 96, 131, 141, 148–9
Theoi Adelphoi ("Sibling Gods") 25, 26, 29, 94, 98
Theoi Soteres ("Savior Gods") 25, 26–7, 148–9
Thersites 77–8, 81
Theseus 36, 40, 48, 189–90, 211
time ("honor") 141, 164–5

Trambelus 201–2, 213
travel writing 46–7
Triton 2, 112, 152, 154–5, 165
Troilus 195, 201–9, 234
    vase paintings, in 203–4
Turnus 209, 232, 234–5
Twelve Gods 22, 152
Tyche ("Fortune") 8
Tydeus 211

Unnamed Gods (also Unknown Gods) 8, 116, 143–4, 145, 161, 185
usurpation 62–3, 81, 194–5

Valerius Flaccus 205
variatio 190, 196
Virgil 226
    Aeneid 13, 18, 78, 202, 224–35
    Argonautica, influence of 226–7, 230–1
    family in 233–5
    gods in 227–8
    pietas in 228–33
wine 78–9
women
    honors, public 101–2
    strife, associated with 92–3
    treachery of 126–7

Xenophon 8, 175

Zarathustra 175
Zenodotus 32–3
Zeus 15, 42, 147, 148, 164, 235
    cosmic influence 45
    justice, straight 50–1, 168–9, 176–9, 185–6, 192, 201, 223
    sexuality 44–5
    wrath 143, 165, 172, 179, 180–1, 187, 192, 196–7, 201, 222–3
Zeus-Amon 14–15, 17, 21, 148, 151